SUSTAINABLE RAILWAY FUTURES

Despite the hopes for a worldwide 'railway renaissance' there was as yet no comprehensive coverage of its multiple dimensions and challenges. This book now fills this gap. It brings together some of the best international experts to discuss the different aspects of the interface between railways and societal development in a very well informed, balanced, and accessible way. For those wanting to understand how railways might help making transport more sustainable, there is no better place to start.

Luca Bertolini, University of Amsterdam, the Netherlands, and co-editor of *Cities on Rails, and Transit Oriented Development: Making it Happen*

Loo and Comtois offer a comprehensive assessment of the promise of enhanced railway systems as a key component of the infrastructure needed to assure sustainable mobility of people and goods. Their co-edited volume shows how railways are critically needed to support economic development while minimizing human impacts on the environment. Transport policymakers, students and academics will benefit greatly from the compendium of challenges and opportunities facing future railway system developments outlined in this book.

Blas L. Pérez Henríquez, University of California, Berkeley, USA

This co-edited volume provides a unique look into the future of railways through the lens of sustainability. Contributions covering passenger and freight, urban and inter-urban, and developed and developing systems, critically examine the geographic, environmental, social and environmental characteristics of a technology that, if not yet undergoing a full-blown renaissance, is very much alive and kicking.

John Preston, University of Southampton, UK

Transport and Mobility Series

Series Editors: Richard Knowles, University of Salford, UK and Markus Hesse, Université du Luxembourg and on behalf of the Royal Geographical Society (with the Institute of British Geographers) Transport Geography Research Group (TGRG).

The inception of this series marks a major resurgence of geographical research into transport and mobility. Reflecting the dynamic relationships between socio-spatial behaviour and change, it acts as a forum for cutting-edge research into transport and mobility, and for innovative and decisive debates on the formulation and repercussions of transport policy making.

Also in the series

Institutional Challenges to Intermodal Transport and Logistics
Governance in Port Regionalisation and Hinterland Integration
Jason Monios
ISBN 978-1-4724-2321-4

Port-City Interplays in China
James Jixian Wang
ISBN 978-1-4724-2689-5

The Geographies of Air Transport
Edited by Andrew R. Goetz and Lucy Budd
ISBN 978-1-4094-5331-4

Innovation in Public Transport Finance
Property Value Capture
Shishir Mathur
ISBN 978 1 4094 6260 6

Hub Cities in the Knowledge Economy
Seaports, Airports, Brainports
Edited by Sven Conventz, Ben Derudder, Alain Thierstein and Frank Witlox
ISBN 978 1 4094 4591 3

Institutional Barriers to Sustainable Transport
Carey Curtis and Nicholas Low
ISBN 978 0 7546 7692 8

Sustainable Railway Futures
Issues and Challenges

Edited by

BECKY P.Y. LOO
University of Hong Kong, China

CLAUDE COMTOIS
University of Montreal, Canada

Routledge
Taylor & Francis Group

LONDON AND NEW YORK

First published 2015 by Ashgate Publishing

2 Park Square, Milton Park, Abingdon, Oxfordshire OX14 4RN
711 Third Avenue, New York, NY 10017

Routledge is an imprint of the Taylor & Francis Group, an informa business

First issued in paperback 2018

British Library Cataloguing in Publication Data
A catalogue record for this book is available from the British Library

The Library of Congress has cataloged the printed edition as follows:
Sustainable railway futures : issues and challenges / [edited] by Becky P.Y. Loo and Claude Comtois.
    pages cm. – (Transport and mobility)
  Includes bibliographical references and index.
  ISBN 978-1-4094-5243-0 (hardback)
1. Railroads. 2. Railroads and state. I. Loo, Becky P.Y. II. Comtois, Claude, 1954-
HE1031.S87 2015
385–dc23

2014031726

ISBN 978-1-4094-5243-0 (hbk)
ISBN 978-1-138-54694-3 (pbk)

Contents

List of Figures		*vii*
List of Tables		*ix*
Notes on Contributors		*xi*
Foreword by David Banister		*xv*
Acknowledgements		*xvii*
List of Abbreviations		*xix*

SECTION I   RAILWAYS AND SUSTAINABILITY

1	Prospects for Sustainable Railways *Becky P.Y. Loo*	3

SECTION II   TRANSFORMING PLACE AND SPACE: GEOGRAPHICAL DIMENSIONS

2	Structuring Effects of Rail Terminals *Jean-Paul Rodrigue*	23
3	National Railway System *John Black*	39
4	Railways and Borders: The International Dimension *Roger Vickerman*	57

SECTION III SAVE OUR EARTH!: ENVIRONMENTAL DIMENSIONS

5	Transit-Oriented Development and the Urban Fabric *Robert Cervero*	75
6	Airline and Railway (Dis)Integration *Moshe Givoni*	95
7	The Transfer of Freight from Road to Rail Transport *Antoine Frémont*	109

SECTION IV EQUITY AND ACCESSIBILITY: SOCIAL DIMENSIONS

8	The Promotion of Social Equity through Railways *Linna Li and Becky P.Y. Loo*	129

9   The Rise of Localism in Railway Infrastructural Development   145
        David Chapman

10   Regional and Local Line Rail Freight Transport in North America   167
        John C. Spychalski

SECTION V   MAKING ENDS MEET: ECONOMIC DIMENSIONS

11   Exporting Railway Technologies   185
        Tin Kin Ho

12   Property Models for Financing Railway Development   201
        Siman Tang and Hong K. Lo

13   Intermodal Transportation   219
        Brian Slack

SECTION VI: LOOKING FORWARD

14   The Resilience of Railways   235
        Claude Comtois

Index   *255*

List of Figures

1.1   A schematic representation of an inland port distribution system   7

2.1   Structuring effects of rail terminals   25
2.2   Typology of rail terminals   26
2.3   Configuration of an intermodal rail terminal   32
2.4   Types of intermodal rail terminals   33

4.1   Rail passenger journeys by country (thousand passengers)   62
4.2   Air passenger traffic within the EU by departure (thousand passengers)   63
4.3   Rail transport of goods by country in 2010 – in million tkm   66
4.4   Evolution of EU-27 road freight transport 2004–2010 (based on tkm, 2004=100)   67
4.5   Share of international transport in total road freight transport (% in tkm)   67

5.1   Transit ridership and VKT per capita among global cities   77
5.2   Population density and transit ridership among global cities   77

6.1   The integrated hub model of H&S operation   96

7.1   Share of railways in the modal split of freight transport in European countries in 2010 (% in total inland freight ton-km)   111
7.2   Share of railways in the modal split of freight transport in selected countries in 2008 (% in total inland freight ton-km)   111
7.3   Evolution of the share of railways in the modal split of freight transport in selected European countries, 1970–2008 (% in total inland freight ton-km)   112
7.4   Evolution of the share of railways in the modal split of freight transport in Australia, USA, India and Japan, 1970–2008 (% in total inland freight tonnes-km)   112
7.5   The modal split transition: The share of railways in the modal split of freight transport   114
7.6   Spread strategy of the road industry versus freight rail corridors   118
7.7   The integration of the combined transport chain   119
7.8   The business model of Hupac Intermodal   121

9.1   Arnstein's (1969) 'ladder of citizen participation'   147
9.2   The Pegasus concept of 'diagonal coordination' (EUROCITIES 2004: 4)   148
9.3   Schematic diagram of the HPHVCRP area   155
9.4   Schematic diagram of Evergreen 3 stage 2   157
9.5   Schematic diagram of HS2 route and phasing   159

11.1   The 3 categories of Turnkey projects   191

12.1   Rate of MTR real fare increases and rail transit service supplies
       over years   205
12.2   The cost and turnover of MTR over the past two decades   206
12.3   Influence diagram of the 'Build' decision   212
12.4   Influence diagram of the 'Fund' decision   213
12.5   Influence diagram of the 'Own' decision   215

13.1   Growth of intermodal traffic in the US, 1961–2011   222
13.2   Rail modal split comparison between US and EU15   223
13.3   Future capacity constraints in the US rail network, 2035   227

14.1   Railways in Africa   238
14.2   Railway densities in North America   240
14.3   Railway border crossings in China   243
14.4   Railway and Panama Canal   245

List of Tables

2.1   Structuring effects of HSR and intermodal terminals   35

3.1   Case study national railway systems (Australia, Indonesia and Japan) and comparative data compared with world's top ten systems ranked by railway track length   40

4.1   High-speed rail services between France and Belgium   64
4.2   Forecast and actual passenger flows on LGV-Nord   64

5.1   Transit ridership, VKT, and GDP among global cities   78
5.2   Mode splits for journeys with destination in Stockholm county   82

6.1   The potential for mode substitution at London Heathrow airport in January 2012 (data include only the flights departing Heathrow airport)   101
6.2   Share of airline alliances in air transport services in January 2013   103

7.1   Major combined transport operators in Le Havre, Antwerp and Rotterdam, 2011   120

8.1   Modal split of passenger travel in selected countries   135
8.2   Top ten private investment railway projects, 1984–2011   140

10.1   Prominent regional/local railway holding companies   173
10.2   Determinants of performance for regional and local railways   175

12.1   Mass railway transit services and patronage   203
12.2   Roles of public and private partners in alternative public-private partnership models   209

14.1   Selected indicators for railway performance   249

Notes on Contributors

John Black is Emeritus Professor of Transport Engineering at the University of New South Wales, Sydney and a Research Fellow in its Institute of Environmental Studies. He has lived in Indonesia and Japan, and has travelled extensively on the rail networks of the three case study countries. He has acted as a high level consultant to governments on rail in Australia and Indonesia and as a Japan Society for the Promotion of Science Fellow has conducted research into the impacts of high-speed rail.

Robert Cervero is Professor and Chair of City and Regional Planning at the University of California, Berkeley, where he is also Director of the Institute of Urban and Regional Development (IURD) and Director of the University of California Transportation Center (UCTC). His research centres on the nexus between urban transportation and land-use systems. Professor Cervero has authored or co-authored six books, more than 50 research monographs, and over 200 journal articles in this area, including *Transforming Cities with Transit* (2013, World Bank).

David Chapman is Professor of Planning and Development in the Birmingham School of the Built Environment at Birmingham City University in the UK, where he was Head of the School of Planning for 10 years. Now semi-retired, he continues to teach and research in the interrelated areas of planning, transportation, urban design, architecture, landscape architecture and education. He is a full member of the Institute of Historic Building Preservation and is retired from the Royal Town Planning Institute, the Royal Institute of British Architects and the Landscape Institute. He holds an MA in Education and his research also explores pedagogy and social learning in his professional areas of interest.

Claude Comtois is Deputy Director of the Interuniversity Research Centre on Enterprise Networks, Logistics and Transportation and Professor of Geography at Montreal University. He has over 10 years experience as transport project director for the Canadian International Development Agency. He has supervised or participated in more than 40 research projects. He is the author or the co-author of over 140 scientific publications and 250 communications. He currently supervises projects on the competitiveness of transport systems, on transport mitigation and adaptation measures to environmental changes and on the development of logistics platforms.

Antoine Frémont, holder of the Agregation of geography (1988), received his PhD from the University of Le Havre (1996) and accreditation to supervise research from the University of Paris Panthéon Sorbonne (2005). He is Director of Research at the IFSTTAR, the French Institute of Science and Technology for Transport, Development and Networks. His research addresses the role of shipping lines in globalization, the organization of intermodal transport chains and the logistics in metropolitan areas. He is currently project leader in Réseau Ferré de France, the French railway infrastructure manager. He is in charge of the relations between spatial planning and the rail projects.

Moshe Givoni is a Senior Lecturer at the Department of Geography and Human Environment and Head of the Transport Research Unit at Tel-Aviv University. He is also a Visiting Research Associate at the Transport Studies Unit, Oxford University and an Associate Editor for *Transport Reviews* journal. Moshe gained his PhD at the Bartlett School of Planning, University College London and received a Marie Curie postdoctoral fellowship which was undertaken at Vrije Universiteit (VU) Amsterdam. He was also a Research Fellow at Wolfson College, Oxford University.

Tin Kin Ho was awarded BEng and PhD by the School of Electronic and Electrical Engineering, University of Birmingham, UK. He has been involved in a range of railway-related research and consultancy projects in UK, Hong Kong, China and Australia. His research interests include railway engineering, simulation and modelling, market deregulation and privatization, asset management, signalling and system assurance. He is now an Associate Professor of Rail Logistics at the SMART Infrastructure Facility of the University of Wollongong, Australia, leading research on railway systems and their interfaces with other infrastructure systems and human users.

Linna Li is a PhD candidate in Department of Geography at the University of Hong Kong. Her research interest is on railway development and sustainable transportation. From a geographical perspective, she focuses on the role of railways in reducing carbon emission, promoting social equity and improving accessibility. With a focus on inter-city rail transit of China, she is currently exploring the competition and cooperation between high-speed railways and other transport modes as well its implications on sustainable transport in China.

Hong K. Lo is Associate Dean of Engineering and Professor of Civil and Environmental Engineering of the Hong Kong University of Science and Technology. He is Convener of the International Scientific Committee of the conference series Advanced Systems for Public Transportation (CASPT), Founding Editor-in-Chief of *Transportmetrica B: Transport Dynamics*, Managing Editor of the *Journal of Intelligent Transportation Systems*, and on the editorial boards of many journals, including *Transportation Research Part B*, *Public Transport*, *ASCE Journal of Urban Planning and Development*, *International Journal of Sustainable Transportation*, among others.

Becky P.Y. Loo is Professor of Geography and Director of the Institute of Transport Studies at the University of Hong Kong. Her research interests are transportation, e-technologies and society. In particular, she is interested in applying spatial analysis, surveys and statistical methods in analysing pertinent issues related to sustainable transportation. She is Founding Editor-in-Chief of *Travel Behaviour and Society* and Associate Editor of the *Journal of Transport Geography*. She is on the editorial boards of major research journals, including *Asian Geographer*, *Injury Epidemiology*, *International Journal of Shipping and Logistics*, *International Journal of Sustainable Transportation*, *Journal of Urban Technology*, and *Transportmetrica A: Transport Science*, among others.

Jean-Paul Rodrigue received a PhD in Transport Geography from the Université de Montréal (1994) and has been a Professor at Hofstra University since 1999. Dr Rodrigue's research interests mainly cover the fields of transportation and economics as they relate to logistics and global freight distribution. Area interests involve North America, Latin America and the Caribbean, and East and Southeast Asia. Specific topics over which he has published extensively cover maritime transport systems and logistics, global supply chains and production networks, gateways and transport corridors. Dr Rodrigue is a member of the World Economic Forum's Global Agenda Council on Advanced Manufacturing (2011–2013).

Brian Slack is a retired Professor of Geography from Concordia University, Montreal, Canada. He is Distinguished Professor Emeritus of that University and holds a PhD from McGill University and an Honorary Doctorate from the University of Le Havre. He has published extensively in the fields of ports and shipping for over 40 years. Much of this work has an intermodal perspective, and he has undertaken research in rail intermodal transport for the Canadian government. His recent research has focused on three areas: cost and time factors in container shipping; port performance indicators; and, the locational relationships between transportation and the logistics industry.

John C. Spychalski is Professor Emeritus of Supply Chain Management at The Pennsylvania State University. His research interests focus on the economic performance, management and history of domestic and international transport systems, and on public policy toward transport. He served as editor of the *Transportation Journal* for many years. His current transport-related public service duties include membership on the board of directors of a public authority that owns rail track at five different locations in central Pennsylvania on which service is operated under contract by a private enterprise company.

Siman Tang received his doctorate in Civil Engineering from the Hong Kong University of Science and Technology with research focus on transportation. He has published a number of research papers on public transportation and public-private partnership. He has been in the profession of urban transport and railway operations for over 25 years.

Roger Vickerman is Professor of European Economics at the University of Kent, UK. He specializes on the relationship between transport, economic development and integration in the European Union and has particularly been working on the role of high-speed rail. He is the author of the textbook *Principles of Transport Economics*, with Emile Quinet, joint editor of the *Handbook of Transport Economics* and editor of *Recent Developments in the Economics of Transport*. He is Editor-in-chief of *Transport Policy*.

Foreword

David Banister

More than 170 years ago there was a 'bubble' associated with the new rail technology in the UK. The age of the railway had begun, with the consequent lowering of transport costs, new levels of speed (and comfort), and substantial investment in the network. The railway mania of the 1840s in the UK resulted in more than 10,000 km of new track being built over a 10 year period. Bristol, for instance, was now only three hours from London, including a compulsory stop at Swindon for refreshments, when previously it had taken two days, and time zones across the UK were standardized according to railway clock time and the new national timetable.

Much of the financing was speculative, with the price of railway shares increasing, but many companies collapsed and some of them siphoned the investment into other enterprises. Low interest rates made railways an attractive proposition, and shares could be bought for a 10 per cent deposit with the remainder being open to call later. Many of the newly rich middle class lost all their savings when the bubble collapsed, and the companies claimed the balance of payments. There were few controls over setting up companies to build the railways, and as interest rates rose again the government bonds became a safer investment.

Despite many losing all their savings, the railway mania led to a rapid expansion of the rail system in the UK, most of which were funded by the private sector. But the experience in the UK was typical of the cycle of boom and bust elsewhere, as many railway lines were not built to join the growing industrial cities, as in the UK, but to link ports to their hinterlands, and to open up new inland areas that had been inaccessible in the past. This type of investment was extremely risky. By 1900, there were more than 800,000 km of railway lines across the world, and this figure rose to over 1,100,000 km by 1913. The current figure is about 1,375,000 km.

Over the last 100 years, the railway system has been a declining element in the total transport network as other forms of transport have taken over. But this is now changing again. Although over 150 countries have rail systems, there are only 23 with networks in excess of 10,000 km. Much of the funding comes from the public sector and the international agencies, and not the private sector as in the early days. The debate is currently over the role that high-speed rail should play in the transport system, and the important contribution that railways can play as part of a sustainable transport system, and its role in enhancing urban development.

This book brings together an international group of leading authors to present a range of different perspectives on some of the main issues that will determine the second railway age that has followed the first railway age some 170 years later – this is a true renaissance.

Acknowledgements

The Editors of this book, Becky P.Y. Loo and Claude Comtois, wish to express their whole-hearted appreciation to the contributing authors of this volume for sharing their research findings and valuable insights. The original idea of this edited volume was developed in January, 2011 when Claude Comtois was visiting the University of Hong Kong and Becky Loo was Associate Dean of Social Sciences. They would like to thank the Dean of Social Sciences then, Ian Holliday, for funding the visit and his insightful leadership and strategic support to international research collaboration initiatives during his Deanship. In addition, Becky Loo also wants to acknowledge the kind support of the current Dean of Social Sciences, John Burns, for supporting her sabbatical leave in 2013–2014. This long-awaited sabbatical leave has enabled her to complete this edited volume in a timely manner.

David Banister, Director of the Transport Studies Unit, Oxford University, has been supportive of this initiative ever since the idea was first shared with him. The Editors are most grateful for his reassurance of the academic value of this endeavour, and agreement to write the Foreword without hesitation. They are also indebted to the assistance and feedback of Richard Knowles and Markus Hesse, the Series Editors of the Transport and Mobility Series, the anonymous book reviewers, and Katy Crossan of Ashgate. Winnie W.Y. Lam, Yoki Lam, Linna Li, Bingxia Sun and Ada Shenjun Yao have helped in the formatting and editing of this book. Tina Tsang has provided cartographic support. We also thankfully acknowledge the permissions from the relevant publishers/copyright holders (listed in brackets) to reproduce Figure 1.1 (Routledge), Figure 2.4 (The Equipment Leasing and Finance Foundation) and Table 6.1 (OAG Aviation Worldwide Limited).

Many authors of this volume also wish to record gratitude for the support that they received for their respective chapters. John Black thanks the following who have either provided data or helped improve an earlier draft of Chapter 3: Kym Norley, doctoral candidate at the University of New South Wales and former employee at Australian National Railway; Gen Okajima, General Manager, Central Japan Railway Company (JR Tokai); Danang Parakesit, Universitas Gadjah Mada, Indonesia; Murti Pradana, PT SMI, Jakarta, Indonesia, and Lynton Ulrich, Indonesian Infrastructure Initiative, Jakarta, Indonesia. He takes full responsibility for the interpretations.

Moshi Givoni would like to thank Frédéric Dobruszkes for producing Table 6.1 in Chapter 6.

Linna Li and Becky P.Y. Loo wish to acknowledge that the study of Chapter 8 was supported by the General Research Fund (GRF) HKU748912H on 'Revisiting the "Three Ds" in Transit-oriented Development (TOD): A People Centred and Place-based Perspective' of the Research Grants Council of the Hong Kong Special Administrative Region Government.

David Chapman of Chapter 9 gratefully acknowledges the contribution of practitioners who, being actively engaged in railway infrastructural development, have immediate experience of the impacts of the rise in Localism in the UK. In doing so they have expressed their own views and their comments are not those of their companies or authorities. Special thanks are due to Mike Rose, Project Officer of the High Peak and Hope Valley Community

Rail Partnership; Stephen Barker, Chief Project Engineer of The Chiltern Railway Company Ltd; and Mel Jones, Projects Leader-Transportation Policy Growth & Transportation, and her colleague Tim Mitchell of Birmingham City Council. Sincere thanks also go to Ken Cronin of Birmingham City University for his work in drawing and redrawing the figures used to illustrate the chapter. The author is also indebted to Becky P.Y. Loo, Professor of the Department of Geography, The University of Hong Kong and Theresa Yeung, Director at ARUP Hong Kong for their contributions to the international context for railway infrastructural development and Localism in China, and to Claude Comtois, Professeur titulaire de géographie, Université de Montréal, and Alex Champagne-Gelinas, Université de Montréal, for their contributions to the international context for railway infrastructural development and Localism in the United States.

Siman Tang and Hong K. Lo wish to acknowledge that the study of Chapter 12 was supported by Public Policy Research Fund HKUST6002-PPR-11 of the Research Grants Council of the Hong Kong Special Administrative Region Government.

Last but not least, the Editors would like to thank their families for their love and lasting support. Claude Comtois would like to thank his wife Suzanne whose understanding and support of a scholar's life is deeply appreciated. Becky Loo wishes to thank her husband, two sons, Wilbert P.S. Ng and Fabian P.W. Ng, and daughter, Concordia P.L. Ng, for the endless joy and inspirations that they have given her in their everyday life. 'Choo-choo … choo-choo … ' are the sounds of trains when they play games at home. In the old days, the typical image of a train was often one running through picturesque countryside, often supported by marvellous engineering works of bridges and tunnels over mountains and difficult terrains. Puffs of steam came out of the dark locomotive that ran on steel rails, with perhaps a friendly train captain standing by the doorstep of the moving train with one hand holding the handrail and the other waving. Nowadays, the image of a train is perhaps very different with the bright bullet train design, which reflects high-technology aerodynamics for reducing air friction. As the railway technology advances, the society is also changing. The success of a transport mode, such as the automobiles in the 1970s, cannot be supported by technological innovations alone. While many favourable conditions for a renaissance of railways are emerging, will it eventually come? We believe that the answer will lie in whether people's lifestyle will really change. With a vision, changes can be fostered by an awareness of the opportunities and determination to overcome challenges related to the environmental, economic and financial, social, and geographical aspects of modern railways.

List of Abbreviations

AAR	Association of American Railroads
ACoRP	Association of Community Rail Partnerships
ADA	American with Disabilities Act
AN	Australian National Railways Commission
APL	American President Lines
ARTC	Australian Rail Track Corporation
ASLRRA	American Short Line and Regional Railroad Association
ATN	Australian Transport Network
ATO	Automatic Train Operation
BAPPENAS	Badan Perencanaan dan Pembangunan Nasional
BFOOD	Build, Fund, Own, Operate, Develop Property
BNSF	Burlington Northern and Santa Fe
BOO	Build-Own-Operate
BOOT	Build-Own-Operate-Transfer
BOT	Build-Operate-Transfer
BUMN	Badan Usaha Milik Negara
CAC	Citizen Advisory Committee
CBD	Central Business District
CCLRT	Central Corridor Light Rail Line
CEF	Community Engagement Forum
CFM	Linea Coahuila Durango SA de CV
CIL	Community Infrastructure Levy
CME	Coordinating Ministry of Economic Affairs
CN	Canadian National Railway
COFC	Container on Flat Car
COMECON	Council for Mutual Economic Assistance
CO_2	Carbon Dioxide
CR	Chiltern Railways
CRH	China Railways Highspeed
CRPs	Community Rail Partnerships
DB	Deutsche Bahn
DfT	Department for Transport
DtC	Duty to Cooperate
EC	European Commission
EIR	Environmental Impact Report
ERP	Electronic Road Pricing
ERS	European Rail Shuttle
ESPON	European Observation Network for Territorial Development and Cohesion
EU	European Union
FCO	Forced Car Ownership

GDP	Gross Domestic Product
GHG	Greenhouse Gas
GTO	Gate-Turn-Off
HIA	Health Impact Assessment
HPHVCRP	High Peak and Hope Valley Community Rail Partnership
HSR	High-Speed Railway
HS2	High-Speed 2
H&S	Hub and Spoke
IPC	Infrastructure Planning Commission
IPO	Input-Process-Outcome
ISO	International Standards Organization
ISTEA	Intermodal Surface Transportation Efficiency Act
JARC	Job Access Reverse Commute
JICA	Japan International Cooperation Agency
JNR	Japanese National Railways
JR Central	Central Japan Railway Company
JR East	East Japan Railway Company
JR Hokaido	Hokkaido Railway Company
JR Kyushu	Kyushu Railway Company
JR Shikoku	Shikoku Railway Company
JRTT	Japan Railway Construction, Transport and Technology Agency
JR West	West Japan Railway Company
KCR	Kowloon-Canton Railway
KPI	Key Performance Indicators
KCSI	Kansas City Southern Industries
LCCs	Low-Cost Carriers
LCD	Liquid Crystal Display
LED	Light Emitting Diode
LTBs	Local Transport Bodies
LTPP	Long Term Planning Process
MAP-21	Moving Ahead for Progress in the 21st Century Act
MLIT	Ministry of Land, Infrastructure and Transport
MOR	Ministry of Railways
MPO	Metropolitan Planning Organization
MTC	Metropolitan Transportation Commission
MTR	Mass Transit Railway
MTRC	Mass Transit Railway Corporation (Hong Kong)
NAFTA	North American Free Trade Agreement
NERSA	Northeast Rail Services Act
NPS	National Policy Statements
NSIP	Nationally Significant Infrastructure Projects
NSHR	North Shore Railroad System
OECD	Organisation for Economic Co-operation and Development
PACT	Pilot Actions for Combined Transport
PC	Penn Central Transportation Company
PPP	Public-Private Partnerships
PTC	Positive Train Control

PT KAI	Perseron Terbatas Kerata Api Indonesia
PT KCJ	Perseron Terbatas Kerata Api Indonesia Commuter Jabodetabek
PT SMI	Perseron Terbatas Sarana Multi Infrastruktur
R+P	Rail+Property program/model
RTS	Rapid Transit System
RUS	Route Utilisation Strategy
SAFETEA-LU	Safe, Accountable, Flexible, Efficient Transportation Equity Act: A Legacy for Users
SAP	Station Area Plan
SAR	Special Administrative Region
SEU	Social Exclusion Unit
SMART	Sonoma-Marin Area Rail Transit District
STB	Surface Transportation Board
SWOT	Strength, Weakness, Opportunity, and Threats
TAD	Transit-Adjacent Development
TBA	Trenes de Buenos Aires
TDM	Transport/Transportation Demand Management
TEA-21	Transportation Equity Act for the 21st Century
TEN-T	European Union's Trans-European Transport Networks
TEU	Twenty-Foot Equivalent Unit
TFM	Transportation Ferroviaria Mexicana
TGV	Train A Grande Vitesse
TOC	Train Operating Company
TOD	Transit-Oriented Development
TOFC	Trailer on Flat Car
TOICA	Tokai IC card
UIC	International Union of Railways
UP	Union Pacific
USS	United States Steel Corporation
VKT	Vehicle Kilometres Travelled
WCT	Wisconsin Central Transportation Company
3R Act	Railroad Revitalization and Regulatory Reform Act

SECTION I
Railways and Sustainability

Chapter 1
Prospects for Sustainable Railways

Becky P.Y. Loo

Background

This book aims to provide a comprehensive overview of the key issues and challenges of developing railways as a sustainable transport (both passenger and freight) mode in modern societies. The importance of railways is put in the wider context of comprehensive sustainability, which encompasses sustainable development, social and economic equity and community livability (Greene and Wegener 1997, Preston and O'Connor 2008). Sustainable development emphasizes the interface between the environment and the economy. In particular, railways in modern societies have the potentials of minimizing the negative environmental impacts of transport and supporting continual growth and development of the economy (Banister and Hall 1993, Bauer et al. 2009, Bristow et al. 2008, Eusebio and Rindom 1994, Givoni et al. 2009, Kim and van Wee 2009, Lee et al. 2009). Social and economic equity emphasizes the interface between the economy and the society. Railways, as a mass transport mode, can provide affordable mobility to people who do not own or use cars, and ensure fair accessibility to various opportunities across different social strata (Litman 2006, Loo et al. 2010, Lucas 2004, State of Victoria 2008). Finally, community livability addresses the interactions between the environment and the society. Railways can make local communities more livable with less noise and air pollution, traffic injuries and congestion (Cervero 1995). Together with the higher usage of active transport modes like cycling and walking, people can enjoy better health and quality of life (Clifton et al. 2007, Steg and Gifford 2005).

Ever since the nineteenth century, the profound impacts of railways on the overall economic development of different countries and the spatial patterns of urban and economic development have received much attention. Historically, railway expansion played a catalytic role in spearheading development at a national or even continental scale (Coatsworth 1979, Hurd 1975, Owen 1964, Rostow 1960). In the seminal work of Rostow (1960) on the *Stages of Growth*, economies developed by undergoing various development stages from the 'precondition for take-off', 'take-off', 'drive to maturity' and 'age of high mass-consumption'. In particular, Rostow (1960: 55) remarked that 'the introduction of the railroad has been historically the most powerful single initiator of take-offs'. This approach of sequential (irreversible), linear and uniform path is described as the modernization paradigm. In transportation, Taaffe, Morril and Gould (1963) theorized the sequential transport development model into six phases. Railway development characterized the second phase of 'penetration lines and port concentration', which was described as 'the most important single phase in the transportation history of an underdeveloped country' (Ibid.: 506). Similarly, Owen's (1964, 1987) 'Stages of Mobility' considers transport mechanization, particularly railroads, to be instrumental in enabling industrialization.

Nonetheless, Fogel's social savings arguments (1979) in the USA sparked much academic debate on the role of railways from an economic history perspective. Railways' contribution to economic development was found to be much smaller in the counterfactual scenario, that is, had railways not been built in the USA (David 1969, Fogel 1979, O'Brien 1977, Fishlow 1965, White 1976). Similar debates about the relative economic contribution of river navigation and canals versus railways were also found in Britain (Hawke 1970) and Italy (Fenoaltea 1972). While some social saving studies casted doubts on the significance of railways in economic development, railways have withstood stringent economic analyses in countries like Argentina (Summerhill 2005b), Mexico (Coatsworth 1979) and Spain (Herranz-Loncán 2006). Economically, railway expansion was found to be critical to the market unification of food grains in India (Hurd 1975) and Russia (Metzer 1974). Moreover, railways were considered to be important in integrating Northeast America with the Midwest to form the 'Manufacturing Belt' (Chandler 1965, Lakshmanan and Anderson 2007).

The focus of the above research was primarily put on freight transport. Yet, the profound impacts of railway expansion on other aspects of the society have also been widely recognized. As early as the 1950s, Abramovitz (1955: 174) stated that 'it is not too much to say that the transition from the capital markets of the early nineteenth century to the complex, highly specialized and organized capital markets on which twentieth century industry depends was largely based on the activity engendered by railway finance'. In relation, railway investments increased productivity significantly in Brazil (Summerhill 2005a). Moreover, railways also played key non-economic roles, such as political and military roles (Wolfe 1963, Leung 1980). On the one hand, railways were instrumental in the political and economic colonialization in Africa and Latin America, particularly for raw material exports (Mabogunje 1989, Pirie 1982). On the other hand, railways played an important role in the formation and integration of nations. It was described as 'the political power of iron rails' and was notably demonstrated in the case of Argentina (Alberdi 1933 quoted in Fleming 1987: 4). Similarly, considerations of political integration, rather than economic growth, underlined the major railway extensions in the People's Republic of China (PRC) from 1949 to 1979 (Leung 1980).

The rapid growth of automobiles, together with extensive highway extensions, has diverted much academic attention in the mid-1970s. Many more academic studies have focused on the impacts of highways on the economic and urban development of cities and countries (Berechman et al. 2006, Cooper and Edwards 1982, Crane 1999, Foster et al. 1991, Forkenbrock and Foster 1990, Guiliano 1986, Gwilliam 1970, 1979, Wilson 1966, Wheeler 1976). In urban geography, the post-war suburbanization of American cities throughout the 1980s and 1990s, and the urban sprawl in the post-1990s were both intrigued by massive highway expansion (Downs 1998, Ewing 1997, Ewing et al. 2003, Gillham 2002, Muller 1995). In retrospect, the shift of focus from railways to highways was well-predicted and described in classical transport models, like the Taaffe-Morrill-Gould model. While railway development dominated the second phase of the 'ideal-typical sequence of transport development', road development began to become more important in the third phase; and 'the dominance of road over railroad' was considered as the 'most marked characteristic' of the fourth phase (Taaffe et al. 1963: 514). Furthermore, the beginning of mass air travel since the 1960s (Graham and Goetz 2008) and its rapid growth with the increasing affluence of the world population has caught the attention of numerous scholars (Debbage and Delk 2001, Dennis 1995, B. Graham 1998, A. Graham 2000, Goetz 2006, O'Connor 1995, 2010, Rakowski and Johnson 1979, Vowles 2000, Wright 1992, Zhang 1998).

In the review paper of Silverleaf and Turgel (1983), it is mentioned that railway investment in OECD countries was 'primarily required for renewal and maintenance'. As mentioned throughout this book (particularly in Chapters 4, 6, 7 and 10), advances in railway technologies have been made throughout the 1980s and 1990s, especially in Japan and France. However, it is clear that both the geographical extent, and the speed and scale of investment in modern railways were limited from a global perspective. While railways in the former Soviet bloc had continued to receive heavy investment throughout these two decades, the dominance of railways in these countries was often seen as a burden after many of them turned to the market economy (Buchhofer 1995, Jauernig and Roe 2000, Kovács and Spens 2006, Loo and Liu 2005). Fullerton (1975) described the 'Railway Age' as the period of 1850 to 1920. In a more explicit manner, C. Buchanan (1963) wrote 'Poor Sir Peter Parker – he talks of the Age of the Train, but the Age of the Train came to an end in 1919 and for the last 60 years we have lived in the Age of the Motor Vehicle or, as I prefer to put it, the Age of the Cart in which the railways were but a short-lived intrusion'. His paper concluded by demanding a 'recognition of the fundamental point that the motor vehicle has ousted the railways' (C. Buchanan 1963). Actually, the official statistics of the United Kingdom (UK) show an overall decline of almost all forms of public transport as well from 1952 to 1997 – with 'cars, vans and taxis' clearly 'ousted' not only 'rail' but also 'buses and coaches' and 'pedal cycles' (Department of the Environment, Transport and the Regions 1999). These striking trends in the UK were well captured and analyzed by M. Buchanan (2004: 29).

The Twenty-first Century

Major changes, however, happened around the turn of the twenty-first century. Some scholars have described the twenty-first century as a period of renaissance for railways (Haywood 1999, Loo and Hook 2002, Woodburn 2001). While these authors have used the term rather loosely, it broadly refers to the 'revival' of the significance of railways vis-à-vis other transport modes in all major areas like academic research, policy discussion and planning, investment and capacities, passenger ridership and freight turnovers. One of the early awakening calls of the possible 'revival' of railways as a transport mode was the special issue of *Built Environment* edited by Banister and Hall (1993) entitled 'The Age of the Train', which focuses on the opportunities brought about by high-speed railways (HSRs). Among other earlier advocates of the 'renewed' general significance of railways is Lowe (1993: 121), who states that 'many transport problems of the twentieth century can be addressed by creating a diverse system in which rail plays a *major* role'. Instead of blaming railways for not making sufficient way to motorways, railways are increasingly seen as a potential 'solution' to many problems caused by the negative transport externalities of automobiles, such as the consumption of non-renewable energy, air pollution, noise, traffic injuries and congestion. About 15 years after 1993, Givoni and Holvad (2009) asked the question 'Is the Second Railway Age Still Here or Yet to Begin?' in another special issue of the *Built Environment* in 2009 entitled 'Railways in Europe: A New Era?'. And their conclusion, though not without qualifications, is that 'overall, European rail transport has certainly made a comeback and once again it is expected to take a leading role in fulfilling the mobility needs of society' (Givoni and Holvad 2009: 9).

The reasons for the new expectations on railways as a sustainable transport mode in the twenty-first century are multifold. First and foremost are the worldwide awareness and concerns over negative environmental impacts, particularly air pollution, caused by the heavy reliance of automobiles and air transport (Akerman and Hojer 2006, Banister 2003, Bristow et al. 2008, Committee on Climate Change 2008, European Commission 2012, Newman et al. 1995). Historically, the environmental concerns were very much focused on energy consumption, oil depletion and its associated high costs (a sizeable literature can be found on the Oil Crisis and Peak Oil) (Gillham 2002, Ullman 1954). Nonetheless, transport pollutants, particularly greenhouse gases (GHG) and the associated impacts on climate change, were getting more attention in the twenty-first century (Akerman and Hojer 2006, Deakin 2002). In this regard, the potential contribution of railways in reducing carbon emissions and energy consumption has been studied in both developed (Akerman and Hojer 2006, Bristow et al. 2008, Department for Transport 2008, Gudmundsson and Höjer 1996, Holden and Hoyer 2005, McCarthy 2010, Tight et al. 2005, US Department of Transportation 2010) and developing countries (Imura and Mitra 2003, Loo and Li 2012, Ramanathan and Parikh 1999, Ribeiro and Balassiano 1997, Wang et al. 2007). In particular, the argument of railways being more environmentally friendly has been put forward in a strong manner in Europe (Committee on Climate Change 2008, European Commission 2012, Janic 2007, Lewis et al. 2001, van Ierland et al. 2000).

Secondly, there is an increasing awareness that other drastic alternative solutions, such as the substitution of transportation by telecommunication (Loo 2012, Mokhtarian 1990, Sloman 2003, Tayyaran and Khan 2003) or the widespread use of alternative fuel automobiles (Adler et al. 2003, Bunch et al. 1993, Li and Loo 2014, Sperling 1988, 1995), are not going to work in the foreseeable future. People are not making less trips over time (Banister 1999). In addition, many of these trips were of longer distances and duration due to the increasing separation of people's homes and their activities, ranging from work to education, leisure and recreation (Banister 2005, Cervero and Wu 1997, Ewing 1997). In cities, a sustainable transport mode which can fulfill people's desire for high mobility with low negative environmental, social, economic and financial impacts arouse new academic interest (Holden and Hoyer 2005). The term sustainable mobility emphasizes that 'the output from transport' is to be maintained or increased but 'the energy inputs, particularly in terms of the use of non-renewable resources' are to be reduced (Banister 2007: 91). Against such background, the eminent position of railways becomes most obvious. Metro systems are in a prime position among other transport modes, especially vis-à-vis road transport, in the sustainability hierarchy for short-distance passenger transport within large metropolitan cities. In relation, the importance of metro systems within cities is also receiving more attention in the broader context of promoting rail-based transit-oriented development (TOD) (Currie 2006, Kain and Liu 1999, Kuby et al. 2004, Litman 2006, Loo et al. 2010).

Thirdly, the process of globalization has meant that many goods and services consumed at a locality are no longer produced in the vicinity (Dicken 2007). Despite the fact that the global economy has passed the stage of industrialization, people are demanding and consuming more and more goods rather than fewer of them. These goods need to be transported for longer distances and the total freight volume of the entire world has grown continuously. While long-distance sea transport relying on the container technology has solved part of the problem, the transport problems of getting manufactured goods from factories to ports remain significant. Figure 1.1 illustrates the underlying concept of inland load centres and the key role of railways in an intermodal freight transport system schematically. Accordingly, there have been more research papers on rail freight services at the national and even continental scale (Alix et al. 1999, DeWitt and Clinger 2000, Edmonds 1993, Hayuth 1987, Heaver 1993, Loo and Liu 2005, Slack 1990, van Klink and

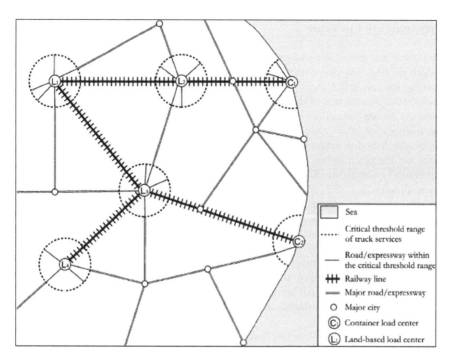

Figure 1.1   A schematic representation of an inland port distribution system
Source: Loo and Liu 2005: 560.

van den Berg 1998). Nowadays, the rapid industrialization of many developing countries actually presents policy makers with a choice of building nationwide highways or railways.

Fourthly, it is the technological advance. The advanced technology of railways has dramatically transformed the 'tarnished' image of railways as being slow, noisy and dirty. In particular, the electrification of railways has not only made this transport mode faster and more reliable but also changed its fundamental nature from a 'dirty' to a 'clean' transport mode. HSRs have put railways in a much better position than other transport modes, especially vis-à-vis air transport, in the sustainability hierarchy for medium- to long-distance passenger transport among cities at the national and international levels. This view was expressed by Hall (2009: 68) who remarks that 'on the evidence so far, high-speed rail in Europe is a technology *whose time has come*'. Much attention has also been put on the economic case of HSRs (Campos and de Rus 2009, US Department of Transportation 2009), and the importance of HSR networks in national and regional socio-economic integration (AECOM and Infrastructure Partnerships Australia 2010, Director-General for Mobility and Transport 2010) and spatial restructuring (Hall 2009, Kim 2000, Peeters et al. 2000). With a longer-term view, the development of HSRs for freight has also received some attention (Pazour et al. 2010).

Key Issues and Challenges

In light of new expectations on railways in the twenty-first century and the lack of a book which provides a synthesis on the renewed interest on railway expansion and their wide-ranging environmental, socio-economic and even political implications, this book is based both on the research of the Editors in the area over the last decade or so and those of others who are experts the railway developments in other parts of the world. It aims to provide an overview of where railways have succeeded and where they do not have a chance from a realistic but optimistic perspective. The fundamental belief is that the 'Railway Era' has the potentials of 'reviving' itself against the broad conceptual framework of sustainability. Nonetheless, there are many challenges and one should not make a sweeping generalization that 'railways will work everywhere and under all circumstances'. In fact, railways may not represent a more sustainable option in some circumstances, even from an environmental or economic perspective (van Ierland et al. 2000, Lee et al. 2009). Based on the above understandings, the rest of this book is structured around several key issues and challenges identified to be crucial in understanding the dynamics and impacts of modern railways. Following the conceptual framework of sustainability, these issues and challenges are organized along the major dimensions of sustainability, that is, the geographical (Section II), environmental (Section III), social (Section IV), economic and financial (Section V) dimensions.

Section II: Transforming Place and Space: Geographical Dimensions

This first major section looks at the geographical dimensions of railways in transforming place and space. The key theme is to promote a better integration of the railway systems with, firstly, the surrounding environment, society, economy, and, secondly, other connecting or nearby railway systems. It consists of three chapters. Chapter 2 is devoted to the structuring impacts of mega-railway terminals which provide the interconnections both among different railway lines (city, inter-city and even international) and other transport modes. The successful planning of these mega-railway terminals is of great importance. For passenger railways, these mega terminals are often based on HSR stations. Some examples are Hongqiao at Shanghai, China and the Crossrail interchange station at London, UK. For freight railways, these mega rail-based transshipment terminals are also particularly important in shaping future rail geography (Ballis and Golias 2002, Wiegmans et al. 2007, Rodrigue 2008). Rodrigue (2008: 233) has put forward the concept of 'Thruport' to describe facilities 'designed to handle high volume of transmodal rail shipments'. This chapter will focus on issues pertinent to the planning, construction and operations of these railway mega terminals.

Chapter 3 looks at issues and challenges of railway integration at the national scale. The key challenge is to promote 'seamless' integration of different railway lines (even systems) at different spatial scales. In the USA, for instance, there were 23 different railroad track gauges in use at the time of the American Civil War; and the use of uniform track gauges in the USA, Canada and Russia was only achieved in 1869, 1885 and 1904 respectively (Knowles 2006). Nowadays, problems of gauge differences still exist widely (Jauernig and Roe 2000). This chapter, therefore, focuses on system wide issues within the railway sector like gauges, technologies, and specific issues like costly and time-consuming interchanges and tariffs for passenger railways and transshipment for freight railways.

Finally, Chapter 4 focuses on cross-border railway integration at the continental scale and examines issues and challenges related specifically to cross-border passenger and freight transport. While differences in national gauges are major issues, the solutions are very different for railway systems involving more than one country. The problems of HSR in Europe with 'different electrical power systems, different signalling systems, different safety requirements and even different track beds' were highlighted by Hall (2009: 62). In relation, the successful experience of the European Union in overcoming many of these hurdles is expected to be the focus of this chapter. Nonetheless, this chapter will also highlight areas which may be unique to Europe and not transferable to other major cross-border railway networks.

Section III: Save Our Earth!: Environmental Dimensions

This section consisting of three chapters, looks at various issues about the environmental sustainability of railways. In particular, it is recognized that specific environmental benefits and costs of different transport modes differ widely among different countries (Ramanathan and Parikh 1999, van Ierland et al. 2000). Generally, environmental benefits of railways hinge on a modal shift *away* from other less environmentally-friendly modes; and not newly-generated traffic induced by new or improved railway infrastructure (Ribeiro and Balassiano 1997). Hence, this section focuses on case studies and factors which affect modal shifts in particular railway sectors. Several strategies are particularly relevant in promoting a modal shift of passenger and freight transport from other less environmentally friendly transport modes. Chapter 5 examines various aspects of TOD in diverting passenger traffic from automobiles for short- to medium-distance travel within cities. Metro systems, which are able to maximize mobility in a high-density environment with minimal land uptake, are the focus. Yet, metro systems are not universally suitable for cities of all population sizes and income levels (Loo and Cheng 2010, Loo and Li 2006). Technically, metro systems are not as flexible as private cars or other on-road mass transit modes to respond to vagaries in travel demand both spatially within networks and temporally at different times (Givoni et al. 2009). Apart from Asia, more success has been achieved in Europe (Bratzel 1999, Knowles 2006). In this chapter, TOD is critically examined as a land conservation tool and a sustainable solution to the traffic gridlock in cities.

Chapter 6 examines factors affecting the ability of HSRs in diverting passenger traffic from air and road transport for medium- to long-distance travel. This modal shift is particularly important because the carbon emissions of international air travel (and international shipping) are currently excluded from the Kyoto Protocol due to difficulties of assigning these emissions to specific countries (Potter and Bailey 2008). Despite some recent efforts to levy international tax on gasoline used in air transportation, 'the aviation industry is effectively "free-riding" the efforts of other sectors of the economy to reduce CO_2 emissions' (Ibid.: 46). Research so far indicates that the relative attractiveness of HSRs vis-à-vis air and other inter-city road transport depends on various factors, such as 'car affection', environmental knowledge, journey time and other level-of-service attributes (Gonzalez-Savignat 2004, Givoni et al. 2009, B. Graham 1998, Nilsson and Pyddoke 2009).

Lastly, Chapter 7 analyzes the potential of railways in diverting freight traffic from road transport. This modal shift is potentially environmentally friendly and is related to the broader concept of green logistics (Bauer et al. 2009, Rodrigue et al. 2001). Apart from the reduced air pollution, lower noise pollution and road safety hazards are major potential benefits (Forkenbrock 2001). This chapter examines several key issues involved in realizing the potential emission, noise and safety benefits of modern freight railways. Notably, van Ierland, Graveland and Huiberts (2000) and Lee et al. (2009) have argued that new rail freight lines were not 'better solutions' in the contexts of Rotterdam in the Netherlands, and the San Pedro Bay Ports complex of Los Angeles and Long Beach in Southern California respectively.

Section IV: Equity and Accessibility: Social Dimensions

This section, consisting of three Chapters, deals with issues about the social sustainability of railways and its impacts on equity and accessibility. Case studies are selected around the key themes of people-based mobility (Chapter 8), place accessibility (Chapter 9) and small markets (Chapter 10).

Chapter 8 focuses on the transport disadvantaged, especially those who do not own a car in developed economies. Railways can reduce social inequity by providing non-car-users with high accessibility to opportunities. In this chapter, the transport disadvantaged concept is not limited to those who do not own a car. It also encompasses people with low income (who may own a car), children and youngsters (who may come from car-owning households), women, the elderly, the disabled (including temporary ones), ethnic minorities and all those who suffer from the 'mobility gap' and are 'accessibility deficit' (Knowles 2006). This chapter will present some cases of successful railway development that facilitates various transport disadvantaged groups in gaining higher accessibility to opportunities, particularly jobs, education and training.

Chapter 9 examines the issues and implications of the rise of localism that is becoming increasingly evident in many places internationally. The research focuses on the issues that can arise from public engagement in strategic infrastructure planning and development, and the processes which railway infrastructural projects may undergo in order to make modern railway services available. Many challenges face large-scale infrastructural development in democratic societies (Doherty 1999). Building and operating modern railways, especially HSRs, are expensive. Critically, different places will not benefit equally from increased accessibility and some may experience great environmental harm without commensurate social or economic benefits. The chapter takes three case studies of railway development at quite different scales in the UK to explore these challenges and to identify potential strategies for promoting railway infrastructural development while supporting a greater emphasis on localism.

Chapter 10 looks at the challenges of serving small markets and maintaining services with limited traffic. To what extent can railways play a role in promoting social and economic equity, and redressing spatial imbalance? Specifically, Spychalski and Swan (2004: 165) remark that 'financial practices in some mergers have had negative impact on the ability of carriers to meet public service needs'. Moreover, one of the unintended consequences of higher speed of railways is the 'peripheralization of the periphery', whereby railways 'may increasingly concentrate on profitable traffic between large urban centres while bypassing smaller and less profitable places' at the regional scale (Hall 2009: 63). Freight rail traffic concentration and the closing down of stations with insufficient traffic are expected (Larson and Spraggins 2000, Slack 1990). However, how can these undesirable effects be better addressed? Is there a way out? This chapter addresses the various key issues and challenges involved.

Section V: Making Ends Meet: Economic Dimensions

Making ends meet is important to ensure the long-term economic and financial sustainability of railways, either for passenger or freight. In fact, the need for long-term subsidies has always been a major criticism for railways. This section (Section V) consists of three chapters which examine various specific 'models' or strategies that aim to turn railways from a liability to an asset. Chapter 11 discusses the issues involved in the strategy of developing or even exporting modern railway technologies (including hardware and software) as a source of income. In some cases, these railway-related technologies are exported overseas to generate foreign exchange. Some examples of railway-related hardware include locomotives (especially high-speed trains), tracks and electricity and signalling systems. Apart from these high-technology industries, railway engineering and management expertise can be provided as services to generate income. Examples from France, Germany, Japan and China are included.

Chapter 12 examines the rail-cum-property model in financing both the railway infrastructure and its operating expenses. An overview of major railway systems worldwide shows that many are not financially viable. This is partly due to the expensive initial capital investment of all major transport infrastructural projects. For instance, Flyvbjerg et al. (2003) examine 258 transport projects in 20 countries, they found that 90 per cent had cost underestimates or overruns averaging 28 per cent. In particular, traffic forecasts for rail projects were often too optimistic (Flyvbjerg et al. 2003, Gibb 1994, Loo 2009). With the rail-cum-property model, the Mass Transit Railway Corporation in Hong Kong has managed to maintain its financial viability. Nonetheless, there are various pros and cons of using this model to finance railway infrastructure and its operating expenses. This chapter will systematically examine the pros and cons of the rail-cum-property model and critically examine its applicability beyond Hong Kong.

Chapter 13 looks at the strategy of enhancing intermodalism to make railway operations financially viable at the national or even continental scale. Examples of freight railways in Europe and North America are included. In particular, double-stack railways with excellent connections with ports and other transport modes were considered as reasons for the revival of the freight railway system (Edmonds 1993, Luberoff and Walder 2000). Moreover, railway mergers and acquisitions involving transport operators with experience in intermodal service were often instrumental in making railway operations profitable again (Alix et al. 1999, Bezar 1997, McCalla 1999). This chapter, in addressing the intermodalism issue, will also touch on the key issues of railway privatization, mergers and acquisitions.

Section VI: Looking Forward

The discussion above lays the background for the rest of the book and puts railways in the wider context of comprehensive sustainability. Back in 1993, Banister and Hall (1993: 157) remarked that 'transport technologies seldom make a comeback, save in nostalgia trips for well-heeled tourists. Stagecoaches have not made a reappearance on the Bath Road, nor sedan chairs on the streets of London. But there is a spectacular exception: railways, written off 30 years ago as a Victorian anachronism destined to atrophy before the steady growth of motorway traffic, have suddenly become one of the basic technologies of the twenty-first century'. The optimism, which was also reflected by other researchers (Haywood 1999, Loo and Hook 2002, Woodburn 2001), was very much based on the key premise that modern railways rank high on the sustainability hierarchy in both passenger and freight transport. Some of the major arguments are being presented in this chapter.

Nonetheless, it should be recognized that these potential benefits remain promises only. In this book, there is no attempt to evaluate whether railways have revived themselves in a cross-sectional study of countries in different parts of the world. It is recognized that railways are not yet the dominant transport mode even in Europe where the HSR networks are the most comprehensive. Moreover, reverse trends of countries transforming from rail-dominant to road-dominant transport are still reported, especially in developing countries (Ramanathan and Parikh 1999). In fact, it is believed that railways can play different roles in different parts of the world, at different scales and with specific circumstances. For instance, the success of the metro system in New York City is not easily transferable to other American cities. Therefore, the focus of the rest of this book is put on identifying the key issues and challenges pertinent to understanding whether and how railways have the potential to 'revitalize' themselves as a transport mode in different parts of the world, and how best to support railways in realizing their potential of contributing to the environmental, social, economic and financial and geographical dimensions of comprehensive sustainability. If the 'Railway Era' is to be 'revived', the coming decades will present a golden opportunity.

References

Abramovitz, M. 1955. The economic characteristics of railroads and the problem of economic development. *Far Eastern Quarterly*, 15, 169–78.

Adler, T., Wargelin, L., Kostyniuk, L.P., Kavalec, C. and Occhuizzo, G. 2003. *Incentives for Alternate Fuel Vehicles: A Large-Scale Stated Preference Experiment.* Paper to the 10th International Conference on Travel Behaviour Research, Luzern, Switzerland, 10–15 August 2003.

AECOM and Infrastructure Partnerships Australia. 2010. *East Coast High Capacity Infrastructure Corridors*. Sydney: AECOM Australia PTY Limited.

Akerman, J. and Hojer, M. 2006. How much transport can the climate stand? Sweden on a sustainable path in 2050. *Energy Policy*, 34, 1944–57.

Alix, Y., Slack, B. and Comtois, C. 1999. Alliance or acquisition? Strategies for growth in the container shipping industry, the case of CP ships. *Journal of Transport Geography*, 7(3), 203–8.

Ballis, A. and Golias, J. 2002 Comparative evaluation of existing and innovative rail-road freight transport terminals. *Transportation Research A*, 36(7), 593–611.

Banister, D. 1999. Planning more and travel less: land use and transport. *Town Planning Review*, 70(3), 313–38.

Banister, D. 2003. Introduction: transport policy and the environment, in *Transport Policy and the Environment*, edited by D. Banister. New York: Routledge, 1–16.

Banister, D. 2005. *Unsustainable Transport: City Transport in the New Century*. London and New York: Routledge.

Banister, D. 2007. Sustainable transport: challenges and opportunities, *Transportmetrica*, 3(2), 91–106.

Banister, D. and Hall, P. 1993. The second railway age. *Built Environment*, 19(2/3), 157–62.

Bauer, J., Bektas, T. and Crainic, T.G. 2009. Minimizing greenhouse gas emissions in intermodal freight transport: an application to rail service design. *Journal of the Operational Research Society*, 61, 530–42.

Berechman, J., Ozmen, D., and Ozbay, K. 2006. Empirical analysis of transportation investment and economic development at state, county and municipality levels. *Transportation*, 33(6), 537–51.

Bezar, F.A. 1997. The emerging intermodal market in China. *Transportation and Distribution*, 38(12), 82–7.

Bratzel, S. 1999. Conditions of success in sustainable urban transport policy change in 'relatively successful' European cities. *Transport Reviews*, 19(2), 177–90.

Bristow, A.L., Tight, M., Pridmore, A. and May, A.D. 2008. Developing pathways to low carbon land-based passenger transport in Great Britain by 2050. *Energy Policy*, 36(9), 3427–35.

Buchanan, C. 1963. *Traffic in Towns*. London: H.M.S.O.

Buchanan, M. 2004. More or less traffic in towns? *Proceedings of the Institution of Civil Engineers-Transport*, 157(1), 27–41.

Buchhofer, E. 1995. Transport infrastructure in the Baltic States during the transformation to market economies. *Journal of Transport Geography*, 3(1), 69–75.

Bunch, D.S., Bradley, M., Golob, T.F., Kitamura, R. and Occhiuzzo, G.P. 1993. Demand for clean-fuel vehicles in California: a discrete-choice stated preference pilot project. *Transportation Research A*, 27(3), 237–53.

Campos, J. and de Rus, G. 2009. Some stylized facts about high-speed rail: a review of HSR experiences around the world, *Transport Policy*, 16(1), 19–28.

Cervero, R. 1995. Sustainable new towns. *Cities*, 12(1), 41–51.

Cervero, R. and Wu, K.L. 1997. Polycentrism, commuting and residential location in the San Francisco Bay Area. *Environment and Planning A*, 29, 865–86.

Chandler, A.D. 1965. The railroads: pioneers in modern corporate management. *The Business History Review*, 39(1), 16–40.

Clifton, K.J., Smith, A.D.L. and Rodriguez, D. 2007. The development and testing of an audit for the pedestrian environment. *Landscape and Urban Planning*, 80(1–2), 95–110.

Coatsworth, J.H. 1979. Indispensable railroads in a backward economy: the case of Mexico. *Journal of Economic History*, 34(4), 939–60.

Committee on Climate Change. 2008. *Building a Low-carbon Economy: The UK's Contribution to Tackling Climate Change*. London: TSO.

Cooper, J.S.L. and Edwards, P. 1982. *Roads and Industrial Development*. Paper to the PTRC Summer Annual Meeting, Warwick, England, 12–15 July 1982.

Crane, R. 1999. *The Impacts of Urban Form of Travel: A Critical Review. Lincoln Institute of Land Policy*. Working Paper WP99RC1 [Online]. Available at: http://www.lincolninst. edu/workpap/wpap13.html.

Currie, G. 2006. Bus transit oriented development-strengths and challenges relative to rail. *Journal of Public Transportation*, 9(4), 1–21.

David, P.A. 1969. Transport innovation and economic growth: Professor Fogel on and off the rails. *Economic History Review*, 22, 506–25.

Deakin, E. 2002. Sustainable transportation U.S. dilemmas and European experiences. *Transportation Research Record*, 1792, 1–11.

Debbage, K.G. and Delk, D. 2001. The geography of air passenger volume and local employment patterns by US metropolitan core area: 1973–1996. *Journal of Air Transport Management*, 7(3), 159–67.

Dennis, N. 1995. Airline hub operations in Europe. *Journal of Transport Geography*, 2(4), 219–33.

Department of the Environment, Transport and the Regions (DETR). 1999. *A Better Quality of Life: A Strategy for Sustainable Development for the UK, CM 4345*. London: DETR.

Department for Transport (DfT). 2008. *Building Sustainable Transport into New Developments: A Menu of Options for Growth Points and Eco-towns*, London: DfT.

DeWitt, W. and Clinger, J. 2000. *Intermodal Freight Transportation*. [Online: Transportation Research Board]. Available at: http://onlinepubs.trb.org/onlinepubs/ millennium/00061. pdf [accessed: 30 January 2012].

Dicken, P. 2007. *Global Shift: Mapping the Changing Contours of the World Economy*. 5th Edition. London: Sage; New York: Guilford.

Director-General for Mobility and Transport. 2010. *High-speed Europe*. Luxembourg: Publications Office of the European Union.

Doherty, J.A. 1999. The railway policy debate in Japan and its domination by old debt. *Journal of Transport Economics and Policy*, 33(1), 55–110.

Downs, A. 1998. How America's cities are growing: the big picture. *Brookings Review*, 16(4), 8–12.

Edmonds, J.A. 1993. Canadian railways in the double-stack era: an operator's view. *Journal of Transport Geography*, 1(3), 195–7.

Eusebio, V.E. and Rindom, S.J. 1994. Community impacts of local and regional railroad: a Kansas case study. *Transportation Research Record*, 1450, 53–8.

European Commission. 2012. *The Contribution of Transport to Air Quality*. Luxembourg: Office for Official Publications of the European Union.

Ewing, R. 1997. Is Los Angeles-lifestyle sprawl desirable? *Journal of the American Planning Association*, 63(1), 107–26.

Ewing, R., Pendall, R. and Chen, D. 2003. Measuring sprawl and its transportation impacts. *Journal of the Transportation Research Board*, 1831, 175–83.

Fenoaltea, S. 1972. Railroads and Italian industrial growth, 1861–1913. *Explorations in Economic History*, 9(1), 325–51.

Fishlow, A. 1965. *American Railroads and the Transformation of the Antebellum Economy*. Cambridge: Harvard University Press.

Fleming, W.J. 1987. *Regional Development and Transportation in Argentina: Mendoza and the Gran Oeste Argentino Railroad*. New York: Garland Pub.

Flyvbjerg, B., Skamris, H.M.K. and Buhl, S.L. 2003. How common and how large are cost overruns in transport infrastructure projects? *Transport Reviews*, 23(1), 71–88.

Fogel, R.W. 1979. Notes on the social saving controversy. *Journal of Economic History*, 39(1), 1–54.

Forkenbrock, D.J. 2001. Comparison of external costs of rail and truck freight transportation. *Transportation Research A*, 35(4), 321–37.

Forkenbrock, D.J. and Foster, N.S.J. 1990. Economic benefits of a corridor highway investment. *Transportation Research A*, 24(4), 303–12.

Foster, N.S.J., Forkenbrock, D.J. and Pogue, T.F. 1991. Evaluation of a state-level road program to promote local economic development. *Transportation Quarterly*, 45(4), 493–515.

Fullerton, B. 1975. *The Development of British Transport Networks*. London: Oxford University Press.

Gibb R.A. 1994. *The Channel Tunnel: A Geographical Perspective*. Chichester: Wiley.

Gillham, O. 2002. *The Limitless City: A Primer on the Urban Sprawl Debate*. Washington, DC: Island Press.

Givoni, M. and Banister, D. 2007. Role of the railways in the future of air transport. *Transportation Planning and Technology*, 30(1), 95–112.

Givoni, M., Brand, C. and Watkiss, P. 2009. Are railways 'climate friendly'? *Built Environment*, 35(1), 70–85.

Givoni, M. and Holvad, T. 2009. The prospects for European railways: is the second railway age still here or yet to begin? *Built Environment*, 35(1), 5–11.

Goetz, A.R. 2006. Air passenger transportation and growth in the U.S. urban system, 1950–1987. *Growth and Change*, 23(2), 217–38.

Gonzalez-Savignat, M. 2004. Competition in air transport. *Journal of Transport Economies and Policy*, 38(1), 77–108.

Graham, A. 2000. Demand for leisure air travel and limits to growth. *Journal of Air Transport Management*, 6(2), 109–18.

Graham, B. 1998. Liberalization, regional economic development and the geography of demand for air transport in the European Union. *Journal of Transport Geography*, 6(2), 87–104.

Graham, B. and Goetz, A.R. 2008. Global air transport, in *Transport Geographies: Mobilities, Flows and Spaces*, edited by R.D. Knowles, J. Shaw and I. Docherty. Oxford: Blackwell, 137–55.

Greene, D.L. and Wegener, M. 1997. Sustainable transport. *Journal of Transport Geography*, 5(3), 177–90.

Gudmundsson, H. and Höjer, M. 1996. Sustainable development principles and their implications for transport. *Ecological Economics*, 19(3), 269–82.

Guiliano, G. 1986. Land-use impacts of transportation investments: highway and transit, in *The Geography of Urban Transportation*, edited by S. Hanson. New York: The Guilford Press, 237–73.

Gwilliam, K.M. 1970. The indirect effects of highway investment. *Regional Studies*, 4, 167–76.

Gwilliam, K.M. 1979. Transport infrastructure investments and regional development, in *Inflation, Development, and Integration: Essays in Honour of A J. Brow*, edited by J.K. Bowers. Leeds: Leeds University Press, 241–62.

Hall, P.V. 2009. Magic carpets and seamless webs: opportunities and constraints for high-speed trains in Europe. *Built Environment*, 35(1), 59–69.

Hawke, G.R. 1970. *Railways and Economic Growth in England and Wales, 1840 1870*. Oxford: Clarendon Press.

Hayuth, Y. 1987. *Intermodality: Concept and Practice: Structural Changes in the Ocean Freight Transport Industry*. London: Lloyd's of London Press.

Haywood, R. 1999. Land development implications of the British rail freight renaissance. *Journal of Transport Geography*, 7(4), 263–75.

Heaver, T.D. 1993. Rail freight service in Canada: restructuring for the North American market. *Journal of Transport Geography*, 1(3), 156–66.

Herranz-Loncán, A. 2006. Railroad impact in backward economies: Spain, 1850–1913. *Journal of Economic History*, 66(4), 853–81.

Holden, E. and Hoyer, K.G. 2005. The ecological footprints of fuels. *Transportation Research D*, 10(5), 395–403.

Hurd, J. 1975. Railways and the expansion of markets in India, 1861–1921. *Explorations in Economic History*, 12, 263–88.

Imura, H. and Mitra, A.P. 2003. *The Budgets of GHGs, Urban Air Pollutants and Their Future Emission Scenarios in Selected Mega-Cities in Asia*. Kobe: APN.

Janic, M. 2007. Modelling the full costs of an intermodal and road freight transport network. *Transportation Research D*, 12(1), 33–44.

Jauernig, C. and Roe, M. 2000. International freight transport in Lithuania. *Transport Reviews*, 20(4), 447–68.

Kain, J.F. and Liu, Z. 1999. Secrets of success: assessing the large increases in transit ridership achieved by Houston and San Diego transit providers. *Transportation Research A*, 33(7–8), 601–24.

Kim, K.S. 2000. High-speed rail developments and spatial restructuring. *Cities*, 17(4), 251–62.

Kim, N.S. and van Wee, B. 2009. Assessment of CO2 emissions for truck-only and rail-based intermodal freight systems in Europe. *Transportation Planning and Technology*, 32(4), 313–33.

Knowles, R.D. 2006. Transport shaping space: differential collapse in time-space. *Journal of Transport Geography*, 14(6), 407–25.

Kovács, G. and Spens, K.M. 2006. Transport infrastructure in the Baltic States post-EU succession. *Journal of Transport Geography*, 14(6), 426–36.

Kuby, M., Barranda, A. and Upchurch, C. 2004. Factors influencing light-rail station boardings in the United States. *Transportation Research A*, 38(3), 223–47.

Lakshmanan, T.R. and Anderson W.P. 2007. Transport's role in regional integration processes, in *Market Access, Trade in Transport Services and Trade Facilitation*, edited by T.R. Lakshmanan and W.P. Anderson. Paris: OECD-ECMT, 45–71.

Larson, P.D. and Spraggins, H.B. 2000. The American railroad industry: twenty years after Staggers. *Transportation Quarterly*, 54(2), 31–45.

Lee, G., You, S., Ritchie, S.G., Saphores, J-D., Sangkapichai, M. and Jayakrishnan, R. 2009. Environmental impacts of a major freight corridor: a study of I-710 in California. *Journal of the Transportation Research Board*, 2123, 119–28.

Leung, C.K. 1980. *China, Railway Patterns and National Goals.* Chicago: University of Chicago Press.

Lewis, I., Semeijn, J. and Vellenga, D. 2001. Issues and initiatives surrounding rail freight transportation in Europe. *Transportation Journal*, 41(2/3), 23–31.

Li, L. and Loo, B.P.Y. 2014. Alternative and transitional energy sources for urban transportation. *Current Sustainable/Renewable Energy Report*, 1(1), 19–26.

Litman, T. 2006. *Rail Transit in America: A Comprehensive Evaluation of Benefits.* Victoria, BC: Victoria Transport Policy Institute, 1–54.

Loo, B.P.Y. 2009. How would people respond to a new railway extension? The value of questionnaire surveys. *Habitat International*, 33, 1–9.

Loo, B.P.Y. 2012. *E-society.* New York: Nova Science.

Loo, B.P.Y., Chen, C. and Chan, E.T.H. 2010. Rail-based transit-oriented development: lessons from New York City and Hong Kong. *Landscape and Urban Planning*, 97, 202–12.

Loo, B.P.Y. and Cheng, A.C.H. 2010. Are there useful yardsticks of population and income level for building metro systems? Some worldwide evidences. *Cities*, 27, 299–306.

Loo, B.P.Y. and Hook, B. 2002. Interplay of international, national and local factors in shaping container port development: a case study of Hong Kong. *Transport Reviews*, 22(2), 219–45.

Loo, B.P.Y. and Li, D.Y.N. 2006. Developing metro systems in the People's Republic of China: policy and gaps. *Transportation*, 33(2), 115–32.

Loo, B.P.Y. and Li, L. 2012. Carbon dioxide emissions from passenger transport in China since 1949: implications for developing sustainable transport. *Energy Policy*, 50, 464–76.

Loo, B.P.Y. and Liu, K. 2005. A geographical analysis of potential railway load centers in China. *Professional Geographer*, 57(4), 558–79.

Lowe, M.D. 1993. Rediscovering rail, in *State of the World, 1993: A Worldwatch Institute Report on Progress toward a Sustainable Society*, edited by L. Starke. New York: Norton, 120–38.

Luberoff, D. and Walder, J. 2000. U.S. ports and the funding of intermodal facilities: an overview of key issues. *Transportation Quarterly*, 54(4), 23–45.

Lucas, K. 2004. *Running on Empty: Transport, Social Exclusion and Environmental Justice*. Bristol: Policy Press.

Mabogunje, A.L. 1989. Movements of goods and services, in *Development Process: A Spatial Perspective*. 2nd Edition. London: Unwin Hyman, 276–303.

McCalla, R.J. 1999. Global change, local pain: intermodal seaport terminals and their service areas. *Journal of Transport Geography*, 7(4), 247–54.

McCarthy, J.E. 2010. *Cars, Trucks and Climate: EPA Regulation of Greenhouse Gases from Mobile Sources*. n.p.: Congressional Research Service.

Metzer, J. 1974. Railroad development and market integration: the case of Tsarist Russia. *Journal of Economic History*, 34(3), 529–49.

Mokhtarian, P.L. 1990. A typology of relationships between telecommunications and transportation. *Transportation Research A*, 24(3), 231–42.

Muller, G. 1995. *Intermodal Freight Transportation*. 3rd Edition. Greenbelt, MD: Intermodal Association of North America.

Nilsson, J.E. and Pyddoke, R., 2009. High-speed railways – a climate policy sidetrack. *Report to the Expert Group for Environmental Studies 2009*. Stockholm: Swedish Ministry of Finance.

Newman, P., Kenworthy, J. and Vintila, P. 1995. Can we overcome automobile dependence? *Cities*, 12(1), 53–65.

O'Brien, P. 1977. *The New Economic History of the Railways*. London: Croom Helm.

O'Connor, K. 1995. Airport development in Southeast Asia. *Journal of Transport Geography*, 3(4), 269–79.

O'Connor, K. 2010. Global city regions and the location of logistics activity. *Journal of Transport Geography*, 18(3), 354–62.

Owen, W. 1964. *Strategy for Mobility: Transportation for the Developing Countries*. Honolulu: East-West Center Press.

Owen, W. 1987. A global overview, in *Transportation and World Development*. Baltimore: Johns Hopkins University Press, 1–16.

Pazour, J.A., Meller, R.D. and Pohl, L.M. 2010. A model to design a national high-speed rail network for freight distribution. *Transportation Research A*, 44(3), 119–35.

Peeters, D., Thisse, J.F. and Thomas, I. 2000. On high-speed connections and the location of activities. *Environment and Planning A*, 32, 2097–112.

Pirie, G.H. 1982. The decivilizing rails: railways and underdevelopment in Southern Africa. *Tijdschrift voor Economische en Sociale Geografie*, 73(4), 221–8.

Potter, S. and Bailey, I. 2008. Transport and the environment, in *Transport Geographies: Mobilities, Flows and Spaces*, edited by R.D. Knowles, J. Shaw, and I. Docherty. Oxford: Blackwell, 29–48.

Preston, J.M. and O'Connor, K. 2008. Revitalised transport geographies, in *Transport Geographies: Mobilities, Flows and Spaces*, edited by R.D. Knowles, J. Shaw, and I. Docherty. Oxford: Blackwell, 227–37.

Rakowski, J.P. and Johnson, J.C. 1979. Airline deregulation: problems and prospects. *Quarterly Review of Economics and Business*, 19(4), 65–78.

Ramanathan, R. and Parikh, J.K. 1999. Transport sector in India: an analysis in the context of sustainable development. *Transport Policy*, 6(1), 35–45.

Ribeiro, S.K. and Balassiano, R. 1997. CO_2 emissions from passenger transport in Rio de Janeiro. *Transport Policy*, 4(2), 135–9.

Rodrigue, J-P. 2008. The Thruport concept and transmodal rail freight distribution in North America. *Journal of Transport Geography*, 16(4), 233–46.

Rodrigue, J-P., Slack, B. and Comtois, C. 2001. Green Logistics, in *Handbook of Logistics and Supply-Chain Management*, edited by A.M. Brewer, K.J. Button and D.A. Hensher. Amsterdam: Pergamon, 339–50.

Rostow, W.W. 1960. *The Stages of Economic Growth: A Non-Communist Manifesto*. New York: Cambridge University Press.

Silverleaf, A. and Turgel, J. 1983. Reflections on transport in the future. *Transport Reviews*, 3(4), 303–27.

Slack, B. 1990. Intermodal transportation in North America and the development of inland load centers. *Professional Geographer*, 42(1), 72–83.

Sloman, L. 2003. *Less Traffic Where People Live: How Local Transport Schemes Can Help Cut Traffic*. London: Royal Commission Exhibition of 1851 Built Environment Fellowships, Transport 2000 and University of Westminster.

Sperling, D. 1995. *Future Drive: Electric Vehicles and Sustainable Transportation*. Washington, DC: Island Press.

Sperling, D. 1988. *New Transportation Fuels: A Strategic Approach to Technological Change*. Berkeley: University of California Press.

Spychalski, J.C. and Swan, P.F. 2004. US rail freight performance under downsized regulation. *Utilities Policy*, 12, 165–79.

State of Victoria. 2008. *Improving Options and Reducing Barriers – Addressing Transport Disadvantage: A Status Report*. Victoria: Department of Transport, Victorian Government, 1–12.

Steg, L. and Gifford, R. 2005. Sustainable transportation and quality of life. *Journal of Transport Geography*, 13(1), 59–69.

Summerhill, W.R. 2005a. Big social savings in a small laggard economy: railroad-led growth in Brazil. *Journal of Economic History*, 65(1), 72–102.

Summerhill, W.R. 2005b. *Profit and Productivity on Argentine Railroads, 1857–1913*. Los Angeles: Department of History UCLA (Mimeo).

Taaffe, E.J., Morrill, R.L. and Gould, P.R. 1963. Transport expansion in underdeveloped countries: a comparative analysis. *Geographical Review*, 53, 503–29.

Tayyaran, M.R. and Khan, A.M. 2003. The effects of telecommuting and intelligent transportation systems on urban development. *Journal of Urban Technology*, 10(2), 87–100.

Tight, M.R., Bristow, A.L., Pridmore, A. and May, A.D. 2005. What is a sustainable level of CO2 emissions from transport activity in the UK in 2050? *Transport Policy*, 12(3), 235–44.

Ullman, E. 1954. Amenities as a factor in regional growth. *Geographical Review*, 44(1), 119–32.

US Department of Transportation. 2009. *Vision for High-speed Rail in America*. Washington, DC: US Department of Transportation.

US Department of Transportation. 2010. *Transportation's Role in Reducing U.S. Greenhouse Gas Emissions, Volume 1: Synthesis Report*. Washington, DC: US Department of Transportation.

van Ierland, E., Graveland, C. and Huiberts, R. 2000. An environmental economic analysis of the new rail link to European main port Rotterdam. *Transportation Research D*, 5(3), 197–209.

van Klink, H.A. and van den Berg, G.C. 1998. Gateways and intermodalism. *Journal of Transport Geography*, 6(1), 1–9.

Vowles, T.M. 2000. The geographic effects of US airline alliances. *Journal of Transport Geography*, 8(4), 277–85.

Wang, C., Cai, W., Lu, X. and Chen, J. 2007. CO2 mitigation scenarios in China's road transport sector. *Energy Conversion and Management*, 48(7), 2110–18.

Wheeler, J.O. 1976. Locational dimensions of urban highway impact: an empirical analysis. *Geografiska Annaler*, 58(2), 67–78.

White, C.M. 1976. The concept of social saving in theory and practice. *Economic History Review*, 29, 82–100.

Wiegmans, B.W., Stekelenburg, D.T., Versteegt, C. and Bontekoning, Y.M. 2007. Modeling rail-rail exchange operations: an analysis of conventional and new-generation terminals. *Transportation Journal*, 46(4), 5–20.

Wilson, G.W. 1966. Concepts and approaches: a critique, in *The Impact of Highway Investment on Development*, edited by G.W. Wilson, B.R. Bergmann, L.V. Hirsch and M.S. Klein. Washington, DC: Transport Research Program, Brookings Institution, 162–73.

Wolfe, R.I. 1963. *Transportation and Politics*. Princeton, NJ: Van Nostrand.

Woodburn, A.G. 2001. The changing nature of rail freight in Great Britain: the start of a renaissance? *Transport Reviews*, 21(1), 1–13.

Wright, P. 1992. Air passenger transport. *Impact of Science on Society*, 162, 191–200.

Zhang, A. 1998. Industrial reform and air transport development in China. *Journal of Air Transport Management*, 4(3), 155–64.

SECTION II
Transforming Place and Space:
Geographical Dimensions

Chapter 2
Structuring Effects of Rail Terminals

Jean-Paul Rodrigue

Introduction: The Renewed Importance of Rail Terminals

Rail Terminals, Then and Now

In the nineteenth and twentieth century the development of rail transport brought significant changes in the mobility of passengers and freight with rail playing a fundamental role in the expansion of resource, industrial and urban landscapes. New resources became available on regional and global markets, some fuelling an emerging industrial and manufacturing sector (e.g. Pred 1964, Fogel 1964). The historical link between railway development and urbanization is also well established (Atack et al. 2010, Fishlow 1965), including its urban spatial structure (e.g. Muller 2004). Several of the first rail lines to be built were portage segments within canal systems or routes aiming at complementing existing canals and filling the gap in their spatial structure. Rail terminals were initially developed to complement the shortcomings of other modes, implying that its structuring effects were the outcome of service gaps in fluvial (canal) and maritime transportation. Because of its cost and time advantages, rail was able to supplant canal services in inland transportation to become the main driver of spatial change in industrializing regions of the world. The space/time convergence effect of rail systems was significant, reducing travel time and improving interactions (Janelle 1968).

Globalization has been associated with a reorientation of trade flows, impacting cities, their regions and their interactions (Hall and Hesse 2013). Like maritime and air transportation, modes significantly impacted by globalization, rail is a heavily terminal dependent activity for its operations. This implies that its structuring effects and added value are dominantly terminal-related since they influence passenger and freight flows and their surrounding economic activities. Considering the new role that rail is expected to play in the twenty-first century, particularly because of intermodal transportation and high-speed train networks, it is relevant to look at what were the main structuring effects of rail terminals in the past and how these effects may unfold in the future (Goetz and Rodrigue 1999). Like any transport mode, rail systems are the outcome of economic and political decisions subject to a regulatory environment pertaining to ownership, capital investment and operations. Thus, due to modal preferences the structuring effects of rail terminals will vary in scale and scope according to the regions where they are operating.

Adjacency, Accessibility and Network Effects

The three main structuring effects of rail terminals involve three tiers: adjacency, accessibility and network effects (Figure 2.1).

Adjacency is a structuring effect where land uses directly adjacent or in close proximity to a rail terminal are strongly influenced by the nature and the level of terminal traffic. Once a specific level of spatial accumulation is attained, they form a cluster benefiting from economies of scale (more traffic leads to lower costs per unit of traffic handled) and agglomeration. For passenger terminals, activities such as hotels, retail outlets, restaurants and offices are usually in close proximity with a good share of their function attributed to the presence of the terminal. New passenger terminal developments, particularly high-speed rail stations, offer the opportunity to establish office parks, including hotels, large surface retail and convention centres. Still, these developments often take place not particularly because of the presence of a high speed station, but because of land availability and road connectivity. For freight terminals, the adjacency effect is also significant and has been observed since the setting of rail systems in the late nineteenth and early twentieth century. Due to their ponderous nature, the storage of several commodities takes place directly adjacent to rail terminals, particularly dedicated single use facilities. Heavy industries such as steel, chemical and cement plants commonly have rail spurs servicing their heavy inputs and outputs. A more recent form of development concerns the setting of large logistics zones that are co-located with intermodal terminals. This mostly takes place in suburban or exurban sites.

Accessibility is a structuring effect where the users of a terminal are impacted by a distance decay function which is related to their intensity and frequency of use. The more reliant the user is on the rail terminal the more likely sites with high accessibility to the facility will be preferred. This effect is generally small as most passengers do not use rail regularly, so as long as the rail terminal is accessible through road or public transit systems, it is said to be reaching a user base. Freight terminals have their own customer base accessible through a drayage distance, which is usually less than a day (about 400 km). The significance of the drayage distance is related to the frequency and intensity of rail use and the relative transport cost in relation to the cargo value.

Network is a structuring effect where a set of interconnected rail terminals are supporting the specialization and interdependency of locations. Networks underline the centrality of some locations, while others assume intermediacy between different systems of circulation (Fleming and Hayuth 1994). For passengers, the network is a reflection of a regional urban system with increasing inter-city commercial and social interactions. While this effect has endured in Europe, India, China and Japan, it has ceased to be relevant in North America with the exception of the Northeast. Yet, high-speed rail systems are permitting the setting of new network effects with increasing interaction levels between cities along the corridors they service, with some terminals, such as Brussels, becoming hubs and thus reflecting and coordinating a new urban hierarchy. For freight, the conventional networking effect of commodities that has supported the interactions between agricultural, mining, energy and forest regions and main manufacturing and consumption markets is being expanded by intermodalism. This is particularly the case with the setting of landbridges in North America and inland load centre networks across the world. The rail terminal becomes an element of a transport chain that can be global in reach. In Europe where intermodal rail played a marginal role until recently, an emerging network effect is being observed with the setting of rail shuttle services between ports and inland terminals.

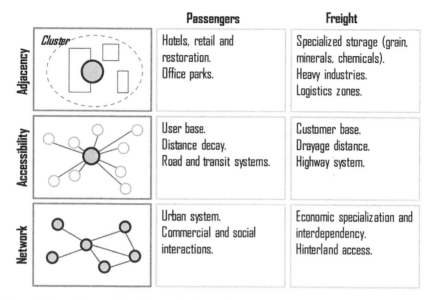

	Passengers	**Freight**
Adjacency	Hotels, retail and restoration. Office parks.	Specialized storage (grain, minerals, chemicals). Heavy industries. Logistics zones.
Accessibility	User base. Distance decay. Road and transit systems.	Customer base. Drayage distance. Highway system.
Network	Urban system. Commercial and social interactions.	Economic specialization and interdependency. Hinterland access.

Figure 2.1   Structuring effects of rail terminals
Source: Author.

This chapter will thus look at the main structuring effects of rail terminals, particularly high-speed rail and intermodal rail. These two types of terminal have been significant drivers of the new and expanded role that passenger and freight terminals play in twenty-first century mobility. First, a review of the locational dynamics of rail terminal will be undertaken, particularly the role each type of terminal plays in passenger or freight transport systems. Then, an overview of the structuring effects of high-speed rail and intermodal terminals will be provided as an example of new infrastructure developments associated with the renaissance of rail. The chapter will conclude with some of the implications of the spatial re-bounding of rail terminals and their impacts on the future of rail.

Rail Terminals and Location

Typology of Rail Terminals

Even if they share the same infrastructure, a separation between passenger and freight terminals occurred early the development of rail transportation since both process were linked with different locational dynamics. Although some terminals may handle both passenger and rail traffic, they are uncommon and serve very specific niches (e.g. mail). Rail terminals can be categorized by the passenger and freight markets they service with the function of shunting accounting for an intermediary form used by both systems (Figure 2.2). Passenger and freight terminals can also be differentiated by their locational setting, such as if they are in an urban or suburban setting and the type of terminal servicing function they may fulfil.

The inter-city rail terminal, often taking the form of a central station, is the standard passenger terminal and a distinctive urban landmark since many have been present for decades and have helped defined urban centrality. Commuter rail covers metropolitan regions with stations of a simpler design and function since waiting time is of short duration. Urban transit systems are also serviced by rail, namely subway and light rail, and depending on density levels are shaping urban dynamics through their network structure. There is thus a whole hierarchy of rail stations depending on their size and the passenger traffic they handle, ranging from simple quay along a commuter line to large central stations that the hub for inter-city, commuter and urban transit rail systems. A much more recent type of rail terminal involves high-speed rail stations which has either required the adaptation of existing central stations to provide spurs connected to the high-speed rail network or the construction of new dedicated terminals in suburban areas that can act as new poles of urban development. The growth of air transportation has conferred new opportunities for rail, with the airport becoming a hub for inter-city, commuter and urban transit. In some instances, a high-speed rail station is part of the airport terminal complex.

For bulk, rail freight terminals tend to be commodity specific with dedicated facilities for either loading or unloading (both activities rarely take place at the same terminal). Roll-on/roll-off terminals are even simpler since a simple ramp is required to load or unload the equipment, but a large amount of parking space is needed to store the vehicles. Break-bulk rail terminals concern a wide variety of activities where the loading and unloading often take

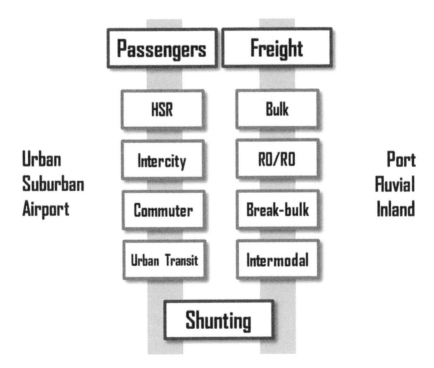

Figure 2.2   Typology of rail terminals
Source: Author.

place at small privately owned facilities serviced by rail spurs. It is the intermodal terminal that has seen the most developments with the setting of facilities handling international and domestic containers. The locational setting of rail freight terminals is usually centred along port terminals, fluvial terminals (less common) or inland locations providing accessibility to markets or resources.

While shunting yards are not necessarily a terminal since they do not handle passengers or cargo, they are a fundamental element of rail operations. The shunting of passenger rail cars is important but less frequent and often takes place at maintenance yards or at yards near central stations (also known as coach yards). For freight, particularly non-intermodal cars, shunting is an important function to assemble, sort and breakdown train units based upon a variety of cargoes, origins and destinations.

Passenger Terminals

Passenger rail terminals tend to be facilities with a simple functionality including platforms for passengers to embark or disembark and a common area for ticket purchase, waiting, and for activities present when there are large volumes of people such as retail and refreshment. Like any other terminal facility, rail terminals have a size and complexity directly related to the amount of passengers they serve. Some are simple facilities with only a platform requiring a short stop so that passengers can embark or disembark, while at the other end of the spectrum there are large terminal facilities at the nexus of inter-city corridors composed of enclosed facilities with multiple piers and amenities. The importance of passenger rail terminals is reflected in the rail network structure (Bertolini and Spit 1998).

The development of high-speed rail systems has offered new opportunities for rail terminals as the public and private sectors provided capital for infrastructure development. Several existing facilities, many of which are at central railway stations, were renovated while new facilities were constructed, many in suburban areas. The centrality of rail stations within the urban landscape became a positive factor in the development of high-speed rail systems. Even if most cities have seen a decline of their central business district (CBD) to the advantage of suburban areas, the CBD still offered a density of commercial activities and employment that was within direct reach of central rail stations well serviced by public transit systems. In many cases the high-speed rail station became a new nexus of activity with co-located real estate developments such as office buildings, retail stores, hotels and parking facilities.

An additional level of integration and structuring effect concerns the design of airport terminals incorporating high-speed rail stations, such as Charles de Gaulle (Paris), Schiphol (Amsterdam) and Pudong (Shanghai). The connectivity of such airports to air transport networks is expanded by the regional accessibility HSR confers. Over specific corridors in France, Belgium, Spain and Germany, high-speed rail stations are effectively competing with airports. Some air carriers such as Air France and Lufthansa are starting to offer services that include a rail segment, implying that the train station becomes a proxy for the airport. In some instances such as Hong Kong, a centrally located public transit station servicing an airport terminal with a rail connection (light or heavy rail) and offer ticket and luggage check-in services. Such practices are bound to be adopted elsewhere. A better integration between passenger rail and air transportation therefore enables substitution of air travel and the possibility to use rail stations as *satellite airport terminals*. This is linked with new forms of airport competitiveness and additional structuring effects for rail stations able to connect with airports.

Freight Terminals

Unlike passenger terminals, rail terminals do not require to be centrally located since their dynamics are related to different transport chains. The space requirement of their multiple tracks is much more extensive than passenger stations which leads to their location in greenfield sites at the edge of cities. However, rail yards tended to attract manufacturing activities able to use the distribution capabilities of rail, and thus became important industrial zones. When dealing with bulk commodities, rail terminals will locate in proximity to the source as they are the main means for these commodities to be shipped to markets. They also vary in complexity because of the different freight markets they service (e.g. grain, coal, cars, containers) which requires specialized loading/unloading facilities and equipment.

For instance, the grain elevator is a fundamental element of the structuring effect of rail on the resource landscape through the dynamics of collection, sorting and distribution of grain in agricultural regions. The terminal is simply a rail spur where grain wagons can be loaded on the side of the facility. Grain is brought by truck to the facility where it will be sorted and stored by type. Large grain unit trains can be assembled to carry the output of a series of grain elevators to port facilities and then to international markets.

When introduced in the nineteenth century, there was roughly one grain elevator and its associated rail terminal every 10 to 15 km along a rail line. This represented the radius around which agricultural resources could effectively be collected by road transportation. Three significant processes transformed this spatial relation by reducing the number of terminals required to collect the output of agricultural regions. The first was the general improvement in road transportation which enabled agricultural commodities to be carried in greater quantities, over longer distances and at a lower cost. The second was the application of economies of scale in rail transportation, enabling the assembly of longer unit trains. Better services and lower transport rates were offered to facilities that could handle a greater amount of rail cars at their siding. The third involved changes in the commercial environment with agricultural ownership and practices moving towards corporate farming as well as rail deregulation where rail companies abandoned several unprofitable services, which included spurs to smaller grain elevators (Miller et al. 1977, Mac Donald 1989).

By the end of the twentieth century, the location dynamics of many industries that previously relied on rail changed, so facilities located around rail yards relocated or disappeared, leaving large tracks of abandoned land of marginal use. This incited an indirect structuring effect of (former) rail terminals that provided real estate for urban redevelopment in accessible locations. Former rail terminals have been among the most important redevelopment areas due to their large scale, central location and site (often waterfront). Their renovation has had a major influence on the surrounding areas and a factor of urban dynamism to which many cities benefited.

At the same time, new intermodal practices emerged, notably lifting trailers or containers directly onto rail cars. Rail intermodalism required capital investments in equipment as well as large terminal surfaces for storage of trailers and containers. The principle of economies of scale that intermodalism reinforced implied that only terminals with sufficient size and volume could be profitable. Some rail yards closed, either because they were too small for intermodal operations or because of a decline of the local traffic base as the offshoring of manufacturing took place. In spite of a growth of intermodal traffic, the number of intermodal terminals declined, as terminals got larger and correspondingly covered a larger market area.

One of the important growth factors for rail transportation has been its closer integration with maritime shipping. This is particularly the case at port terminals with new on-dock container rail facilities. The term on-dock can itself be a misleading since a direct ship-to-rail transshipment actually rarely takes place. A dray carries the container from alongside the ship to alongside the rail track (and vice versa), but frequently the containers are brought back and forth from a stack. Transloading, the practice of transferring loads between truck and rail transportation, has also experienced a remarkable growth in recent years. As long distance trucking is getting increasingly expensive due to growing energy costs and congestion, many shippers see the advantages of using rail transportation to a location in the vicinity of their markets. At this location, freight loads are broken down into smaller loads and then shipped by short distance trucks to their final destinations. Many port authorities and terminal operators are actively involved in improving the capacity and efficiency of their hinterland reach, implying a growing role of rail in the regionalization of port activities and its structuring effects (Notteboom and Rodrigue 2005).

New Rail Terminals and the Spatial Structure

This section focuses on the structuring effects of two types of rail terminals that have accounted for a large share of the renewed dynamism of rail in the late twentieth and early twenty-first century: high-speed rail and intermodal rail.

High-Speed Rail Terminals

The structuring effects of high-speed rail networks

High-Speed Rail (HSR) systems were set to support high density and high income urban corridors by promoting their accessibility and by filling a gap between the short range mobility offered by the automobile and the mobility offered by air transportation, which covers longer distances. HSR networks were initially set as corridors between city-pairs (point to point services with a few stops in between) and their growth led to an integrated system spanning large urban regions, such as Japan and Western Europe (Givoni 2006). For many HRS systems the simple corridor remains dominant, if not the only type for service, in more complex systems nodes (hubs) have emerged that enable the linking of several HSR corridors. HSR systems are mainly found in three regions of the world where they have contributed to the structuring of inter-city mobility and favouring space-time convergence by cutting rail travel time by half. Readers may refer to Rodrigue (2013) for the figures of world high-speed rail systems 2012.

In Asia, Japan was the first to build an HSR system in 1964, which eventually grew to service most the major metropolitan areas of the country with a particularly high density of services along the Tokyo-Osaka corridor (Smith 2003). South Korea and Taiwan have also built their own HSR systems as a corridor between their two largest cities (Seoul-Busan and Taipei-Kaohsiung respectively). China has embarked on an ambitious infrastructure plan to build a national HSR system leading to a growing level of integration of its urban system. With a network of 8,000 km in 2010, China HSR system has grown rapidly and is already the world's most extensive with 9,300 km being operational at the end of 2012. For instance, the world's longest high-speed rail service between Beijing and Guangzhou was inaugurated in December 2012, taking approximately 8 hours to link both cities. It is expected that by 2020, China's HSR system will total 16,000 km. India has several high speed corridors projects planned, but high capital requirements and securing rights of way are serious challenges.

In Europe, HSR systems have permitted a growing level of inter-city integration, particularly between France, Belgium, the Netherlands, and Germany. They are a strategic component of the development of a trans-European network advocated by the European Union. The completion of the Eurotunnel in 1994 linked London to the European HSR system and favoured the development of a hub at Lille. Spain and Italy have also experienced notable space-time convergence effects where HSR reinforces the national urban system (De Urena 2012). Northern European countries (Norway, Sweden and Finland) have mostly developed their HSR corridors through the reconversion of existing lines, a strategy that reflects the relatively short distances involved and lower population densities. As the 6,600 km European HSR system is getting more integrated, HSR hubs connecting different corridors are emerging, notably Brussels (Charlier 2008).

In North America, the Boston and Washington Acela line is the only operating HSR, but technical requirements limit the speed along several segments of the corridor. Only the New York-Washington segment can be considered high speed. The setting of HSR corridors linking regional urban systems has been debated for more than two decades, with many corridor projects clearly identified and advocated. Yet, the prominence and relatively low cost of the road and air transport have been factors playing against the development of HSR systems. As congestion and capacity constraints become more apparent at airports, the advantages of linking the central areas of large North American cities could stimulate the development of such services. Therefore, the structuring effect of HSR networks in North America is almost insignificant but could become notable pending large sums of capital investment in the development of such networks along major corridors in the Northeast, California, the Midwest, Florida and Texas.

The high-speed rail station as a growth pole

The development of HSR networks and stations underline a new geography of inter-city movements and land use developments. It brings forward a variety of spatial structuring issues for planners and developers, first at the regional level with long term and permanent decisions such as routing, the number and the spacing of stops. This planning and design process brings contentious issues about which cities get serviced and receive infrastructure investments, such as new (or renovated) rail stations. At the local level the location of stations, including their design and integration to urban transport systems, is at the forefront. Local communities have expectations that the station will add a new growth pole and urban real estate development opportunities, particularly around central business districts. Evidence is diverging in terms of what are the structuring effects of HSR stations on regional and local economies and if they may capture new opportunities or facilitate existing activities (Pol 2002). One expectation is that the increasing accessibility HSR confers will expand the economic scope of urban activities and bring added value and tax revenue that will compensate the large capital investment they require, particularly since fares usually do not cover operational and capital costs. As a result, estimating return on investments is not clear for HSR stations since not all added value can be expressed in monetary terms.

Like airport terminals that have been active at capturing added value from activities not directly related to air operations, including real estate development, the HSR station may also trigger such structuring effect. Here, an analogy can be made with the concept of Aerotropolis where the airport terminal becomes the hub of a cluster of airport-related activities (e.g. hotels, convention centres, office towers, distribution centres), all of which are closely integrated in a transport system composed of highways and transit corridors linking the airport with the central urban district (Kasarda and Lindsay 2011). However, in a number of cases involving the development of new stations, the reason why developers are investing in adjacent developments is not necessarily to benefit from the accessibility that the HSR station may confer, but to take advantage of the available real estate, often subsidized by the public sector to promote development. Activities located in rail-centric office parks have generally a low usage of high-speed rail, which questions the direct structuring effect of HSR terminals (Facchinetti-Mannone 2006). Private actors see the development of the commercial function of HSR terminals for the purpose of revenue generation, including residential projects. The HSR station thus represents an opportunity for public-private partnerships with the public sector providing investment in terminal facilities while the private sector focuses upon commercial real estate development. The case of Europe underlines that the structuring effects of HSR terminals are significant, but tends to reinforce the most important urban centres (Pol 2002).

Intermodal Rail Terminals

With globalization and the growth of long distance trade, container rail terminals have come to play a growing role in the structure of regional economic landscapes. This structuring effect can be observed at different scales: the locational and operational constraints of terminal facilities, through the setting of satellite terminals and extended gates, and through the co-locational effects of inland ports (also known as dry ports).

Rail terminal facilities
The intermodal rail facility has specific locational and operational characteristics, which by their nature, have structuring effects. Three major components interact in intermodal terminal operations; rail track operations, storage yard operations and gate operations. The purpose is to ensure that each operation interacts efficiently with the other since a delay with one operation will have impacts on the others. For instance, a problem with storage yard operations will create delays both at the rail track and gate operations and have an impact on the terminal productivity and the quality of its services. An intermodal rail container terminal is commonly composed of the following main elements, each performing a specific function (Figure 2.3):

- *Intermodal yard.* The core of the terminal where unit trains are loaded and unloaded by cranes (rubber-tired gantries) or lifts (side-loaders). They can be more than 2 km in length due to the large size of container unit trains (100 cars). In many cases, namely when the yard is of older design, unit trains are broken down in two or more parts, which leaves a midway crossing for the circulation of chassis within the yard (otherwise movements between the storage area and unit trains would be much longer). Containers are brought trackside or to the storage area by hostlers. Higher intensity terminals are operated with rail-mounted gantry cranes able to straddle over several tracks (up to about eight) and are able to use track-side stack piles; therefore part of the storage area is within the intermodal yard.
- *Storage area.* Acts as a buffer between the road system (drayage) and the intermodal yard. It often covers an area similar in size than the intermodal yard as modern rail intermodal yards are heavy consumers of space. Storage in the intermodal yard can

be grounded where containers are stored by stacking them upon one another, or wheeled with containers stored on chassis. In wheeled terminals, which are common in North America, containers are directly transferred to a chassis waiting to be picked up for delivery, and thus the chassis is an active element of terminal operations. Empties are commonly kept in a specific part of the yard and often as an off-site empty container depot. There are also some storage areas for reefers (refrigerated containers) with power outlets, but this accounts for a small amount of the total storage capacity: 1 to 5 per cent. Users are commonly given a dwell time of 48 hours where their cargo is stored at the terminal at no charge, which gives enough time for outbound loads to be assembled or for customers to prepare for the pick-up of their inbound cargo once they have been notified of its arrival at the terminal.

- *Classification yard.* Can be present if the terminal has been upgraded from a regular freight to a container terminal, but for most modern intermodal rail terminals the classification yard will be absent. Its function is mainly related to the assembly and break down of freight trains carrying other types of cargo. This is necessary because each rail car can be bound for a different destination and can be shunted on several occasions. This mainly takes place at the origin, destination or at an intermediary location (such as Chicago or North Platte). Classification yards are often operated independently from the intermodal yard and have a tendency to be located at different locations.

- *Gate.* This is where the truck driver presents proper documentation (bill of lading) for pick up or delivery. Most of the inspection is done remotely with cameras and intercom systems where an operator can remotely see for instance the container number of an existing truck and verify if it corresponds to the bill of lading. If international cargo is concerned, then it must have been first cleared by customs. To simplify matters and increase throughput, there are often separate entry and exit gates and dedicated lanes for empties or chassis returns.

The synthetic representation of Figure 2.3 underlines that modern intermodal terminals require large sites, are equipment intensive and are associated with a continuous flow of container loads between the terminal and the distribution centres using them. As intermodal

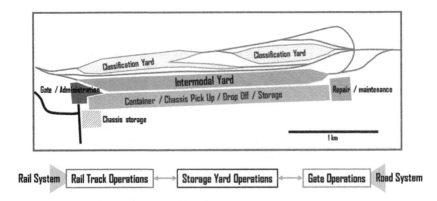

Figure 2.3   Configuration of an intermodal rail terminal
Source: Author.

transportation and international trade grew from the 1990s, the structuring effects of intermodal rail terminals around the world became more apparent.

Inland intermodal terminals
The emergence of inland intermodal terminals is the outcome of several forces, namely the strategies of port authorities, terminal operators and rail operators to more effectively access and compete over the hinterland. The promotion of economies of scale for inland transportation has logically benefitted rail and required the setting of dedicated inland intermodal terminals, which led to the development of dry ports (Roso and Lumsden 2010, Rodrigue and Notteboom 2012). Such initiatives also require the development of long distance rail corridors having the capacity to accommodate growing intermodal volumes. One key advantage of North America is double stacking along major rail corridors, which expands the structuring effect of these corridors through strategic decisions made by governments and rail operators to provide capital investment to improve their efficiency. In many developing economies, the lack of rail corridors is inhibiting the development of inland ports, leaving them to be truck-based facilities (Ng and Cetin 2012). Thus, looking at the structuring effects of intermodal rail requires the consideration of the whole inland transport chain (Figure 2.4).

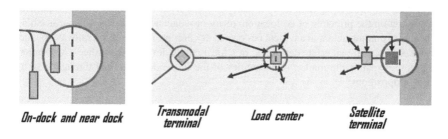

On-dock and near dock   **Transmodal terminal**   **Load center**   **Satellite terminal**

Figure 2.4   Types of intermodal rail terminals
Source: Rodrigue and Hatch 2009.

At the head of an inland corridor rail terminals are linked with port terminals through on-dock and near-dock facilities. While for an on-dock rail terminal containers can be moved directly from the dock (or the storage areas) to a railcar using the terminal's own equipment, accessing a near-dock facility requires clearing the terminal's gate, using the local road system and clearing the gate of the near-dock rail terminal. Near-dock facilities tend to have more space available and can thus play a significant role in the maritime / rail interface, particularly if they are combined with transloading activities. In North America, transloading has been a significant structuring effect with the setting of distribution centres between port terminals and near or off-dock rail facilities. Transloading enables the transfer of the contents of about three international containers of 40 foot into two domestic containers of 53 foot, improving the capacity of inland intermodal rail. Such practices are much less common in other parts of the world due to the shorter inland distances (e.g. Europe); maritime containers are brought directly to inland destinations. The satellite terminal is mainly a facility located at a peripheral and less congested site that often performs activities that have become too expensive or space consuming for the maritime terminal (Slack 1999).

Rail satellite terminals can be linked to maritime terminals through rail shuttle or truck drayage (more common) services.

A load centre is a standard intermodal rail terminal servicing a regional market area. If combined with a variety of logistical activities, namely freight distribution centres, it can take the form of a dry port. The surge of inland long distance containerized rail traffic also require transmodal (rail to rail) operations as freight is moved from one rail network to the other. This can be done by switch carriers or trucking containers from one terminal to the other (Rodrigue 2008). While such as network structuring effect is active in North America due to the size of the network and the regional markets of rail operators, it has yet to emerge elsewhere, such as in Europe (Bontekoning and Priemus 2004). Dedicated rail-to-rail terminals are likely to eventually emerge, providing a new form of connectivity for regional rail freight networks.

The structuring effects of co-location
Most of the dry ports initially developed where intermodal facilities acting as nodes of convergence for regional freight distribution enabling a modal shift away from road and freight diversion and away from congested areas. These two key paradigms have been expanded with a more comprehensive approach leaning on the principle of co-location. As dry port projects become increasingly capital intensive and prone to risk because of their size, required equipment and infrastructure, the need for a higher value proposition is now set on the principle of co-location, many of which are public-private partnerships. The most common actors in a typical co-located dry port project involve a railway operator and a commercial real estate developer, or a local public development office. Co-location, therefore, expands the market opportunities of the intermodal terminal through a set of value propositions:

- *Real estate.* Logistic zone projects tend to occupy a large amount of space to accommodate existing and anticipated freight distribution activities. Most co-located projects occupy at least 250 acres and several projects are well above 1,000 acres. Larger projects tend to have lower land acquisition costs. Also, since co-located projects usually involve at least two large players, a commercial real estate developer and a railway company, they are able to tap into capital pools with better conditions than a smaller actor (e.g. interest rates). Another important aspect is that a co-located logistic project enables the joint planning of facilities.
- *Specialization.* A co-location project enables both actors involved to focus on their core competencies, creating multiplying factors. For instance, the rail operator can focus on terminal development and operations while the real estate promoter can develop and manage the freight distribution facilities.
- *Interdependency.* Both the terminal operator and freight distribution activities at the logistic zone are their respective customers, implying that both partners have vested interests in the efficiency of their operations. The possibility of joint marketing where the logistic zone is promoted as a single intermodal package is also common since the terminal is sold as a value proposition to potential customers.
- *Drayage.* A co-location project offers notable operational advantages for drayage, not just because of close proximity, but because trucks can have a priority access through the terminal's gates (e.g. pre-registration, advance notification, RFID). Drivers are able to perform more deliveries per day and the reliability of these deliveries improves.

- *Asset utilization.* Intermodal transportation assets are capital intensive and there are pressures to increase their utilization level to achieve better returns on investments. Containers and chassis tend to be the assets that are the most prone to such strategies, namely through the setting of chassis pools and empty container depots.
- *Information technologies.* A co-location project offers the possibility to jointly plan information systems for terminal operations and the related supply chains, creating a community system where users can have access to real time information about the status of their shipments. Both terminal operations and their related supply chains benefit.

One drawback is that co-located logistics activities are dependent on the performance of the terminal as well as the level of service offered by the rail operator. If for any reason the rail operator has other priorities within its network, then the efficiency of the co-located logistic zone is compromised.

Conclusion: The Spatial Re-bounding of Rail Terminals

While rail was a dominant vector structuring the economic, political and social geography of territories in the late nineteenth and early twentieth centuries, the later part of the twentieth century saw its structuring effects overshadowed by air and road transportation. The twenty-first century is likely to see a spatial re-bounding of rail, implying a closer integration between terminals and the spatial structure. Higher energy prices, stringent mobility demands, public policy and investments, global value chains, environmental and sustainability concerns are all inciting new forms of structuring effects by rail terminals. This chapter looked at two new types of rail terminals: the HSR station and the intermodal terminal. In both cases, their structuring effects started to come into play only 30 years ago and have yet to fully pan out. Still, several of their structuring effects can be assessed in terms of adjacency, accessibility and network effects (Table 2.1).

Table 2.1   Structuring effects of HSR and intermodal terminals

	Passengers	Freight
Adjacency	HSR station redevelopment Office parks	Transloading / Satellite terminals Inland ports (Dry ports)
Accessibility	Development of connecting infrastructure (road and public transit)	Port regionalization
Network	Regional space / time convergence HSR hubs	Global value chains Freight corridors Transmodal hubs

Source: Author.

The location of HSR stations remains a salient issue as suburban locations are advantageous from an availability of land perspective. However, suburban locations tend to be not well connected to the local transport system and are remote from central areas, which is commonly the destination for most passenger traffic. The impacts of new HSR stations as poles for urban growth and development remain so far elusive; their structuring effect is less evident. However, the structuring effects of intermodal rail terminals are far more evident. The setting of global value chains and of logistical chains supporting them has incited the development of freight corridors along which dry ports act as load centres. The co-location of logistical activities is a salient structuring effect combining intermodal terminal operations and freight distribution, leading to a cluster of activities that has become apparent. These developments are often supported by well capitalized actors trying to achieve economies of scale and of agglomeration.

As passenger and freight rail services and networks are expanded, so will the structuring effects of rail terminals. The capital investments required as well as the complexity of operations, including interactions with regional passengers and freight markets will require a closer collaboration between public and private actors. The rail terminal will continue its ongoing integration with road, air and maritime modes leading to new transport chains and new forms of intermodalism. Developing economies will be at the forefront of these forms of developments, which will play a salient role in addressing pressing passenger and freight mobility challenges.

References

Atack, J., Bateman, F., Haines, M. and Margo R.A. 2010. Did railroads induce or follow economic growth? Urbanization and population growth in the American Midwest, 1850–1860. *Social Science History*, 34(2), 171–97.

Bertolini, L. and Spit, T. 1998. *Cities on Rails: The Redevelopment of Railway Station Areas.* London: E & FN Spon.

Bontekoning, Y.M. and Priemus, H. 2004. Breakthrough innovations in intermodal freight transport. *Transportation Planning and Technology*, 27(5), 335–45.

Charlier, J. 2008. Bruxelles, premier eurohub de la grande vitesse ferroviaire. *Bulletin de l'Association des Géographes Français*, 4, 487–93.

De Urena, J.M. 2012. *Territorial Implications of High-Speed Rail: A Spanish Perspective.* London: Ashgate.

Facchinetti-Mannone, V. 2006. Gares ex-urbanisées et développement urbain: le cas des gares TGV bourguignonnes. *Revue Géographique de l'Est*, 46(1–2), 15–23.

Fishlow, A. 1965. *American Railroads and the Transformation of the Antebellum Economy.* Cambridge: Harvard University Press.

Fleming, D.K. and Hayuth, Y. 1994. Spatial characteristics of transportation hubs: centrality and intermediacy. *Journal of Transport Geography*, 2(1), 3–18.

Fogel, R.W. 1964. *Railroads and American Economic Growth: Essays in Economic History.* Baltimore: Johns Hopkins University Press.

Givoni, M. 2006. Development and impact of the modern high-speed train: a review. *Transport Reviews*, 26(5), 593–611.

Goetz, A.R. and Rodrigue J.-P. 1999. Transport terminals: new perspectives. *Journal of Transport Geography*, 7, 237–40.

Hall, P.V. and Hesse, M. 2013. *Cities, Regions and Flows.* Abingdon and New York: Routledge.

Janelle, D.G. 1968. Central place development in a time-space framework. *Professional Geographer*, 20, 5–10.

Kasarda, J.D. and Lindsay, G. 2011. *Aerotropolis: the Way We'll Live Next*. New York: Farrar, Straus and Giroux.

Mac Donald, J.M. 1989. Railroad deregulation, innovation, and competition: effects of the staggers act on grain transportation. *Journal of Law and Economics*, 32(1), 63–95.

Miller, J.J., Baumel, C.P. and Drinka, T.P. 1977. Impact of rail abandonment upon grain elevator and rural community performance measures. *American Journal of Agricultural Economics*, 59(4), 745–9.

Muller, P.O. 2004. Transportation and urban form: stages in the spatial evolution of the American metropolis, in *Geography of Urban Transportation*, 3rd Edition, edited by S. Hanson and G. Giuliano. New York: Guilford, 59–84.

Ng, A.K.Y. and Cetin, I.B. 2012. Locational characteristics of dry ports in developing economies: some lessons from Northern India. *Regional Studies*, 46(6), 757–73.

Notteboom, T. and Rodrigue, J-P. 2005. Port regionalization: towards a new phase in port development. *Maritime Policy and Management*, 32(3), 297–313.

Pol, P.M.J. 2002. *A Renaissance of Stations, Railways and Cities. Economic Effects, Development Strategies and Organisational Issues of European High-Speed-Train Stations*. Delft: Delft University Press.

Pred, A.R. 1964. The intrametropolitan location of American manufacturing. *Annals of the Association of American Geographers*, 54(2), 165–80.

Rodrigue, J-P. 2013. *Geography of Transport Systems*. 3rd Edition. London: Routledge.

Rodrigue, J-P. 2008. The thruport concept and transmodal rail freight distribution in North America. *Journal of Transport Geography*, 16, 233–46.

Rodrigue, J-P and Hatch, A. 2009. *North American Intermodal Transportation: Infrastructure, Capital and Financing Issues*. Washington, DC: The Equipment Leasing and Finance Foundation.

Rodrigue, J-P. and Notteboom, T. 2012. Dry ports in European and North American intermodal rail systems: two of a kind? *Research in Transportation Business and Management*, 5, 4–15.

Roso, V. and Lumsden, K. 2010. A review of dry ports. *Maritime Economics and Logistics*, 12(2), 196–213.

Slack, B. 1999. Satellite terminals: a local solution to hub congestion? *Journal of Transport Geography*, 7, 241–6.

Smith, R.A. 2003. The Japanese Shinkansen. *Journal of Transport History*, 24(2), 222–37.

Chapter 3
National Railway System

John Black

Introduction

This chapter looks at issues and challenges of railway integration at the national scale. The key challenge is to promote 'seamless' integration of different railway lines (even systems) at different spatial scales, where problems of gauge differences still exist widely. By 'seamless' is meant that passengers and freight can transfer easily and efficiently from one railway to another. In addition to the countries mentioned in Chapter One (Loo 2014), the three countries included as case studies of national railways – Australia, Indonesia and Japan – have been plagued historically by gauge differences that have offered opportunities in the case of Japan and constraints in the case of Australia (where state governments adopted different gauges). However, the three countries are also island continents or archipelagos where it is unnecessary for integration with other national railways. A new age of inter-city passenger transport was heralded by the Japanese with the opening in 1964 of the Tokaido-Shinkansen (where previously there existed freight and passenger limiting capacities on the narrow gauge railway between Tokyo and Osaka) to the extent that its success encouraged several nations to change their minds about the role of railways – 'a so called "railway renaissance" began in a number of nations' (Straszak 1981: 49).

The focus is on system-wide issues within the railway sector such as gauges, technologies, and specific issues like costly and time-consuming interchanges and tariffs for passenger railways and transshipment for freight railways. It examines various technical and non-technical issues of 'seamless' integration of railway systems at the national scale, based on a case study approach. The selection of case studies is justified in the first section where some simple comparative statistics are given with the 10 longest national railway systems of the world. This is followed with a description of railway institutions and governance in the three case study countries. The next section offers an evaluation of segmentation in the railway system focusing on spatial, institutional and operational concepts and the issues and challenges facing railway managers in general ('seamless' transport, funding new investment with a public-private partnership model and sustainability) and specific issues for each country in particular, such as the introduction of high-speed rail (Australia and Indonesia) and freight strategies in Japan. The concluding section highlights the necessity to develop new tools embedding environment and governance in railway planning.

Selection of National Railway Case Studies

According to Jane's Railways (Harris 2010: 2) there are 134 countries in the world that operate railways. The inclusion of only three national railway systems as case studies to articulate some of the issues and challenges in the 'railway renaissance' therefore requires substantial justification. There is a compelling argument to include Japan as the

Sustainable Railway Futures

leading example of the railway renaissance with its introduction of high-speed, inter-city rail in 1964. In Europe, the French introduced the TGV between Paris and Lyon in 1981 followed by the German ICE between Frankfurt and Koln in 1991. Although the Germans have been successfully operating a test track in Emsland for magnetic levitation since 1987, the only commercial application of TRANSRAPID is in Shanghai between Pudong and the international airport (30.5 km), the Japanese are committed to applying its superconducting maglev technology for inter-city services following an inland route for security reasons with speeds around 500 km/h between Tokyo and Nagoya (Chuo Shinkansen) by the end of the next decade, then westwards to Osaka. As shown in Table 3.1, Japan is second only to Germany in terms of the density of railway penetration (area per km of track).

Table 3.1   **Case study national railway systems (Australia, Indonesia and Japan) and comparative data compared with world's top ten systems ranked by railway track length**

Country	Railway length (km) Rank in the world	Area (km²) / km track and rank in table	Population per km track and rank in table
USA	226,427 (1)	43.40 (4)	1, 379 (8)
Russia	128,000 (2)	133.58 (9)	1, 117 (= 9)
China (PRC)	98,000 (3)	105.46 (8)	14, 722 (3)
India	65,000 (4)	51.19 (6)	18, 846 (2)
Canada	46,552 (5)	174.51 (10)	468 (12)
Australia	*38,445 (6)*	*199.94 (11)*	*572 (11)*
Germany	37,679 (7)	9.47 (1)	2, 210 (5)
Argentina	35,897 (8)	77.45 (7)	1, 117 (= 9)
South Africa	31,000 (9)	49.79 (5)	2, 066 (7)
France	29,901 (10)	21.53 (3)	2, 201 (6)
Japan	*23,474 (14)*	*16.10 (2)*	*5, 451 (4)*
Indonesia	*8,529 (25)*	*223.31 (12)*	*27, 853 (1)*

Source: based on website data available at: http://en.wikipedia.org/wiki/List_of_countries_by_rail_transport_network_size [accessed: 6 February 2013].

Australia is representative of a country with railways covering a vast territory, as with Canada, China, India, Russia and the USA, and has the sixth longest track length in the world (Table 3.1). Also, it is a case study where air transport is in direct competition over the longer distances between origins and destinations. All of these jurisdictions built railways at an early time from different points using different technologies, and, significantly for the concept of a national, integrated, rail system, with different gauges. Australia is a good example of countries attempting to modernize and reform work practices based on essentially nineteenth century technologies, and who hold aspirations to introduce high-speed rail based on imported technology. In terms of financing the construction, operation and maintenance of major economic (and social) infrastructure, Australia is recognized as a world leader (along with Canada and the UK) with experience in public-sector private-sector partnerships (PPP). When public infrastructure is delivered under a PPP modality various risks are apportioned by governments to the private sector such as design, construction, maintenance and operations with finance (equity and debt) bundled into the contractual arrangement.

There are many developing countries throughout the world that have inherited railways from former colonial powers and who have not yet embraced the 'railway renaissance' and continue with largely obsolete technologies, governance structures, institutional arrangements and management practices. Indonesia is a case in point: it inherited its railways from the Dutch in the East Indies but now, as an independent nation, it aims to be the twelfth largest economy in the world by 2025. Today its network length ranks 25 in the world but amongst the top 10 longest rail systems of the world and of our three case studies it has by far the greatest population per km of track (Table 3.1). Its railways carry relatively modest amounts of passengers and freight yet to meet national development goals there is an imperative to reform the national railway system. Whilst the challenges and spatial detail may be particular to Indonesia there are general principles that can be distilled for many developing countries wanting to embrace a 'railway renaissance'.

Railway Institutions and Governance

All case study countries were importers of railway technology that, in later decades, presented specific challenges: Australia (from the British); Indonesia (from the Dutch); and Japan (the narrow gauge was recommended by the British on the first railway between Edo, now Tokyo, and Yokohama). Before describing the current institutional arrangements and key policy initiatives in each country, some relevant background history is outlined.

Historical Backdrop

In the nineteenth century, the construction of railways in the colonies of Australia was universally supported in the expectation that frontier expansion would parallel developments occurring in North America – 'the railway was the sacred and only symbol of progress' (Donovan and O'Neil 1991: 31). Private companies built many of these earliest railways as developmental lines into the agricultural hinterlands of the major cities, but the huge costs meant community expectations turned to the various colonial territorial governments to build and operate them (using loans from the British Government). At Federation in 1901 the Australian Constitution vested the governance of railways with the State and Territory Governments (the Constitution permits 'the acquisition, with the consent of a State, of any railways of the State on terms arranged between the Commonwealth and the State'). By the late 1960s, on a continent with five mainland states (Tasmania is an island) with three different gauges, plus a Commonwealth Government control of disparate railways running in the mainly arid parts of the country (Donovan and O'Neil 1991: 13–27), there were six mainland rail deficits escalating out of control with declining passenger traffic, and severe freight competition from road.

Thus, the Commonwealth of Australia Government (Federal Government) has had relatively limited involvement with railways but it did establish the Australian National Railways Commission in 1978 – whose corporate history describes it as a railway 'from nowhere to nowhere' (Donovan and O'Neil 1991: 13–27). Australian National was to conduct its business safely and efficiently based on sound commercial principles (annual corporate plans, financial targets and pricing policies). It made rapid progress in closing down unprofitable railway lines, services and stations, reducing the workforce, and concentrating business on long-distance and bulk haul freight. Objectives for the 1990s under the 11th Corporate Plan aimed to further transform Australian National so as to 'earn sufficient surplus from operations to sustain the commercial business; to provide for investment needs ... to generate an appropriate return on assets employed' (Donovan and O'Neil 1991: 191). Despite this Federal Government intervention between 1978 and 1988, most Australians would not think there is a 'national' railway system – the country being ranked sixth in the world in terms of route length in 2012 at 38,445 km.

A colonial government also developed railways in Indonesia. The first railway in the East Indies (now the Republic of Indonesia) was a line built by the Dutch from Semarang to Tanggung on the island of Java, which opened in 1867. It was built to standard (1,435 mm) gauge, but this proved uneconomical for further extension on account of the terrain and low amounts of expected traffic. During 1942–1945, the Japanese re-layed these various gauges to its own 1,067 mm standard (also called the Cape Gauge) that was retained by the returning Dutch colonial administration. When Indonesia gained its independence all further development was constructed to narrow gauge, predominantly 3 feet 6 inches (1,067 mm). At their greatest extent, there were railways on the islands of Java, (4,807 km) Sumatra (1,860 km), Madura (130 km) and Sulawesi, but today there remains an inter-connected network of lines serving most parts of the densely populated island of Java (3,327 km), together with three unconnected groups of lines on Sumatra (1,348 km). The concept of a 'national' railway system is unthinkable in Indonesia because of its geography dictating, among other things, the necessity for inter-island sea transport.

By the end of the nineteenth century, Japan, as with the Australian colonies, experienced the full effects of modernization on transport and communications (Meany 2007: 14). From 1872 there was a rapid expansion of government and private railways adopting the narrow rail gauge based initially on British advice. Just prior to the fall of the Tokugawa shoganate in 1867 the Government issued a grant to the American diplomat Anton L.C. Portman to construct a line from Yokohama to Edo but, after considerable diplomatic manoeuvring with the American mission, the new Meiji Government of Japan (1868) decided to build a railway using British finance and technology. Much later, it was the carrying capacity constraints imposed by this narrow gauge that eventually led to plans for a high-speed rail network using standard gauge whose implementation heralded the 'railway renaissance', and, significantly, *the* Japanese symbol of national progress (Hood 2006: 1). Paradoxically, when the Tokaido Shinkansen was being planned by Japan National Railways in the 1950s – with civil aviation re-opening and expressways being built – many Japanese politicians and university professors were highly critical, advocating the ultimate embarrassment of the 'railway downfall theory' (Straszak 1981: 54–60).

Australian Institutions

In Australia, the ownership and management of rail infrastructure and rail operations is performed by a mix of Government and private-sector operators. Despite policy reforms by the Whitlam Federal Labor Government of 1973, and the (failed) offer of the Commonwealth to take over the State railways, politics intervened (Whitlam 1991). Today, the governance of much of the Australian railway system remains a state government responsibility, unlike in other federal nations – USA, Canada, India and Germany – who pay no regard to state boundaries in their management of railways.

Generally, these institutional functions are divided into track management ('below' rail) and operators of trains and rolling stock ('above' rail). It is doubtful whether most Australians perceive there is a 'national' railway system both because of railway history dating back to when the British divided the continent into colonial states and territories and there were three different rail gauges, and because of the 1901 Constitution proclaimed that railways (and most other economic infrastructure) were the sole responsibility of the state and territorial Governments. Railway reforms were part of the more general microeconomic reforms of the 1980s to achieve greater productivity, whereby government monopoly providers were opened up for competition from the private sector. The stated objective of National Competition Policy, as it applies to the public sector, is to achieve the most efficient provision of publicly-provided goods and services through reforms designed to minimize restrictions on competition and promote competitive businesses. In November 1996, the Australian Federal Government announced a major rail reform package that included: the sale of Australian National Railways Commission (AN); the sale of National Rail Corporation; and the establishment of a Rail Track Corporation to manage access to the inter-state rail network. The objective of these reforms was to respond to rail's decreasing market share by increasing private-sector involvement to lower the cost of transport to industry, better meet the needs of customers, and provide long-term employment in the rail sector.

The Australian Government sold AN's interstate freight and interstate passenger services to three operators, transferred the 'below' rail (track and signalling) infrastructure to the newly formed Government-owned Australian Rail Track Corporation. Great Southern Railways took over passenger services (The Indian Pacific, The Ghan and the Overland). Australian Southern Railroad (now Genesee and Wyoming Australia Pty Ltd) took control of the SA rail freight businesses, and, from 1 December, 2010, the Tarcoola to Darwin line following a purchase of the assets of the line's previous owner, FreightLink Pty Ltd. Following Tasmanian Government ownership, the New Zealand-based corporation TranzRail took ownership of Tasrail in 1997, before passing ownership to Australian Transport Network (ATN) from 2000. In February 2004, ATN sold its Tasmanian Rail holdings to Pacific National. Having assumed responsibility for the above rail assets in 2007, in late 2009 the Tasmanian Government purchased the remaining business assets back from Pacific National. In December 2009, the Tasmanian Government established a new government-owned corporation to own and operate the rail lines in the state.

In November 1997, the Australian Transport Council (now the Standing Council on Transport and Infrastructure), State and Commonwealth Transport Ministers signed an Intergovernmental Agreement to establish the Australian Rail Track Corporation (ARTC) to provide a single point of access for the standard gauge interstate track. ARTC is a public company, incorporated on 25 February 1998 under the Corporations Law, whose shares are wholly owned by the Australian Government. While the AN train services were all privatized, the AN main-line interstate track was transferred to the Australian Rail Track Corporation. The functions of ARTC include (available at: http://www.infrastructure. gov.au/rail/trains/background/index.aspx): providing efficient and seamless access to the interstate rail network by entering into access agreements with track owners; managing track maintenance and construction, train pathing, scheduling, timetabling and train control on track owned or controlled by the company; improving the interstate rail infrastructure through better asset management, and by managing (in consultation with rail operators and track owners) a programme of commercial and public funded investment for the interstate rail network; and promoting operational efficiency and (by working with other track owners) uniformity of operating, technical and safety standards and practices on the interstate rail network. ARTC owns or leases the interstate track from Kalgoorlie in the west to the Acacia Ridge in Queensland.

Indonesian Institutions

The Institutional framework for the Indonesian rail sector has been slowly modified after independence from the Dutch resulting in many, and powerful, national government institutions: the Ministry of Transport Directorate General of Railways (technical expert agency); the state-owned enterprises ministry (BUMN) as the holder of the government's share in corporatized components of former state agency enterprises; the Ministry of Finance (authority for government finance for railway undertakings proposed by the National Development Planning Agency [BAPPENAS]); BAPPENAS; the Coordinating Ministry of Economic Affairs (CME) as the integrator of sector and inter-sector plans; together with numerous inter-agency coordination committees at both national and provincial level. Unsurprisingly, there is an 'absence of a clearly articulated rail sector strategy' (Indonesia Infrastructure Initiative 2010: 9).

From the proclamation of independence from the Dutch in 1945 to the present, a single, vertically integrated public monopoly has managed railway infrastructure and passenger and freight services. The colonial rail network was run by civil service public entities until 1991 when the national government's desire for greater efficiency led to a more autonomous and commercially oriented 'public corporation', or state-owned enterprise, although retaining its important public service obligations. Law no. 13/1992 strengthened this expected commercialization of operations that included improving management functions, modernizing operating regulations, and encouraging private-sector participation. Government Regulation no. 19/2007 created PT KAI (Perseron Terbatas Kerata Api Indonesia), a state-owned enterprise, to provide high quality rail services that are competitive and profitable, and to allow private-sector investment. According to the Indonesian Infrastructure Initiative, railway reform has been disappointing with passenger and freight volumes stagnant between 1998 and 2008 against a rapidly growing economy and various reforms have never been adopted (Indonesian Infrastructure Initiative 2010: 22–3). This resulted in the current Law no. 23/2007 with its mandate to create a national rail master plan that is discussed in the next section on issues and challenges.

Japanese Institutions

Private companies were the major players in the early stages of railway development in Japan. During the First Sino-Japanese War and the Russo-Japanese War the government recognized the strategic functions of transport and planned to directly control a unified railway network. In 1906, the Railway Nationalization Act was introduced to nationalize many trunk railway lines, where the government purchased, at generous prices, 17 leading private railway companies. Only 20 private steam railway companies continued operating. Generally, these companies operated short lines, and only four had a network of more than 50 km. In addition, there were other railways operating electric, horse-drawn and man-powered trains, running mainly on tramways (Aoki 1995).

From this time, Japan Government Railways became the major Japanese railway network which had suddenly expanded the route kilometres from 2,500 km to 7,150 km and the market share from less than 50 per cent to 90 per cent – almost monopolizing the railway business in Japan. This investment resulted in the government not having the funds to further expand the network to the countryside. The government passed the Light Railway Act 1910 encouraging smaller private operators to build at an even narrower 762 mm gauge.

An entirely new institution for railway governance was imposed on the Japanese. Post-war Japan was run by the Allied Occupation Forces: a letter from General MacArthur dated 22 July 1948 instructed the Japanese government to reorganize Japanese Government Railways as a public corporation called Japanese National Railways (JNR) which commenced on 1 June 1949 (Imashiro 1995). The public corporation model was little understood by railway managers and did not suit Japanese business culture. From the 1970s onwards, 'rampant capital expenditure and irresponsible management' (Okada 2010: 1) caused Japan National Railways to sink further into debt. Upon declaration of bankruptcy in 1987, JNR was privatized and broken up into JR Freight, West Japan Railway Company (JR West), Central Japan Railway Company (JR Central), East Japan Railway Company (JR East), Kyushu Railway Company (JR Kyushu), Shikoku Railway Company (JR Shikoku), and Hokkaido Railway Company (JR Hokaido), with all companies operating narrow gauge and international standard gauge railways and high-speed rail except on Shikoku, Kyushu and Hokkaido at the time over a network of 23,474 km.

Before privatization the annual budget and the number of persons employed had to be approved in congress but with the division of operations in April, 1987, such matters were determined by each company. By 2006, all of the shares of JR East, JR Central and JR West had been offered to the market and they are now publicly traded. On the other hand, all of the shares of JR Hokkaido, JR Shikoku, JR Kyushu and JR Freight are still owned by the Japan Railway Construction, Transport and Technology Agency (JRTT) who build new lines, provide subsidies to weak railway companies and conduct research and development. Another nearly 3,400 km of routes are operated by major private railways and by what are known in Japan as third sector railways – new companies, financed with private and local government funds – which absorbed some of Japanese National Railways' rural lines. The Ministry of Land, Infrastructure and Transport (MLIT) classifies private railways into different groups. Fifteen of the most important companies are classified as major private railways. One serves Nagoya, one serves Fukuoka, and the rest are all in Tokyo and Osaka. Some other railways operating in or near large metropolitan centres are classified as quasi-major private railways but there are no clear distinctions between these railways and major private railways (Terada 2001).

Whereas the separation of infrastructure and operations has become common in Europe (EU Directive 91–440), in Japan, these companies develop rolling stock, structures, track, electrical and signalling, manage operations and maintenance. The companies promote many affiliated businesses through their subsidiaries to maximize operating and flexibility such as coach transportation, merchandise and food, real estate, and other services such as hotels and travel tours. If we take JR Central as an example (the market area contains about 60 per cent of the national population and almost two-thirds of prefectural GDP), with its 552.6 km Tokaido Shinkansen and 12 narrow gauge lines of 1418.2 km, 85.4 per cent of revenue comes from the high speed line, 8.2 per cent from other railways, 5.7 per cent from other railway revenues (track usage fees, land leasing fees at stations, usage fees from store operators at stations, and advertising) with less than one per cent coming from other businesses (Central Japan Railway Company 2011: 4). Revenues from affiliated businesses are growing relative to revenue from high speed lines.

Issue and Challenges

There are three broad generic challenges for railways in the case study countries that are common to most national railway systems. First, the creation of a 'seamless', integrated passenger transport system covering international and domestic airports, ground access to the nearest population centre then onward rail services to other destinations. Secondly, is the challenge of how to fund new railway infrastructure, including the role of PPP. Thirdly, is the challenge of how policy makers and railway managers respond to issues of sustainable transport, especially the International Union of Railways (UIC 2012) Declaration on Sustainable Mobility and Transport. Finally, each case study country is taken in turn and some country-specific challenges are highlighted.

Economic globalization and increasing productivity are drivers of 'gateway' projects that create 'seamless' passenger transport connections between international airports, major domestic cities, and other destinations. Japan is the only case study country to achieve this inter-modal integration, where the Shinkansen high-speed rail network is synonymous with the international 'railway renaissance'. For example, all major economic activity areas in the Kanto (Tokyo), Kansai (Osaka) and Nagoya regions have international air services with the urban core areas connected by express rail services, with convenient interchange to the high-speed rail system. JR Central has a special discount membership service – 'Express Reservation' and 'EX-IC' – that enables passengers to make reservations on the Tokaido and Sanyo Shinkansen from mobile phones or PCs, and to board the train directly from the entry gates without waiting in line at the ticket office window. Furthermore, passengers can transfer easily between the Shinkansen and conventional lines by simultaneously touching the ticket gates with a 'EX-IC' card and a conventional line card such as TOICA (Tokai IC card) or PASMO used in Tokyo, Kansai, Kyushu and Hokkaido areas from Spring 2013 (Japan Central Railways 2012: 22).

In contrast, the major Australian airports are less well integrated into their urban networks. Furthermore there are no onward fast rail connecting services between the major capital cities of Adelaide, Brisbane, Sydney, Canberra and Melbourne along the east coast of Australia. The nation's two largest metropolitan areas are good examples of inadequate ground access. Sydney Airport's domestic and international terminals are connected by a (relatively new) rail line to the CBD (9 km) – opened in time for the 2000 Sydney Summer Olympic Games (Black 1999). However, there is no dedicated airport rail rolling stock (Sydney suburban rolling stock runs along the airport rail line) and high airport station access charges at the international and domestic terminals deter users and do not contribute to airport-CBD airport international success factors (Scott and Black 1998). Since its opening in 1970, Melbourne's Tullamarine International Airport (22 km from the CBD) has had six rail feasibility studies, a state government elected on the promise of building a rail link, and an announcement of a feasibility study of a bus rapid transit system (Lucas 2010, Chandu 2012). Of the other major capital cities, only Brisbane has rail connections (operated by Airtrain – a private-sector consortium) between the international and domestic airport terminals and the CBD.

Indonesia faces severe problems with airport ground access into its major gateway, Jakarta, whose region has some 35 million people. The terminal design capacity of 22 million annual passengers is well exceeded (about 40 million annual passengers in 2010, according to PT Angkasa Pura II, the state-owned enterprise operator of the Soekarno-Hatta International Airport), although there is a master plan currently being implemented with expansion of terminal facilities. Access travel to and from the centre of Jakarta and the airport (about 35 km to Blok M) is constrained by the one main highway available for passengers or vehicles. The Cengkareng (Prof. Sediyatmo) toll road, despite recent widening, is predicted to be over capacity in the year 2013. Travel times are highly variable, exacerbated by traffic accidents or water on the road pavements caused by flooding from tropical storms. A rail pre-feasibility study between the airport and Manggarai station is being conducted because of problems of route identification.

This project preparation is funded by loans from the Japan International Cooperation Agency (JICA) but responsibility for further project preparation was taken over by the Government of Indonesia. The regulation governing this policy is the Minister of Finance Decree No. 126/PMK.01/2011 concerning the Soekarno Hatta Airport-Manggarai Railway Project where preparation was entrusted to PT Sarana Multi Infrastruktur (Persero) ('PT SMI'), established on 26 February 2009 with the purpose of accelerating infrastructure development in Indonesia. In December 2010, the Ministry of Transport decided to re-tender and disqualify three companies passing the prequalification stage at the time, namely PT Railink (a subsidiary of PT Kereta Api and PT Angkasa Pura II), China Harbour from China, and Mitsui from Japan. The preliminary project cost is an estimated Rp. 10 trillion (US$102.7 million), of which a government contribution of Rp. 3.2 trillion (US$32.9 million) has been prepared – Rp. 1.5 trillion (US$15.4 million) for land acquisition (a major constraint to transport development across Indonesia) and Rp. 1.7 trillion (US$17.5 million) for construction (available at: http://www.indii.co.id/news_daily_detail.php?id=129 [accessed: 13 August 2011]). The pre-feasibility study will determine estimated project costs, the likely financing from the private sector and the government contribution needed from the Indonesian Infrastructure Guarantee Fund (available at: http://iigf.co.id/Website/Home.aspx) which is building on relevant international experiences involving the use of government guarantees to leverage private financing of infrastructure.

The private financing of railway infrastructure and operations is a challenge for all countries. Along with Canada, Australia is one of the world leaders in the PPP model for economic and social infrastructure development, and has learnt continuously from transport project experience from the mid-1980s (Black 2012). This includes institutional frameworks at both national and state levels and clear regulatory frameworks and guidelines (Infrastructure Australia and its state government equivalents), project management experience by the private sector (consulting and construction), a strong financial sector and railway value-added businesses such as transit-oriented development (although Hong Kong is the world leader with MTR station developments). Japan, on the other hand, has world-leading construction technologies, but, despite a recent change in the law, has no experience of PPP with major economic infrastructure such as toll roads (Japan learnt from the British Private Financing Initiatives of the late 1990s but has experience limited to small, local government projects such as city halls and school buildings). The Indonesian Government recognizes in its *Vision 2025 – The Indonesian Economic Development Plan 2011–2025* to become the twelfth largest economy in the world (available at: http://www.ekon.go.id/media/filemanager/2011/07/06/m/p/mp3ei-english_final.pdf), and its complementary document, the Master Plan for the Acceleration and Expansion of Indonesia's Economic Development (MP3EI), that private financing of infrastructure is essential, as is continuous reform at national, provincial and local government levels (Parakesit et al. 2008, 2010).

In pursuing private finance for economic infrastructure, governments must not neglect their environmental responsibilities. The International Union of Railways has a strong tradition of working on sustainability issues – both in supporting members to improve their sustainability performance, as well as communicating on the sector level to key external stakeholders in order to support the development of sustainable transport systems (UIC 2012: 3). A recent brochure highlights the achievements that UIC members around the world have made in the field of sustainable development. Case studies and examples were submitted by many of the 50 members who have signed the UIC Declaration on Sustainable Mobility and Transport (including East Japan Railway Company). Consistent with the United Nations Global Compact, there is a public commitment to implementing sustainable development measures and to providing regular and transparent progress reports. The challenge for railway managers and decision makers, especially in Australia and Indonesia, is: to embrace the paradigm shift and make railways the backbone for sustainable mobility and transport systems for society (macro-economic advantages, impacts on climate change and the environment); to focus on customers; and to provide leadership in corporate governance and social and environmental responsibility.

Australia

One of the challenges for Australia is to develop a national freight logistics network where rail has a role in the system. As a maritime nation, Australia's ports are an important gateway for freight. Consequently, ports and associated infrastructure are of the utmost economic and social importance. (Here, we ignore the Australian mineral railways that employ world-class technology between mine and port because they are essential part of an industrial production process and arguably not part of a national railway system.) Commercial ports are currently planned by state and territory jurisdictions with the involvement of the Commonwealth and local governments, where appropriate, so the release of the national port strategy (Australian Government Infrastructure Australia and National Transport Commission 2010) was welcomed by industry for a more coordinated approach, including rail access for freight and supply chains. Constraints include a lack of planning for freight activities, a lack of clarity about the capacity for growth, and poor interoperability across infrastructure networks, all of which lead to congestion, low reliability and unexploited opportunities for investment.

Infrastructure Australia is a statutory body that advises governments, investors and infrastructure owners on Australia's future infrastructure needs; mechanisms for financing infrastructure investments; policy, pricing and regulation. One national theme is to improve Australia's productivity and international competitiveness through a national land freight network strategy where railways are integrated into a multi-modal approach:

> Rail and road freight infrastructure planning and investment can no longer be undertaken in isolation from each other, or worse, in competition with each other ... A new national freight strategy needs to be developed for our freight networks to improve planning, investment and decision making. (Australian Government Infrastructure Australia 2011: 2)

The long-term 'national' freight network would aim at interoperability by including specifications for rail, roads, communications, corridors and shipping. These challenges for Australia imply a long-term direction towards: availability of a standard gauge freight priority rail line from principal freight nodes to the designated inter-state network; standard gauge rail tracks/freight priority routings in capital cities, the Inland Rail Route, and further rail standardization in Queensland, Victoria and Western Australia; a single rail control system or seamless interface with city train control systems; the identification of opportunities to use smart technology in infrastructure and operations; and greater intermodal terminal capacity in the capital cities, in major cities and at strategic interchange points (Australian Government Infrastructure Australia 2011: 4).

Possibly the greatest challenge to implement an Australia 'national' passenger rail network is whether a high-speed rail system will ever connect the capital cities of Brisbane, Sydney, Canberra and Melbourne given the difficulty of obtaining political agreements amongst the three levels of government and its high cost. The dream started in June 1984 when the Commonwealth Scientific and Industrial Research Organisation (CSIRO) presented a proposal to the Hawke Federal Government for a route between Sydney, Canberra and Melbourne using French TGV technology (Clark 2011: 35–7). Government rejected the proposal when it was realized that construction costs had been substantially underestimated. Another unsolicited private-sector proposal (the Very Fast Train Joint Venture) from BHP, Elders IXL, Kumagai Gumi and TNT for the same route (later Brisbane was included) at 'no cost to government' was also rejected on the grounds that the proposed tax breaks would have cost the Federal Government Aus $1.4 billion (Clark 2011: 36, Black 1989).

Phase 1 of a study of high-speed rail (HSR) along the East Coast of Australia for the Federal Department of Transport and Infrastructure (AECOM et al. 2011) identified feasible routes and indicative costs. The phase 2 study released in April, 2013, built on the work of phase 1, but was considerably broader and deeper in objectives and scope, and refined many of the phase 1 estimates, particularly the demand and cost estimates. The network would comprise approximately 1,748 km of dedicated route between Brisbane-Sydney-Canberra-Melbourne, with construction costs at Aus $114 billion (in 2012 dollars). Once fully operational (from 2065), high-speed rail could carry approximately 84 million passengers each year, with express journey times of less than three hours between Melbourne-Sydney and Sydney-Brisbane. However, the HSR programme, and the majority of its individual stages, 'are expected to produce only a small positive financial return on investment. Governments would be required to fund the majority of the upfront capital costs' (AECOM et al. 2013). On the eve of the Federal Election of 7 September, 2013 both major political parties are being lobbied by the infrastructure industries to protect land from development along the proposed corridors.

Indonesia

Indonesia too has plans to introduce high-speed rail on Java as part of the *Vision 2025 – The Indonesian Economic Development Plan 2011–2025*. A decision will have to be taken to build a standard gauge new railway to capitalize on the growing international competition between manufacturers in Europe, Japan and China for high-speed rail technology (see Clark 2011). The Director General of Railways, in the longer term, must start planning with a preliminary development plan and a slow start to land acquisition for the new railway line (Indonesian Infrastructure Initiative 2010: 182). The National Railway Master Plan recommends that a pre-feasibility study commence around 2020–2024 (Indonesia Infrastructure Initiative 2010: 43). If the Indonesian economy continues to grow rapidly, such a high-speed railway may be profitably built by 2030.

The short-term challenges are to improve railway management and revitalize the whole of the railway system, including the heavily-used passenger services in the major metropolitan areas of Jakarta (Jabodetabek) and Surabaya. The major infrastructure issues in Indonesia are that the capability and capacity of the system is constrained by: many kilometres where train control is provided by mechanical semaphore signalling systems with *maximum* operating speeds on main lines (60 to 100 km/h); low axle loadings (9 to 18 tons); and light rails predominantly R54 (54 gm/m), R50 and R40, with some R33 on the main lines. The topography of Indonesia requires many bridges, culverts and drainage structures. Generally, the national network is single track (with some double track on Java and multiple tracks at stations). The passenger and freight rolling stock are outdated with a large proportion of the locomotive and diesel multiple unit fleet beyond their economic life, locomotive depots are hindered because of the lack of spare parts, and 35 per cent of freight wagons are already operating beyond their economic lives (Indonesia Infrastructure Initiative 2010: 98–9).

The National Railway Master Plan (Indonesia Infrastructure Initiative 2010) has considered the railway sector goals of increasing market share in passenger transport from approximately 4 per cent to 10 per cent by 2015 and 25 per cent by 2025, and to increase railway freight market share from a low base (data are unreliable but one estimate is 3 per cent of national ton-km) to 5 to 10 per cent of ton-km by 2020. Freight targets require network improvement and expansion on Java, and exploiting coal and other bulk commodities on Sumatra and Kalimantan where road transport would have adverse environmental impacts (Indonesia Infrastructure Initiative 2010: 129).

As in Australia, resource extraction and export is important to the Indonesian economy. In 2011, construction commenced on a new standard (1,435 mm) gauge 130 km freight railway in the East Kalimantan province, connecting the Muara Wahau coal mine with a new industrial complex and port facility at Bengalon. Land is in the process of being acquired for the construction of a new 307 km railway in southern Sumatra, connecting mines at Banko Tengah with the port of Srengsem in Lampung province in Kalimantan. In the passenger market segment, network expansions will begin with PPP initiatives for urban commuter services. For example, PT Kerata Api Indonesia Commuter Jabodetabek (KCJ) has targeted 2.2 million daily passengers as a goal, but this can only be supported by major improvements in railway operating practices, signalling and rolling stock.

The National Railway Master Plan also addresses key issues in institutional development in order to achieve the aspirations just described for revitalizing the rail sector (Indonesian Infrastructure Initiative 2010: 72–96): regulatory frameworks (written regulations and processes) supported by capacity building to implement, update and enforce these regulations. An economic regulator/dispute resolution body needs to be established within the Ministry of Transport. There needs to be a transition from government dominated to a more commercially-oriented railway business with the withdrawal of state ownership and complete privatization with the separation of infrastructure management functions and train operations. A new structure should encourage intra-modal competition (such as special bulk commodity railways, port access projects and metropolitan commuter services) where feasible. To achieve this, the Director General of Railways's core responsibility would be the definition of a clear policy on access charges that produce an equitable sharing of the fixed cost burden of PT KAI and any new entrant using established infrastructure.

Under Law No, 23/2007, private investors are encouraged to enlarge the economic and environmental role of railways with private finance and commercial management skills. The investment requirements to upgrade the existing main lines in Indonesia to a minimum 22.5 ton continuous axle load capability and to construct infrastructure that will support 150 km/h operations on the Java North Coast line are substantial (Indonesian Infrastructure Initiative 2010: 129–30). The cost of infrastructure enhancements (track, turn outs, level crossings, bridges, clearances to allow bi-level passenger equipment, signals) would be US$7,740 million over the first 5-year period (2010–2014). A further US$4,700 is required to simply replace the existing rolling stock (whose mean age ranges from 13 years for electrical motor units to 35 years for freight wagons).

Japan

As in Australia, international competitiveness for freight and logistics is a pressing issue for Japan. In 2011, the Ministry of Land, Infrastructure, Transport and Tourism formulated its policy on international container port strategy that promotes international competitive through the creation of tactical ports (for example, the 'Keihin' ports of Kawasaki, Tokyo and Yokohama and the 'Hanshin' ports of Osaka and Kobe). Much of the freight volume passes through ports on the Sea of Japan side that entails expensive domestic landside transport costs (together with issues such as road traffic incidents and the declining numbers of long-distance truck drives where the average age has exceeded 50 years). To make ports in Eastern Japan more competitive a more efficient nation-wide feeder transport system (road and rail) is required (Yamaguchi 2011). For example, between 1998 and 2010, JR Freight (Yoshizawa 2012) operates a dedicated rail service for sea containers between Yokohama Honmoku Station (on the Kanagawa Coastal Rail Line Company) and Sendai Port station (on the Sendai Coastal Rail Line Company). Foreign trade and inter-modal freight to selected regions of Japan involves JR 12-foot containers and international 20-foot and 40-foot containers. With rail freight operations running to schedule, it is possible to adhere to the loading programme for export vessels in ports. With rail and sea modes integrated there is an environmental benefit with reduced carbon dioxide emission compared to air cargo. Furthermore, government reforms of domestic container distribution have allowed JR Freight to develop a business model for the feasibility of transporting bonded containers on round trips (Yoshizawa 2012).

Possibly the greatest challenge is how best to maintain the vast railway system against a back-drop of an ageing population, reduced government income from taxation, and a lack of central and local government capacity to provide the required subsidies. One way is to separate the owner of the infrastructure from the rail operator (the franchise model), as in the European Union, but policy reform and transitions from existing arrangements to new ones have proved to be difficult in the Japanese political and cultural context. Most profitable lines are owned by private entities and the new model would force operators into an internal subsidy of the less lucrative services with the beneficiary being the government with reduced subsidies. Whatever the institutional arrangements there is the problem of maintaining ageing infrastructure such as tunnels and bridges where the average age of these infrastructure maintained by governments is 32 years (*Nikkei Shinbun,* 2 February 2013) and the collapse in early December 2012 of the Sasago motorway tunnel highlights the risks of lack of investment (available at: http://www.news.com.au/world/motorway-tunnel-caves-in/story-fndir2ev-1226528288752 [accessed: 6 February 2013]).

The IC ticketing system including affiliated usages has supported the on-going renaissance of the Japanese railway system and facilities a 'seamless' system. The IC ticketing makes journeys very easy, smooth and less stressful. In addition, IC ticketing is not just ticket but also electric money that can be used in many restaurants, supermarkets, convenient stores, book stores, drug stores, cafés, taxis, vending machines, and so on. Stations are spaces to use the card: railway companies are renovating station buildings, making stations destinations to spend time and money. For example, JR Central Towers at Nagoya station is almost a city in itself, called 'eki-naka' business, where there are businesses inside/above/below a station. Furthermore, the IC card can be a photo ID/

security card for companies and facilities, and even combined into one credit card. The IC card is increasingly playing a part in a security system. For example, when children arrive at school, they touch a device located at school, where automatically emails are sent to their parents to confirm they safely arrived at school.

In terms of further promoting the next generation of 'railway renaissance', there can be no greater challenge for Japan in linking the three major metropolitan areas of Tokyo, Chukyo (Nagoya) and Kinki (Osaka) by the Chuo Shinkansen utilizing the superconducting maglev system with its operation speed of 500 km/h. Fundamentally, at the heart of the issue of whether governments or the private sector should run railways, is the ability of governments to take a long-term view in the 'national interest' (for example, the shinkansen programme and national unity) or short-term profit maximization of the private sector. For example, when JR Central announced the decision of building the Maglev Chuo Shinkansen and opening it in 2045, its stock price plunged. In May 2011, the Ministry of Land, Infrastructure, Transport and Tourism reported that it was appropriate to utilize the maglev technology on the inland Southern-Alps route and designated JR Central as the construction authority between Tokyo and Osaka (and to finance the construction) and also as the railway operator (Central Japan Railway Company 2012: 24), subject to obtaining the consent following an assessment of environmental impacts by the Central Government (currently underway). Miyazawa (2012: 12) outlines the major time-lines in this decision making process. The superconducting maglev technology has been proven on the 18.4 km (under extension to 42.8 km at a cost of 355 billion yen) Yamanashi Maglev Test Line, where, between April 1997 and June 2011, 850,000 km of cumulative running tests had been performed (Central Japan Railway Company 2012: 25). The Central Japan Railway Company aims to build the first section between Tokyo and Nagoya with operations unlikely to commence much before the end of the next decade.

Towards National Railway Renaissances?

Drivers of climate change induced by anthropocentric activities, such as greenhouse gas emissions from transport, and the international recognition of the need for sustainable development, have forced governments to consider the role of railways in moving people and freight across their territories. According to the UIC database, countries of the world have railways of vastly different lengths that cover the smallest state to the largest territory. Countries at different stages of economic development – as the case studies of Australia, Indonesia and Japan have illustrated – will have their unique issues and challenges for railway development. However, there are a number of common requirements for a national railway system to achieve world's best practice. A personal view of some pointers towards improvements necessary in national railway systems follows.

Central governments must set the strategic directions for the development of multi-modal, integrated national transport systems including the role for railways. Sustainability targets by specified dates that are quantifiable for the national transport system, and key performance indicators (KPI), focus the mind of managers on meeting targets. Railway managers need, in addition to running a railway, a greater understanding of sustainability issues as, for example, in the UIC *Railways and Sustainable Development: A Global Perspective* – and this requires extensive capacity building. Governments should formulate the regulatory environment, provide (in consultation with industry) the technical guidelines and funding framework for infrastructure, including railways (see, for example, the Indonesian *National Railway Master Plan*).

The key 'railway' institutions will differ somewhat in each country but a good working principle is to separate ownership and management of 'below' track and 'above' track (as in parts of the Australian railway network). Another important economic principle is a government policy to open up any government monopoly to competition and create 'contestable markets' (the National Competition Policy in Australia). There is accumulating evidence that set within appropriate regulatory frameworks, the private sector can introduce greater innovation, productivity and efficiencies in the rail sector of the economy. In any analysis of railway institutions it is important to recognize public-private partnerships (PPP) in the funding of rail tracks, signalling, rolling stock and associated development around railway stations (such as JR Central complex of offices, commercial facilities, hotel and bus terminal above Nagoya station, Japan).

Finally, the role of leadership should not be underestimated in any reform to transform current national rail systems so that there is a sustainable, worldwide 'railway renaissance'. The charismatic leadership is epitomized in Australia by the then Labor leader of the Federal Opposition, Gough Whitlam, who, in his policy speech, advocated a national rail system and attempted to drive change through when in government (Whitlam 1991, Donovan and O'Neil 1991: 21–3). The successful completion of the Tokaido Shinkansen in 1964 was 'due to the President of the JNR, Mr. Sogo … ' (Straszak 1981: 7). Books abound on 'management styles' to transform business organizations so there should be no shortage of expertise to help any national railway system based on the cultural values and political imperatives to become part of the global 'railway renaissance'.

References

AECOM, GRIMSHAW Architects, KPMG and SKM. 2011. *Executive Summary: High Speed Rail Study – Phase 1*. Sydney: AECOM Australia.

AECOM, Grimshaw, KPMG, SKM, ACIL Tasman, Booz & Co and Hyder. 2013. *High Speed Rail Study – Phase 2 Report: Key Findings and Executive Summary*. Sydney: AECOM Australia.

Aoki, E. 1995. Japanese railway history 5 – construction of local railways. *Japan Railway & Transport Review*, 5, 34–7.

Australian Government Infrastructure Australia. 2011. *National Land Freight Strategy: Discussion Paper*. Canberra: Infrastructure Australia.

Australian Government Infrastructure Australia and National Transport Commission. 2010. *National Ports Strategy: Infrastructure for an Economically, Socially and Environmentally Sustainable Future*. Canberra: Infrastructure Australia.

Black, J.A. 1989. Very Fast Trains: Developments Overseas and the Proposal for Australia. New South Wales Parliamentary Library Background Paper. Sydney: New South Wales Parliamentary Library.

Black, J. 1999. Transport, in *Staging the Olympics: The Event and its Impact*, edited by R. Cashman and A. Hughes. Sydney: University of New South Wales Press, 93–105.

Black, J. 2012. *Public-Sector Private-Sector Partnership in the Australian Infrastructure Sector: Empirical Evidence*. Keynote Address at the International Seminar on Investment Aspect of the Sunda Strait Special Economic Zones, Bali, Indonesia, 14–15 June 2012.

Central Japan Railway Company. 2011. *Central Japan Railway Company: Annual Report 2012 For the Year Ended March 31 2011*. Tokyo: Central Japan Railway Company.

Central Japan Railway Company. 2012. *Central Japan Railway Company: Annual Report 2012 For the Year Ended March 31 2012*. Tokyo: Central Japan Railway Company.

Chandu, A. 2012. Wait for train to Tullamarine now 55 years. *The Age* [Online, 31 December]. Available at http://www.smh.com.au/opinion/politics/wait-for-train-to-tullamarine-now-55-years-20121230–2c1c1.html#ixzz2GaVnfb29 [accessed: 31 December 2012].

Clark, P. 2011. *High Speed Trains*. Dural: Rosenburg Publishing.

Donovan, P. and O'Neil, B. revised and updated by Jay, C. 1991. *The Long Haul: Australian National 1978 – 1988*. Double Bay: Focus Books.

Harris, K. 2010. *Jane's World Railways, 2010–2011*, 52nd Edition. Coulsden: HIS Global.

Hood, C.P. 2006. *Shinkansen: From Bullet Train to Symbol of Modern Japan*. Abingdon: Routledge.

Indonesian Infrastructure Initiative. 2010. *National Railway Master Plan Consolidated Background Papers*. Jakarta: Australia Indonesia Partnership.

Imashiro, M. 1995. Japanese railway history 9 – dawn of Japanese national railways. *Japan Railway & Transport Review*, 10, 46–9.

Loo, B.P.Y. 2014. Prospects for Sustainable Railways, in *Sustainable Railway Futures: Issues and Challenges*, edited by B.P.Y. Loo and C. Comtois. Farnham: Ashgate Publishing.

Lucas, C. 2010. Train derailed by buck-passing and vested interests. *The Age*, [Online, 26 June 2010]. Available at: http://www.theage.com.au/travel/travel-news/train-derailed-by-buckpassing-and-vested-interests-20100625-z9sx.html [accessed: 31 December 2012].

Meany, N. 2007. *Towards a New Vision: Australia and Japan Across Time*. Sydney: UNSW Press.

Miyazawa, K. 2012. *Semi-Annual Investors Meeting FY2013.3 (Fiscal Year Ending March 31, 2013)*, 5–15 [Online]. Available at: http://english.jr-central.co.jp/company/ir/brief-announcement/_pdf/fr54.pdf [accessed: 6 February 2012].

Okada, M. 2010. *Japanese Case Study: Planning, Implementing and Operating a Successful HSR Network*. Paper to the High Speed Rail World, Sydney, Australia, August 2010.

Parikesit, D., Black, J., Lea, J., Santoso, P., Dillian, H.S. and Novitarini, R. 2008. *New Directions in Transport Reform*. Australian Indonesia Governance Reform Program, Policy Brief 11 [Online: The Australian National University, Crawford School of Economics]. Available at: http://www.aigrp.anu.edu.au/docs/projects/1021/black_en.pdf [accessed: 13 February 2013].

Parakesit, D., Black, J., Lea, J., Santoso, P., Dillon, H.S. and Novitarini, R. 2010. *New Directions in Transport Reforms*. Australian-Indonesian Governance Research Partnership: Research Projects 2007–2010. Canberra: Crawford School, ANU and Australia Indonesia Partnership, Canberra, 20.

Scott, F. and Black, J. 1998. *CBD – Airport Rail Access: Institutional Arrangements and Decision Making*. Australasian Transport Research Forum, 22nd ATRF, Sydney, 30 September to 2 October, 22, Part 1, 411–27.

Straszak, A. 1981. *The Shinkansen Program: Transportation, Railway, Environmental, Regional, and National Development Issues*. Laxenburg: International Institute for Applied Systems Analysis.

Terada, K. 2001. Railway operators in Japan 1: railways in Japan – public & private sectors. *Japan Railway & Transport Review*, 27, 48–55.

UIC. 2012. *Railways and Sustainable Development: A Global Perspective*. Paris: International Union of Railways (UIC).

Whitlam, E.G. 1991. A perspective, in *The Long Haul: Australian National 1978–1988*, edited by P. Donovan and B. O'Neil, revised and updated by C. Jay. Double Bay: Focus Books, 7–11.

Yamaguchi, S. 2011. International strategic freight ports policy and Yokohama Port's approach. *Cargo Handling JAPAN*, 56(3), 1–10.

Yoshizawa, J. 2012. JR Freight Company's quest for intermodal freight transport. *ICHCA'S Cargo World*, December 2011, 10–18.

Chapter 4
Railways and Borders: The International Dimension

Roger Vickerman

Introduction

Railways transformed inland transport. They enabled goods to be brought from coastal ports to inland cities and furthered the exploitation of natural resources in locations other than those accessible by navigable rivers. As a result the interiors of continents such as North America and Africa were opened up and the industrialization of large countries such as Russia, India and China was facilitated. We can argue over the precise contribution the railways made to the social dividend, and over the direction of causality, did the railways cause the economic development or simply facilitate that development which would have occurred anyway? But the association of railways with economic development in the late nineteenth and early twentieth centuries is clear. The economic debate started with Fogel's (1964) study of the railroad in the development of the US economy, but there has been much discussion of the issue since. Wolmar (2009) provides a more romantic account of the role of railways in transforming the world.

Much of the work on the role of railways has, however, been conducted at the national level. The connection between railways and the performance of the economy is easier to identify within countries and clearest within the large countries mentioned above (or in the case of Africa where colonial powers controlled contiguous countries allowing landlocked territories access to the oceans). The story is more ambiguous where national borders were less permeable. In Europe, for example, the railways were developed on a national basis and for various reasons the nature of that development reinforced national boundaries and potentially retarded economic development, especially in regions adjoining those borders. In part this was because, in many countries, railways were developed by the State. In Germany, where the railways were developed by the individual States before the unification in the late nineteenth century, this fragmentation was even greater. Coupled with the corresponding polycentric urban geography, this led to the absence of a coherent national network of the form developed in France or Great Britain.

More recently there has been a renaissance of the railway for both passengers and freight. For passengers, the development of the high-speed train using new dedicated track has challenged both the automobile and the airplane for middle distance journeys, providing both shorter journey times and greater reliability. For freight, rail has adapted from its traditional role as primarily a carrier of bulk products to be one element in an integrated multi-modal transport chain. In both of these cases, and particularly in Europe, rail has particular advantages when used in international transport as the new rail modes are able to overcome some of the traditional disadvantages rail has faced when confronted with borders.

In this chapter we examine first the economic arguments about the role of railways, before looking more closely at the changes in rail usage in international transport, and finally at the way in which attempts at revitalizing railways may have differential effects on the distribution of economic activity.

The Economic Role of Railways

There are two sets of issues which we need to explore here. First is the debate on the social dividend or social savings attributable to the development of railways. Secondly is the role of national borders on trade and communications across them with a view to exploring: first, how the development of railways has been affected by the existence of national frontiers and, secondly, how attempts to reduce the effects of these borders through new rail developments are being made.

Social Dividend

The historical juxtaposition of the development of railways and the industrial revolution led to a natural conclusion that railways were a decisive factor. Economic historians such as Savage (1959) argued that the role of railways 'could hardly be overemphasised' and Rostow (1960) believed them to be 'decisive' in America's take off into self-sustained growth. It was the work of Fogel (1964) which attempted to quantify this effect though the concept of social savings. Recent contributions include Crafts and Mulatu (2006) and Leunig (2006) and the debate is well surveyed in Leunig (2010).

The social savings idea is an attempt to quantify the extent to which an economy's output is higher as a result of the introduction, as here, of a new mode of transport. The argument is that the new mode of transport, as with any innovation, will only be successful if it is cheaper to use than existing modes. The extent to which it leads to economic growth therefore depends on assumptions made about the elasticity of demand for activities which use the mode and the extent to which the new mode is a perfect substitute for the old mode. It also depends on the assumption that the introduction of railways did not put back the possible introduction of an even more efficient mode of transport by gaining a first-mover advantage. Leunig (2010) details results of 19 studies from 11 different countries at different times which claim social savings which range from less than 1 per cent to over 30 per cent of GDP. As Leunig points out, these are all studies undertaken by different authors and are only single country studies, although they presumably include the possible benefits from the use of railways for importing and exporting goods.

More recent arguments, also outlined by Leunig (2010), explore the extent to which allowing for imperfect competition in the transport-using industries might itself lead to a further increase in output in that sector which the social savings method would fail to capture. On the other hand if output expansion in one location was at the expense of output in another there may be less of a net increase in output; this is an argument which continues to dominate discussions on the wider economic impacts of new transport projects.

Borders and International Trade

We know from evidence on trade flows (Anderson and Wincoop 2004, Bröcker 1988, Peschel 1982) that borders impose an added cost to transport. Anderson and Wincoop (2003) estimate that borders reduce trade by 20 to 50 per cent. In the European Union it has been estimated (Peschel 1981) that even between major contiguous countries such as France and Germany flows across the border are similar to those over longer distances of up to 500–600 km within the country. Most international trade is carried by shipping, or for high-value low-weight goods by air, both of which have seen a significant reduction in unit costs in recent decades through technological advance (Hummels 2007). Of course landlocked countries suffer a disadvantage as they cannot benefit to the same extent. Similarly, interior regions of countries face the extra costs of land transport and transshipment. Limão and Venables (2001) estimated that variations in infrastructure provision accounts for 40 per cent of the variation in transport costs between coastal countries, but up to 60 per cent in landlocked countries. Behar and Venables (2011), provide a recent summary of evidence, including an estimate from a World Bank study that waiting times at borders could be equivalent to the time taken to travel 1,600 km inland.

Studies of both ocean shipping and air freight have emphasized the role which competition (or the lack of it where shipping conferences and airline alliances are present) plays in determining freight rates. Land transport is equally subject to restrictions which keep prices above costs. As Behar and Venables note, evidence from studies of the deregulation of trucking have shown how prices have fallen, not least from the reduction of power of truckers' trade unions. A railway industry which is still largely a nationalized industry in many countries demonstrates to an even greater extent the way the lack of competition has kept both freight rates and passenger fares above the levels which could be justified by costs. Costs themselves have often been higher as a result of the failure to invest when constrained by public sector expenditure controls.

Evolving Transport Policy towards Borders

Nevertheless there is a view that transport is a means by which borders can be reduced in significance and economic space unified. Through its Single Market programme the European Union sought to remove remaining non-tariff barriers to intra-EU trade. These included the need for customs posts and multiple sets of documents, exacerbated by the need often to cross multiple borders. Vickerman (1992) quotes estimates that taking a truck from London to Milan, a distance of 1,260 km, would take around 60 hours longer than an equivalent distance entirely within the UK; the extra time, even after discounting the need for a Channel crossing, is taken up by delays at borders and the subsequent additional rest breaks needed to comply with drivers' hours regulations.

But road transport does at least have the advantage of reasonably standardized conditions of operation. There are some differences in maximum truck weights allowed in different countries, and four island countries of the EU drive on the left, but a single driver and truck can complete a journey across the EU without any additional requirements. What has become known as interoperability is thus relatively straightforward, although even this is in the process of being compromised by the adoption of different technologies for the tolling of trucks on main highways in different countries. The situation in rail transport is entirely different. European Union countries operate more than four different track gauges on their main networks (ignoring the many narrow gauge railways) and at least as many different electrification voltages. Electrification systems and signalling systems differ not only between countries but even within countries. As if this were not sufficient to prevent a continent-wide rail system, differences in working practices, not least the role of trade union pressure made it impossible to operate international rail services without lengthy border delays to change drivers and in most cases locomotives. Interoperability in the railways was at a very low level (for a fuller discussion see Vickerman 2007).

The European Union's Trans-European Transport Networks (TEN-T) programme as recently updated (European Commission 2010) is based on the premise that completing a European network (or networks) will have a positive effect on both growth and integration (European Commission 1997). The example usually chosen for illustrating this is the US Inter-State Highway System, which has been argued to have had a major impact on the development of the economic space in the US (Mohring and Harwitz 1962). This may have been an accidental corollary of a network which was initially conceived for military defence purposes. This is itself not unlike the way railways were developed as an effective way of moving military equipment and personnel in the First World War (see Wolmar 2009, for a useful account) or the original Autobahnen in 1930s Germany.

The TEN-T were argued to have a dual purpose: they would enhance European competitiveness by reducing transport costs and enabling the integration of markets across borders; but they would also promote cohesion through the reduction of disparities between regions by reducing differences in accessibility. But there is an inherent problem in this argument (see Vickerman 1995) since, as suggested by the new economic geography approach advanced by Krugman (1991), the enhanced competitiveness may well be achieved by a greater concentration of economic activity, not necessarily in the geographic core of the EU, but at least in its major centres of population (see, for example, Brülhart 1998, Martin 1998, Midelfart-Knarvik and Overman 2002). Vickerman et al. (1999) demonstrated how the completion of the TEN-T for rail would have relatively little impact on the relative accessibility of Europe's major cities as those with already higher levels accessibility would benefit from the expansion of the high-speed network as much if not more than those in the periphery. Moreover those centres connected to the enhanced networks would benefit at the expense of their hinterlands. This reflects the fact that new networks, especially those devoted to international travel, such as air and high-speed rail, are essentially discontinuous in space such that measures based on continuous measures of accessibility (e.g. Gutiérrez and Urbano 1996) may overestimate the likely impact on some regions and underestimate the impact on others.

The Economics of Borders

The evidence from both theoretical and empirical studies is thus that all borders have an impact on trade. This may arise both from the administrative barriers which national frontiers present and from the incomplete nature of transport networks across frontiers. The network effects arise from gaps in the physical networks, from technical differences in the networks and from differences in the method of organizing the operation of the network.

For border regions, the existence of the border can have mixed effects. On the one hand national borders dramatically reduce the hinterland for firms in the region. This impacts both on the market area for output and on the available market areas for inputs, including labour. On the other hand the need for border posts and, where railways are concerned, for the facilities for the changing of crews and locomotives and marshalling yards for the storage of wagons or whole trains during the border crossing process, creates economic activity and employment. The reduction or removal of these border effects may thus enable firms to exploit cross-border opportunities in the longer run, but the short-term effect is often one of reducing employment opportunities. This is likely to be particularly pronounced in cases where new infrastructure is associated with the reduction of the border effect.

In looking for evidence of the effects of borders we need therefore to examine flows across them, how these flows are handled and how they change with new infrastructure and technological change. Thus for the railways we can observe how the development of international high-speed rail services has changed patterns of passenger travel and how the development of containerization and the block-train has changed patterns of freight transport. This is most clear in the emerging changes arising from the completion of a borderless single market in the European Union coupled with a series of railway packages designed to create a single rail market, supported by the TEN-T policy for infrastructure enhancement.

Changing Border Effects in Europe

Cross-border Passenger Traffic

Detailed data on international rail passenger transport flows on particular routes in Europe is increasingly difficult to identify given the commercial confidentiality where operators face potential new entrants through open access requirements. Eurostat (2012) reports that national journeys constitute over 90 per cent of total rail passenger journeys for every EU member state except Luxembourg where international flows comprise almost 30 per cent of the total. The next largest proportions are found in Lithuania (8.25 per cent), Denmark (6.63 per cent) and Sweden (6.11 per cent). Data is not available for France or the Netherlands on the same basis but the corresponding figures for Italy are 0.59 per cent, for Germany 0.48 per cent and for the UK 1.31 per cent. For small countries in core geographical positions in Europe the figures are also remarkably small: for Belgium, 2.99 per cent, and Switzerland, 3.57 per cent.

As Figure 4.1 shows international passenger journeys are virtually indiscernible against the total volume of rail passenger journeys in EU countries.

In contrast air passenger journeys within the EU are primarily international (Figure 4.2). Only in Italy, France, Germany, UK, Sweden and Finland do domestic journeys by air amount to more than 20 per cent of the total intra-EU departures.

In order to examine this more closely we take as an example traffic flows, as evidenced by the supply of services, across one internal border of the EU, that between France and Belgium. Although data is more difficult to establish we know from traffic counts that even by road traffic is less by a significant factor on sections of route across national borders. This is also true for rail. For example Table 4.1 shows the number of trains per day between Paris, Lille and Brussels; Lille is the centre of a metropolitan area of over 1 million inhabitants situated close to the Franco-Belgian border. Whereas there are similar numbers of weekday trains between Paris and Lille (220 km, 1 hour) as between Paris and Brussels (305 km, 1 hour 20 minutes), the number between Lille and Brussels (110 km, 35 minutes) is only a little over half of that figure.

Similarly passenger flows using the LGV-Nord high-speed line between Paris-Lille-Brussels and London (Table 4.2) demonstrate the much greater effective intensity of internal traffic in France than to the more significant economic destinations in the adjoining countries. Note also that these passenger numbers were all significantly below those forecast at the time of the French Enquête Publique in 1988, especially for the cross-Channel link to the UK, suggesting a much greater problem in forecasting cross-border traffic. Although even the figures for internal traffic in France demonstrate that forecasting for rail projects is, as noted by Flyvbjerg et al. (2005), notoriously subject to over-optimism bias.

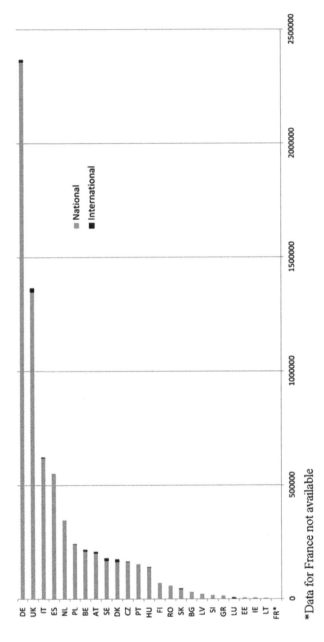

*Data for France not available

Figure 4.1   Rail passenger journeys by country (thousand passengers)

Source: Eurostat.

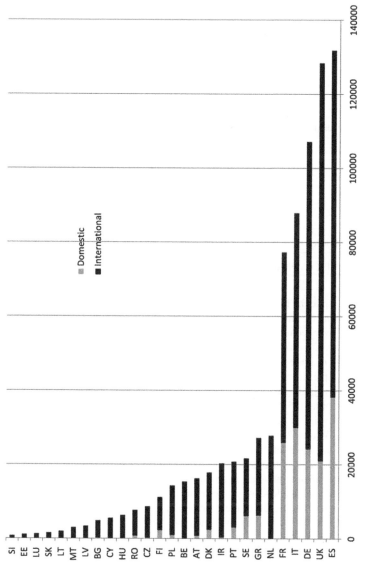

Figure 4.2   Air passenger traffic within the EU by departure (thousand passengers)

Source: Eurostat.

Table 4.1   High-speed rail services between France and Belgium

	Lille	Brussels
Paris	25	26
Lille		14

Source: Calculated from Thomas Cook European Rail Timetable Winter December 2011 Edition.

Table 4.2   Forecast and actual passenger flows on LGV-Nord

	Forecast passengers (mn) 2002	Actual passengers (mn) 2002	Error as % forecast
Paris-Northern France	10.9	6.4	41.3
Paris-Brussels/ Amsterdam/Köln	7.2	5.5	23.6
Paris/Brussels/Lille-London	20.6	7.3	64.6

Source: Bilan LOTI de la LGV Nord, RFF, May 2005.

Interestingly, despite the high density of population either side of the Franco-Belgian border and the extent of daily commuting (according to Boutillier et al. 2001, more than 6,000 Belgians were commuting into France every day in 1999 with more than 16,000 travelling in the opposite direction), available rail transport is very limited. In part this reflects the difficulty of joined-up inter-regional policy making in an international context (Vickerman 2008). Apart from the Lille-Brussels service, there are only three other cross-border rail services. Lille to Kortrijk, a distance of just 30 km, supports only an hourly service and Lille-Tournai (25 km) an irregular service about once every 90 minutes. The third service is the vestige of the old main line between Paris and Brussels via Maubeuge and Mons which in Winter 2011/12 had only seven local trains a day across the border between Charleroi and Jeumont. The coastal link between Dunkerque and De Panne is served by a five times daily bus service. Maubeuge in particular shows how an urban centre previously on an international main line can be effectively by-passed by new infrastructure and reduced to a level of service reflecting its status at the effective end of a branch line to a frontier. This is part of the general trend noted in Vickerman et al. (1999) towards rail interactions dominated by inter-metropolitan flows and to the detriment of smaller town in border regions.

Knowles and Matthiessen (2009) show that even where traffic on an international link has exceeded the forecast levels, in this case the Øresund Bridge, it is considerably lower than on the internal Great Belt Link within Denmark. This applies to both road and rail traffic and is despite average journey distances for traffic on the Great Belt being around 5 times longer than on the Øresund crossing. Unlike the cross-Channel link between England and France, the Øresund crossing links two sizeable metropolitan areas, Copenhagen and Malmo, where it would be expected that the potential for trip generation would be much greater.

Cross-border Freight Traffic

We noted above that freight traffic by rail was even more impaired by border controls than passenger traffic. Overall, however, rail has been losing modal share to road, falling from over 20 per cent of total tonne-km in the EU in 1995 to just over 15 per cent by 2009, although the rate of loss has slowed and there was a marginal recovery in 2010. Much of the loss in the EU as a whole was concentrated in the new member states of Central and Eastern Europe. Total rail tonne-km in these countries fell by almost 50 per cent between 1990 and 2010 and this can be explained by the way that markets were re-oriented from carrying heavy goods to markets to the east to finding new markets in the west not well served by rail, or where rail had been allowed to deteriorate. In Western Europe, some countries experienced a renaissance of rail freight in this period prior to the most recent recession. Rail freight grew by 40 per cent in the UK between 1990 and 2005 and by 65 per cent in Germany between 1995 (after the initial fall following the reunification of Germany) and 2008. This experience was not repeated everywhere; in France and Italy for example, where deregulation proceeded less markedly, rail freight remained remarkable constant.

However, compared with passenger traffic the situation is somewhat different. International traffic constitutes a significantly larger share of freight tonne-kilometres (Figure 4.3). Notice in particular the large share of a very large total in Germany, and the larger shares in Italy, Austria and Poland. Perhaps surprising is the much smaller share of the total for France – a figure which has knock-on effects for those countries which need to transit through France to reach the main markets in Europe. It should be noted that the freight figures are in tonne-km whereas the available passenger figures are counted in journeys. Passenger kilometre figures would be expected to suggest a larger share of international travel than the evidence discussed above as international journeys will on average be significantly longer than national journeys which include a high proportion of shorter distance commuting trips in most countries.

Comparison with road freight (Figure 4.4) shows that international transport has tended to decline in the most recent years, especially in 2008–09 mirroring the drop in trade in the recession, but cabotage traffic, that performed by non-nationals in or between other countries, grew strongly. 2010 did see strong growth in all forms of international traffic. Given the extent of national road freight traffic in the larger countries it is not surprising that international traffic accounts for a relatively small proportion, less than 20 per cent, of total traffic in these (Figure 4.5).

It remains a concern that road freight can respond much more flexibly to changing economic circumstances than rail. Road provides door to door service for shippers using public infrastructure. Rail requires most shippers to transship goods at rail depots and, even where private rail freight companies are used, these need to obtain slots from the rail infrastructure operator. In many EU countries the infrastructure operator is still closely related to the national rail carrier despite the separation of infrastructure and operation required by the EU in Directive 91–440 (Nash 2011). And it is to this issue of the development of the competitive and regulatory environment we now turn.

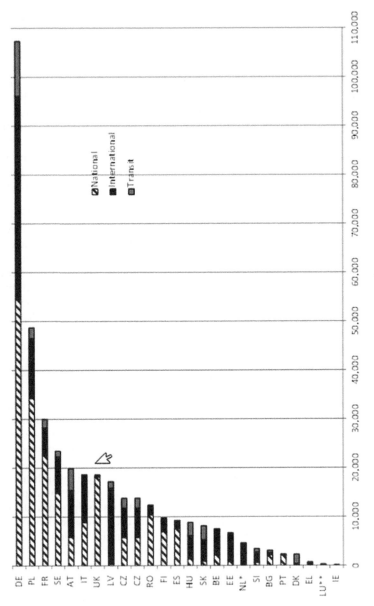

Figure 4.3   Rail transport of goods by country in 2010 – in million tkm

Note: *NL: Only the total transport is presented as the breakdown between national and transit is not available due to confidentiality; **LU: 2009 data.
Source: Eurostat.

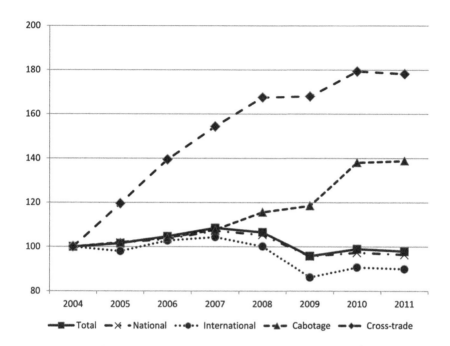

Figure 4.4   Evolution of EU-27 road freight transport 2004–2010 (based on tkm, 2004=100)

Source: Eurostat.

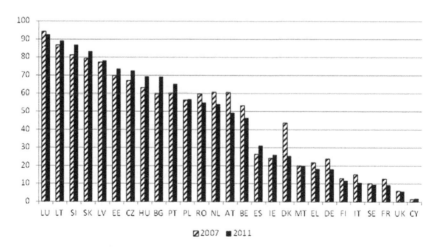

Figure 4.5   Share of international transport in total road freight transport (% in tkm)

Source: Eurostat.

The Competitive and Regulatory Environment

Whereas passenger services have seen the development of new international operators such as Thalys and Eurostar as joint ventures between the national operators to operate largely on the new high-speed infrastructures, interoperability remains more problematic in traditional freight. The joint venture passenger operators have had the advantage that they can operate international services as unified end to end services using common rolling stock and crews. There remain issues of technical compatibility due to differing signalling systems and the need for multi-voltage stock when operating off the dedicated high-speed lines, but these new international services have proved effective and have led to both a significant diversion from air over the affected routes and a growth in the total market on routes such as London-Paris and Paris-Brussels.

These services have had the advantage of being operated by joint ventures of the relevant national operators giving easier effective access to slots controlled by national infrastructure agencies. Open access has only recently become a requirement for international passenger services under the EU's third railway package (see Nash 2011, for a fuller discussion). However, although there has been a considerable exploitation of the franchising model now used in most EU countries for regional passenger services by non-national operators, there is relatively little exploitation of open access in the international market. This is limited by the need for technical homologation and slot acquisition (see House of Lords 2011, for a detailed discussion of these issues). It has also been pointed out in this report how the lack of a simple interoperable ticketing system militates against the easy transition between different operators when making longer international journeys requiring more than one operator, even when these operators are linked through an alliance, Railteam, supposedly similar to that of airlines.

The traditional way in which railways have been run as national networks, with little regard for the need to be flexible with respect to international traffic, has been more resistant to change in freight markets. Deregulation and the development of new approaches to rail freight have been largely confined to national markets. Thus in the United Kingdom, privatization led to a largely deregulated and competitive market for freight services and this has allowed the private sector to respond effectively with considerable innovation in services. Although much of the early competition has disappeared through consolidation, low entry costs keep the prospect of competition alive. The revival of freight services has been helped by the structure of track access charges where freight only bears the additional costs of making routes available to freight. Alongside the development of new marketed services, a number of major logistics operators have diversified into the rail market often finding that any disadvantages of transshipment are outweighed by increased reliability given increased road congestion. Similar changes have occurred in Germany and it is no surprise that the freight division of German railways, DB Schenker, is heavily involved as the major freight operator in the UK and a number of other countries.

The impact on international rail freight has been less marked, however, despite this internationalization of ownership and control of national freight operators. Only on certain corridors, designated as part of the TEN-T network and primarily involving Germany, such as the major North-South axis through the Alps and the so-called Via Baltica linking the countries around the Baltic Sea, has there been significant expansion of through international freight services under the control of a single operator. In other cases access to slots remains problematic and the need to deal with multiple track access charges has proved a less economical alternative to road freight. A good example of this is through rail freight services via the Channel Tunnel which suffer from high access charges in the Tunnel itself and the lack of priority on the rail networks in the UK and France (House of Lords 2011). Despite original forecasts that through rail services could carry 6 million tonnes a year the figure for 2011 was only a little over 1.3 million tonnes, 17 years after opening.

Although Directive 91–440 provided for open access for certain categories of international freight this was only extended to all freight, including domestic freight, through the second and third railway packages, by 2007. There remained considerable concern that genuine open access was not being provided and thus certain borders in Europe remained significant barriers to the development of a genuine EU-wide rail freight network (House of Lords 2005, 2011).

Some Lessons

The Impact on Economic Activity

We have noted in the above discussion that the way in which both the passenger and freight railway have been modernized to overcome the effect of borders has been to focus on non-stop integrated services between main centres. To this extent the modern railway has moved from the concept of a public service railway serving all communities equally to one which focuses on that traffic which can be carried profitably.

This centralizing effect of new transport is one of the paradoxes which recent work has tried to explain, where a development which is designed to improve overall accessibility actually results in increasing disparities (for a useful recent review see Lafourcade and Thisse 2011). This arises in two ways. First, it enables activities in the more developed central locations to take greater advantage of the resulting reduction in transport costs in a condition of imperfect competition. This is the effect noted first by Krugman (1991) in terms of core-periphery relationships and discussed in detail in SACTRA (1999). Secondly, there is a bifurcation in accessibility between locations which have good access to the new infrastructure and those which do not; this is the discontinuity effect which high-speed rail with its more limited intermediate stations and new freight services which link only major terminals will display.

As Vickerman (2008) has explored in greater detail, these effects have particular significance in border regions which are both peripheral and intermediate. These are regions through which new improved infrastructure passes, but which cannot exploit their location effectively. This arises not least because the economics of such services is prejudiced against stops for small numbers of passengers (in the case of high-speed rail) since the extra revenue does not compensate for the time penalty which stopping imposes on the end to end passenger. Thus despite attempts to reduce the impacts which borders have for physical and organizational reasons, border regions face new barriers for economic and commercial reasons.

Other Experiences

This chapter has focused on experiences in the European Union, a focus which can be justified on two main grounds: European countries are typically smaller and face more border challenges than in many other parts of the world, but have a highly developed and dense network of rail services; and, through the European Union, has a clear objective and mechanism to develop a greater degree of cross-border integration.

The changes in the organization of railways which we have observed in the EU can be encountered in many other parts of the world, however. Deregulation and privatization can be encountered in the Americas, Asia and Australasia. The passenger railway has largely disappeared in a number of countries outside the major metropolitan areas and the freight railway has diminished substantially in the face of road competition. Only in Japan can one encounter a nationwide railway which looks broadly similar to the European model, revived by high-speed rail, a solution now looked to in a number of other countries. But in very few of these other instances are there services which operate in an international context. In South America, for example, most of the international connections of the once very dense railway network of Argentina have been lost. There are grand projects, for example to revitalize the rail route between Europe and Central and East Asia through a new trans-Siberian route providing a high-speed freight service which would reduce the time currently taken by shipping and avoid the riskier areas of the Gulf and the Suez Canal. These are perhaps like some of the grand designs of the nineteenth century which would have provided through rail services between Europe and India or the Cape to Cairo railway in Africa, projects which were largely derailed by the conflicts of the early twentieth century and subsequently overtaken by the growth of road and then air transport.

Concluding Remarks

It would seem that the real role of the railway in the twenty-first century is to recapture the ascendency in middle distance transport, up to 1,000 km, in densely populated regions, where it can compete effectively with any other mode of transport. But to do this may require both a greater commitment to interoperability and a better balancing of the traditional public service obligation of the railways with the pressure to benefit from the perceived advantages which deregulation and competition bring. This could lead to a genuine reduction in the barriers which the borders between countries and rail operators still impose.

Ironically, it may also be the case that where privatization has moved furthest such as in the UK, where franchised passenger services are the new norm, this has led to a degree of fragmentation of the national network. This may have introduced new barriers to easy movement at the borders between the franchise areas. This shows clearly that the focus of reform needs to be on the provision of information and service to the prospective customer and not just on the technical and administrative issues on the supply side of the railway.

References

Anderson, J. and van Wincoop, E. 2003. Gravity with Gravitas: a solution to the border puzzle. *American Economic Review*, 93, 170–92.

Anderson, J. and van Wincoop, E. 2004. Trade costs. *Journal of Economic Literature*, 42, 691–751.

Behar, A. and Venables, A. 2011. Transport costs and international trade, in *A Handbook of Transport Economics*, edited by A.de Palma, R. Lindsey, E. Quinet and R. Vickerman. Cheltenham: Edward Elgar.

Boutillier, S., Coppin, O., Laperche, B. and Mudard, N. 2001. *Les migrations transfrontalier entre la Belgique et le bassin dunkerquois des origines du capitalisme à la fin du XXème siècle*. Rapport, Dunkerque: Laboratoire Redéploiment Industriel et Innovation, Université du Littoral-Côte d'Opale.

Bröcker, J. 1988. Interregional trade and economic integration: a partial equilibrium analysis. *Regional Science and Urban Economics*, 18, 252–81.

Brülhart, M. 1998. Economic geography, industry location and trade: the evidence. *The World Economy*, 21, 775–802.

Crafts, N. and Mulatu, A. 2006. How did the location of industry respond to falling transport costs in Britain before World War I? *The Journal of Economic History*, 66, 575–607.

European Commission. 1997. *The Likely Macroeconomic and Employment Impacts of Investments in Trans-European Transport Networks*. Commission Staff Working Paper, SEC(97)10. Brussels: Commission of the European Communities.

European Commission. 2010. Decision No 661/2010/EU of the European Parliament and of the Council of 7 July 2010 on Union guidelines for the development of the trans-European transport network. *Official Journal of the European Union*, 204, 1–129.

Eurostat. 2012. *Railway Passenger Transport Statistics-Quarterly and Annual Data* [Online]. Available at: http://epp.eurostat.ec.europa.eu/statistics_explained/index.php/Railway_passenger_transport_statistics_-_quarterly_and_annual_data [accessed: 30 November 2012].

Flyvbjerg, B., Skamris Holm, M. and Buhl, S.L. 2005. How (in)accurate are demand forecasts in public works projects? The case of transportation. *Journal of the American Planning Association*, 71(2), 131–46.

Fogel, R.M. 1964. *Railroads and American Economic Growth: Essays in Economic History*. Baltimore: Johns Hopkins Press.

Gutiérrez J. and Urbano P. 1996. Accessibility in the European Union: the impact of the trans-European road network. *Journal of Transport Geography*, 4, 15–25.

House of Lords. 2005. *Liberalising Rail Freight Movement in the EU*. 4th Report of the European Union Committee, Session 2004–5, HL52. London: The Stationery Office.

House of Lords. 2011. *Tunnel Vision? Completing the European Rail Market*. 24th Report of the European Union Committee, Session 2010–12, HL229. London: The Stationery Office.

Hummels, D. 2007. Transportation costs and international trade in the second era of globalization. *Journal of Economic Perspectives*, 21(3), 131–54.

Knowles, R.D. and Matthiessen, C.W. 2009. Barrier effects of international borders on fixed link traffic generation: the case of Øresundsbron. *Journal of Transport Geography*, 17, 155–65.

Krugman, P. 1991. Increasing returns to scale and economic geography. *Journal of Political Economy*, 99, 483–99.

Lafourcade, M. and Thisse, J-F. 2011. New economic geography: the role of transport costs, in *A Handbook of Transport Economics*, edited by A. de Palma, R. Lindsey, E. Quinet and R. Vickerman. Cheltenham: Edward Elgar, 67–96.

Leunig, T. 2006. Time is Money: a re-assessment of the passenger social savings from Victorian British Railways. *Journal of Economic History*, 66, 635–73.

Leunig, T. 2010. Social savings. *Journal of Economic Surveys*, 24, 775–800.

Limão, N. and Venables, A. 2001. Infrastructure, geographical disadvantage, transport costs and trade. *World Bank Economic Review*, 15(3), 451–79.

Martin, P. 1998. Can regional policies affect growth and geography in Europe? *The World Economy*, 21, 757–74.

Midelfart-Knarvik, K. and Overman, H. 2002. Delocation and European integration: is structural spending justified? *Economic Policy*, 35, 321–59.

Mohring, H. and Harwitz, M. 1962. *Highway Benefits: An Analytical Framework*, Evanston: Transportation Center, Northwestern University.

Nash, C. 2011. Competition and regulation in rail transport, in *A Handbook of Transport Economics*, edited by A. de Palma, R. Lindsey, E. Quinet and R. Vickerman. Cheltenham: Edward Elgar, 763–78.

Peschel, K. 1981. On the impact of geographic distance on the interregional patterns of production and trade. *Environment and Planning A*, 13, 605–22.

Peschel, K. 1982. International trade, integration and industrial location. *Regional Science and Urban Economics*, 12, 247–69.

Rostow, W.W. 1960. *The Stages of Economic Growth: A Non-Communist Manifesto*. Cambridge: Cambridge University Press.

SACTRA (Standing Advisory Committee on Trunk Road Assessment). 1999. *Transport and the Economy*. London: The Stationery Office.

Savage, C.I. 1959. *An Economic History of Transport*. London: Hutchinson.

Vickerman, R.W. 1992. *The Single European Market: Prospects for Economic Integration*. London: Harvester Wheatsheaf.

Vickerman, R.W. 1995. The regional impacts of trans-European networks. *Annals of Regional Science*, 29, 237–54.

Vickerman, R.W. 2007. Policy implications of dynamic globalized freight flows in Europe, in *Globalized Freight Transport: Intermodality, E-commerce, Logistics and Sustainability*, edited by T. Leinbach and C. Capineri. Cheltenham: Edward Elgar, 219–37.

Vickerman, R.W. 2008. Multi-level policy making in transport: the problems for border regions. *International Journal of Public Policy*, 3, 228–45.

Vickerman, R.W., Spiekermann, K. and Wegener, M. 1999. Accessibility and regional development in Europe. *Regional Studies*, 33, 1–15.

Wolmar, C. 2009. *Blood, Iron and Gold: How the Railways Transformed the World*. London: Atlantic Books.

SECTION III
Save Our Earth!:
Environmental Dimensions

Chapter 5
Transit-Oriented Development and the Urban Fabric

Robert Cervero

Policy Context for TOD

Over the next several decades, around 90 per cent of the world's urban population growth will be in the Global South (UN Habitat 2011). If developing countries continue on their trajectories of the past decade – i.e., annual population growth rates of 2.5 per cent and a decline in built-up densities of 1.5 per cent a year – the world's cumulative area of built-up, impervious surfaces will double in 17 years and triple in 27 years (Angel 2011). The long-term ecological consequences of converting land from natural habitats and open space to urban functions – diminished water supplies, the release of more pollutants into the air, heat-island effects, and lost agricultural land – could be devastating.

The role of public transport and its ability to support more sustainable patterns of urban development is increasingly recognized as a way to moderate climate change, curb auto dependence, and increase the mobility of the poor. This is particularly so for rapidly urbanizing and motorizing developing countries. At the 2012 Rio+20 Conference, international development banks announced a 'game changer' commitment to sustainable transport and pledged substantial financial support over the next decade for this purpose (World Resource Institute 2012).

The coupling of public transport investments and urban development – what can broadly be defined as Transit-Oriented Development, or TOD – yields arguably the most efficient and sustainable type of cityscape (Calthorpe 1993, Cervero et al. 2002, Curtis et al. 2009). Experiences show that well-designed TOD not only increases ridership by drawing more travellers out of cars and into trains and buses, it can also serve as a hub for organizing community development and revitalizing long-distressed urban districts (Bernick and Cervero 1997, Cervero 1998). TOD is thus about much more than simply inducing transit ridership. It aims to be the focal point of local communities – a place to not only 'pass through' but also 'to be', whether for public celebrations, demonstrations, outdoor concerns, farmers markets, or any other activity that helps build community (Bernick and Cervero 1997, Bertolini and Spit 1998).

Today, TOD is most fully developed in Europe, and in particular Scandinavia. Case experiences in Scandinavia are reviewed later in this chapter. Linking public transport investments and urban development in those parts of the world where they might have the greatest long-term impact – i.e., rapidly developing cities – is far more challenging than in Scandinavia. In China, for example, a number of cities have officially embraced TOD. Beijing and Shenzhen, for instance, have adopted TOD as a guiding design principle in their most recent long-range master plans (Li and Huang 2010). Failure to articulate densities (e.g., tapering building heights with distances from stations), the siting of stations in isolated superblocks, poor pedestrian access, and a lack of co-benefiting mixed land uses, however, have undermined TOD efforts in these and other Chinese cities (Zhang 2007, Cervero and Day 2008). Also hampering the coordination of public transport and land development is the reality that the benefits are often not evident until a decade or more in the future. Nevertheless, opportunities abound and simply cannot be overlooked when massive public transport investments are being made in some of the world's fastest growing and congested cities.

This chapter highlights best-case examples of advancing TOD by linking rail investments to urban development, focusing on central-city settings. Case experiences are cited for two fairly mature Scandinavian cities – Stockholm and Copenhagen – and two economic juggernauts of southeast Asia – Singapore and Hong Kong. First, the economic rationale for linking transit investments and urban development are reviewed followed by discussions on types of TOD and the roles they can play in advancing sustainable growth. The chapter concludes with discussions on the challenges of translating best-case global experiences to rapidly urbanizing cities of the world.

The Economic Rationale

The case for aggressively expanding transit services are often rooted in social-equity and environmental arguments however just as important, at least among those who make tough urban decisions (i.e., politicians), are economic ones. Increasingly, elected officials are drawn to the economic development potential of transit investments. In its Liveanomics series, the Economist Intelligence Unit (2011) found that 61 per cent of surveyed mayors reported that 'improving public transport/roads' was the most important thing that could be done to make their city more competitive for business on the global stage. This was nearly twice the share that felt investing in schooling and education was the key to being economically competitive.

Transit-oriented built environments, I would argue, are fully consistent with economic prosperity and productivity. Global examples shed light on this. The International Association of Public Transport, or UITP, published a Mobility in Cities Database which provides background data on a number of international cities, including several discussed later in this chapter. Vehicle Kilometres Travelled (VKT) per capita is widely viewed as the best aggregate-level metric to gauge sustainability in the urban transport sector. As VKT per capita increases, so does fossil-fuel consumption, tailpipe emission (e.g., carbon dioxide and photochemical smog), and land consumption from roadway expansion. Figure 5.1 reveals a strong negative association between transit usage and VKT per capita. Cities like Stockholm, Hong Kong, and Curitiba stand out for their comparatively small environmental footprints. The positive association between population density and transit ridership is shown in Figure 5.2. While not sufficient, compact patterns of development – a signature feature of TOD – are a necessary feature of successful transit services, at least when measured on the basis of per capita transit ridership.

How transportation/urban-form relationships influence economic productivity has garnered increased policy attention in recent years. Past research has found compact and highly accessible cities to be associated with relatively high levels of labour productivity (Prud'homme and Lee 1999, Cervero 2001, 2009). Well-designed cities and efficient pricing of infrastructure that slows the VKT growth can also promote economic growth. A US report on Growing Wealthier, for example, found that states with lower VKT per capita tend to have higher GDP per capita (Kooshian and Winkelman 2011). While correlations do not

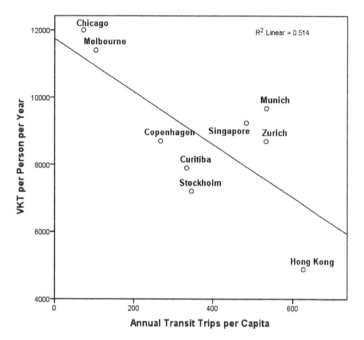

Figure 5.1   Transit ridership and VKT per capita among global cities

Source: Data from International Association of Public Transport 2002.

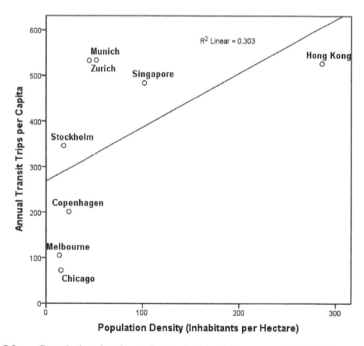

Figure 5.2   Population density and transit ridership among global cities

Source: Data from International Association of Public Transport 2002.

prove causality and other researchers have reached opposite conclusions (QuantEcon 2009), most would agree that the aim should be less about encouraging physical movement and more about designing communities and pricing resources to maximize economic and social interactions. For the first-world cities in the UITP database, Table 5.1 suggests that low VKT and high transit ridership is at least not associated with low economic performance. European cities with world-class transit systems, like Zurich and Munich, for example, average high GDP per capita and at the same time transit ridership and relatively modest VKT per capita. Zurich is not only one of the wealthiest cities in the world, its high per capita levels of transit ridership is matched by: among the highest commercial real-estate values in the world (Bahnhoffstrasse); highest worldwide ranking in quality of life (Arthur D. Little 2002); one of the lowest vehicle ownership rates in the developed world (40 per cent of households have no cars); and among the cleanest air quality of any European city.

Table 5.1   Transit ridership, VKT, and GDP among global cities

	Transit Trips/person/yr	VKT/person/yr	GDP/person (US$)
Hong Kong	627	4,880	$27,600
Zurich	533	8,690	$41,600
Munich	534	9,670	$45,800
Singapore	484	9,240	$28,900
Stockholm	346	7,210	$32,700
Curitiba	334	7,900	$6,800
Copenhagen	268	8,700	$34,100
Chicago	73	12,000	$40,000
Melbourne	105	11,400	$22,800

Source: International Association of Public Transport 2002.

TOD Typologies

TODs do not automatically sprout around transit stations, in a vacuum, but rather are the products of both market forces and strategic planning efforts to channel growth into desired settings. The economic drivers of clustered development around urban rail stops include market demand in employment sectors that benefit from agglomeration and spatial clustering (e.g., knowledge-based industries and services). Employment growth in fields such as finance, law, real estate, and architectural design mean a market demand for clustered development that allows knowledge transfers and face-to-face deal-making (Venables 2007). Transit stations in major urban districts are where such businesses naturally gravitate. These basic-employment jobs in turn spawn business-serving sub-clusters as well as demand for housing, some of which can similarly end up near transit stations. Making sure they do means preparing station-area transit plans that identify the functional roles and urban design qualities of station catchments, backed up with effective implementation tools and strategies.

Defining the future roles of various station areas along a system often starts with creating a typology of TODs. Typologies are generally defined in terms of:

1. land uses – predominantly employment, predominantly residential, or balanced/ mixed use;
2. market scale – regional, sub-regional/district, or community/neighbourhood;
3. urban intensity – high-density, medium-density, low-rise; and
4. market activity – strong, emerging, or static.

For successful TOD to take shape, every station can and should be classified in terms of these four characteristics. In the case of Portland, Oregon, America's most successful TOD region, such an approach toward building TOD typologies has been in place over the past decade. There, factors like trends in land prices and building densities as well as urban design features (e.g., average block sizes and street connectivity indices) have been used to classify each of the region's 57 existing and planned rail stations. Station areas with a mix of strong real-estate market trends and transit-supportive built environments are targeted for pro-active TOD planning and public-sector leveraging. This means preparing specific station-area TOD plans as well as introducing supportive land-use zoning and complementary infrastructure investments (e.g., sidewalk enhancements, expanded sewerage trunk-line capacities). In neighbourhoods with more tepid local real estate markets for which TOD is desired for social or environmental reasons, financial incentives like property tax abatements and low-interest loans might also be introduced to entice private investors.

If a station is to be more than a jumping-off point to catch a fast train or bus, it is important to define its role along a spectrum of node versus place. The absence of TODs in many parts of the world often reflects the inherent tension between the place-making versus logistical roles of stations (Bertolini and Spit 1998, Dittmar and Ohland 2004). On the one hand, stations are logistical nodes wherein cars, buses, taxis, delivery trucks, pedestrians and cyclists converge for accessing transit and allowing inter-modal transfers. Here, function takes precedence over form. The engineer's perspective wins out over the architect's or planner's. On the other hand, stations and their immediate environs can also be places for creating or rebuilding community hubs. In such a role, a TOD serves both functionally and symbolically as the centrepieces of communities. Here, form takes precedence over function. In terms of physical designs, architecture and urban planning subsumes engineering. Such place- and people-oriented TODs aim to not only increase transit ridership but also enliven community life, build social capital, and increase commerce and economic activities.

Absent efforts to build TOD typologies and define stations on the place-versus-node spectrum, functionality almost always precedes form, due to factors like statutory design codes and liability concerns. Whenever the logistical needs of a station win out, the resulting road designs and parking layouts often detract from the quality of walking, creating more of a transit-adjacent development (TAD) than a transit-oriented one (TOD).

With limited institutional capacities and resources to conduct strategic planning, many cities designing and building TODs give little thought to the functional roles of specific stations. Stations planned for a more residential orientation will be best suited for place-making roles. Those with more commercial and logistical orientations are apt to be better suited for nodal and intermodal roles. Failure to define the function roles of stations and create a typology of TODs can result in some stations taking on a schizophrenic persona – trying to play both place-making and logistical roles and as a result doing neither particularly well.

The cases that follow are examples where the role of rail transit improvement and ancillary land development in advancing a particular vision of urban futures was well articulated. To a significant degree, this meant defining transit's role in leveraging specific hoped-for outcomes, such as green urbanism (in the case of Stockholm) and financial profitability (in the case of Hong Kong). That is, in keeping with the derived nature of urban travel, the rail transit improvements and the development they spurred were envisaged as a means to a larger end, one that extends well beyond moving people swiftly and safely along railway corridors.

Stockholm, Sweden: First-Generation Transit Necklace; Second-Generation Urban Regeneration

In Greater Stockholm, the last half-century of thoughtful strategic regional planning has helped create regional settlement and commutation patterns that have substantially lowered car-dependency in middle-income suburbs. Stockholm's investment in radial rail lines has given rise to a 'string of pearls' urban form, and a balanced use of land for work and housing (Cervero 1998). Stockholm planners consciously created a jobs-housing balance along rail-served axial corridors. This in turn has produced directional-flow balances in commuting periods. During peak hours, 55 per cent of commuters are typically travelling in one direction on trains and 45 per cent are heading in the other direction.

Stockholm's transit modal share is nearly twice that found in bigger rail-served European cities like Berlin and even higher than inner London's market share. Perhaps most impressive, Stockholm is one of the few places where automobile travel is receding. Between 1980 and 1990, it was the only city in a sample of 37 global cities that registered a per capita decline in car use – a drop off of 229 annual kilometres of travel per person (Kenworthy and Laube 1999). As revealed previously in Table 5.1, its VKT per capita remains among the lowest in the world. An independent analysis by Siemens/McKinsey (2008) found Stockholm's CO_2 emissions from the transport sector to be particularly low relative to global cities, including New York, Tokyo, and London, a product mostly of low VKT.

These statistics do not mean that Stockholm is 'anti-car'. In fact, Stockholm has a relatively high level of car ownership (555 cars per 1,000 inhabitants). In a well-designed transit metropolis like Stockholm, residents simply drive less. Notably, they are more judicious and discriminate in their use of the private car than car owners in other cities. Most Stockholmers use public transport for the daily grind of going to work, selectively using cars where they have natural advantages, such as for grocery shopping or long weekend excursions.

Stockholm is credited for spearheading transit-oriented development in the age of the motorway, in the form of master plans for new towns like Vallingby. There, the Tunnelbana rail stop sits squarely in the town centre. Upon exiting the station, one steps into a car-free public square surrounded by shops, restaurants, schools, and community facilities. The civic square, often adorned with benches, water fountains, and greenery, is the community's central gathering spot – a place to relax, socialize, and a setting for special events, whether national holidays, public celebrations, parades, or social demonstrations. Sometimes, the square doubles up as a place for farmers to sell their produce or street artists to perform, changing chameleon-like from an open-air market one day to a concert venue the next. The assortment of flower stalls, sidewalk cafes, newsstands, and outdoor vendors dotting the square, combined with the musings and conversations of residents sitting in the square, retirees playing chess, and everyday encounters among friends, adds colour and breathes life into the community. Thus, a community's rail station and its surroundings are more than a jumping off point. As lively urban districts, they should be the kinds of places people are naturally drawn to. If done well, TODs are 'places to be', not 'places to pass through' (Bertolini and Spit 1998). In Stockholm's case, suburban rail's place-making role has been every bit if not more important than its logistical role. Form has rarely been subsidiary to function.

While the first-generation of TOD in metropolitan Stockholm was on former greenfields (e.g., Vallingby and Kista), in recent times a push has been made to redevelop former brownfields. The most notable example of this is Hammerby Sjöstad, an eco-community that has taken form along a recently built inner-ring tramway.

Green TOD of Hammarby Sjöstad

The development of Hammarby Sjöstad marked an abrupt shift in Stockholm's urban planning practice. After decades of building new towns on peripheral greenfield sites, Hammarby Sjöstad is one of several 'new-towns/in-town' created following Stockholm's 1999 City Plan that set forth a vision of 'Build the City Inwards'. Consisting of some 160 hectares of brownfield redevelopment, Hammarby Sjöstad today stands as Stockholm's largest urban regeneration projects to date. Because the urban regeneration project focuses on a new inner-city transit line in addition to being design for energy self-sufficiency and minimal waste, it has been called a 'Green TOD' (Cervero and Sullivan 2011). Just as the greenfield new town of Vallingby pioneered TOD, Hammarby Sjöstad is a paragon of TOD with green urbanism and green architecture.

Green transportation in Hammarby Sjöstad

Hammarby Sjöstad's signature transit element is a new orbital tramway, Tvärbanan, which runs through the heart of the community along a 3-km boulevard (Hammarby Allé and Lugnets Allé). Fully opened in 2002, it carried 44,000 people per weekday in 2007 (Hall 2014). In TOD fashion, Hammarby Sjöstad's taller buildings (mostly six–eight stories) cluster along the transit spine and building heights taper with distance from the rail-served corridor. Trams run every 7 minutes in the peak and provide 5-minute connections to Stockholm's metro underground network and commuter trains. Rail stations are well-designed, fully weather protected, and provide real-time arrival information. Hammarby Sjöstad's buses, moreover, run on biogas produced by local wastewater processing.

Parks, walkways and green spaces are also prominent throughout Hammarby Sjöstad. Where possible, the natural landscape has been preserved. Bike lanes run along major boulevards, ample bike parking can be found at every building, and bike and pedestrian bridges cross waterways. Design features that are integral to TOD, like buildings that go up to sidewalk line (i.e., no set-backs), offer comfortable and secure walking corridors with clear sight-lines. As in the case of Vallingby, they also bring destinations together and through side friction end up slowing traffic.

The presence of three car-sharing companies which together provide access to 37 low-emission vehicles has further reduced the need for owning a car in Hammarby Sjöstad. Also, the project was designed at just 0.25 parking spaces per dwelling unit, though this rate has inched up in recent years. All commercial parking, moreover, is for a fee and rates discourage long-term parking. The neighbourhood also sits just outside Stockholm's congestion toll boundary, which adds a further incentive to use public transport, walk or bike when heading to the central city.

Green urbanism in Hammarby Sjöstad
Hammarby Sjöstad's green urbanism is found in energy production, waste and water management, and building designs. The energy use of buildings in Hammarby Sjöstad has been set at 60 kWh/year, a third less than for the city as a whole. All windows are triple glazed and walls thoroughly insulated. Other conservation measures include extra heat insulation, energy-efficient windows, on-demand ventilation, individual metering of heating and hot water in apartments, electrically efficient installations, lighting control, solar panels, fuel cells, reduced water flow, and low-flush toilets.

The ecological feature of Hammarby Sjöstad that has garnered the most attention is the fully integrated closed loop eco-cycle model. This clever system recycles waste and maximizes the reuse of waste energy and materials for heating, transportation, cooking and electricity. Also impressive is Hammarby Sjöstad's approach to water management. All stormwater, rainwater and snowmelt is collected, purified locally through sand fibre, stormwater basins, and green roofs and released in purified form into a lake. A preserved oak forest, ample green surfaces, and planted trees help collect rainwater to ensure cleaner air and provide a counterbalance to the dense urban landscape.

Environmental and transportation impacts
Hammarby Sjöstad is well on its way to becoming a low-carbon eco-community. The project's reductions relative to conventional development were: emissions and pollution (air, soil and water) – 40–46 per cent; non-renewable energy use – 30–47 per cent; and water consumption – 41–46 per cent. Similar to the rest of Stockholm, 95 per cent of all waste produced by Hammarby Sjöstad's household is reclaimed.

In terms of transportation, environmental benefits have accrued from Hammarby Sjöstad's relatively high share of non-motorized (walking and bicycling) trips. In 2002, the project's modal splits were: public transport (52 per cent), walking/cycling (27 per cent), and private car (21 per cent) (Brick 2008). Non-car travel shares are thought to be considerably higher today and even in 2002 well exceeded that of comparison suburban neighbourhoods of Stockholm with similar incomes (Table 5.2). Residents' transit modal splits even exceed those of inner-city Stockholm. Also, 62 per cent of Hammarby Sjöstad's households had a car in 2007, down from 66 per cent in 2005 and in line with averages for the denser, core part of Stockholm city (Brick 2008). Studies show that residents' carbon footprint from transportation in 2002 was considerably lower than comparison communities: 438 versus 913 kg CO_2 equivalent/apartment/year (Brick 2008). This is in keeping with the goal of the city of Stockholm to become fossil-fuel free by 2050.

Table 5.2   **Mode splits for journeys with destination in Stockholm county**

	Inner City	Southern Suburbs	Western Suburbs	Hammarby Sjöstad**
Car	17%	39%	43%	21%
Public Transport	36%	28%	23%	52%
Bike/Walk	47%	32%	34%	27%

Source: Brick 2008.

Another barometer of Hammarby Sjöstad's environmental benefits is the relatively healthy local economy – i.e., a higher median household income and lower unemployment rate relative to the city as a whole in 2006. Also, land prices and rents have risen more rapidly over the past decade than most other parts of the Stockholm region.

Other Urban Regeneration Elements

An important component of creating a functional and livable core city has been the introduction of congestion pricing. Stockholm's Electronic Road Pricing (ERP) scheme, introduced in 2004 on a trial basis, charges motorists for entering the central city on weekdays using a graduated price scheme. Buses, taxis, eco-fuel cars, and those coming and going from isolated island of Lidingo are exempted. As traffic conditions and the quality of public transit services improved, citizens' support grew steadily (Eliasson et al. 2009). A referendum in 2007 resulted in 53 per cent of Stockholm residents voting to make the road pricing trial permanent. During the first two years of the permanent scheme, peak-period traffic volumes within the pricing zone fell by 25 per cent (removing one million vehicles from the road each day), CO_2 emissions fell by 14 per cent, and around US$300,000 per day in toll revenues were collected (Eliasson et al. 2009).

Revenues from congestion tolls have gone to enhance transit services but mostly to upgrade road facilities, such as the South City tunnel project (Sodra Lanken), that help remove through traffic from central-city surface streets and a western bypass project. Revenues are also going for a major inner-city land reclamation project in the Slussen area. Guided by a master plan of noted architect Norman Foster, Slussen – what has been called a tangled bunch of highway overpasses – is to become a pedestrian- and transit-oriented central-city infill project. Slussen will feature attractive public spaces and water terraces that link pedestrians on a historic route into the old city.

Copenhagen: Transit-Oriented and Bike-Friendly

A text-book example of long-range planning visions shaping rail investments which in turn shaped urban growth comes from Copenhagen, with its celebrated 'Finger Plan'. As in Stockholm, Copenhagen planners identified corridors for channelling overspill growth from the urban centres early in the planning process, and rail infrastructure was built, often in advance of demand, to steer growth along desired growth axes. As importantly, greenbelt wedges set aside as agricultural preserves, open space, and natural habitats were also designated and accordingly major infrastructure was directed away from these districts. In keeping with Scandinavian tradition, rail transit's critical role in shaping urban growth according to a widely embraced vision of the future and defining 'place' has been an overriding determinant of how and where rail was built.

Pro-Cycling and Pedestrian Programs

On the periphery of Copenhagen are new towns that are every bit as bike- and pedestrian-friendly as those in greater Stockholm. Suburban towns of 10 to 30 thousand inhabitants, like Ballerup, Brønby, and Høje-Taastrup, are laced by greenways that connect neighbourhoods, schools, retail centres, and pocket parks to inviting rail stops. Around half of residents of these middle-class master-planned new towns take a train to work and four out of five walk, bike, or bus to their community's rail station.

Copenhagen planners have long embraced the notion that industrial progress should not encroach on the rights and needs of pedestrians and cyclists. They created one of the first and the longest car-free streets in Europe, Strøget, which during summer days accommodates some 55,000 pedestrians, often shoulder-to-shoulder. Street life is not viewed only in terms of foot traffic but also with regards to stationary activities. Jan Gehl, a noted urban designer from Copenhagen, sold city leaders on the idea that great public spaces accommodate not only busy pedestrians but also causal sitting, relaxation, and mulling around. Today, some 80,000 square metres of public squares – big and small, grandeur and modest – dot central Copenhagen.

One of the chief ways of tending to the needs of cyclists has been the expropriation of car lanes and curbside parking for exclusive use by bicyclists. Since 1980, Copenhagen's inventory of bike lanes has increased from 210 to 460 kilometres within an area of about 90 km^2 (Hall 2014). Over the same period, the number of bike trips has jumped 80 per cent. Today, fully one-half of journeys to work or school in Copenhagen are by bicycle, by far the highest modal split of any capital city in Europe (Gemzøe 2013). The city's most recent master plan, 'Eco-Metropolis', commits Copenhagen to become 'the world's best city for bicycling'. Copenhagen has set a high bar of 50 per cent of its citizens biking to work or school by 2015. New separated cycle-tracks are being added in hopes of achieving this goal.

To give cycling a further boost, Copenhagen introduced a short-term bike lease programme, called City Bike, in 1995. While commonplace in many parts of the world today, Copenhagen was a trailblazer, having actively pursuing bike-sharing for going on two decades. City Bikes provide on-demand access to train stations with more than 2,000 white bikes in place at some 140 bike stands throughout the city. Besides improving rail access, the programme has also reduced on-vehicle carriage of bikes, freeing up train capacity for passengers. The City Bikes are overseen by a local non-profit organization that hires hundreds of rehabilitees to maintain the shared bikes. The organization reports that 55 per cent of the rehabilitees get a job afterwards.

Statistics reveal how well-articulated Copenhagen's 'access-shed' is for transit riding (Suzuki et al. 2013). A recent survey of 15 suburban rail stations found that walking captured 38 to 100 per cent of access trips up to 1 km; for trips 1 to 2 km away, cycling accounted for 40 per cent of access trips. Beyond 2 km, buses handled two-thirds of access trips. Even 4 km from stations, twice as many access trips were by bicycle as by car. Danish designers have found that acceptable walking and cycling distances can be stretched considerably by creating attractive, visually stimulating, and safe travel corridors. It is for such reasons that carbon dioxide emissions per capita have fallen by 25 per cent since 1990.

Other Initiatives

A transit-oriented and pedestrian/bike-friendly built form is not the only factor that accounts for Copenhagen's low annual VKT per capita of 8,700, shown earlier in Table 5.1. Also critical have been national policies that aim to moderate car ownership and usage. Since World War II, the Danish national government has issued policy guidelines every four years aimed at shaping the land-constrained country's physical development. A series of national directives have over the years called for targeting greater Copenhagen's future growth around rail-transit stations.

National infrastructure funds are tied to the compliance of these directives. Also, while they do not exactly carry the force of law, Denmark's national directives clearly imply that localities are to make good faith efforts in encouraging TOD. If the nation's Ministry of Environment feels otherwise, it has veto power over proposed local development projects. These veto powers have been exercised sparingly over the years, in large part because most localities strongly support sustainable patterns of development.

Besides national directives that mandate major trip generators to be sited near rail stops, Denmark adds taxes and fees that typically triple the retail price of a new car. Copenhagen's 250 motor vehicles per 1000 inhabitants is around half that found in large German cities like Hamburg and Frankfurt.

Local policies have also restricted car travel. In Copenhagen, central-city road capacity has been kept constant since 1970 and outside the core city, additional road capacity must be matched by at least as many square metres of additional bike-lanes and bus-lanes. Parking supplies have also been restricted, particularly near rail stops. The outsourcing of parking to peripheral areas has led to a 3 per cent annual reduction in core-area parking supplies (Hall 2014). Central-city bus services have been enhanced by a system of reserved lanes and signal prioritization.

Also strengthening Copenhagen's standing as a transit metropolis has been the expansion of rail services. New rail 'fingers' have been built, notably an automated, fully grade-separated line to the new-town/in-town of Ørestad. Rail services preceded development in Ørestad, a clear case of building transit first to guide development. From the start, Ørestad was a true mixed-use community, designed to be a place to live, work, shop, learn, and play. Particular attention was paid to the livability of the new community. Housing was built close to parks and canals, and connected by plazas and pathways. Cafes and squares were intentionally sited to attract customers who arrive by foot. A variety of neighbourhood parks were designed to meet the diverse recreational needs of new residents. In contrast to the rather drab, standardized appearance of Copenhagen's early generation TODs, Ørestad also features a variety of architectural styles carefully planned to interact and blend with each other. Many of Ørestad's signature buildings were designed by world-class architects and several have won prestigious design awards. Ørestad's diversity is underscored by one of the largest car-free housing developments anywhere, called 'Urbanplanen'.

Another notable rail line that is being built in the region follows a circular route, providing 'cross-finger' connections. This Cityringen metro line will serve a number of districts outside of the city proper not served by the S-Train commuter rail system. The sale of land whose values have appreciated in anticipation of new rail services has helped finance new investments like Cityringen, the Ørestad line, and Copenhagen's first light-rail Line, Letbanen, being built parallel to the region's third ring road.

Collectively, Copenhagen's suite of pro-transit/auto-restraint measures as well as TOD, both new and old, have helped create a '5 minute city' – one where everything is close at hand, and eventually, it is hoped, the vast majority of trips will be by foot, bicycle, train, or bus. Thus far, the results have been spectacular: though car ownership rose by 40 per cent between 1995 and 2004, usage only went up by 10 per cent while bicycle use increased by nearly 50 per cent; thus, kilometres cycled have increased by twice as much as kilometres driven, while average journey times on transit have fallen 23 per cent (Hall 2014).

Singapore: TOD Empowered by TDM

The city-state of Singapore is internationally renowned for its successful integration of transit and regional development, placing the urbanized island of 5.1 million inhabitants on a sustainable pathway, both economically and environmentally. Its transformation over the post-Second World War period has been remarkable, from a backwater port awash in third world poverty to a dynamic, modern industrialized city-state. As part of a national economic development strategy, Singapore has embraced Scandinavian planning principles that call for radial corridors that interconnect the central core with master-planned new towns. Its structure plan, called the Constellation Plan, reflects its namesake – from plan view, it has the appearance of a constellation of satellite 'planets', or new towns, that orbit the central core, interspersed by protective greenbelts and interlaced by high-capacity, high-performance rail transit. Radial rail links inter-connect Singapore's high-rise urban core with the hierarchy of sub-centres and a looping mix of heavy and light rail lines connect sub-centres amongst themselves. Like Stockholm and Copenhagen, this rail-served settlement pattern has produced tremendous transportation benefits: low VKT per capita (among the lowest of any urbanized region worldwide with per capita GDP over US$25,000) and high transit modal splits (484 annual transit trips per capita in 2006).

Singapore adopted the approach of building new towns that are not independent, self-contained units but rather nodes with specialized functions that interact with and depend upon other new towns. Some satellite centres are primarily industrial estates, some are predominantly dormitory communities, and most are mixed-use enclaves. Around three-quarters of residents of master-planned new towns work outside of their area of residence. Most, however, commute within the radial corridor that connects their new town to Singapore's Central Business District. This means travel is predominantly within, not between, rail-served corridors. Also, the dispersal of mixed land uses along corridors has created two-way travel flows and spread travel demand more evenly throughout the day.

Singapore is also noted for its progressive 'transit first' policies that complement its transit-oriented Constellation Plan. The city has introduced a three-tier fiscal program that comes as close to 'getting the prices right' within the urban transport sector as any city in the world. The first tier of charges is subscription fees for owning a car. Comprised of high registration fees, import duties for automobile purchases, and a licensing surcharge based on a quota system (Certificate of Entitlement that is indexed to congestion levels), these charges principally cover fixed costs associated with providing basic levels of road infrastructure and parking facilities. The second tier of charges are use-related, in the form of fuel taxes and parking fees, that cover incremental costs for scaling road capacity to traffic volumes and maintaining roadway infrastructure. The third set of charges – in the form of real-time electronic road pricing (ERP) – force motorists to internalize the externalities they impose in using their cars during peak hours. Fees fluctuate according to congestion levels, meaning motorists bear some of the costs they impose on others such as time delays and air pollution. Within a month of initiating electronic road pricing in 1998, traffic along a main thoroughfare fell by 15 per cent and average rush-hours speeds rose from 36 to 58 kph. Vehicle quotas, congestion prices, and an assortment of fees and surtaxes (that add as much as 150 per cent to a car's open market value) have reduced Singapore's annual vehicle population growth from 6 per cent in 1991 to under 3 per cent in 2006, a remarkable achievement for a city where per capita incomes have risen faster over the past two decades than virtually anywhere in the world.

Charging motorists more to own and use cars is but one form of transportation demand management (TDM) found in Singapore. For instance, as in Europe, car sharing has gained a foothold in Singapore, the only Asian city where this is the case. Singapore also has an off-peak vehicle licensing scheme that allows vehicles holding such licenses to be used only during the morning and evening off-peak periods from Mondays to Saturday and anytime Sunday.

While higher prices and TDM have boosted transit usage, their influences are being eclipsed by rising incomes that continue to push up Singapore's rates of car ownership and motorization. Part of the reason is that Singapore has among the most affordable housing (due to government provisions of mass produced units), freeing up personal income for the second most costly durable goods purchased by households, the private car. In the early 1990s, the ratio of average housing price to income was 2.3 compared to ratio of 3.7 of average new-car price to income. Over the 1974 to 1995 period, one study reported a price elasticity for car ownership of -0.45 compared to an income elasticity of 1.00 (Chu et al. 2004). Even if automobile prices increase at twice the rate of household incomes, such elasticities suggest motorization rates will continue to rise in Singapore. Rising congestion is reflected by statistics on the density of cars on land-constrained Singapore's fairly fixed supply of road supply: on a per kilometre of road basis, from 180 vehicles in 1995 (the year the vehicle quota system was introduced) to 250 vehicles in 2010. While car ownership only increased by 11 per cent from 2000 to 2005, it increased by 39 per cent from 2005 to 2010. For such reasons, Singapore is turning to higher congestion tolls as a way to temper motorization. The logic of raising congestion tolls is expressed in the long-term master plan: 'While congestion charges such as encourage motorists to consider whether and when to drive, ownership costs are sunk costs and may in fact result in motorists driving more rather than less. Hence, as we expand the ERP system, we will continue to shift the focus of our demand management strategies from ownership taxes to usage charges' (Singapore Land Transport Authority 2008).

Singapore's centralized form of governance has allowed land development and transit services, overseen by different authorities (Urban Redevelopment Authority and Land Transport Authority), to be closely coordinated, both institutionally and financially. Revenues generated from high vehicle ownership and usage charges, for instance, go to the general treasury that in turn get channelled into not only vastly enhanced and expanded transit services, but also the construction of the armature (e.g., sidewalk networks, civic squares, bus staging areas) of rail TODs. It is because of the island-state's world-class transit service offerings and TOD built form that congestion tolls are politically possible – for a significant share of trips, transit is a faster mobility option than the private car. Of 8.9 million daily motorized trips made in Singapore in 2010, 4.5 million, or just over half, are by rail or bus transit (Singapore MRT 2011). Long-range planning goals call for raising this share to two-thirds.

Rail transit's role in capturing larger shares of motorized trips has increased and is slated to continue to do so in coming years. The length of Singapore's MRT rail system has more than doubled to 138 km in 2011 from 67 km in 1990, leading to a doubling of ridership, to nearly 2,000,000 riders a day, from a little under 1 million in 1998. In 1999, Singapore added automated light rail services to the mix, with trackage increasing from 8 km in 1999 to 29 km in 2010. Bus ridership is now only one and a half times higher than total rail ridership, while it was three times higher than rail in 1998. Singapore's latest land transport master plan, released in 2008, embraces 'making public transport a choice mode' and 'managing road usage' as strategic thrusts toward retaining its status as a world-class transit metropolis.

Hong Kong: Profitable Transit

Any visitor to Hong Kong instantly recognizes that public transit is the lifeblood of the city. Hong Kong boasts a rich offering of transit services, including a high-capacity railway network, surface-street trams, ferries, and an assortment of buses and minibuses. In late-2007, the city's main passenger rail operator, MTR Corporation, merged with the former Kowloon-Canton Railway Corporation, forming a 168 km network of high-capacity, grade-separated services in Hong Kong island, the Kowloon peninsula, the Northern Territories (to the Chinese border), and, through a recent extension, to Hong Kong's new international airport. Today, over 90 per cent of all motorized trips in Hong Kong are by public transit, the highest market share in the world (Lam 2003).

The combination of high urban densities and high-quality public transport services has not only produced the highest level of transit usage in the world (570 annual public transport trips per capita) but has also substantially driven down the cost of motorized travel. In 2002, over half of all motorized trips made by Hong Kong residents were a half hour or less (ARUP 2003). Motorized travel consumes, on average, around 5 per cent of Hong Kong's Gross Domestic Product (GDP). This contrasts sharply with more automobile-oriented global cities such as Houston and Melbourne, where upwards of one-seventh of GDP goes to transportation (International Association of Public Transport 2002). Hong Kong residents enjoy substantial travel cost savings even in comparison to much larger global cities with extensive railway networks, like London and Paris.

Transit Value Capture in Hong Kong

Hong Kong is one of the few places in the world where public transport makes a profit, courtesy of the city's rail operator – MTR Corporation – pursuing what is called the 'Rail+Property' programme, or R+P for short (Cervero and Murakami 2009). R+P is one of the best examples anywhere of transit value capture in action. Given the high premium placed on access to fast, efficient and reliable public-transport services in a dense, congested city like Hong Kong, the price of land near railway stations is generally higher than elsewhere, sometimes by several orders of magnitude. MTR has used its ability to purchase the development rights for land around stations to recoup the cost of investing in rail transit and turn a profit. The railway has also played a vital city-shaping role. In 2002, around 2.8 million people, or 41 per cent of Hong Kong's population, lived within 500 m of a railway station (Tang et al. 2004).

Profit motive accounts for MTR's active involvement in land development. As a private corporation that sells shares on the Hong Kong stock market, MTR operates on commercial principles, financing and operating railway services that are self-supporting and yield a net return on investment. Effectively, the fully-loaded costs of public-transport investments, operations, and maintenance are covered by supplementing fare and other revenues with income from ancillary real estate development – e.g., the sale of development rights, joint venturing with private real-estate developers, and running retail outlets in and around subway stations. Hong Kong's government is MTR's majority stockholder, ensuring the company weighs the broader public interest in its day-to-day decisions. However, the sale of 23 per cent of MTR's shares to private investors exerts a market discipline, prompting the company to be entrepreneurial. During the 2001–2005 period, property development produced 52 per cent of MTR's revenues. By contrast, railway income, made up mostly of farebox receipts, generated 28 per cent of total income. MTR's involvement in all property-related activities – i.e., development, investment, and management – produced 62 per cent of total income, more than twice as much as user fares.

Timing is crucial in MTRC's recapturing of the rail's value-added on land-price. MTRC purchases development rights from the Hong Kong government at a 'before rail' price and sells these rights to a selected developer (among a list of qualified bidders) at an 'after rail' price. The differences between land values with, versus without, rail services are substantial, easily covering the cost of railway investments. When bargaining with developers, MTRC also negotiates a share of future property-development profits and/or a co-ownership position from the highest bidder. Thus MTRC receives a 'front end' payment for land and a 'back end' share of revenues and assets in-kind.

MTRC has hardly been the sole financial beneficiary of R+P. Society at large, reflected by the city of Hong Kong's majority ownership of MTRC, has also reaped substantial rewards. For the 1980 to 2005 period, it is estimated that Hong Kong has received nearly US$140 billion (in today's Hong Kong dollars) in net financial returns. This is based on the difference between earned income ($171.8 billion from land premiums, market capitalization, shareholder cash dividends, and initial public offer proceeds) and the value of injected equity capital ($32.2 billion from land grants). Thus the government of Hong Kong has enjoyed tremendous finance returns and seeded the construction of a world-class railway network without having to advance any cash to MTR. The $140 billion figure, of course, is only the direct financial benefit. The indirect benefits – for example, higher ridership through increased densities, reduced sprawl, air pollution, and energy consumption – have increased net societal returns well beyond $140 billion.

Sustainable Finance and Sustainable Urbanism

Hong Kong has long had tall towers perched above railway stations, however density alone does not make a good TOD. What was often missing was a high-quality pedestrian environment and a sense of place. Most first generation R+P projects featured indistinguishable apartment towers that funnelled pedestrians onto busy streets and left them to their own devices to find a way to a subway entrance. Growing discontent over sterile station-area environments and sagging real-estate market performance of older buildings prompted MTRC to pay more attention to principles of good town planning. In 2000 MTR created a town-planning division within the corporation to pursue land-development strategies that met corporate financial objectives while also enhancing station-area environments. Prior to this, R+P projects followed rather than anticipated development. With an in-house town planning department, MTR became more pro-active. This has taken the form of the company being ahead of market demand, building high-quality, pedestrian-friendly TODs to steer growth. Research shows the design of high-quality walking environments has yielded even higher financial returns per square metre for R+P projects (Cervero and Murakami 2009). In Hong Kong, pedestrian-friendly R+P projects have contributed to sustainable urbanism as well as sustainable finance. These benefits have been capitalized into land prices.

Close

An overarching principle followed by the cities reviewed in this chapter is that successful transit and land-use integration requires a cogent and coherent vision of the future city.

Importantly, visions of how the city should grow and the role of transportation investments and policy in achieving this urban-form vision were well articulated in all cases. In some instances this translated into a vision of compact, mixed-use, often lineal corridors that produced necklace-of-pearls built forms and induced sustainable mobility choices. In others it meant regenerating once-depressed urban districts and reallocating scarce public resources, including funds, land, and road space, to promote inherently sustainable modes, notably cycling and transit. It is this unwavering commitment to link transit investments and urban development in mutually beneficial and reinforcing ways that distinguishes successful global cases.

As urban growth shifts to cities in the developing world and more and more large-scale rail systems get built, unprecedented opportunities exist for linking land development and transit infrastructure. Worldwide, one and a half billion or more inhabitants will be added to cities between 2013 and 2035 (UN Habitat 2013). This means not only transporting but also clothing, feeding, sheltering and educating the equivalent of seven new megacities – that is, seven 'Jakarta's', 'Shenzhens', or 'Lagos's' – each year over the next two decades. The huge scale of city-building in the Global South over the next several decades will be unlike anything seen anywhere in the past. Growing populations combined with growing wealth will trigger rapid increases in vehicle ownership, energy consumption, and GHG emissions. How growing cities are designed and mobility choices are shaped by transport investments will strongly impact the patterns of future travel and the resources called upon to support it. Once cities are built, patterns become very hard to change. Thus capitalizing upon rail investments to help leverage and create more sustainable urban forms – broadly defined – is more urgent today than ever.

It is indeed fortuitous that opportunities for capitalizing on rail investments are greater than ever. Worldwide, a major rail revival is underway. Urban rail services have dramatically increased in recent times, faster than bus services – from 1995 to 2005, for instance, rail seat kilometres per person increased by more than 30 per cent in US and European cities, compared to less than 10 per cent growth in bus seat kilometres per person (Newman et al. 2013). Moreover, the quality of rail services has been trending upwards, reflected by a jump in the ratio of average urban rail speeds to road speeds from 0.88 in 1960 to 1.13 in 2005 (Newman et al. 2013). Fast-growing Asian cities like Kuala Lumpur, Bangkok, Manila, Delhi, Kolkata, Mumbai and Seoul have built a variety of rail-based systems including above-ground metros or monorails, underground metros, and light-rail system. In China, 82 cities have built or are in the midst of building metros. China also boasts the world's large high-speed inter-city rail network.

A number of significant barriers need to be overcome if rapidly growing and motorizing cities are to follow in the footsteps of creating transit-supportive urban places like Stockholm and Singapore. Among these will be the need to balance the current focus on enhancing mobility in the near term with an ethos of forward-looking, strategic planning that promotes not only sustainable movement but also sustainable urban growth. In many developing cities, the fragmented institutional structures for planning transportation systems and managing urban growth will also have to be revamped (Gakenheimer 2011, Cervero 2013). One way to overcome barriers and bring about change would be for international aid organizations and donor agencies to tie financial assistance for metrorail projects to bona fide local efforts to improve the coordination and integration of transit and land development projects. Pilot-demonstrations of innovative ideas, like Green TOD, are also needed. Prodding local governments to introduce value-capture schemes would be a way to generate much-needed revenues to help jump-start TOD. As experiences in cities like Hong Kong show, a virtuous cycle can be set into motion in which denser, high-quality TOD generates income which can go into creating future high-quality TODs, which further increases income and so on.

On the global stage, TOD, it would seem, has strong upside potential (Chen 2010, Suzuki et al. 2013). As long as urban ills like traffic congestion and air pollution – and global concerns like oil dependency and climate change – persist or worsen, TOD will gain credence as a desirable form of urbanism. Rapid urbanization, combined with equally rapid urban and inter-city rapid rail construction, such as in China, suggests that TOD will find particular acceptance in former third-world countries that are rapidly industrializing and modernizing – the very places where radical transformations in urban landscapes are most urgently needed.

References

Angel, S. 2011. *Making Room for a Planet of Cities*. Cambridge, MA: Lincoln Institute of Land Policy.

Arthur D. Little, Inc. 2002. *Worldwide Quality-of-Life Survey*. New York: Mercer Human Resource Consulting.

ARUP. 2003. *Travel Characteristics Survey 2002: Final Report*. Hong Kong: Transport Department, Hong Kong Special Administrative Region.

Bernick, M. and R. Cervero. 1997. *Transit Villages for the 21st Century.* New York: Mc-Graw Hill.

Bertolini, L. and Spit, T. 1998. *Cities on Rails: The Redevelopment of Railway Station Areas*. London: E & FN Spon.

Brick, K. 2008. *Report Summary – Follow Up of Environmental Impact in Hammarby Sjöstad: Sickla Udde, Sickla Kaj, Lugnet and Proppen*. Stockholm: Grontmij, AB.

Calthorpe, P. 1993. *The New American Metropolis: Ecology, Community, and the American Dream.* New York: Princeton Architectural Press.

Cervero, R. 1998. *The Transit Metropolis: A Global Inquiry*. Washington, DC: Island Press.

Cervero, R. 2001. Efficient urbanisation: economic performance and the shape of the metropolis. *Urban Studies*, 38(10), 1651–71.

Cervero, R. 2009. Transport infrastructure and global competitiveness: balancing mobility and livability. *The Annals of the American Academy of Political and Social Science*, 626(1), 210–25.

Cervero, R. 2013. Linking urban transport and land use in developing countries. *Journal of Transport and Land Use*, 6(1), 7–24.

Cervero, R. and Day, J. 2008. Suburbanization and transit oriented development in China. *Transport Policy,* 15, 315–23.

Cervero, R., Ferrell, C. and Murphy, S. 2002. *Transit-Oriented Development and Joint Development in the United States: A Literature Review* (Research Results Digest, Number 52), Washington, DC: Transit Cooperative Research Program.

Cervero, R. and Murakami, J. 2009. Rail and property development in Hong Kong: experiences and extensions. *Urban Studies*, 46(10), 2019–43.

Cervero, R. and Sullivan, K. 2011. Green TODs: marrying transit-oriented development and green urbanism. *International Journal of Sustainable Development & World Ecology*, 18(3), 210–18.

Chen, X. 2010. Prospect of the transit-oriented development in China. *Management Research and Practice*, 2(1), 83–93.

Chu, S., Koh, W. and Tse, T. 2004. Expectations formation and forecasting of vehicle demand: an empirical study of the vehicle quota auctions in Singapore. *Transportation Research A*, 38(5), 367–81.

Curtis, C., Renne, J. and Bertolini, L. 2009. *Transit Oriented Development: Making it Happen*. Surrey: Ashgate.

Dittmar, H. and Ohland, G. 2004. *The New Transit Town: Best Practices in Transit-Oriented Development*. Washington: Island Press.

Economist Intelligence Unit. 2011. *Lievanomics: Urban Liveability and Economic Growth*. London: The Economist.

Eliasson, J., Hultkrantz, L., Nerhagen, L. and Rosqvist, L.S. 2009. The Stockholm congestion-charging trial 2006: overview of effects. *Transportation Research Part A*, 43(3), 240–50.

Gakenheimer, R. 2011. Land use and transport in rapidly motorizing cities: contexts of controversy. *Urban Transport in the Developing World: A Handbook of Policy and Practice*, edited by H.T. Dimitriou and R. Gakenheimer. Cheltenham: Edward Elgar Press, 40–68.

Gemzøe, L. 2013. Cities for people: Copenhagen studies in urban life, in *Cities & Cycling Around the World: Creating Liveable & Bikeable Cities*, edited by J. Dextre, M. Hughes and L. Bech. Lima: Fondo Editorial de la Pontificia Universidad Católica del Peru, 101–10.

Hall, P. 2014. *Good Cities, Better Lives: How Europe Discovered the Lost Art of Urbanism*. London: Routledge.

International Association of Public Transport. 2002. *Mobility in Cities Database*. [Online] Available at: http://uitp.org/publications/Mobility-in-Cities-Database.cfm [accessed: 22 January 2014].

Kenworthy, J.R. and Laube, F.B. 1999. Patterns of automobile dependence in cities: an international overview of key physical and economic dimensions with some implications for urban policy. *Transportation Research Part A: Policy and Practice*, 33(7–8), 691–723.

Kooshian, C. and Winkelman, S. 2011. *Growing Wealthier: Smart Growth, Climate Change and Prosperity*, Washington, DC: Center for Clean Air Policy.

Lam, W.H.K. 2003. *Advanced Modeling for Transit Operations and Service Planning*. Oxford: Elsevier.

Li, W.L. and Huang, J. 2010. The conception of transit metropolis in Guangzhou. *Proceedings of the 2010 International Conference on Mechanics Automation and Control Engineering*, Singapore, 26–28 June 2010.

Newman, P., Kenworthy, J. and Glazebrook, G. 2013. Peak car use and the rise of global rail: why this is happening and what it means for large and small cities. *Journal of Transportation Technologies*, 3(4), 272–87.

Prud'homme, R. and Lee, G. 1999. Sprawl, speed and the efficiency of cities. *Urban Studies*, 36(11), 1849–58.

QuantEcon, Inc. 2009. *Driving the Economy: Automotive Travel, Economic Growth, and the Risks of Global Warming Regulations*. Portland: Cascade Policy Institute.

Singapore MRT. 2011. *SMRT Annual Report 2011*. Singapore: SMRT Corporation Ltd.

Singapore Land Transport Authority. 2008. *Long Term Master Plan: A People-Centred Land Transport System*. Singapore: Land Transport Authority.

Suzuki, H., Cervero, R. and Iuchi, K. 2013. *Transforming Cities with Transit: Transit and Land-Use Integration for Sustainable Urban Development*. Washington: World Bank.

Tang, B.S., Chiang, Y.H., Baldwin, A.N. and Yeung, C.W. 2004. *Study of the Integrated Rail-Property Development Model in Hong Kong*. Hong Kong: The Hong Kong Polytechnic University.

UN Habitat. 2011. *Global Report on Human Settlements 2011: Cities and Climate Change.* London and Washington, DC: Earthscan.

UN Habitat. 2013. *Global Report on Human Settlements 2011: Planning and Designing for Sustainable Urban Mobility.* London and Washington, DC: Earthscan.

Venables, A. 2007. Evaluating urban transport improvements: cost–benefit analysis in the presence of agglomeration and income taxation. *Journal of Transport Economics and Policy*, 41(2), 173–88.

World Resource Institute. 2012. *Statement: Development Banks Announce 'Game Changer' for Sustainable Transport at Rio+20* [Online]. Available at: http://www.wri. org/press/2012/statement-development-banks-announce-game-changer-sustainable-transport-riot20 [accessed: 22 January 2014].

Zhang, M. 2007. Chinese edition of transit-oriented development. *Transportation Research Record*, 2038, 120–27.

Chapter 6
Airline and Railway (Dis)Integration

Moshe Givoni

Introduction

The inauguration of High-Speed Rail (HSR) services in Japan in 1964 was never meant to provide an alternative to the aircraft, but to increase capacity on the Tokyo-Osaka route in order to meet growing demand. Similar was the case in France about 20 years later when the French TGV services began operation (Givoni 2006). In Europe in those years, rail transport was experiencing a decline in patronage, largely attributed to increase in car ownership and the corresponding increase and reliance on car use, and also the increase in competition from the airlines as flying became more affordable. Demand for air transport in those days was growing, facilitated by the process to liberalize European air transport and, as a result, the emergence of the Low Cost Carriers (LCCs).

Economic growth coupled with other changes led to an overall increase in demand for transport, resulting in congestion increasingly becoming a problem and a 'worry' for policy makers concerned with the associated 'waste of time'. Congestion and accompanied delays became also a major issue for air transport, especially in the main airports that often serve as hubs. At the same time, increased environmental awareness and concern with the environmental impact of transport and its potential contribution to climate change became a major problem faced by the air transport industry. Attention then turned to the railways that started experiencing an increase in demand and signs of a renaissance, attributed also to the HSR and the new image it gave the railways. Mode substitution – from air transport to rail transport – became then an increasingly popular idea promising to be a win-win policy in the context of sustainable transport and airport congestion. For some reason it was not perceived as a 'winning' policy in the context of revitalizing the railways.

In 2005, the model of Airline and Railway Integration was suggested (Givoni 2005, Givoni and Banister 2006) that promised to offer important benefits also to rail transport (Givoni and Banister 2007). The research on airline and railway integration ended with the assumption that air and rail integration will be widespread as its benefits are obvious and its potential will only increase. Close to 10 years on, when the HSR network around the world is fast developing and expanding and the notion of mode substitution is still apparent in contemporary transport policy, for example that of the EU (CEC 2001, EC 2011 and see below) air and rail transport are still largely disintegrated. This is a missed opportunity. A missed opportunity to advance sustainable transport, a missed opportunity for a different approach to air transport provision, and even more so a missed opportunity for advancing the renaissance of the railways. Although not a panacea for any of the above challenges, and although it could be counterproductive for sustainable transport,[1] the idea of airline and

---

1 The environmental paradox of mode substitution is that although an HSR journey of up to about 1,000 km will almost for sure result in less emissions if replacing an aircraft service per seat-km (Givoni 2007), it is likely that such mode substitution will result in a long-haul flight taking up

railway integration holds great potential. Trying to understand why this opportunity is being missed is the main aim of this chapter as well as trying to still argue the case for airline and railway integration.

The chapter continues by revisiting the model of airline and railway integration, followed by a brief review of the literature on air-rail substitution to highlight the dominance of 'competition' rather than complementarity in the debate. Two examples to illustrate the potential for integration and why it is a missed opportunity are then described, also showing the current disintegration between the modes. Finally, some conclusions are drawn.

Revisiting the Model of Airline and Railway Integration

One of the consequences of deregulating the US air transport market in 1978 was the emergence of Hub and Spoke (H&S) operation by the major airlines. Liberalization of other air transport markets, and notably the European market, together with the process of moving towards open-skies agreements between countries meant that H&S was adopted by many of the large international airlines. In an H&S network, passengers are flown between different nodes (airports) in the airline network through a central node, the hub. While an operating strategy for airlines, the main impact of adopting such a strategy is on the airport, which sees demand for runway capacity substantially increasing as a result. Hub airports are the busiest and most congested airports, and where the potential for mode substitution is the largest.

Two types of hub airports are recognized: the Hinterland model where short-haul flights feed traffic into long-haul flights, and the Hourglass model where short-haul services are 'squeezed-out' by the more profitable long-haul flights (Doganis and Dennis 1989, Button and Stough 2000). A third model is the integrated hub model where short-haul services are provided by the airlines using the railways and not aircraft to feed traffic into the airlines' long-haul services (Figure 6.1).

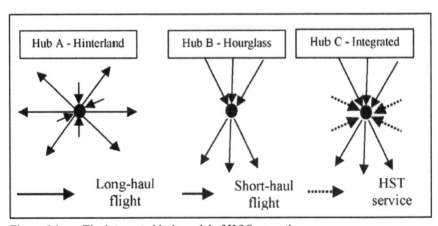

Figure 6.1   The integrated hub model of H&S operation

Source: Adapted by the author from Givoni 2007.

---

the runway capacity freed by the short haul flight transferred to the HSR, thus overall increasing the environmental impact from air transport.

In the integrated hub model, rail services could be to destinations where currently the airline offers services using aircraft, in this case mode substitution takes place, and it could also be to destinations the airline currently does not serve, thus expanding the airline's network. Although Figure 6.1 suggests that the rail services offered by the airline should be HSR services this does not have to be case. Any rail service can be used to feed traffic into the routes served by aircraft from the hub airport. Naturally, where the rail service is to substitute an aircraft service, change of mode from aircraft to rail is more likely to remain attractive to the passenger, and hence the airline, if it does not carry a substantial travel time penalty and this often requires the use of HSR.

An important aspect of airline and railway integration, as originally envisaged, is close commercial cooperation between the airline and the Train Operating Company (TOC). The idea is that the airline continues to offer the service, which is fully integrated into its network, but should not actually operate the service. The commercial agreement between the airline and the TOC can naturally vary, as do agreements between airlines when they collaborate and jointly offer services. In the airline industry the most common type of agreement is code-sharing, whereby one airline operates the flight but many can offer it to their passengers. This agreement can be extended to include TOCs. Lufthansa operates HSR services as part of its network on a few routes, like Frankfurt-Stuttgart and Frankfurt-Cologne, where the service is operated by DB (Deutsche Bahn) and carries a Lufthansa code. Over the years airlines have extended and developed the types of commercial agreements between them, including the formation of airline alliances, but the railways have largely remained outside these agreements.

A prerequisite for airline and railway integration is a railway station at the airport. Ideally, and to make the railways a suitable and attractive substitute to the aircraft, railway stations at airports should be integrated into the main passenger terminal(s), as in the case of Amsterdam Schiphol airport, to allow a seamless as possible transfer between the modes. It should also be a station that offers a high frequency service to many destinations, thus a central node on the rail network. This often requires the station to be a through station rather than an end-of-the-line station. For more elaboration on airline and railway integration see Givoni and Banister (2006, 2007) and Givoni and Rietveld (2008).

The Dominance of Competition in the Air-Rail Substitution Debate

The parallel development and success of the HSR, especially in Europe, on the one hand and the growing concern about the congestion and environmental problems of the air transport industry on the other hand led to increasing interest in air-rail intermodality and mode substitution. While the relations between the air and rail modes can take many forms, the debate on such relations focuses almost entirely on competition between them. There is some attention given in the context of air-rail intermodality to complementarity between the modes, largely in the form of rail services as access modes to airports. The idea of close cooperation, or integration, is largely ignored. One of the earliest studies on the subject, 'optimizing rail/air intermodality in Europe' (Buchanan and Partners 1995) was limited to rail access to airport. A more extensive research, a few years later and also intended for the European Commission (EC), called 'interaction between high-speed and air passenger transport' (EC 1998) focused on the competition aspect of mode substitution and seemed to set the trend.

The situation looked set to change when the notion of integrated transport started to take central place in transport policy, and especially the policy of the EU. Integrated transport was one of the strategies adopted in the EU's 2001 White Paper, especially in order to promote modal shift, for example from air to rail transport (CEC 2001).[2] '[N]etwork planning should therefore seek to take advantage of the ability of HSR to replace air transport and encourage rail companies, airlines and airport managers *not just to compete, but also to cooperate*' (CEC 2001: 53, emphasis in original text). The same notion is evident in the follow up, recent EU White Paper on transport published in 2011. In its recent policy document, the EU outline 10 goals for transport policy one of them (number 6) states that 'By 2050, connect all core network airports to the rail network, preferably high-speed … ' (EC 2011: 9). Yet, the debate on mode substitution continues to be dominated by concern with competition between the modes, with little regard to other options.

Friederiszick et al. (2009) examined railway alliances in European long-distance passenger transport with the aim to find out whether cooperation between HSR service providers might impede competition between operators. As expected, they pay significant attention to air transport, as a benchmark sector that was opened up for competition and as a competitor to HSR services, but they do not consider cooperation between the sectors, a point returned to below. A study by Goldman Sachs (2010, cited in Fu el al. 2012) also focused its analysis on the air-HSR competition effects after HSR entry into service in China.

Two recent studies examined the effect of new HSR services on air transport and on airlines in particular. Both these studies, in Spain and China, focus on competition. In Spain there are no HSR connections to the main airports and it is natural that only competition between the modes resulted. Jiménez and Betancor (2012) find for Spain that HSR has won the race with air carriers for the Spanish transport market. Fu et al. (2012) ask if China's airline industry will survive the entry of HSR and focus on the competition that the airlines are facing, and will increasingly face, from the HSR, they only note in passing that airlines and HSR companies may cooperate.

China experienced rapid economic growth and fast expansion of transport infrastructure in recent years. This has led to a rapid expansion of domestic as well as international air transport – the number of civil airports increased from 94 in 1990 to 175 in 2010 and is expected to reach 244 in 2020 (Fu et al. 2012). At the same time, China is fast developing its HSR network, like in Japan and France, also largely to accommodate the increase in demand for rail transport, i.e. for capacity reasons (ibid.). According to the UIC (2012) China had in 2012, 6,403 km of high speed lines in operation, additional 4,235 km were under construction and 2,901 km were still planned. These figures make China already today the largest HSR network in the world and an almost ideal case for airline and railway integration, considering also the regulatory environment that might be more open for cooperation between the modes. In terms of the infrastructure, the need to integrate the air and rail networks has been identified and more than 32 Chinese airports are planning HSR links and turning the airports into transport hubs (Fu et al. 2012). One such hub, the Shanghai Hongqiao International Airport – one of the largest airports in China, includes a new terminal (Terminal 2) and adjacent to it a large HSR station with 16 platforms. It is also planned to be a station on the future MAGLEV train network. However, although the infrastructure is provided, there are no signs that airline and railway integration is a

---

2   Even before the EU White paper, integrated transport was the central principle in the UK transport policy when the 1998 transport White Paper was published (DETR 1998).

strategy pursued by the airlines, the TOC, or the authorities and the focus seems to still be on competition between the modes.

There are some exceptions in the debate on air-rail intermodality. Janic (2011) does recognize some potential for airline and railway integration (the reference made is to complementarity between the modes) at London Heathrow airport. He believes that mode substitution through competition can account for 50–60 per cent of the services which are candidates for mode substitution; the rest could be substituted through some form of integration, but after the airport is connected to the HSR network. There is no elaboration on what services are better to be substituted through competition and not integration and why. Chiambaretto and Decker (2012) argues that use of air-rail intermodal agreements has expanded over recent decades, but the evidence they provide suggest these agreements are not common and are not seen as an important strategy by the 'big' players in either the airline or rail industries.

The air and rail industry evolved separately, with relatively little overlap in their services and this is also true after the development of the HSR, although the overlap between the modes increases with the spread of the HSR network and services. The fact that the majority of the rail 'business' is not where the airline 'business' is, and vice versa, indicates that the potential for cooperation rather than competition between the modes is probably greater. Yet, competition is the dominant element in the relation between the modes and respective industries. There are two main explanations for this. First, the dominance of the 'market economy' and the *laissez-faire* approach to governing the economy results in competition being seen as something sacred and while cooperation as unfavourable. Second, the governance and governing of the transport system is predominantly uni-modal in nature and this acts as a major barrier to integrated transport and to reaping the benefits of cooperation when such potential exists. These two explanations together explain the dominance of airline and railway disintegration over airline and railway integration.

Illustrating the Potential for Airline and Railway Integration

Two examples for the dominance of airline and railway disintegration are presented below to illustrate the scope for airline and railway integration and the opportunities that are being missed, not only by the air and rail industries but, even more, by policy makers.

Re-examining the Potential for Airline and Railway Integration at London Heathrow Airport

Givoni and Banister (2006) showed the potential for mode substitution, and hence for airline and railway integration, at London Heathrow airport. Using flight frequency data for 2002 and based on the assumption that passengers would favour using HSR and not aircraft from the airport if it led to travel time savings (or small travel time penalty) they found that 10 routes, from less than 200 in total, would be suitable for mode substitution. These routes, to Manchester, Leeds/Bradford, Brussels, Newcastle, Paris, Cologne, Glasgow, Amsterdam, Edinburgh, and Dusseldorf[3] accounted together for 20.9 per cent of the flights at the airport in 2002.

---

3   The cities are ordered by travel time savings if substituting from the aircraft to the HST. 48 minutes saving to Manchester, 8 to Paris, and travel time penalty thereafter with 16 minutes longer travel time to Dusseldorf (see Givoni and Banister 2006).

In 2010, Heathrow airport was fourth largest airport in the world with 66.7 million passengers, but only thirteenth in the world in terms of flight frequency, 454,883 air transport movements (atms).[4] Operating with only two runways, as in 2002, analysis for January 2012 based on route distance shows that up to 21 routes, from the 175 routes operating from the airport, could be candidates for mode substitution (Table 6.1). These routes took up almost 30 per cent of Heathrow's runway capacity and just over 20 per cent of the number of seats 'flown' through the airport.[5] Considering the cities listed in Table 6.1 and the fact that 'rail' distance is often longer than 'aircraft' distance, hence travel time is likely to be longer than suggested by the geographic distance, it is more realistic to expect mode substitution on the first 12 routes. To serve these 12 routes about 18 per cent of the airport runway capacity was required and 12 per cent of the seating capacity. An even more cautious analysis of the potential for mode substitution would consider only Manchester, Paris, Brussels, and Newcastle. These destinations together took up 7.6 per cent of Heathrow's runway capacity in terms of flights and 5.2 per cent in terms of seats, about a yearly capacity of 35,520 flights and 4.86 million seats. Janic (2011) estimated the potential for mode substitution to be 15 per cent of the total daily flights scheduled at Heathrow airport.

Table 6.1 only reveals part of the potential for mode substitution. It includes only five destinations in the UK, which shows the limited access of UK's cities and residents to the country's main gateway to the world and its international network of services. Most UK's regional airports have direct flights to the main hubs in mainland Europe, like Amsterdam Schiphol, but not to Heathrow. By rail, Heathrow airport is even less accessible from outside London, although the rail network in the country is one of the densest in Europe. This is because the airport is not a node on the rail network. Rail access to Heathrow airport is only from London and via London Paddington railway station.

Current air transport policy in the UK, as reflected in the draft aviation policy framework (DfT 2012b) has not changed since the 2003 Aviation White Paper (DfT 2003). It still prioritizes air transport contribution to economic growth, maintaining the UK's air transport connectivity, while acting to minimize air transport impact on the environment. The focus when trying to achieve these objectives, and in the order listed, is on Heathrow airport. Givoni and Banister (2006) explained how airline and railway integration can serve to better achieve these objectives and better reconcile between them. The same arguments hold today, perhaps even more, as explained below and largely due to the fact that the policy remained unchanged, and so is the supply of runway capacity, but demand has increased.

While the policy remains generally unchanged, so is the debate on additional runway capacity in London and Southeast England. While the options of a third runway at Heathrow airport, new runways at the other London airports, or a new London airport are always on the agenda, with political support shifting between these options, there has not been change in the provision of runway capacity in the London area for a long time. The last runway (airport) to be opened in London was City airport, which is a relatively small airport (handled about 3 million passengers in 2010) and a short runway that cannot even

---

4   Airport Council International. Available at: http://www.aci.aero/ [accessed: 14 January 2013].

5   The data given in Table 6.1 is for January 2012 and include only services departing from Heathrow. Assuming the level of service (flight frequency) and the number of seats supplied are similar on the services arriving to Heathrow, and that on other months of the year similar level of service is provided (it is more likely to be higher) then the percentages reported and discussed apply to the yearly potential for mode substitution as well.

Table 6.1 The potential for mode substitution at London Heathrow airport in January 2012 (data include only the flights departing Heathrow airport)

| | | Runway utilization at Heathrow (January, 2012): ATM: 19,632 Number of seats: 3,912 million | | | Runway utilization | | | |
| | | | | | Route level | | Cumulative | |
	Destination (Code)	Dist.	ATM	Seats	ATM	Seats	ATM	Seats
1	Manchester (MAN)	241	444	56,945	2.3%	1.5%	2.3%	1.5%
2	Paris (CDG)	346	475	67,734	2.4%	1.7%	4.7%	3.2%
3	Brussels (BRU)	349	267	35,858	1.4%	0.9%	6.0%	4.1%
4	Paris (ORY)	365	116	14,875	0.6%	0.4%	6.6%	4.5%
5	Amsterdam (AMS)	367	528	68,122	2.7%	1.7%	9.3%	6.2%
6	Newcastle (NCL)	404	178	27,380	0.9%	0.7%	10.2%	6.9%
7	Düsseldorf (DUS)	501	312	42,501	1.6%	1.1%	11.8%	8.0%
8	Luxembourg (LUX)	512	62	7,963	0.3%	0.2%	12.1%	8.2%
9	Cologne/Bonn (CGN)	533	78	9,672	0.4%	0.2%	12.5%	8.5%
10	Edinburgh (EDI)	533	453	64,526	2.3%	1.6%	14.8%	10.1%
11	Glasgow (GLA)	554	285	47,318	1.5%	1.2%	16.3%	11.3%
12	Aberdeen (ABZ)	647	346	34,678	1.8%	0.9%	18.1%	12.2%
13	Frankfurt (FRA)	653	578	87,538	2.9%	2.2%	21.0%	14.4%
14	Hannover (HAJ)	702	84	4,116	0.4%	0.1%	21.4%	14.5%
15	Basel (EAP)	718	160	20,923	0.8%	0.5%	22.2%	15.1%
16	Hamburg (HAM)	744	264	37,095	1.3%	0.9%	23.6%	16.0%
17	Geneva (GVA)	752	438	64,071	2.2%	1.6%	25.8%	17.7%
18	Lyon (LYS)	755	93	12,171	0.5%	0.3%	26.3%	18.0%
19	Stuttgart (STR)	755	144	16,357	0.7%	0.4%	27.0%	18.4%
20	Zurich (ZRH)	785	390	56,161	2.0%	1.4%	29.0%	19.8%
21	Toulouse (TLS)	880	92	11,803	0.5%	0.3%	29.5%	20.1%

Note: ATM = Air Traffic Movements (take-off only). Code = IATA airport code, Dist. = Distance.
Source: OAG 2012.

accommodate aircraft like the Boeing 737 and Airbus A320. Before that London Stansted airport opened around 1970. While there are many plans, there is no decision that will likely change the situation in the near future. Change however is taking place.

The UK government gave the green light to the HS2 (High-Speed 2) project – the HSR line from London to the north stopping first at Birmingham[6] (Phase 1 of the project) and continuing in Phase 2 from Birmingham to Manchester (the Northwest arm of the Y shape network originating from London) and from Birmingham to Leeds (the Northeast arm of the Y). In the future the two arms will possibly be extended to Scotland serving Glasgow and Edinburgh respectively. HS2 is also planned to be connected with HS1 – the HSR line connecting London and Europe through the Channel Tunnel. In planning Phase 1 of HS2 the so-called Heathrow connection received considerable attention. After considering the additional costs, largely additional construction cost and travel time penalty to passengers not using the airport, and the benefits, in terms of rail accessibility to the airport and the benefits of air-rail cooperation, it was decided to not include the airport in Phase 1 of the project and consider connecting it to the HSR line only in Phase 2 and via a spur to the airport from the main HSR line. This contradicts the model of airline and railway integration and likely limit, if not eliminate, the potential for mode substitution.

In a report for HS2 Ltd by Arup (High Speed Two Limited, undated) several options to include Heathrow in HS2 were considered. The travel time by HSR between London and Birmingham without intermediate stops was estimated to be 41 minutes and 26 seconds, increasing to 44 minutes and 9 seconds with an additional stop in London at Old-Oak Common and to 48 minutes and 27 seconds with another stop, this time at Birmingham international (next to the airport). Both of these two additional stations are included in the plan that was approved. Compared to this, a route alignment for HS2 that will only include one intermediate stop between London and Birmingham at Heathrow airport will require 50 minutes and 22 seconds – additional travel time of less than 2 minutes. The difference in the cost between the two options is estimated at around £2 billion (ibid.). For comparison, the cost of constructing Terminal 5 at Heathrow was over £4 billion.

A later report published by the Department for Transport (DfT) (2012a) concluded that with respect to serving Heathrow airport, the option for a spur from the preferred London to Birmingham 'performs better than a through route stopping close by the airport' (DfT 2012a: 32). Largely for technical reasons, it was concluded that an HSR station at the airport is not feasible, or too costly, and therefore the only real option to serve the airport is through a station near the airport, not at the airport. Compared to this the alternative of serving the airport through a spur is better, it was concluded.

It is outside the scope of this analysis to go into more details about the evaluation of the options to include Heathrow as a through station on the emerging UK HSR network. It is clear, however, that one of the largest airports in the world, serving over 70 million passengers per year – over 40 million of which are non-transfer passengers, considered vital to the UK's economy, hub for the UK's largest airline, competing with rival European hub airports and experiencing congestion almost throughout the day and year will remain disintegrated with the rail network. This is a missed opportunity that will be almost impossible to change once construction of the HS2 line begins.

---

6   Birmingham is the second largest city in the UK. Birmingham airport is the seventh largest airport in the UK, with close to 9 million passengers in 2010 serving directly many of the European major airports, but not Heathrow (which is too close to support air services).

Airline and Railway Alliances

The adverse effect of competition between the modes in terms of wasteful capacity and duplication of services can be seen on the routes to Manchester, Paris and Brussels (Table 6.1). On these routes, which currently each take 2.4 per cent of Heathrow capacity (Paris), 2.3 per cent (Manchester) and 1.4 per cent (Brussels), there is already a good rail alternative that captures the majority of the market. Yet, airlines for different reasons still offer high frequency service on these routes. The main reason is the importance of these air links to passengers and airlines in terms of network connectivity. In the absence of rail, and HSR in particular, connection to Heathrow, airline and railway integration is not an option, and airlines must use aircraft to keep these routes in their network.

For different commercial reasons and due to the regulatory barriers that prevent airlines from merging or taking over one another, airlines form strategic cooperation through global alliances.[7] A large part of airline services worldwide is offered in connection with one of the three major global alliances: Star, Sky team, and Oneworld (Table 6.2). Gudmundsson and Lechner (2006) explains that membership of an international alliance has become a key component of business strategy for many airlines, partly also as a means for differentiating airlines from low-cost competitors in terms of quality of service offered. Due to airline alliances, competition between airlines is less a matter of individual firms competing against individual firms but more a matter of airline groups competing against airline groups, or, to be more precise, competition of (alliance) networks against networks. Being part of a multilateral alliance allows airlines to exploit scope and density economies across geographical boundaries largely through different network economies related to schedule convenience (frequency), connectivity (more connections and more options to connect between two points), and flow improvement (reducing total travel time between any nodes in the network) (ibid.). In these circumstances and given the nature of airline alliances, there is no reason for these global networks of services to not include rail networks and especially existing and emerging HSR networks.

Table 6.2   Share of airline alliances in air transport services in January 2013

	ATM		Seats (million)		ASKs (billion)	
Oneworld	58,167	10%	8.3	11%	18.4	14%
Sky Team	95,731	17%	13.0	18%	24.4	19%
Star	144,929	26%	18.2	24%	34.8	27%
Airline alliances	*298,827*	*53%*	*40*	*53%*	*78*	*60%*
Low Cost Carriers	106,603	19%	16.5	22%	19.9	15%
Un-Aligned	160,270	28%	18.3	25%	32.5	25%
TOTAL	565,700	100%	74	100%	130	100%

Note: ATM = Air Transport Movements, ASK = Available Seat-KM.
Source: Innovata http://www.airtransportnews.aero/analysis.pl?id=1330 [accessed: 15 January 2013].

7   These regulatory barriers are the result of concern about competition or market concentration and the requirement by many countries that airlines should be 'substantially owned and effectively controlled' by nationals of the country in which the airline is registered.

In Europe, low-cost carriers (LCCs) accounted for 31 per cent of the intra-European air transport market, steadily taking a market share from the incumbent, or traditional airlines, mainly those known as the flag carriers (Dobruszkes 2013). Between 1995 and 2012, LCC accounted for 70 per cent of the increase in the number of intra-European flights or seats and 64 per cent of the number of seat-km (ibid.). Airlines which do not adopt the low-cost model find it increasingly hard to sustain their domestic European network, often needing to increase service frequency from the most congested airports, to maintain it and to keep feeding traffic into their long-haul services through the hubs. Many of these airlines face competition from both the LCCs and the HSR, in some cases resulting in bankruptcy.

Expansion of airline services into the HSR network through competition with the existing TOCs can almost be ruled out. It seems unlikely that the first AiRaiLine will be created anytime soon. The operation of rail and air services is so different that airlines would not be capable of operating rail services and, more important, have no incentive to learn to do it. Acquisition of a TOC by an airline also seems unlikely, probably for the same reason and in part due to the fact that HSR services are often a small part of a TOC's services. However with companies like Eurostar and Thalys, which operate only HSR services, such acquisition is more likely. Yet some form of cooperation is more likely and will be more beneficial to both sides, for example through code sharing.

There are some examples of agreements between airlines and TOCs in Europe, but these are more exceptions to the rule and are on a relatively small scale. At the same time, there exists an alliance of European HSR operators. The Railteam alliance, founded in 2007, include Deutsch Bahn (the German operator with 25 per cent share in the alliance), SNCF (France, 25 per cent), SNCB (Belgium, 10 per cent), NS Highspeed (The Netherlands, 10 per cent), ÖBB (Austria, 10 per cent) and SBB (Switzerland, 10 per cent) and two associated members Thalys and TGV Lyria. The alliance covers large parts of Western Europe (Readers may refer to the Railteam alliance route network available at: www.railteam.co.uk). In the same way the three major airline alliances consider whether to invite or accept a new airline into the alliance, largely based on the network of services it provides, a TOC can be considered.

After the liberalization of air transport in Europe has been completed, the EU initiated a liberalization of the rail market. This has been going on through the adoption of different so called packages. The third package is aimed at opening up international passenger rail traffic for competition. The Railteam alliance can be seen as a response of rail companies to the likely opening of the market for competition. Similar to commercial agreements between companies in other sectors, including airlines, there is concern that agreements between rail companies will compromise competition (see for example Chiambaretto and Decker 2012). This results in a paradox. The EU is eager to encourage competition in rail transport, hoping rail transport can imitate air transport in many respects, but at the same time it is also concerned about market concentration in rail transport, and especially in the HSR passenger transport market. This concern led the EU to insist, when the Railteam alliance was formed, that members of the alliance must continue to compete on prices.

A solution that is oddly not considered is for TOCs, especially those operating HSRs services, to join different global airline alliances and to compete head on with each other. It is reasonable to assume that only by seeing the air and rail markets as one market for long-distance passenger transport, where different companies compete and cooperate based on prices and networks and regardless of the vehicle they operate, that the rail transport market can witness the kind of market transformation the air industry has undergone following deregulation and opening of the skies. Airline and railway integration which call for full cooperation between the modes, is also the key to achieving competition in rail transport by having a few large *Global Air-Rail Alliances* competing around the globe.

From Airline and Railway Disintegration to Integration

Givoni (2005) writes in the research conclusions:

> It is predicted that within a time period of 30–40 years major global airlines around the world, an evolution of today's major alliances, will operate a network of air and rail services. By then, passengers will be used to transferring between aircraft and rail services (some of which will be HST [HSR] services) and to begin or end their air journey at the (city-centre) railway station. (Givoni 2005: 263)

There are no signs that any progress towards such a future is being made. Nevertheless the prediction remains. With concern about the environmental impact of air transport increasing, mounting congestion at the major airports, and the rapid expansion of the HSR network, airline and railway integration seems bound to take place maybe even sooner than later. Givoni et al. (2012) demonstrate that the potential for mode substitution worldwide exists and is quite considerable. Under favourable assumptions, this potential could reach about 20 per cent of the worldwide flights and 7 per cent of the seat-km provided by the world airlines in January 2010 (ibid.).

What stands in the way of airline and railway integration relates to several issues. First of all, it is the (economic) mindset in which competition is 'good' and should be encouraged while cooperation or integration is considered less optimal. Second, there is still a world difference between the industries in their way of operation, thinking and as a result culture; even though the development of the HSR brought the railways much closer to the airlines in terms of business strategies and marketing (e.g. the adoption of yield management). Third and in the long term, the main barrier for airline and railway integration is the separate, very much disintegrated, planning of air and rail transport infrastructure.[8] At the moment, it seems that the two first barriers stand in the way of an integrated planning of air and rail networks, and thus in the way of realizing the benefits of airline and railway integration.

But the situation is bound to change and is already changing. The mediating actor standing between the air and rail industries, the airport operator, is still much more concerned with the airside than the landside part of its operations. The balance however starts to shift, even if not yet changing, when airports in relatively close geographical proximity start to compete for passengers and at the same time for airlines, and for keeping airlines at the airport (Vespermann and Wald 2011, Starkie 2012). Competition for passengers between airports is very much through ground access services, and rail and HSR in particular play a crucial role in this respect. The expansion of the HSR is also reaching a critical mass, in Europe but maybe more importantly in China, and is relatively successful in taking market share from the airlines, probably making the airline industry more open to consider tighter cooperation with the railways. Adding to that, the success of the LCCs is another important incentive for traditional airlines and to the HSR service provider to join forces, as both need to face the LCC threat.

---

8 See Givoni and Rietveld (2008) for more elaboration on this through a comparison between three European hub airports with respect to rail access infrastructure.

Mode substitution is commonly discussed from an air transport perspective but it is equally important and an opportunity for the rail industry. The HSR, through airline and railway integration, could be the stepping stone to an integrated transport network where rail is integrated with air transport networks on the one side and the urban (public) transport network on the other. Airline and railway integration holds the potential for revitalizing the railways, for a true railway renaissance, and for making the railways, once more, the backbone of the transport system.

References

Airport Council International (ACI). 2013. *ACI Data & Statistics* [Online: ACI]. Available at: http://www.aci.aero/ [accessed: 14 January 2013].

Buchanan and Partners. 1995. *Optimising Rail/Air Intermodality in Europe.* London: Colin Buchanan and Partners.

Button, K. and Stough, R. 2000. *Air Transport Networks: Theory and Policy Implications.* Cheltenham: Edward Elgar.

Commission of the European Communities (CEC). 2001. *European Transport Policy for 2010: Time to Decide.* Brussels: European Commission.

Chiambaretto, P. and Decker, C. 2012. Air–rail intermodal agreements: balancing the competition and environmental effects. *Journal of Air Transport Management*, 23, 36–40.

Department of the Environment, Transport and the Regions (DETR). 1998. *A New Deal for Transport: Better for Everyone.* London: Department for Transport.

Department for Transport (DfT). 2003. *The Future of Air Transport.* London: DfT.

Department for Transport (DfT). 2012a. *Review of London to West Midlands Route Selection and Speed.* London: DfT.

Department for Transport (DfT). 2012b. *Draft Aviation Policy Framework.* London: DfT.

Dobruszkes, F. 2013. The geography of European low-cost airline networks: a contemporary analysis. *Journal of Transport Geography*, 28, 75–88.

Doganis, R. and Dennis, N.P.S. 1989. Lessons in hubbing. *Airline Business,* March, 42–5.

European Commission (EC). 1998. *Interaction between High Speed and Air Passenger Transport.* Final Report on the Action COST 318, Luxemburg: European Commission.

European Commission (EC). 2011. *Roadmap to a Single European Transport Area – Towards a Competitive and Resource Efficient Transport System.* Brussels: EC.

Friederiszick, H., Gantumur, T., Jayaraman, R., Röller, L-H. and Weinmann, J. 2009. *Railway Alliances in EC Long-Distance Passenger Transport: A Competitive Assessment Post-Liberalization 2010.* Berlin: ESMT European School of Management and Technology.

Fu, X., Zhang, A. and Zheng, L. 2012. Will China's airline industry survive the entry of high-speed rail? *Research in Transportation Economics*, 35, 13–25.

Givoni, M. 2005. *Aircraft and High Speed Train Substitution: The Case for Airline and Railway Integration.* Unpublished Ph.D. Thesis, University College London.

Givoni, M. 2006. The development and impact of the modern High Speed Train. *Transport Reviews*, 26(5), 593–612.

Givoni, M. 2007. Environmental benefits from mode substitution: comparison of the environmental impact from aircraft and high-speed train operation. *International Journal of Sustainable Transport*, 1(4), 209–30.

Givoni, M. and Banister, D. 2006. Airline and railway integration. *Transport Policy*, 13, 386–97.

Givoni, M. and Banister, D. 2007. The role of the railways in the future of air transport. *Transport Planning and Technology,* 30(1), 95–112.

Givoni, M. and Rietveld, P. 2008. Rail infrastructure at major European Hub Airports: the role of institutional settings, in *Decision-Making on Mega-Projects: Cost-benefit Analysis, Planning and Innovation,* edited by H. Priemus, B. Flyvbjerg and B. van Wee. Cheltenham: Edward Elgar, 281–303.

Givoni, M., Dobruszkes, F. and Lugo, I. 2012. Uncovering the real potential for air-rail substitution: an exploratory analysis, in *Energy, Transport and the Environment: Assessing the Sustainability Mobility Paradigm,* edited by O. Inderwildi and D. King. London: Springer, 495–512.

Goldman, S. 2010. *China Transportation: Airlines: High Speed Rail Less of a Threat Than You May Think.* Report issued on 28 October 2010.

Gudmundsson, S.V. and Lechner, C. 2006. Multilateral airline alliances: balancing strategic constraints and opportunities. *Journal of Air Transport Management,* 12, 153–8.

High Speed Two Limited (undated) *Options for Connecting to the Heathrow Airport Area: Final Report* [Online: Arup]. Available at: http://www.airtransportnews.aero/analysis. pl?id=1330 [accessed: 15 January 2013].

Janic, M. 2011. Assessing some social and environmental effects of transforming an airport into a real multimodal transport node. *Transportation Research D,* 16, 137–49.

Jiménez, J.L. and Betancor, O. 2012. When trains go faster than planes: the strategic reaction of airlines. *Transport Policy,* 23, 34–41.

OAG. 2012. *OAG Historical Schedules.* OAG Aviation.

Railteam. *High Speed Europe* [Online: Railteam]. Available at: www.railteam.co.uk [accessed: 15 January 2013].

Starkie, D. 2012. European airports and airlines: evolving relationships and the regulatory implications. *Journal of Air Transport Management,* 21, 40–49.

UIC. 2012. High speed lines in the world. *UIC.* [Online, July]. Available at: http://www.uic.org/ IMG/pdf/20120701_a1_high_speed_lines_in_the_world.pdf [accessed: 24 January 2013].

Vespermann, J. and Wald, A. 2011. Intermodal integration in air transportation: status quo, motives and future development. *Journal of Transport Geography,* 19, 1187–97.

Chapter 7
The Transfer of Freight from Road to Rail Transport

Antoine Frémont

Introduction

Since the advent of the industrial revolution in the nineteenth century, the volume of freight carried and distance covered has increased continuously. This applies to both national and international traffic. The beginning of a Post-Fordist economy in the 1970s did not signal a reversal of this pattern. Never has there been so much merchandise produced and used.

Road transport is the dominant mode of transport. Despite its performance in answering transport demand, it is increasingly being called into question because of the negative environmental externalities it generates, notably carbon dioxide (CO_2) emission and congestion in major metropolitan areas. Modal transfer from road to rail is considered a viable option to mitigate the negative effects of road transport. This objective is widely supported by several countries and explains the planned implementation of policies to favour this modal shift as exemplified by the European Union (European Commission 2001, 2011).

This chapter highlights the necessary conditions for the realization of an effective modal transfer from road to rail. The modal shift issue can only be considered for the movement of goods answering the needs of shippers in terms of price, reliability and time and thus applied to manufactured goods in particular. These factors barely apply for the movement of bulk commodities where road transport is not competitive. The main hypothesis is that the implementation of a mass and intermodal transport system, including a rail component and door-to-door service, is the essential condition to achieve a modal shift from road to rail.

The first part of the chapter describes the main trends leading to a dominance of road transport. The notion of 'modal shift transition' provides an explanation of the uneven modal share between countries. The understanding of the dynamics of road transport is fundamental for assessing the conditions of modal shift from road to rail. In the second part, the analysis of containerization allows the necessary conditions to organize a modal shift from road to rail to be identified. The chapter concludes by assessing the extent to which non-containerized traffic could be considered for modal transfer.

Rail Facing the Domination of Road Transport

The Freight Modal Split: Similarities and Differences

Despite statistical problems in establishing international comparison,[1] there is a general trend in terms of modal distribution. Modal shift is a reality, but it occurs in the opposite direction from the desired effect. Modal transfer does not occur from road to rail but from rail to road. Road transport is largely dominant. It responds to transport demand, in sharp contrast to other modes that are increasingly being marginalized. Rail cannot always meet transport demand. Notwithstanding, in high growth countries such as the emerging economies, the volume of freight carried by rail is increasing although its share in overall freight carried diminishes in favour of road transport. Beyond this general trend, major differences exist between countries. Evidence reveals three types of modal share and their evolution (Figures 7.1, 7.2, 7.3 and 7.4).

The first type corresponds to countries with a small share of rail transport, systematically below 20 per cent of the market. Several countries are confronted with a constant decline of rail transport since the 1970s both in terms of relative share and volume carried. This decline has gained further momentum in recent years despite the political will to promote rail transport as an alternative to road with a modal share above 80 per cent. France and the United Kingdom are examples. Belonging to this category are also the peripheral states of the European Union either Mediterranean or insular (Ireland) but also Asian countries such as Japan and South Korea. The Netherlands is a separate case as the weakness of rail is compensated by the importance of inland waterways.

The second type are countries where the modal share of rail transport is between 20 per cent and 30 per cent. This group includes a large set of conditions. In Europe, it concerns countries located along transit corridors and in the Alps such as Switzerland, Austria and to a certain extent Germany. Rail plays an important role in Anglo-Saxon countries with vast areas of land and valuable natural resources, notably Canada, United States and Australia. This modal share must however be nuanced since statistics do not necessarily take into account short distance transport. In the United States, taking into consideration local traffic and not only inter-city traffic, the modal share of rail transport would only be 25 per cent of total ton-miles. Scandinavian countries with important natural resources and difficult climatic conditions rely heavily on rail with the exception of Norway. Emerging countries such as China, India and Brazil display a modal split profile very similar to countries with vast areas of land. Their rail modal share averages 20–30 per cent but is declining (ESCAP 2011).

The third type corresponds to former East European countries that have been integrated within the European Union since the beginning of the 1990s. The modal share of rail transport was very high when they were part of the Soviet Union's sphere of influence. Since the 1980s Russia continues to have a rail share above 60 per cent. But the other East European countries are experiencing rapid modal shift to road transport. In the early 1990s Poland which had a railway share of freight transport superior to 60 per cent is currently displaying a modal split similar to France.

---

1 It is very difficult to rigorously compare the share of rail freight transport from one country to another. For European countries, Eurostat provides systematic information. Outside Europe, the most systematic source is OECD. But numerous data are not available to allow time series analysis or comparison between countries. We therefore had to draw information from various secondary sources to assess the share of rail in freight transport.

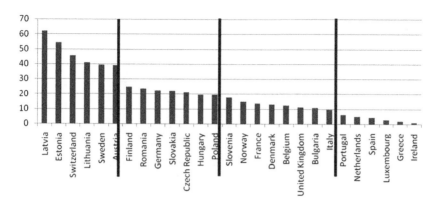

Figure 7.1   Share of railways in the modal split of freight transport in European countries in 2010 (% in total inland freight ton-km)

Source: Adapted by the Author from statistics provided by Eurostat.

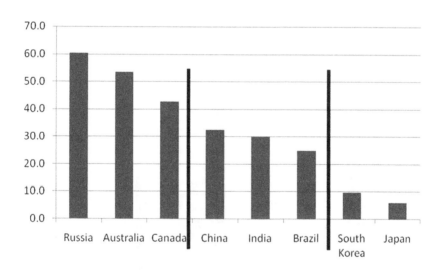

Figure 7.2   Share of railways in the modal split of freight transport in selected countries in 2008 (% in total inland freight ton-km)

Source: Adapted by the Author from statistics provided by International Transport Forum (OECD). For Brazil, Secretary for Transportation National Policy, Marcelo Perrupato (2011), Logistic Infrastructure Scenario in Brazil, Minneapolis, September 20. Available at: www.transportes.gov.br/public/arquivo/arq1318615138.pdf.

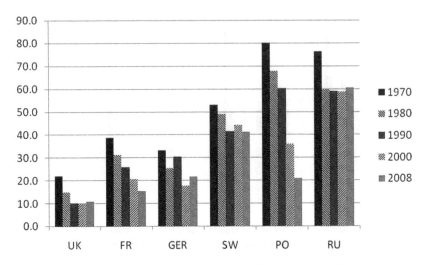

Figure 7.3   Evolution of the share of railways in the modal split of freight transport in selected European countries, 1970–2008 (% in total inland freight ton-km)

Note: UK: United Kingdom   FR: France
         GER: Germany   SW: Switzerland
         PO: Poland   RU: Russia
Source: Adapted by the Author from statistics provided by International Transport Forum, OECD.

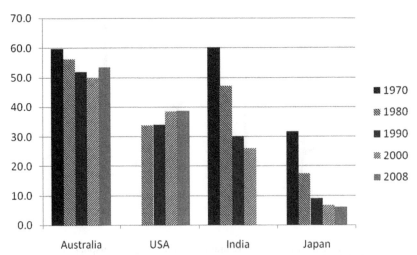

Figure 7.4   Evolution of the share of railways in the modal split of freight transport in Australia, USA, India and Japan, 1970–2008 (% in total inland freight tonnes-km)

Source: Adapted by the Author from statistics provided by:
-      For Australia and Japan: International Transport Forum (OCDE), % of ton-km;
-      For USA: US Department of Transportation 2013 (No data for 1970);
-      For India: Chaudhury 2005. % of ton-km (No data for 2008).

The Modal Split Transition

In order to explain the modal profile described above, we propose the notion of modal transition. By analogy with demographic transition, it is possible to bring to light several phases of modal split in a country's history.

Five sequential steps can be identified (Figure 7.5). They apply notably to European countries. Phase 1 underpins the era prior to the industrial revolution when the amount of freight carried was relatively small due to lack of industrial mass production. Land transport remained difficult and very slow given the poorly developed road networks. Waterways, when available, were the most efficient way to carry large volumes.

Phase 2 corresponds to the industrial revolution. Steamships and railways allowed the movement of large volumes of freight, notably bulk products such as coal and minerals to supply heavy industry as well as cereals to balance the different international food markets. European states established fully meshed and densed railway networks servicing their respective territories. These networks reached their pinnacle at the dawn of the First World War. Rail was not affected by competition except along inland waterway corridors. Railway networks, together with horse-drawn road vehicles, moved all or substantially all freight on land.

Phase 3 corresponds to the modal split transition as such from rail to road. Road transport wins a larger share given its high performance. Road transport can move a variety of freight at any time, rapidly, from one point to another and without intermediate reloading. Road transport is also highly flexible. This flexibility rests on the development of a dense road network and on intense competition insuring low-cost transport services. Simultaneously, the production and distribution systems are progressively being modified. Heavy industries, engines of growth during the three post-war decades, played a decreasing role as a direct consequence a concomitant fall in the volume of land bulk movement. Conversely, the advent of a consumer society is reflected in the demand for an increasing number of manufactured products. These products are lighter and diversified as exemplified by information-based products. They are integrated in transport logistics chains answering production and consumption requirements in the context of just-in-time and zero-stock distribution system while maintaining flexible responses to customer requirements. The large degree of flexibility, efficiency and reliability that road transport offers is in line with trends in goods movement. While adapted to bulk transport, railways have difficulty in competing for manufactured products. Rail imposes transshipment, delays and uncertainty. Railway carriage is more expensive than road transport and is inadequate to satisfy new transport demand. Besides, railway networks have to address increasing demand for passenger movement. The rail freight sector is not being considered as a priority, thus fostering a downward spiral.

This phase in modal split transition concludes with Phase 4 which is the culmination of the preceding phase. In this phase the road transport system reaches its peak. Railways play a marginal role for freight movement and increasingly focus its activities on the movement of passengers.

The subsequent Phase 5 marks the beginning of a new process. This phase is characterized by an increase in rail freight transport and a modal shift from road to rail. This transition phase is widely called for by national policy makers and the broader public. But the conditions that must be met in order to benefit from that modal transition remain to be explained. They require innovation.

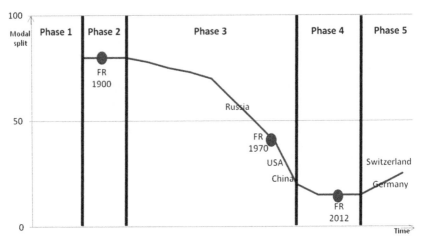

Figure 7.5   **The modal split transition: The share of railways in the modal split of freight transport**

Source: Author.

Countries with Differing Levels of Modal Split Transition

Each country belongs to a specific modal profile which allows an exact positioning in the modal split transition. The socio-economic characteristics of a country may explain at least in part their stage in the modal transition. It is possible to consider the least advanced countries at Phase 1. In sharp contrast to the traditional historical perspective, road transport is dominant but with very poor service quality which relates to the very core of underdevelopment.

At the other end of the modal split transition spectrum, countries such as France, the United Kingdom, Japan or South Korea are currently at Phase 3. Having limited supplies of raw materials, the share of bulk carried by land transport on national territory is small as a result of the concentration of heavy industries in industrial port zones. Heavier products necessary for construction and public works are carried over short distances. Road transport accounts for the movement of manufactured products.

In Phase 2 of the modal split transition are countries such as Canada, the United States and Australia. They differ from countries positioned in Phase 1 by the importance of natural resources carried by land transport on their national territory. Australia and Canada export raw material such as coal from open mines to ocean sea ports by railways. In sharp contrast, the United States mines its own coal to supply their thermal power production and has large exports. Rail with its capacity to achieve scale economies is very competitive with road transport. It is primarily for this reason that the modal share of rail transport expressed in tons-kilometres remains strong in these countries. Railway benefits from specialized traffic and captive customers. Without this specificity, road transport would be as dominant as in countries of Phase 3.

Emerging countries are also at Phase 3 of the modal split transition. But they have not reached the level of economic maturity mentioned above. Their economies still rely on exports of raw materials or cereals (Brazil, Mexico) or imports to feed domestic industries

(China, India). Road transport satisfies part of the freight transport demand that could be carried by railways. In the context of rapid economic growth, these countries are facing bottlenecks notably in ocean ports for lack of efficient rail infrastructures.

Russia is at the beginning of Phase 3 of the modal split transition. Its economic development is based on heavy industries and the export of raw materials. Road transport is seriously limited over large parts of the country. Russia has not completely emerged from the Soviet Era when railway linkages were privileged to ensure complementarity between different industrial complexes. Conversely, the former East European countries have undergone the modal transition process in extremely brutal ways. Their integration within the European Union forced a reorganization of their means of production and external trade in highly different ways. The planned economy of the Council for Mutual Economic Assistance (COMECON) and its rail focus gave way to the market economy of the European Union and road primacy.

Conditions for a Modal Shift: Lessons from Containerization

In emerging and developing countries, the supply of rail infrastructures is necessary to capture bulk traffic, avoid bottlenecks and increase the market share of rail transport. In other countries, modal shift that would signal the entry into Phase 5 of the modal split transition concerns the non-bulk freight. From this perspective, containerization represents a genuine breakthrough. Containerization points to the conditions necessary for rail to provide a credible alternative solution to road transport.

Modal Shift from Road to Rail with Containerization

The success story of the container finds explanation in higher productivity in materials handling (Levinson 2006). It is not freight that is handled but the container as a unit of intermodal transport. In inland haulage, combined transport must demonstrate that it can compete with road transport. Combined transport is an intermodal transport where the major part of the journey is by rail (or by inland waterways) and initial and/or final legs carried out by road which are as short as possible (UN/ECE 2001). Beyond the technical prerequisites which are provided by containerization, certain conditions must be met for combined transport to be set up.

The first condition is that a shared dynamic leads to the use of rail-road transport for hinterland services from maritime ports. The various port stakeholders are all concerned about three issues promoting the use of combined transport: the environment, cost and traffic flow.

Transport is the only major sector of the economy that is responsible for an ever growing percentage of total CO_2 emissions (ECMT 2006), the largest share coming from road transport. Generally, waterways are more energy efficient per ton transported than rail (by a factor of 2 to 1) which itself is more energy efficient than road transport (by a factor of 2.6 to 1) (FEEMA 2006). The environmental problem is primarily being dealt with by the public authorities even if the current deep economic crisis has put this issue further down the agenda. Nevertheless, combined transport receives strong support at local level in Europe as there is very strong social pressure to reduce the negative environmental externalities caused by economic activities, particularly transport. There is thus strong political and social pressure in favour of combined transport. These environmental concerns are increasingly being considered by both shippers and carriers wishing to express their commitment to sustainable development.

Cost is another major issue. Combined transport partially extends further inland the economies of scale that are achieved on the sea by very large vessels. Therefore, even if the organizational complexity of combined transport is greater than road transport, the volumes handled by combined transport reduces costs on the inland transport leg. Double-stack unit trains in North America with a capacity of 400 TEUs are salient examples. In Europe, economies of scale are smaller as the largest block trains only have a capacity of 80–95 TEUs. Consequently, the issue of inland transport costs primarily involve the economic agents such as shippers since it has a direct impact on their operations. Shippers are therefore interested in the development of combined transport as it can result in lower supply chain costs. It is also in the interest of transport operators, such as shipping lines or freight forwarders to provide customers with transport services that are cheaper than road, particularly because of the competition that exists between them.

Promoting combined transport is also in the interests of port managers as a means not only of extending port hinterlands but also to secure their customer base from possible competition from other ports along the same maritime range. Combined transport can extend a port's hinterland, enabling it to compete with another port's immediate hinterland. The neighbouring port will therefore respond by also promoting combined transport in its hinterland in order to protect its catchment area (Robinson 2002). Public opinion is sensitive to these arguments as preserving or increasing port activity means jobs.

Congestion is the last shared issue. Even if port traffic has tended to slow down as a result of global economic crisis, many large ports have experienced an increase in container traffic. Therefore, there is a risk for those ports to suffer from congestion problems. There is risk for these ports that some of the traffic will be transferred to less congested secondary ports, as a result of what is known as the peripheral port challenge (Hayuth 1981). By offering diversified transport supply and higher volumes than is possible by road, combined rail-road transport is one possible way of improving traffic volumes between the port and its hinterland (ECMT 2006). The issue of traffic flow is thus decisive not only for port managers but also for the public authorities as traffic flow is directly responsible for a share of a port's competitiveness (Notteboom and Winkelmans 2001). Using combined transport can therefore be in the interest of shippers if it is more reliable, particularly for meeting the requirements of just-in-time transport operations. Traffic flow is also an important issue for carriers as the reliability of the services they provide to their clients depends on it. The increasing container transport volumes handled in the main seaports have put the issues of sea terminal and hinterland transport capacities and performance on the agenda of terminal operators. They have to deal with the storage of containers at the deep-sea terminal and they also need barge and train services to ensure the fluidity of container movements and reduce dwell times. This explains why some port terminal operators are involved in developing 'extended gates' (Slack 1999, Rodrigue and Notteboom 2009).

Containerization highlights the existence of a window of opportunity favouring combined rail-road transport. The various stakeholders, carriers, shippers, public authorities, environmental or neighbouring associations, share three common issues: environment, transportation cost and congestion. Their interests are different but they share the same goal: the transfer of freight from road to rail transport. This coalition of interests is the first condition enabling a modal shift from road to rail.

The Need for Massified Corridors

Beyond this coalition of interests, there is a need to put in place the conditions to make combined rail-road transport competitive with road transport. The price of combined transport must be lower than road transport. When freight forwarders are accustomed to use road, the door-to-door delivery price of combined transport must be less than 10–20 per cent over road to have a leverage effect in favour of combined transport (Frémont and Franc 2010). Anything that augments the cost of road transport favours combined transport: increases in fuel price, road congestion, strengthening of social legislation.

Massification is the first advantage of rail transport in its capacity to offer a lower transport cost than road. There is thus a need to implement the conditions of massification. On the rail leg of the journey, double-stacking trains allow this massification. Emerging countries are following this trend. China has been running double-stack container train services to and from main coastal ports on selected routes using new specialized wagons and powerful locomotives. In 2007, Chinese railways operated 680 double-stack trains and carried 53,161 TEU, compared to 454 trains carrying 39,437 TEU in 2006. India has also introduced the double-stack concept (ESCAP 2011).

Massification is all the more important in cost reduction when rail distance is considered. A distance of 600 km is generally considered a threshold in Europe for combined transport cost to be competitive over road. This threshold is purely theoretical. Significant and balanced volume in each direction, frequent shuttles and high loading rates allow that limit to be lowered.

Organizing massification requires a concentration of traffic at each end of the main rail corridor. Ports are mandatory points of traffic concentration (Hayuth 1981). But container terminals are often dispersed, contradicting the logic of massification (Slack 2007). It is thus necessary to implement a drayage of containers to a main rail terminal where rail shuttles are assembled. The operation is comparable to a hub-and-spoke system at the port scale. The port of Hamburg has the most important volume of rail freight traffic in Europe. Rail shuttles are assembled in three main terminals. Numerous ports experiencing traffic growth are affected by the geographical spread of their container terminals. In the port of Antwerp, the new container terminals are located on the left bank of the Schelt River while the main rail terminals are on the right bank. At the port of Rotterdam, the new Massvlakte extends the port toward the sea, increasing rail and road distances between existing container and rail terminals. Le Havre has built an intermodal terminal behind the port terminal with a view to concentrating different types of traffic.

The Need for Inland Terminals

At the other end of the rail corridor, upon arrival in urban areas, the challenge of concentrating traffic is even greater. The rationale of road transport dominates. Road freight transport results in a wider distribution of activities and urban sprawl which in turn sustain road transport. This is notably the case of urban areas in North America and Europe (Cidell 2009, Dablanc 2007). The road network offers a high level of accessibility over the entire territory. Warehouses, often concentrated in logistical parks, have become a dominant feature of supply chains supplying industrial plants in intermediate products or retail stores in consumer goods. These logistics clusters assemble products originating from different industries to be redistributed either directly to other industrial customers, to retail stores, or to secondary regional platforms for final distribution. They are nodes that funnel dispersed traffic before redistribution. Evidently, these facilities are located near major production and consumption facilities in large urban areas (Bowen 2008, O'Connor 2010). They require vast surface areas, near road infrastructures and preferably motorway junctions and put pressure on land development. The real estate situation is further exacerbated by the need to reduce negative externalities that may affect residential areas. These platforms are thus compelled to be located in peripheral urban areas far away from city centres. This process increases the distances in the final distribution of goods in the city thus contributing to the suburbanization of logistics movement. The phenomenon favours an almost exclusive use of trucking given the dispersion of traffic (Frémont 2012).

In contrast to this emphasis on road transport, combined traffic require few major terminals located in close proximity to urban agglomerations with a view to concentrate traffic (Notteboom and Rodrigue 2010). The acceptability of these inland rail terminals is a major issue. The oldest, such as in Chicago or Paris, are currently enclosed within the built-up urban area and cannot be extended. They are affected by urban congestion. The establishment of new terminals located on the outskirts of the cities raises important opposition given their considerable size (Hesse 2008). The Canadian Pacific rail company is planning a new terminal in Montreal. The company has earmarked a site in Les Cèdres, located 40 km west of Montreal. The objective is to build an intermodal complex of 300 hectares, with an annual handling capacity of 550,000 TEU. As for infrastructure projects of this magnitude, consultation with the local communities and environmental compensation measures are required to insure its acceptability.

The location of intermodal terminals in urban areas is a determining factor to manage the problems of the 'last kilometre' (Rotter 2004). The road pre- and post-haulage account for 35–50 per cent of the total cost of combined rail-road transport. The average number of daily truck movements has a decisive impact on the cost of pre- or post-haulage. Warehouses

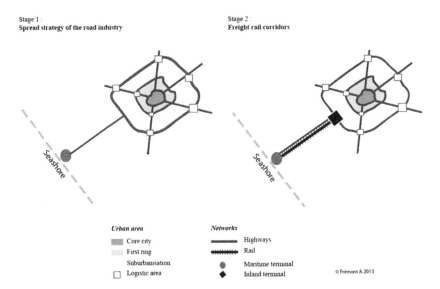

Figure 7.6   Spread strategy of the road industry versus freight rail corridors
Source: Author.

at close proximity to rail terminals, full loads, balanced flows are all favourable factors to lower the cost of road haulage.

This focus on transport corridors requires a business approach unlike road transport. Logistics have to be organized on either side of the corridor with a view to implementing the conditions of modal split transition (Figure 7.6).

The Need for the Integration of the Transport Chain

Contrary to road transport, a combined transport chain is more complex to implement since it necessitates time and space coordination between several modes of transport with a view to offer door-to-door services (Figure 7.7) (Caris et al. 2008). The necessary condition for the development of combined rail-road transport is the use of freight transport chain integrators (ECMT 2006).

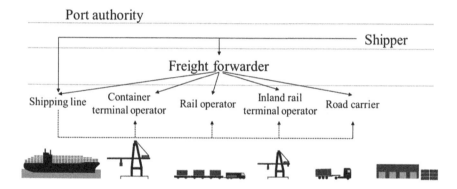

Figure 7.7   The integration of the combined transport chain
Source: Author.

Transport integrators offer shippers door-to-door services between maritime ports and import/export warehouses located in the hinterland. Rail services, inland terminals and final journeys by road are organized and coordinated by the integrator that manages the activities of rail haulage operators, terminal operators and road carriers (Debrie and Gouvernal 2006). Integrators can provide their services directly to shippers but more often have indirect contacts through freight forwarders, shipping lines or port terminal operators. Some integrators are often subsidiaries of one of the actors of the transport chain: forwarders, shippers, rail carriers or stevedoring company (Heaver 2002). The degree of involvement of these firms as combined transport operators varies and depends on corporate strategies, interests and objectives but also on the characteristics of the hinterland being served (Franc and Van Den Horst 2010).

Transport integrators do not necessarily own the means of transport. They can purchase slots from a rail carrier on demand or charter fixed and regular numbers of slots to share the commercial and operational risk with the rail carrier. This can be exemplified by Hupac Intermodal's business model which exploits combined transport (Figure 7.8). Rail haulage and the last few kilometres are undertaken by rail and road carriers. Hupac's customers are freight forwarders and transport companies.

Table 7.1   Major combined transport operators in Le Havre, Antwerp and Rotterdam, 2011

Combined transport operator	Mother company	Core business	Number of weekly services		
			Le Havre	Antwerp	Rotterdam
Hupac	Freight forwarders and railcies	Freight forwarders and railways cies		59	77
Naviland cargo	SNCF	Railways company	24	20	
Inter Ferry Boats	SNCB	Railways company		35	2
European Rail Shuttle	Maersk Line	Shipping line			26
Kombiverkehr	Freight forwarders and DB Logistics	Freight forwarders and railcies			23
TCT Venlo	European Container Terminal/Hutchison	Stevedoring company			22
Rail Link	CMA–CGM	Shipping line	8	6	7
Total			32	120	157

Source: Adapted by the Author from data provided by the web sites of the combined transport operators.

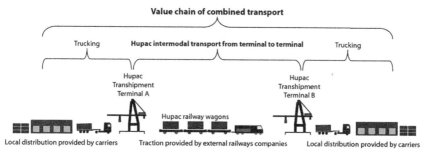

Figure 7.8   The business model of Hupac Intermodal

Source: Adapted by the author from Hupac (2013). Available at: http://www.hupac.ch.

The ultimate consequence is that the shipper must find an interest in using rail services offered by the combined transport operator. The shipper is concerned with low transport costs on the land leg and additional logistics services (customs, storage, …) and environmentally-friendly modes of transport.

Other Potential Traffic Concerned by Modal Shift from Road to Rail

As demonstrated by containerization, the necessary conditions to ensure a modal shift from road to rail are difficult to obtain. This raises the issue of potential modal shift for other types of traffic.

In order to have door-to-door combined transport, goods must be packaged within intermodal transport units. The packaging of manufactured products in train cars is not possible with the exception of selected heavy, bulky products, such as mineral waters. Generally, they are placed in train cars at the plant to be shipped to distribution centres where they will be carried to final destination by trucks.

Pallets are a common management unit for the road industry but they are not suitable for intermodal handling from a trailer to a freight car. This implies costly transshipment and delays. Pallets must be placed directly in larger intermodal transport units in order to achieve combined transport.

Combined transport is based on different techniques: unaccompanied transport of swap bodies, containers, cranable semi-trailers and accompanied transport or a rolling motorway. With rolling motorways, the whole road vehicle is transported on special flat wagons and the driver accompanies his truck during the rail transport in a sleeping car. Combined transport is being developed in Europe. While the techniques are improving, combined transport only accounts for a small share of freight rail traffic. The service is not always profitable. Several reasons may be provided.

In Europe, freight trains lack reliability since priority is systematically given to passenger trains. Major investments have been undertaken or planned to favour rail freight transport. The Betuwe Line is a dedicated freight rail line between the port terminals of Rotterdam and the German border at Zevenaar (The Netherlands) and Emmerich (Germany). The line opened in June 2007 at an initial cost of €5 billion. The construction of transalpine rail tunnels is estimated at €10 billion. These new rail corridors pass through the base of the mountains with minimum slope thus providing a much shorter straight line than the current tunnels. They provide high capacity both for passenger and freight trains and reduce transit times. Two base tunnels are located in Switzerland: the Lötschberg base tunnel opened in 2007 and the Gothard base tunnel is scheduled for 2017. The Lyon-Turin line between France and Italy is a project for a base tunnel of over 50 km. But financing has not been approved and the project faces strong opposition from Italy.

The European Union has set up a policy to develop nine international marked-oriented rail freight corridors at the European scale. According to the EU Regulation 913/2010, they have to meet three challenges concerning:

- the European integration of rail infrastructures by strengthening cooperation between infrastructure managers on investment and traffic management
- a balance between freight and passenger traffic along the rail freight corridors, giving adequate capacity and priority for freight in line with market needs and ensuring that common punctuality targets for freight trains are met
- the intermodality between rail and other transport modes by integrating terminals into the corridor management and development.

The European Union has also favoured opening rail freight to competition since the beginning of 2000. Everywhere the traditional operators have lost market share without significant increase in volume carried. New entrants have often been satisfied with challenging the traditional operators on the most lucrative markets, notably bulk traffic. The main exception is Germany.

The rolling motorway system as experienced in France is highly subsidized, either directly, such as between Perpignan and Bettembourg, from the Spanish border to Luxembourg, or indirectly, such as across the Maurienne valley in the Alps between France and Italy.

The success of combined transport stemmed from constraints imposed on roads. Between the continent and the United Kingdom, Eurotunnel is not competing with the road but with car-ferries. The marine obstacle requires the use of combined transport. This can further be exemplified with the transit traffic through the Alps. The aim of the Swiss transport policy is to shift transalpine goods movement from road to rail by improving the competitiveness of the rail system compared with the road. In 2010 about 1,257,000 vehicles crossed the Swiss Alps on the roads, while 927,000 shipments were carried by intermodal transport. Since 2000, shipments in transalpine combined transport have increased by 72 per cent, whilst shipments by road transport have fallen by 11 per cent. The constraints imposed on road transport by the transit tax (Performance-related Heavy Vehicle Fee), the improvement of rail infrastructures, the provision of efficient combined transport services by transport integrator (i.e. Hupac) and the physical constraint of the mountains all contribute to the relative success of modal shift from road to rail.

The introduction of distance charges for trucks (truck toll system) similar to the one implemented in Germany since 2005 contributes to the increase in the cost of road transport. This increase must however be reflected in the transport price paid by shippers. But the strong competition between road transport enterprises in the European Union keeps transport prices at a low level. In contrast, the toll system represents an important source of income for the development of rail freight. In Germany, over the last eight years, Toll Collect has transferred around €30 billion of toll income to the Federal government. In response to these challenges, the road transport industry is gaining in productivity through higher load factors and better environmental performance (i.e. Euro emission class). Besides, new legislation is being promoted across Europe for truckloads of 38–44 tons in the United Kingdom, Italy, Belgium and France (since 1 January 2013) strengthening the competitiveness of the road sector.

Conclusion

Countries are at different stages in the modal split transition. In some countries road is the dominant mode of transport to move freight. In other countries rail plays an important role for the movement of raw materials. The diversity of modal profile does not make possible the elaboration of a unique model describing the transfer of freight transport from road to rail. Besides, some rail networks are almost entirely dedicated to passenger transport (i.e. Japan and Europe) or mostly servicing freight (i.e. North America).

Despite this diversity, the main issue in modal shift concerns all types of freight from intermediate goods to manufactured products entering into channels of production and distribution before being delivered to consumers. The movement of these goods is currently being captured by an already dominant road system which draws its strength from its great flexibility in answering transport demand in time and space at very low cost.

The implementation of massified and intermodal transport including a rail leg and door-to-door service are the necessary conditions to achieve a modal shift from road to rail. In the current market conditions, massification is the main tool to render combined rail-road transport competitive over road.

The analysis of containerization underlines the necessary conditions for the provision of massified, intermodal and door-to-door services: a coalition of actors with differing interests seeking to attain the goal of modal shift. The strategy rests on offering a counterweight to the geographical spread of road transport. The rationale consists in organizing the massification of freight at both ends of rail corridors, in ocean ports and in dry ports within the logistics chain of combined transport operators.

For non-containerized traffic, these conditions are difficult given the primacy of road transport. It is important to recognize that these types of freight are an integral part of production and distribution processes. It is thus necessary at least initially to concentrate efforts on selected major freight axis building on a few shippers capable of supplying a constant amount of freight volume.

References

Bowen, J.T. 2008. Moving places: the geography of warehousing in the US, *Journal of Transport Geography*, 16(6), 379–87.

Caris, A., Macharis, C. and Janssens, G. 2008. Planning problems in intermodal freight transport: accomplishments and prospects. *Transportation Planning and Technology*, 31(3), 277–302.

Chaudhury, P.D. 2005. Modal split between rail and road modes of transport in India. *Vikalpa*, 30(1), 17–33.

Cidell, J. 2009. Concentration and decentralization: the new geography of freight distribution in US metropolitan areas. *Journal of Transport Geography*, 18, 363–71.

Dablanc, L. 2007. Goods transport in large European cities: difficult to organize, difficult to modernize. *Transportation Research A*, 4, 80–285.

Debrie, J. and Gouvernal, E. 2006. Intermodal rail in Western Europe: actors and services in a new regulatory environment. *Growth and Change*, 37(3), 444–59.

European Conference of Ministers of Transport (ECMT). 2006. *Strengthening Inland Waterway Transport: Pan-European Co-operation for Progress*. Paris: OECD.

Economic and Social Commission for Asia and the Pacific (ESCAP). 2011. *Emerging Issues in Transport: Sustainable Transport Development* [Online]. Available at: http://www.unescap.org/ttdw/MCT2011/EGM/EGM1–8E.pdf [accessed: 14 January 2013].

European Commission. 2001. *European Transport Policy for 2010: Time to Decide* [Online]. Available at: http://www.central2013.eu/fileadmin/user_upload/Downloads/Document_Centre/OP_Resources/EU-transportpolicy2010_en.pdf [accessed: 14 January 2013].

European Commission. 2011. *Roadmap to a Single European Transport Area – Towards a competitive and resource efficient transport system* [Online]. Available at: http://eurlex.europa.eu/LexUriServ/LexUriServ.do?uri=CELEX:52011DC0144:EN:NOT [accessed: 14 January 2013].

Eurostat. 2013. Modal Split of Freight Transport [Online]. Available at: http://epp.eurostat.ec.europa.eu/tgm/table.do?tab=table&init=1&plugin=1&language=en&pcode=tsdtr220 [accessed: 14 January 2013].

Franc, P. and Van Den Horst, M. 2010. Understanding hinterland service integration by shipping lines and terminal operators: a theoretical and empirical analysis. *Journal of Transport Geography*, 18(4), 557–66.

Frémont, A. and Franc P. 2010. Hinterland transportation in Europe: Combined transport versus road transport. *Journal of Transport Geography*, 18(4), 548–56.

Frémont, A. 2012. Quel rôle pour le fleuve dans le Grand Paris des marchandises? *L'Espace géographique*, 3, 236–51.

French Environment and Energy Management Agency (FEEMA). 2006. *Transports combinés rail-route, fleuve-route etmer-route. Tableau de bord national 2006*. Valbonne: Sophia Antipolis.

Hayuth, Y. 1981. Containerization and the load center concept. *Economic Geography*, 57(2), 160–76.

Heaver, T.D. 2002. The evolving roles of shipping lines in international logistics. *International Journal of Maritime Economics*, 4, 210–30.

Hesse, M. 2008. *The City as a Terminal*. Aldershot: Ashgate.

Hupac. 2013. Home [Online]. Available at: http://www.hupac.ch [accessed: 14 January 2013].

International Transport Forum. 2013. *Inland Freight Transport (million t-km)* [Online]. Available at: http://stats.oecd.org/ViewHTML.aspx?Theme=INLAND_FREIGHT_TRANSPORT&DatasetCode=INLAND_FREIGHT_TRANSPORT [accessed: 14 January 2013].

Levinson, M. 2006. *The Box: How the Shipping Container Made the World Smaller and the World Economy Bigger*. Princeton and Oxford: Princeton University Press.

Notteboom, T. and Rodrigue, J-P. 2010. Foreland-based regionalization: Integrating intermediate hubs with port hinterlands. *Research in Transportation Economics*, 27, 19–29.

Notteboom, T. and Winkelmans, W. 2001. Structural changes in logistics: how will port authorities face the challenge? *Maritime Policy & Management*, 28(1), 71–89.

O'Connor, K. 2010. Global city regions and the location of logistics activity. *Journal of Transport Geography*, 18(4), 354–362.

Perrupato, M. 2011. *Logistic Infrastructure Scenario in Brazil, Secretary for Transportation National Policy.* [Online]. Available at: www.transportes.gov.br/public/arquivo/arq1318615138.pdf [accessed: 14 January 2013].

Robinson, R. 2002. Ports as elements in value-driven chain systems: the new paradigm. *Maritime Policy and Management,* 29(3), 241–55.

Rodrigue, J-P. and Notteboom, T. 2009. The terminalization of supply chains: reassessing the role of terminals in port/hinterland relationships. *Maritime Policy and Management,* 36(2), 165–83.

Rotter, H. 2004. New operating concepts for intermodal transport: the mega hub in Hanover/Lehrte in Germany. *Transport Planning and Technology,* 27(5), 347–65.

Slack, B. 1999. Satellite terminals: A local solution to hub congestion? *Journal of Transport Geography,* 7, 241–6.

Slack, B. 2007. The terminalisation of seaports, in *Ports, Cities, and Global Supply Chains,* edited by J. Wang, D. Olivier, T. Notteboom and B. Slack. Aldershot: Ashgate, 41–50.

United Nations/Economic Commission for Europe (UN/ECE). 2001. *Terminology on Combined Transport, United Nations* [Online]. Available at: www.oecd.org/dataoecd/42/32/1941816.pdf [accessed: 14 January 2013].

US Department of Transportation. 2013. *National Transportation Statistics* [Online]. Available at: http://www.rita.dot.gov/bts/sites/rita.dot.gov.bts/files/publications/national_transportation_ statistics/index.html [accessed: 14 January 2013].

SECTION IV
Equity and Accessibility: Social Dimensions

Chapter 8
The Promotion of Social Equity through Railways

Linna Li and Becky P.Y. Loo

Social Equity and Transport Disadvantaged

As one of the three pillars of sustainable development, social equity is often less defined than economic and environmental dimensions (Boschmann and Kwan 2008). Social equity, sometimes called social justice, refers to the equitable distribution of benefits and burdens in society (Beyazit 2010, Litman and Brenman 2012). There are many social equity theories. One important theory is utilitarianism, focusing on the consequence of an act and assuming that equality should be the greatest happiness of the greatest number, which means that the total amount of good should be greater than the total amount of bad (Jost and Kay 2010). Egalitarianism is different from utilitarianism. Egalitarianism advocates that all people should be treated equally and the greatest benefit of the least advantaged members of society should be pursued. Similarly, sufficientarianism supposes that there is a certain threshold of 'sufficient' well-being, and the priority should be given to the improvement of people whose well-being levels are below the threshold (van Wee and Geurs 2011). Traditional transport policy and planning adopts utilitarianism as its principles and tends to neglect the well-being of people with least advantage in transport. It was not until the 1990s that the academia and governments started to pay more attention to transport-related socoal equity (Beyazit 2010). Indeed, most of those who are transport disadvantaged are economically disadvantaged people, who cannot afford the most convenient transport modes (Litman 1997). Other groups may also face transport disadvantage due to a variety of reasons, including people without driver licenses, people with physical or mental disabilities, people too young or too old to drive, and immigrants from developing countries, who face language barriers and social isolation (Litman 2003). Because of transport disadvantages, it is more difficult for them to access either public or private sector facilities, including education, employment, key services and affordable goods, thus a combination of social exclusion problems happens to them. Considering the pervasiveness of transport disadvantage, social equity has been put forward as an integral element of sustainable transport, along with economic development and environmental protection (Button and Nijkamp 1997). Before suggesting strategies to solve social exclusion problems related to transport, we need firstly to understand the main groups of people who are experiencing transport disadvantage (Hine and Mitchell 2001).

Zero-car Households

In developed economies, such as Europe and North America, households that do not own a car are most likely to be transport disadvantaged (Malekafzali 2009). On one hand, due to urban sprawl, transport systems in these countries are mostly automobile-centred and travelling almost everywhere in the cities depends on private vehicles, except for a few centres in the largest cities (Clifton and Lucas 2004). On the other hand, for zero-car households, public transport has not been a good substitute for private cars because of its disinvestment at the neighbourhood level and the lack of services in many places (Lucas 2012). Moreover, most households without a car are low income population with low transport affordability. For instance, the car ownership of the lower income quintile in France, UK and US is 42 per cent, 35 per cent and 74 per cent respectively in 2004, much lower than their car ownership of all households, which is 77 per cent, 72 per cent and 92 per cent respectively (Fol et al. 2007). Therefore, the spatial dispersion and limited mobility makes the zero-car households lack accessibility to jobs, health care and other daily necessities, and accordingly face social exclusion (Pickup and Giuliano 2005).

Low-income People Who May Own a Car

In fact, the car ownership rate in developed economies has increased greatly during the past decades and reached a relatively high level, even for low income households. The US National Travel Survey shows that from 1985 to 2008, the number of households in the low income quintile with car rose by 23 per cent and the car ownership of low income quintile reached 49 per cent in 2008 (Hine 2012). However, it doesn't mean that owning cars has made the low income people less transport disadvantaged, compared with their zero-car counterparts. As a matter of fact, many involuntarily choose to own and use cars because many necessary services are out of reach around the communities due to the low density and sparse development of the city; meanwhile, no other affordable transport options are available. This phenomenon is called 'transport poverty' or 'forced car ownership' (FCO). FCO may lead to high transport costs for these households. An empirical research about FCO households in outer urban Melbourne shows that they made less trips and travelled shorter distances than average car households (Currie et al. 2009). Hence, private car can never be a panacea for the transport-related social problems of the low income population.

Children, Youngsters and Women

Children, youngsters and women can also suffer from transport disadvantage because of their reliance on public transport and safety issues. Children and youngsters cannot drive even if some of their households own a car. So they rely more on public transport, which is in shortage of service provision in most cities. Safety issues, including transport accidents and crimes, can also be reasons for their limited use. In comparison with youngsters, children's mobility is more restricted even in the local area due to their parents' worries about safety. However, youngsters are often constrained by travel cost because fare concessions are generally no longer available for them (Lucas 2004). Women are more reliant on public transport than their male counterparts and they have multiple roles with primary responsibility for child care (Suchorzewski 2005, Hine 2012), so poor public transport services may cause some social exclusion problems for them. Personal safety when using or trying to access public transport services is also a major consideration for women (Ortoleva and Brenman 2004).

The Elderly

In both Europe and North America, their demographic structure is shifting towards aging. Transport, as a means of access to services, resources and cultural opportunities still remains important in ensuring the elderly's quality of life. According to OECD (2001), the elderly who drive usually prefer to continue as long as possible and automobile reliance is pervasive for them. For example, in the UK, 53 per cent of all trips by men over 70 years old were by car. In the US, the elderly made over 90 per cent of their trips by car, and for three-quarters of all car trips the elderly were drivers rather than passengers (Waldorf and Pitfield 2005). On the other hand, they also expect to have access to alternative transport modes to meet their needs when their age is associated with constraints on driving and eventually even with complete driving cessation. However, existing non-automobile transport services are not sufficient as an alternative and thus cause transport disadvantage for the elderly (Donaghy et al. 2005). Difficulties in walking also emerge for old people, including uneven pavements, hills, ramps, traffic and crossing roads, steps, carrying bags (Hine 2012).

The Disabled

The disabled, including wheelchair users and visually impaired people as well as temporary ones, may suffer from unnecessary exclusion from current forms of transport, which is called transport disability (Heiser 1995). Because of disabilities, they usually cannot own a car, drive less, and tend to rely on taxis, minicabs, buses or a car driven by someone else. However, despite some efforts to improve the universal design, difficulties in travel are pervasive for disabled people in most countries. For instance, the disabled in Great Britain are complaining about inaccessibility for getting to and from bus stops or stations, and on and off buses and trains (Wilson 2003). Also, affordable services, more accessible pedestrian environment, more information provision and improved consultation are also needed for them. Transport is an essential element for them to access education, employment, health services, social events and leisure pursuits, the lack of which means social exclusion.

Ethnic Minorities

Inequalities in transport access exist between different races in both US and UK (Sheller 2012). In US, the overt racial discrimination in public transport no longer exists; however, the ethnic minorities still remain disadvantaged in transport. They are inclined to have a low social network and income as well as less access to driver licenses and private vehicles. Over 20 per cent of Black households do not own cars compared with 5 per cent of white households. American Indians, Hispanics, Pacific Islander, Asian and people of mixed race are also less likely to own cars than white Americans (Lucas 2012). It is similar for ethnic minorities in UK, where the black and mixed ethnic origins are less likely to drive to work (Hine 2012). Without good transport alternatives to cars for the ethnic groups, it is more likely for them to experience transport disadvantage and social exclusion.

Balancing Equity and Efficiency in Transport

In theory, social welfare should include both efficiency and equity. Traditional transport policy emphasizes efficiency and generally adopts cost-benefit analysis and transport modelling for the planning in practice. Social equity, however, is mostly neglected. Thus, balancing equity and efficiency in transport becomes important. As two different principles, equity and efficiency have their own objectives and evaluation criteria. Transport equity requires equal impacts on each group and individual, and pays more attention to the transport disadvantaged. It can be divided into three categories:

1. horizontal equity – individuals and groups receive equal share of resources, bear equal costs and be treated the same;
2. vertical equity with regard to income and social class – favour disadvantaged groups and support affordable modes, discount and special services for economically and socially disadvantaged groups, and ensure that disadvantaged groups do not bear an excessive share of external costs;
3. vertical equity with regard to mobility need and ability – support universal design and accommodate people with disabilities and other special needs (Litman 1997).

So, several indicators could be used for its evaluation: horizontal equity (whether otherwise comparable people and groups are treated equally), cost-based pricing (whether consumers bear the costs they impose, excepting where subsidies are specially justified), progressive pricing with respect to income (whether a policy or project benefits or harms lower-income households), benefits to transport disadvantaged (whether a policy or project benefits or harms transport disadvantaged people), and basic mobility improvement (whether a policy or project favours more important transport, such as emergency response, commuting, basic shopping, over less important transport) (Litman 1997). Transport efficiency gets more attention from different professions, and they often have different perceptions. Engineers aim to maximize mobility and safety under a certain cost constraint; planners focus on accessibility; economists emphasize utility; managers try to increase the productivity. So, efficiency of transport system can be measured mainly by four classes of indicators: mobility, which describes how the network facilities movement; utility, the sum of consumers' and producers' surplus; productivity, divided output (ton-km shipped or person-km travelled) by input (capital and labour); accessibility, measure of the ease some locations or activities can be reached (Levinson 2003). Nevertheless, both the efficiency of a transport system and its equity or fairness should be included to reach a sustainable transport system. However, it is not easy to reach the balance because these two principles have different objectives and sometimes could be contradictory. One critical dilemma is about developing public transport. It is expected that public transport can help solve many important social problems. However, most public transit operators are experiencing low efficiency, especially the financial problems caused by rising costs and falling revenues, and have to rely on government subsidies (Nash 2006).

Still, many efforts are made in pursuit of transport equity and efficiency. One measure is by improvement of transport design. It is expected that good design of a transport system can provide better accessibility, improve safety, lower emotional stress, link poor people to opportunity, connect isolated disabled people and stimulate economic development (Malekafzali 2009). Policy response is another important measure to solve social exclusion of transport. These policies try to ensure basic levels of accessibility, by transport costs reduction, information technology development, decentralization, income increase and pro-family and pro-neighbourliness policies (Preston and Rajé 2007). According to the Employment, Social Policy, Health and Consumer Affairs Council of Europe (2004), many countries have adopted policy strategies aiming to mitigate the transport inequity and keep transport efficiency at the same time. In Greece, both public transport and reasonable fares are supported to improve the accessibility of people in poverty or located in the countryside and islands. In France, a 'travel with a handicap' programme is promoted and universal access to transport services has improved. Also, there is a reduced charge for the transport disadvantaged there. In Ireland, policies about disability access and investment in rural transport have been adopted. In Belgium, policies to improve commuter transport are emphasized to help people with employment transport. The government websites of Spain, Canada, New Zealand and South Africa also reveal that policy makers are responding to the transport and social equity agenda (Lucas 2012). In the following section, the UK and the US will be used as examples to illustrate how policies have evolved from efficiency oriented towards transport equity.

The UK Policies

It was not until the mid-1990s that the UK government put forward some transport policies to promote accessibility for the socially excluded population. In 1995, the Disability Discrimination Act was enacted to regulate on access to all kinds of land-based public transport modes for disabled people. Following this act, a ten-year transport plan further concentrates on the promotion of universal design and accessibility of public transport. In 2000, concessionary fares were introduced in its Transport Act to reduce the travel costs of disabled people. The most well-known issue in its policy evolution is the report about transport and social exclusion by the Social Exclusion Unit report (SEU) in 2003 (Titheridge 2004). For the very first time, a systematic process of accessibility planning was introduced to identify and address the transport problems of the transport disadvantaged, which had a great influence on its transport policy (Farrington and Farrington 2005, Shaw 2005). Following these policies, there was some improvement in public transport services, however, the subsidy funding finally ran out and public transport ends up being operated on a commercial model (Lucas 2012), which exactly reflects the difficulty of the trade-off between equity and efficiency.

The US Policies

The US government has made various policies for different groups of transport disadvantaged people. For disabled people, the American with Disabilities Act (ADA) was enacted in 1990, aiming to provide public transport services in an accessible way. Under ADA, disabled people get better bus and rail services; however, for some older stations or bus stops, the difficulty of access still exists. Another programme for improving transport for the elderly and disabled provides funding to states, aiming to assist private sectors in providing transport options for these groups. Besides, some other programmes relate funding for transport infrastructure to the requirement of providing facilities accessible to the disabled. That is to say, the transport infrastructure needs to fulfil the requirement of accessibility to get funding from the government. For minority and low-income populations, the Transportation Equity Act for the 21st Century (TEA-21) was released to promote public participation in transport planning and provide funding for transport investment for their communities. Also, the Job Access Reverse Commute (JARC) Program provides transportation to and from workplaces for low-income individuals and individuals who receive government assistance (AAPD & the Leadership Conference Education Fund 2012). However, there is still a long way to go for the improvement of the public transport system in the US.

Cases of Successful Railway Projects

As mentioned above, transport disadvantage is closely related to the trend of car dependence and the downward trend in bus and transit use. The share of public transport has greatly decreased in developed economies, especially in Europe and North America, as shown in Table 8.1. The share of cars for passenger travel reached 61.67 per cent, 52.03 per cent, 85.35 per cent in the US, Canada and UK respectively. One exception is in Japan, which has a lower share of private car travel and higher share of bus and rail travel. Buses and railways account for 58.47 per cent and 29.02 per cent of its passenger travel. Although the role of public transport in reducing social exclusion has been widely recognized by policy makers around the world (Lethbridge 2008), there is limited recognition about the impact of railway development on social equity. Will railways aggregate or alleviate inequity? It is still a question of great debate. Compared with private vehicles, railways have the characteristics of public transport, which are more affordable and available for socially disadvantaged groups. However, some argue that railways are less socially sustainable than public buses. On the one hand, railways tend to serve higher-income populations than bus services. In the US, rail transit only contributes about a tenth of trips of the poor, and the majority of transit riders are not poor (Pucher 1981). On the other hand, the construction or extension of a railway line may increase the property value and make it difficult for low income or minority populations to afford living at convenient locations (Sanchez et al. 2003). Indeed, railways and buses each have different advantages and shortcomings and they should be applied in different situations and coordinated to promote social equity. Railways can provide faster, longer and more comfortable services than buses. They are usually appropriate for high density transport corridors, particularly useful for commuters (Light Rail Now 2000). Also, they can promote multi-modal transport and transit-oriented development around stations (Litman 2012). Without railway services, the transport disadvantaged may get fewer transport options and be restricted in their mobility (Shaw et al. 2003). Therefore, the role of railways in social equity promotion should be better explored by empirical case studies.

Improving Accessibility for the Poor and Disabled

For the poor who cannot afford a private vehicle and the disabled who cannot drive, railways will improve their accessibility to kinds of social activities. The situations are different for developing and developed countries. In developing countries, railways are usually viewed as a measure to reduce poverty. In Namibia, a developing country in the south of Africa, road transport dominates its transport system and is often the only accessible mode of transport for most communities in both urban and rural areas (Nyambe et al. 2009). Railways, however, are slower but cheaper for passenger travel there. So, the government tries to develop railways to allow poor people to get access to goods and services that are affordable for them. Also, the development around stations promotes employment and increases incomes for the poor communities nearby, especially in the rural area. Its operation is mainly charged by Namibian government and the Trans-Namib Company. The government is responsible for making funds available to the company by national finance and foreign loans, while the company is entrusted to provide non-profit passenger services and depend on cargos for its revenue. Still, it faces underinvestment problems in its infrastructure (Nyambe et al. 2009).

Table 8.1   **Modal split of passenger travel in selected countries**
(Unit: Million passenger-km/ percentage)

	US (2009)		Canada (2003)		UK (2009)		Japan (2008)	
Road	6,354,100	*87.04*	485,800	*93.37*	727,342	*91.27*	906,000	*64.92*
Buses	489,800	*6.71*	21,500	*4.13*	36,588	*4.59*	816,000	*58.47*
Passenger cars	4,502,000	*61.67*	270,700	*52.03*	680,180	*85.35*	90,000	*6.45*
Light trucks	1,326,300	*18.17*	193,600	*37.21*				
Motor cycles	36,000	*0.49*	-	-	5,620	*0.71*	-	-
Pedal cycles	-	-	-	-	4,954	*0.62*	-	-
Rail	57,900	*0.79*	1,400	*0.27*	61,205	*7.68*	405,000	*29.02*
Air	887,900	*12.16*	33,100	*6.36*	8,396	*1.05*	81,000	*5.80*
Water	-	-	-	-	-	-	3,500	*0.25*
Total	7,299,900	*100.00*	520,300	*100.00*	796,941	*100.00*	1,395,500	*100.00*

Source: For US and Canada, North American Transportation Statistics 2011; for UK, Department for Transport Statistics 2011, buses include buses and coaches, passenger cars include cars, vans and taxis; for Japan, Statistics Bureau 2011.

In developed countries, transit-oriented development has become a strategy for improving the livability of different communities. For instance, the Twin Cities region of Minnesota and Saint Paul in US is constructing a Central Corridor Light Rail Line (CCLRT). It is an 11-mile transit corridor with diverse racial communities. Along this corridor, 28 per cent of the population is black or African American, 16 per cent is Asian or Pacific Islander, 7 per cent Latino, 4 per cent two or more races, and 1 per cent American Indian. The poverty rate is 27 per cent in 2009, much higher than in the city and more than a quarter of the population is foreign-born from Southeast Asia, Eastern Africa and Latin America. By health impact assessment (HIA), it is predicted that this new railway line will create job opportunities for residents and promote local business development. For the low income and disabled, access to social opportunities will be increased and coordination of railway with bus, bicycle and pedestrian infrastructure will be promoted. However, many of the residents are still concerned that the improved accessibility brought by the rail will increase their housing and other costs and lead to displacement by higher-income residents (Malekafzali and Bergstrom 2011). Another example is the San Diego Trolley's East Line, which was built in the late 1980s. It mainly serves the city's low income district in the east of the city, attracting many more riders than the bus services. In the 1990s, this line extends to the suburbs and attracts people from higher income classes, but the low income ridership still gets increased and the poor population can get access to employment in the suburb areas (Light Rail Now 2000). Therefore, railways can be a good measure to promote the livability of poor communities, which are easily socially excluded. However, more strategies should be adopted to keep the poor from displacement by higher income population.

Also, for the disabled, more universal design should be taken into consideration to ensure better accessibility to railway stations (Rail Industry Safety & Standards Board of Australia 2011). Universal design is defined as 'the design and composition of different products and environments to be usable by all people, to the greatest extent possible, without the need for adaptation of specialized design'. It has seven principles: equitable use, flexibility in use, simple and intuitive use, perceptible information, tolerance for error, low physical effort, size and space for approach and use (Aslaksen et al. 1997). For train compartments, there are guidelines for the design of seats, hand straps, baggage rocks, doors and others. For the railway station, the concept of universal design covers lifts for wheelchair users, LED (light emitting diode) or LCD (liquid crystal display) information panels, Braille indications, spate smoking and non-smoking carriages, etc. (Kimura 2006). In East Asian region, Hong Kong and Japan could be two cases with good application of universal design in railways. The design of Mass Transit Railway (MTR) facilities has considered the special needs of passengers with different kinds of disabilities (MTR 2011). For visually impaired passengers, there are tactile guide paths, escalator audible warning signals and tactile layout maps in the stations as well as buzzer sounds to remind door closing and colour contrast grad poles inside the compartments of trains. For hearing impaired passengers, the facilities mainly concentrate on helping them to communicate with the customer service centres, such as introduction loops and information cards. For mobility impaired passengers, paths, gates and toilets are designed to allow access for wheelchair users. According to the Travel Characteristics Survey 2002 (Transport Department 2003), most disabled people in Hong Kong preferred to use rail and bus for their travel because they provided the facilities like low-platforms and ramp/gangplanks. Also, for most visually impaired people, rail and taxi were their most preferred modes. The hearing and speech impaired people preferred taking MTR and bus. However, there is still some room for improvement, such as the limited coverage of universal design facilities among all the stations in Hong Kong and the interchange between railways and other transport modes (Lui 2009). In Japan, an aging society (Sekiguchi 2006), universal design features are quite common in its railway stations and trains. Nowadays, escalators are commonly installed in stations of traditional railways. There is also easy access to toilets for the disabled, wheelchair ticket gates and stepless ramps, Braille passenger information for fare and maps, sculpted floor guides, and voice-guidance devices for visually impaired users, etc. In carriages, there are special seats and space for passengers with wheelchairs (Ito 2006). New rail systems in particular emphasize the accessibility features. For instance, on the Nanakuma Line in the city of Fukuoka, there is a strict standard for the gap between trains and platform, within 5 mm gap of 52 mm. The interchange between railway and other transport also shows the feature of universal design. For example, the central Japan International Airport railway station ensures that the airport railway station has no stairs to arrive at the boarding gates. When passengers with large suitcases exit the train, they can get baggage carts soon at the station platform. The moving walkways are wide enough for travellers to walk past wheelchairs. In the public washrooms, users can take their baggage into the stall and place it in a dedicated area. Railway information boards have evolved from LED to LCD panels, a great advance providing much more information. The stations also published brochures offering accessible rail travel tips and information for disabled people (Kimura 2006). The universal design of railways not only relies on thoughtful design, but also need the support of policy. The law of 'Barrier-Free Transportation Law' (2000) further guarantees the application of universal design, especially the installation of escalators and lifts in many Japanese railway stations.

Integrating Peripheral Regions

In regional theories, it is still a debate whether transport improvement would strengthen the core-periphery system of a region or promote the integration towards regional integration. The outcome of a transport system connecting the peripheral regions with the core would either improve the accessibility of peripheral regions and accelerate their growth rate, or otherwise increase the agglomerative advantage of the core and attract the labour and capital away from peripheral regions (Gauthier 1970). The interrelationship between transport development and regional development could be very complicated; however, railways are often built in the hope of improving the accessibility of peripheral regions and providing more opportunities to them. Among different kinds of transport infrastructure, railways have long been constructed to promote regional integration (Hechter 1971). Modern railways connecting with peripheral regions can be better planned from the perspective of spatial equity. For instance, the European high-speed railway (HSR) was expected to link peripheral regions to its geographic, political and economic centre. Some scholars argue that this system is increasing concentration into the main metropolitan centres and has caused inequality to some small towns and rural areas, which could become mere transit areas (Vickerman 1997, Ross 1994). But, considering the short history of HSR, it is still too early to give a conclusion to its role in regional integration. At the city level, rapid rail development seems a good measure to integrate peripheral area with the city centre. In Sweden, the Svealand line was opened in 1997 between Eskilstuna and Stockholm. It has been found that it has significantly increased the accessibility of the peripheral area of Stockholm and more workplaces in the centre can be reached by the labour force in peripheral regions through the Svealand line (Fröidh 2005).

Creating Employment Options

The construction of railway itself can generate some job opportunities for the local people in the short term. In the long term, employment can be created by the regional development promoted by railways. More importantly, the railways can broaden the range of employment for the socially disadvantaged population and thus increase their employment options. Some studies have found that commute transport is closely related to employment. For the employees, difficulties in travel and high travel cost may limit their job options, especially for the poor; for the employers, they may feel that people who have to travel long distances or depend on public transport are not so reliable (Wilson 2003). However, with urban sprawl, spatial mismatch between jobs and housing has become pervasive. Many job opportunities are increasingly located away from low-wage workers, so transport becomes extremely important. What workers need is a relatively fast and affordable transport mode. Light rail systems are generally adopted in cities as a measure to connect the housing and the workplaces (Lau 2011). For instance, the Hiawatha light rail line between downtown Minneapolis and its southern suburb in the US, which opened in 2004, has some impacts on job accessibility. The newly constructed light rail has greatly increased the number of jobs for low income workers because of improved accessibility. Improved accessibility mainly comes from the fast speed of light rail compared to traditional bus services and better integration of rail system with its bus connections. Statistics of districts along the Hiawatha light rail line show that, the number of low-wage jobs accessible within 30 minutes of transit travel increased by 14,000 jobs in rail station areas and an additional 400 jobs by bus connection. After the opening of this light rail, many low-wage workers and low-wage jobs also relocated near the station areas (Center for Transportation Studies 2010). So, the Hiawatha light rail line has improved transport equity in Minneapolis greatly. However, apart from the accessibility improvement brought by the construction of the rail system, many other strategies are also important for the success of the railway system in creating employment. They included subsidies towards the socially targeted populations, integrating the rail system with other transit modes and related land use policies.

Generating Economic Revenues

As an infrastructure providing public service, railway projects usually need large investment for construction and operation; and most are unprofitable. However, there are some exceptions. One example is MTR of Hong Kong. Unlike many railway systems in the world, which are operated by the public sector, Hong Kong MTR is commercially operated. By the 'Rail & Property' development model, the MTR company gets more than half of its income from property development which supports its rail transit operation (Cervero and Murakami 2009). Non-fare income from the property above the metro station keeps the metro system financially sustainable without government subsidy and provides the citizens with quality services at affordable fares. Its experience may enlighten the operation models for other railway systems around the world, especially the railway development in cities with high density and rapid growth (Tang and Lo 2010). Nevertheless, the main contribution of railways to the economic development is through indirect impacts to regional economies (Vickerman and Ulied 2006). After the investment of railways, especially HSR projects, business activities may be developed around the railway stations, including real estate, retail and commerce (Calimente 2009). For instance, the Japanese Shinkansen has promoted the development of Japan at the regional, urban and station levels. The effects include the spillover effects of construction expenditure during construction, reduction in travel times, introduction of private investment and creation of employment due to the influx of new industries and enterprises in areas along the lines (Okada 1994). It is found that regions served by the Shinkansen had higher population and employment growth rates than those without direct Shinkansen services (Givoni 2006).

Strategies for Promoting Social Equity through Railways

Although railways have many advantages in promoting social equity, the main challenges are related to its efficiency in operation and financial sustainability. Because of the large investment needed for their infrastructure and operation as well as maintenance, the public sector is traditionally the exclusive stakeholder of railway projects. However, public sector provision has mostly been performed poorly in efficiency. Without efficiency in terms of productivity, it is hard to provide high quality of services to passengers and further extend the network to serve the more disadvantaged locations and population. Moreover, the number of railway projects is increasing and government funding may not be able to support all of them. Therefore, the participation of private stakeholders becomes a strategy for railway development. The public sector can regulate the service quality and uphold social equity while the private sector can improve the efficiency of railway system to keep its operation. Meanwhile, the cooperation between the two parties can provide more capital for railway construction and operation. Actually, the participation of the private sector in railways has become a trend in the world, shown as Table 8.2. Still, many problems exist in practice and strategies to encourage private stakeholders to take part in railway projects are necessary.

First, the key obstacle for private stakeholder to participate is the intensive capital needed and the long payback periods (Panayotou 1998). So, some tax incentives and other favourable treatment to enhance the attractiveness of the railway projects can be introduced to encourage public-private partnership. The Hong Kong MTR and Japanese Shinkansen experiences show that the most effective strategy is integrating the railway infrastructure with real estate development, so that the private sector can get revenue from property and business development, and therefore be willing to engage in the railway development (American Public Transportation Association 2006).

Second, the participation of private stakeholders also face other institutional obstacles, such as the lack of adequate legislation for private involvement, lack of confidence in private sector among policy makers and unfavourable public opinion (Panayotou 1998). As more countries began to liberalize and deregulate in their railway governance, the institutional environment gets better. For instance, in UK, the railway system was privatized in the mid-1990s. Since then, the government is only responsible for strategic management, such as transport planning, and all service provision has been transferred to private companies. The entry to rail service for the private sector is all through bidding for rail franchises. Although the entry cost is very high, the revenues show a high rate of return and promote the private sector's participation (Lethbridge 2008). However, the institutional environment cannot be changed only by reform in railway sector governance. Other reforms are needed to build a new institutional and legal framework to ensure enforcement of private participation contracts, including enacting adequate legal reforms to allow the private sector to operate efficiently and effectively, developing regulations that are transparent to private sectors, removing unnecessary restrictions on the ability of private enterprises, allowing for dissolution of existing enterprise, expanding opportunities for local private enterprises to develop management capacities, creating incentives and assurances to protect the labours, and redefining the role of government to facilitate and regulate private sector service provision (TERA International Group 2006).

Last but not the least, providing different public-private partnership strategies can also encourage more private sectors to participate in the railway development. Now, the strategies include: service contracts, management contracts, lease arrangement, concessions, BOOT (Build-Own-Operate-Transfer), BOT (Build-Operate-Transfer), BOO (Build-Own-Operate), reverse BOOT (the public entity builds the infrastructure and progressively transfers it to the private sector), joint ownership or mixed companies, and outright sale or divestiture (Panayotou 1998). So, private sector participation can take place both in construction and in the provision of services. It is also suggested that for the construction stage, the participation for private sector in policy decisions is important, while for the services provision stage, the public sector should provide more facilitation through changing procurement guidelines, bidding documents, and renting construction equipment (Social Development Department 2006).

Table 8.2   Top ten private investment railway projects, 1984–2011

Country	Project	Type of private participation	Cost ($US, million)
Russian Federation	Freight One	Partial	4271.0
India	L&T Hyderabad Metro Rail Private Limited	Build, operate, and transfer	3639.5
South Africa	Gautrain light rail concession	Build, operate, and transfer	3483.0
India	Mumbai Metro - Phase II	Build, operate, and transfer	2514.8
Argentina	Trenes de Buenos Aires (TBA)	Rehabilitate, lease or rent, and transfer	2488.2
Mexico	Transportation Ferroviaria Mexicana (TFM)	Rehabilitate, operate, and transfer	2270.0
Brazil	MRS Logistica SA	Rehabilitate, lease or rent, and transfer	2077.1
China	Daqin Railway Co., Ltd	Partial	1850.0
China	Guangshen Railway Company Limited	Partial	1804.0
Brazil	Malha Paulista	Rehabilitate, operate, and transfer	1765.3

Source: World Bank and PPIAF, PPI Project Database. Available at: http://ppi.worldbank.org.

Conclusion

From the above discussion, the potential role of railways in promoting social equity is clear. However, to realize such benefits, there are still many challenges. In the first place, the construction of railways needs large investment and has a long revenue return period. Sometimes the railway connecting peripheral regions may face low economic efficiency. Second, for regional development, only when institution, policy and other infrastructure all match, the improvement of accessibility could work best for poverty reduction. Last but not least, the low fare and good design of railways cannot be maintained without the support of policies, which put the priority on social equity. All these challenges could affect the success of a railway project and the prosperity of a region or livability of a community. So, the key point is to balance equity and efficiency in developing railways for a specific region.

References

AAPD & The Leadership Conference Education Fund. 2012. *Equity in Transportation for People with Disabilities* [Online]. Available at: http://www.aapd.com/resources/publications/transportation-disabilities.pdf [accessed: 19 November 2012].
American Public Transportation Association. 2006. *Public-private Partnerships in Public Transportation: Polices and Principles for the Transit Industry.* Washington, DC: American Public Transportation Association.

Aslaksen, F., Bergh, S., Bringa, O.R. and Heggem, E.K. 1997. *Universal Design: Planning and Design for All.* Oslo: The Norwegian State Council on Disability.

Beyazit, E. 2010. Evaluating social justice in transport: lessons to be learned from the capability approach. *Transport Reviews*, 31(1), 117–34.

Boschmann, E.E. and Kwan, M.P. 2008. Toward socially sustainable urban transportation: progress and potentials. *International Journal of Sustainable Transportation*, 2(3), 138–57.

Button, K. and Nijkamp, P. 1997. Social change and sustainable transport. *Journal of Transport Geography*, 5(3), 215–18.

Calimente, J. 2009. *Rail Integrated Communities in Tokyo.* Unpublished Master Thesis, Simon Fraser University.

Center for Transportation Studies. 2010. *How Light-Rail Transit Improves Job Access for Low-Wage Workers.* Minneapolis: The University of Minnesota.

Cervero, R. and Murakami, J. 2009. Rail and property development in Hong Kong: experiences and extensions. *Urban Studies*, 46, 2019–43.

Clifton, K. and Lucas, K. 2004. Examining the empirical evidence of transport inequality in the US and UK, in *Running on Empty: Transport, Social Exclusion and Environmental Justice*, edited by K. Lucas. Bristol: Policy Press, 15–38.

Currie, G., Richardson, T., Smyth, P., Vella-Brodrick, D., Hine, J., Lucas, K., Stanley, J., Morris, J., Kinnear, R. and Stanley, J. 2009. Investigating links between transport disadvantage, social exclusion and well-being in Melbourne: preliminary results. *Transport Policy*, 16(3), 97–105.

Department for Transport Statistics, UK. 2011. Transport Statistics Great Britain [Online]. Available at: http://webarchive.nationalarchives.gov.uk/20110218142807/dft.gov.uk/pgr/statistics/data tablespublications/tsgb/ [accessed: 5 December 2011].

Donaghy, K., Poppelreuter, S. and Rudinger, G. 2005. *Social Dimensions of Sustainable Transport: Transatlantic Perspectives.* Aldershot: Ashgate Publishing.

Employment, Social Policy, Health and Consumer Affairs Council of European. 2004. *Joint Report by the Commission and the Council on Social Inclusion.* Brussels: European Council.

Farrington, J. and Farrington, C. 2005. Rural accessibility, social inclusion and social justice: towards conceptualisation. *Journal of Transport Geography*, 13(1), 1–12.

Fol, S., Dupuy, G. and Coutard, O. 2007. Transport policy and the car divide in the UK, the US and France: beyond the environmental debate. *International Journal of Urban and Regional Research*, 31(4), 802–18.

Fröidh, O. 2005. Market effects of regional high-speed trains on the Svealand line. *Journal of Transport Geography,* 13(4), 352–61.

Gauthier, H.L. 1970. Geography, transportation, and regional development. *Economic Geography*, 46, 612–19.

Givoni, M. 2006. Development and impact of the modern high speed train: a review. *Transport Reviews*, 26(5), 593–611.

Hechter, M. 1971. Regional inequality and national integration: the case of the British Isles. *Journal of Social History*, 5(1), 96–117.

Heiser, B. 1995. The nature and causes of transport disability in Britain and how to overcome it, in *Removing Disabling Barriers*, edited by G. Zarb. London: Policy Studies Institute, 49–63.

Hine, J. 2012. Mobility and transport disadvantage, in *Mobilities: New Perspectives on Transport and Society*, edited by M. Grieco and J. Urry. Farnham: Ashgate Publishing, 21–40.

Hine, J. and Mitchell, F. 2001. Better for everyone? Travel experiences and transport exclusion. *Urban Studies*, 38, 319–32.

Ito, Y. 2006. Easy-to-access rail: JR East's initiatives. *Japan Railway & Transport Review*, 45, 12–16.

Jost, J.T. and Kay, A.C. 2010. Social justice: history, theory, and research, in *Handbook of Social Psychology*, edited by S.T. Fiske, D.T. Gilbert and G. Lindzey. Hoboken: John Wiley, 1122–65.

Kimura, K. 2006. Universal design for railways: accessibility for everyone. *Japan Railway & Transport Review*, 45, 6–8.

Lau, J.C.Y. 2011. Spatial mismatch and the affordability of public transport for the poor in Singapore's new towns. *Cities*, 28(3), 230–37.

Lethbridge, J. 2008. Public transport, in *Poor Choices: the Limits of Competitive Markets in the Provision of Essential Services to Low-income Consumers*. London: PSIRU, 151–78.

Levinson, D. 2003. Perspectives on efficiency in transportation. *International Journal of Transport Management*, 1, 145–55.

Light Rail Now. 2000. *Light Rail and Lower-income Transit Riders* [Online]. Available at: http://www.lightrailnow.org/myths/m_000004.htm [accessed: 27 November 2012].

Litman, T. 1997. *Evaluating Transportation Equity*. Victoria: Victoria Transport Policy Institute.

Litman, T. 2003. *Social Inclusion as a Transport Planning Issue in Canada*. Transport and Social Exclusion G7 Comparison Seminar. London, 2003.

Litman, T. 2012. *Evaluating Rail Transit Criticism*. Victoria: Victoria Transport Policy Institute.

Litman, T. and Brenman, M. 2012. *A New Social Equity Agenda for Sustainable Transportation*. Paper to the 2012 Transportation Research Board Annual Meeting, Washington, DC, 22–26 January 2012.

Lucas, K. 2004. Transport and social exclusion, in *Running on Empty: Transport, Social Exclusion and Environmental Justice*, edited by K. Lucas. Bristol: Policy Press, 39–54.

Lucas, K. 2012. Transport and social exclusion: where are we now? *Transport Policy*, 20, 105–13.

Lui, W.K.W. 2009. *A Study of Intermodal Transport Coordination and Its Contribution to Sustainable Urban Transportation in Hong Kong*. Unpublished Master Thesis, the University of Hong Kong.

Malekafzali, S. 2009. *Healthy, Equitable Transportation Policy: Recommendations and Research*. Oakland, CA: PolicyLink.

Malekafzali, S. and Bergstrom, D. 2011. *Healthy Corridor for All: A Community Health Impact Assessment of Transit-Oriented Development Policy in Saint Paul, Minnesota*. Oakland, CA: Policy Link.

MTR. 2011. *MTR Facilities for Passengers with Disabilities* [Online]. Available at: http://mtr.com.hk/eng/getting_around/disabled.html [accessed: 18 March 2013].

Nash, A. 2006. *Design of Effective Public Transportation Systems*. Paper to the 6th Swiss Transport Research Conference, Monte Verita/Ascona, Switzerland, 15–17 March 2006.

North American Transportation Statistics. 2011. *North American Transportation Statistics Database* [Online]. Available at: http://nats.sct.gob.mx/nats/sys/index.jsp?i=3 [accessed: 5 December 2011].

Nyambe, J.M., Walubita, B. and Plessis, C.D. 2009. *Fostering Talent Movement in the SADC and ESA Region Does the Railway Sub-sector Contribute to Poverty Alleviation in Namibia?* Windhoek: Namibian Economic Policy Research Unit.

OECD. 2001. *Ageing and Transport: Mobility Needs and Safety Issues Highlights.* Paris: OECD.

Okada, H. 1994. Features and economics and social effects of the Shinkansen. *Japan Railway & Transport Review*, 9–46.

Ortoleva, S. and Brenman, M. 2004. Women's issues in transportation, in *Running on Empty: Transport, Social Exclusion and Environmental Justice*, edited by K. Lucas. Bristol: Policy Press, 257–80.

Panayotou, T. 1998. *The Role of the Private Sector in Sustainable Infrastructure Development.* Cambridge, MA: Harvard Institute for International Development.

Pickup, L. and Giuliano, G. 2005. Transport and social exclusion in Europe and the USA, in *Social Dimensions of Sustainable Transport: Transatlantic Perspectives*, edited by K. Donaghy, S. Poppelreuter and G. Rudinger. Aldershot: Ashgate Publishing, 38–49.

Preston, J. and Rajé, F. 2007. Accessibility, mobility and transport-related social exclusion. *Journal of Transport Geography*, 15(3), 151–60.

Pucher, J. 1981. Equity in transit finance: distribution of transit subsidy benefits and costs among income classes. *Journal of the American Planning Association*, 47(4), 387–407.

Rail Industry Safety & Standards Board of Australia. 2011. *Accessible Rail Services: Code of Practice.* Canberra: Rail Industry Safety and Standards Board.

Ross, J.F.L. 1994. High speed rail: catalyst for European integration? *Journal of Common Market Studies*, 32, 191–214.

Sanchez, T.W., Stolz, R. and Ma, J.S. 2003. *Moving to Equity: Addressing Inequitable Effects of Transportation Policies on Minorities.* Cambridge: The Civil Rights Project at Harvard University.

Sekiguchi, M. 2006. JR East's approach to universal design of railway stations. *Japan Railway and Transport Review*, 45, 9–11.

Shaw, J., Walton, W. and Farrington, J. 2003. Assessing the potential for a 'railway renaissance' in Great Britain. *Geoforum*, 34, 141–56.

Shaw, S.J. 2005. *Tackling Social Exclusion in Transport: Principles into Practice?* Paper to The International Conference on Managing Urban Land. Belfast, UK, 13–15 April 2005.

Sheller, M. 2012. Sustainable mobility and mobility justice: towards a twin transition, in *Mobilities: New Perspectives on Transport and Society*, edited by M. Grieco and J. Urry. Farnham: Ashgate Publishing, 289–304.

Social Development Department, The World Bank. 2006. *Social Analysis in Transport Projects: Guidelines for Incorporating Social Dimensions into Bank-Supported Projects.* Washington, DC: The World Bank.

Statistics Bureau, Japan. 2011. *Japan Statistical Yearbook* [Online]. Available at: http://www.stat.go.jp/data/nenkan/pdf/yhyou12.pdf [accessed: 5 December 2011].

Suchorzewski, W. 2005. Society, behaviour, and private/public transport: trends and prospects in transition economies of central and Eastern Europe, in *Social Dimensions of Sustainable Transport: Transatlantic Perspectives*, edited by K. Donaghy, S. Poppelreuter and G. Rudinger. Aldershot: Ashgate Publishing, 14–28.

Tang, S.B. and Lo, H.K. 2010. On the financial viability of mass transit development: the case of Hong Kong. *Transportation*, 37(2), 299–316.

TERA International Group. 2006. *Best Practices for Private Sector Investment in Railways.* Manila: Asian Development Bank and the World Bank Group.

Titheridge, H. 2004. *Social Exclusion and Transport Policy (Scoping study on Accessibility and User Needs in Transport).* London: Centre for Transport Studies, University College London, UK.

Transport Department. 2003. *Travel Characteristics Survey 2002 Final Report.* Hong Kong: Transport Department.

Vickerman, R. 1997. High-speed rail in Europe: experience and issues for future development. *Annals of Regional Science*, 31, 21–38.

Vickerman, R. and Ulied, A. 2006. *Indirect and Wider Economic Impacts of High Speed Rail.* Paper to the 4th Annual Conference on Railroad Industry Structure, Competition and Investment, Madrid, 2006.

Waldorf, B. and Pitfield, D. 2005. The effect of demographic shifts on non-automobile transportation needs of the elderly, in *Social Dimensions of Sustainable Transport: Transatlantic Perspectives*, edited by K. Donaghy, S. Poppelreuter and G. Rudinger. Aldershot: Ashgate Publishing, 67–89.

van Wee, B. and Geurs, K. 2011. Discussing equity and social exclusion in accessibility evaluations. *European Journal of Transport and Infrastructure Research*, 11(4), 350–67.

Wilson, L.M. 2003. *An Overview of the Literature on Disability and Transport.* London: Disability Rights Commission.

World Bank and PPIAF. 2011. *PPI Project Database* [Online]. Available at: http://ppi. worldbank.org [accessed: 29 November 2012].

Chapter 9
The Rise of Localism in Railway Infrastructural Development

David Chapman

Aim and Scope

This chapter explores the potential impacts of an increasing emphasis on Localism upon railway infrastructural development. A brief exploration of the context for railway infrastructural development and Localism in China, the United States and Western Europe sets the context for a closer exploration of the changing roles and participation of local actors in government, governance and planning in the UK where the idea of Localism has been promoted as a major goal of public policy in recent years. Three small scale case studies are then used to explore how railway projects may be affected by increasing local engagement in decision-making and how local communities can collaborate with private stakeholders in shaping railway infrastructure development; possibly constructing alternative development trajectories and stimulating citizen engagement in the political life of local communities. The chapter concludes that, while a focus upon the local level has clear value for engagement within communities, there are a number of important spatial scales and sectors of policy making that deserve equal consideration and involvement, especially for services of strategic significance beyond the locality. Nevertheless the value of local creativity and volunteering to railway operations is potentially great and it is concluded that citizen engagement could become part of a wider process of social learning and infrastructure development.

Background

Railway infrastructural development today faces many challenges (Docherty 1999) and the complexities of developing modern high-speed railways (HSR) are matched by equal challenges in operating 'classic' railway systems. Both involve significant financial and environmental costs and not all places or localities will benefit equally from increased accessibility. Unequal distribution of costs and benefits creates tensions between self-interest and public good, and questions arise about who is to choose; who should pay and fundamentally who will benefit. These dilemmas are sometimes polarized between local and strategic interests but in reality there is a much more complex tapestry of interlocking spatial scales of interest in between. This chapter explores these complexities and the challenges that are presented for positive public engagement in the processes of railway infrastructural development and operation. It focuses on the UK at a time in the early twenty-first century when localism was declared a goal of public policy and the term 'Localism' was adopted as a banner for a variety of initiatives. Although the research is based largely on the UK experience there are also lessons of international significance.

The term Localism has been used by the UK coalition government to capture the idea ' ... that power should be held at the lowest possible level, whether individuals, communities, neighbourhoods, local institutions or local government' (DCLG 2010). The decentralization of government and the involvement of people and organizations in the delivery of public services are key objectives for what the UK Coalition government has described as the 'Big Society'. The chapter examines these ideas and the impacts that may be presented for railway infrastructural developments. Could railway infrastructural developments also stimulate participation of citizens in the political life of local communities? Evidence from United Kingdom suggests that, while a number of opportunities may arise from this, there are significant issues for railway development projects and how they engage with local communities and stakeholders. The three short case studies presented below illustrate some of the challenges and opportunities and they suggest a number of lessons that are of international interest.

The development of the British railway network *ab initio* and the complex system that evolved presents a challenge today as any vision for the future is heavily constrained by the past. In the 10 years from 1830 the railways of Britain developed from nothing into the skeleton of the 'system' today. 'Yet "system" is a misleading word if it suggests order and plan, for there was little of either' (Simmons 1968: 6). Unlike the developments in Belgium where the state planned and funded the main strategic lines, the UK Government did neither. This ambivalence was manifest at the local level where the terminals for even major strategic routes were forced to locate on the periphery of the destination cities. In the absence of any strategic input at the state level the railways ' ... grew up haphazardly, not necessarily where there was most need for them, but where capital and leadership were most readily forthcoming, and – often quite as important – where opposition to them was weak or negligible' (Simmons 1968: 7). The exuberant innovation of the early days of railway development produced an extensive network of routes; each line being driven by individual enterprise far more than any national strategy. The achievements of early developments were not followed by later projects and what began as a runaway success gradually became unsustainable. Nationalization in 1947 was seen as a way to address the inadequacies of the infrastructure but continued problems led to substantial cuts and closures in the network following the Beeching report by the British Transport Commission (1963). However from the low point of the 1960s there has been a steady growth in demand and the potential of a real renaissance, but the limitations of network capacity poses real questions. Will an increasing emphasis upon Localism in the planning, development and delivery of public services provide a positive or negative force for railway infrastructural development?

Planning and Citizen Engagement

Less than a century ago Lippmann (1922) argued that citizens of democratic societies should have no role in decision-making beyond electing their leaders, but since then there has been a steady demand by citizens for engagement in public decision-making. Arnstein's (1969) well known 'ladder of citizen participation' as illustrated in Figure 9.1 has provided a useful framework for theorists and practitioners, albeit that the idea has been challenged as too directed upon the transfer of power as the object of engagement rather than as a means of improving decision-making (Collins and Ison 2006). Some see increasing citizen participation in governance as beneficial, but others may see increasing engagement a threat to their authority, and while participation could become a powerful process of social

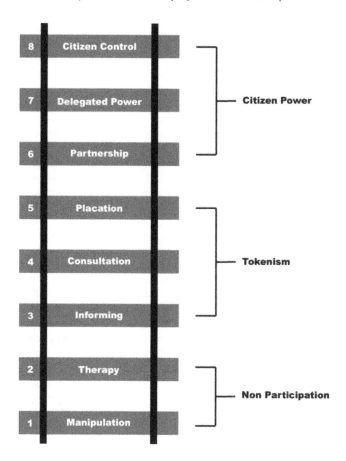

Figure 9.1 Arnstein's (1969) 'ladder of citizen participation'
Source: Redrawn by Ken Cronin.

learning it could perversely produce a subtle form of 'tyranny' (Cooke and Kothari 2001). The value of engaging with places and localizing urban design and development planning has also been examined by Chapman (2011) and this also suggests some key issues for approaches to engagement and social learning.

Before exploring the implications of Localism in railway infrastructural development it is helpful to explore contemporary ideas about the participation of citizens and interest holders in governance and planning. The two expressions, *citizen engagement* and *public participation*, are frequently used interchangeably in debates but neither fully captures the idea of Localism, which suggests devolution of decision-making to the local level much more than simply being consulted 'from outside'. While there is increasing evidence of citizen engagement in complex policy and project development, experience suggests that in most cases systematic processes of engagement do not exist.

A great diversity of approaches to planning can be found internationally as the result of widespread diffusion of systems from more developed countries to those less developed

(Home 1997) and a great deal of selective and synthetic borrowing between countries (Ward 2000). Nevertheless it is possible to discern two broad types of approach (Booth 1996). The first is the prescriptive, regulatory and codified approach typical of the USA and much of mainland Western Europe; and second the discretionary approach typical of Britain and some of its former colonies (Cullingworth and Nadin 2006: 1). Prescriptive approaches reduce uncertainty by providing explicit development principles and designs. Discretionary approaches rely upon policies and principles to guide discretionary decision-making, which may vary from place to place. Knowledge transfer has produced quite complex hybrids between these simplistic typologies, for example by the introduction of more regulatory design coding in Malta in response to challenges encountered in the discretionary approach (Chapman and Cassar 2004).

Two significant ideas have begun to unify this diversity. First *spatial planning* which aims to go beyond land use and development planning to shape the functional dynamics across the whole range of scales. As Albrechts (2004: 748) explains ' … the term "spatial" brings into focus the "where of things" (and) interrelations between different activities … intersections and nodes'. Second *communicative planning* which is concerned with engaging interest holders in collective discourses to support and guide decision-making (Healy 1992). This has been harder to achieve in practice, even when welcomed institutionally, and while in some cases 'Participation has become integral to the delivery of public services, as governments attempt to involve citizens in decision-making through processes of consultation and engagement' (Carpenter and Brownhill 2008: 227) this is still the exception.

These approaches are mutually supportive as spatial planning embraces citizen engagement. For example the EUROCITIES *Pegasus* research explored a variety of

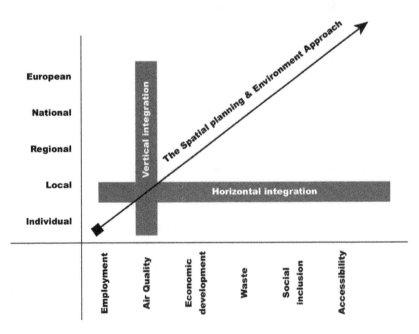

Figure 9.2   The Pegasus concept of 'diagonal coordination' (EUROCITIES 2004: 4)

Source: Redrawn by Ken Cronin.

approaches to engagement throughout Europe, concluding that diagonal integration between citizen engagement and decision-making is critical for spatial integration, and that ' ... vertical and horizontal coordination [is] not sufficient ... ' (EUROCITIES 2004: 4). Figure 9.2 illustrates the concept, but there are layers of complexity which must be appreciated if the idea is to succeed. As Cherry (1974: 79) observed, there is ' ... simply not one way of doing things ... but a variety (depending) on the different assumptions and values held by the groups concerned'.

The International Context

Although this chapter deliberately focuses more closely upon the experiences of the relatively newly declared priority for Localism in the UK with particular reference to its implications for railway infrastructural development, it is important to recognise that these experiences are not necessarily typical of the comparative scene internationally. Nevertheless a number of significant insights are revealed by the case studies from the UK, where the emphasis upon Localism espoused in policy is far from being realised in practice. While it is not possible to attempt anything more than a preliminary introduction to the wider international context the following examples of experiences of railway infrastructural development and local engagement internationally, from China, the United States and Western Europe, when taken together with the UK experiences, do begin to suggest areas for critical reflection and an agenda for future research.

The Context for Localism in the United States

The modal share of railways for passenger transport in the United States remains insignificant (US DOT 2014). Notwithstanding, states and local governments are proposing various projects with the participation of citizens for the development of commuter railways. The Sonoma-Marin Area Rail Transit District (SMART), a passenger rail project in the North Bay region of the San Francisco Bay Area region is a testimony of North American localism as briefly outlined below.

The context for these sorts of initiative has been set by several laws which have been enacted with a view to promote the participation and control of citizens in transportation planning. The Intermodal Surface Transportation Efficiency Act of 1991 (ISTEA) instigated many changes in transportation planning in the country. The Act emphasised non-automobile transportation and established a participatory environment by enhancing the role of Metropolitan Planning Organizations (MPOs). Citizens, representatives of public transport agencies, private providers of transportation and other interested parties must be consulted in the development of transport plans and programmes (Innes and Gruber 2001). Arguably, underrepresented groups such as ethnic minorities, disabled people and senior citizens are given an opportunity to participate in public hearings. In 1998, the Transportation Equity Act for the 21st Century (TEA-21) reaffirmed the importance of public involvement by adding public transit users among stakeholders included in the consultations. This was followed in 2005 by the Safe, Accountable, Flexible, Efficient Transportation Equity Act: A Legacy for Users (SAFETEA-LU) which added users of pedestrian walkways and bicycle transportation facilities in the public participation process and created tools to help citizens understand the terminology used in transportation planning meetings. The Act also underlined the obligation for the MPOs to develop short- and long-term participation plans in consultation with interested parties. In 2012, the Moving Ahead for Progress in the 21st Century Act (MAP-21) updated the SAFETEA-LU by stressing the importance of public involvement in transportation planning.

In addition to these federal acts, the state of California also enacted laws for increasing citizen involvement. The most notable is the Sustainable Communities and Climate Protection Act of 2008 which aims to reduce the emission of greenhouse gases by setting specific targets to each MPO. This suggests more emphasis on environmentally friendly transportation modes such as commuter railways. More importantly it reaffirmed the need for a 'bottom up' approach ensuring that local administrations are involved in the development of regional plans to achieve the GHG reduction target. Thus evidence suggests that communicative planning and localism have been gradually implemented in transportation planning in the United States over the past decades and that the prescriptive approach is no longer the norm.

Initially, the Sonoma-Marin Area Rail Transit District (SMART) project in the North Bay region of the San Francisco Bay Area region involves upgrading the section of the Northwestern Pacific Railroad running between a depot in Healdsburg, Sonoma County and the Ignacio Wye in Marin County. The project proposed a rail extension at both extremities so that the line would run between Cloverdale, Sonoma County and Larkspur's ferry terminal, Marin County. The project also included a bicycle and pedestrian pathway running alongside the line. The objective is to divert some of the traffic from Highway 101, the only north-south transportation infrastructure in the North Bay, and to offer a more ecological way to commute for the inhabitants.

The planning for SMART began officially in 2003 with the creation of the SMART district. In 2006, public exhibitions were held for the Environmental Impact Report (EIR) and copies of the initial draft were made available for citizens, public agencies, elected officials and interested stakeholders to comment. A total of 132 letters and 79 oral comments were received during this phase, all of which were addressed and used to modify the final EIR (Aspen Environmental Group 2006). During this process, alternatives routes and station locations were proposed along with proposition for the creation of quiet zones that would mitigate noise pollution, which had been one of the main concerns of the local population.

The project was eventually submitted for approval at local referendum. The measures asked citizens of Sonoma and Marin counties to accept a quarter cent sales tax increase to finance SMART. In 2006, the proposal fell short of the needed 66 per cent approval rate. The proposal was accepted at the 2008 election when the ballot registered 69.5 per cent yes votes. This process did not only give the population of the counties the power to decide about the project, it also generated debates encouraging citizens to seek information and stimulated their participation. SMART also encouraged smaller communities to participate in the planning process.

Sonoma and Marin counties' citizens were involved in all the different phases of the development of SMART and with local elected representatives from the two counties, and delegates of seven other counties of the Bay Area participated in the writing of regional transportation plans within the San Francisco Bay Area Metropolitan Transportation Commission (MTC) and in the allocation of federal funds. Citizens input on those plans encouraged the MTC to focus investments on mass transit and regional rail services in order to reduce the modal share of automobiles and contribute in reducing GHG emissions. The layout of the line changed several times due to SMART's economic difficulties, but the first phase of the project – the middle part of the line running from Sonoma County Airport station to San Rafael Downtown station – should be completed by 2016.

The second phase of the project is highly contested notably with regards to the exact course of the line and the location of stations. This concerns Larkspur where a crucial section of the line is to be constructed. Since the beginning, citizens have been involved in the planning of the station and its surrounding area. A citizen advisory committee (CAC) was created in Larkspur to draft a Station Area Plan (SAP) in consultation with the local communities to identify the preferred land use and location for the station. The CAC held three different public workshops in order to gather citizens' input pertaining to the urban planning surrounding the station. Plans were subjected to debate and comments in public hearings, which were not only followed by Larkspur's citizens, but also by people from the whole region serviced by SMART as the rail station will be connected with the Larkspur Ferry terminal offering services from the North Bay to San Francisco. One of the key components of the project is based on transit oriented development (TOD) around the station, although this was heavily criticized by a number of citizens who feared that the high density housing coming with TOD will increase pressure on the infrastructures and undermine Larkspur's 'small town' character (Hansen 2013). The final recommendation of the SAP is to promote moderate density housing (City of Larkspur 2012).

Public involvement and localism are currently thriving in the United States and efforts are made in order to offer local communities and citizens the opportunity to comment, not only on local transportation issues, but also on regional projects. While an absolute consensus is rarely achieved, the case of SMART demonstrates that the participation of citizens can enhance spatial planning through the fundamental component of localism.

The Context for Localism in China

Railways have traditionally been very important in China and in the People's Republic of China (PRC) the development of railway lines was primarily governed by political considerations before the Open Policy (Leung 1980) when capital investment, railway alignment and operations were highly centralized under the Ministry of Railways (MOR) (Loo and Liu 2005). Despite the efforts to 'separate politics from enterprise' (*zhengqi fengli*) under the Open Policy, and recent changes in the responsibility for the safety and regulation, inspection and construction and management of railways, central government still plays an enormous and powerful role. Typically, land resumption is facilitated by local governments; and the existing occupants are relocated and compensated by standard packages. Local opposition to the land resumption or to change the alignment of routes were minimal and, at best, sporadic and trivial both in terms of number of people involved or the duration of demonstrations (Tanner 2004). This characteristic has been one of the key reasons for the Chinese government to be able to announce a very ambitious high-speed rail (HSR) in the contemporary world (Cheng, Loo and Vickerman 2013). The building of the HSR network has been going very rapidly and only slowed down a bit with the Wenzhou crash incident in 2011.

Nonetheless there are signs of some limited change in public attitudes and citizen expectations and it seems probable that the process of building railway stations and railway tracks will involve more local engagement in future. One of the interesting case studies of actively engaging local communities in development of railway projects in mainland China is the process of the building of the Lok Ma Chau Spur Line and the planning of the Lok Ma Chau Loop (87 ha). The Lok Ma Chau Loop encompasses the Hong Kong Special Administrative Region (SAR) and Shenzhen across the SAR boundary. Both the Hong Kong SAR and Shenzhen governments were involved in a series of public engagement activities, led by the consultancy ARUP, which took place in 2008. Here the process of engagement of civil society in Hong Kong (Cheung 2011) has been tested on a railway project on mainland Chinese soils for the first time. In the public engagement exercise, the development of the Lok Ma Chau Spur Line railway stations was no longer simply considered in terms of the location of efficient transport nodes but as part of a long-term integrated concept plan to bring about closer integration of socio-economic development of the two cities. The ultimate concept plan (available at http://www.lmcloop.gov.hk and http://www.szpl.gov.cn) was based on the constructing an ecological landscape, promoting a pedestrian priority environment, pursuing low carbon economy, and a vibrant and diversified gateway.

Both the civil engagement process and the concept plan illustrated here are examples that are potentially paving the way for more local involvement in major railway infrastructural development and more integrated railway infrastructural development in China.

The Context for Localism in Western Europe

The European context for railway infrastructural development is strongly influenced, at least at the strategic transnational level by the policy framework of the European Union. This addresses the entire range of social, economic and environmental challenges that are recognized as critical to sustainable development. Within this infrastructure planning and investment is strongly shaped by the EU Territorial Agenda which intends to address the disparities between regions within different countries as well as between countries. The goals of cohesion and equality are addressed in a variety of ways and infrastructure investment is directed at two key goals: increasing connectivity and reducing disparities. Linking centres of growth and connecting peripheral regions are particularly evident objectives in policy formulation.

Within this context policy and investment strategies are powerfully influenced by the spatial relationships that already exist within the EU, and the ways these may be influenced and developed by infrastructure investment. These are fundamental considerations in the formulation of two key instruments. Firstly the European Spatial Development Perspective, which dates back some way to 1999 and seeks to balance social and economic demands with ecological and cultural needs. This has subsequently formed the foundation for on-going policy research and development and has guided the work of the European Observation Network for Territorial Development and Cohesion (ESPON). Secondly the Transnational European Transport Network strategy which was radically overhauled in 2013 when the European Parliament adopted a new framework and voted to triple EU financing for transport infrastructure for the period 2014–2020 to €26.3 billion for roads, railways, airports and canals in order to create a unified trans-European transport network (TEN-T).

It may seem that these wide scale spatial strategies are somewhat distant from the local level but in fact they help to set the scene for national, regional and local levels, with each level enabling engagement of communities and stakeholders at that spatial scale, at least in theory. In practice of course this is clearly not a simple process and there are inevitably serious tensions between stakeholders at all levels. Nevertheless there is considerable evidence that where integration between tiers of governance exists, including the local level, many of the tensions can be reduced and delays avoided. This is particularly evident in those countries in Europe where more 'nested' and codified approaches to policy and planning are used. In these situations strategic decisions can often be addressed and mediated at the most appropriate scale of governance. By contrast the discretionary approach typical of Britain, where today there a wide gulf between central Government and the local level, projects can sadly experience unresolved conflict, as manifest in the on-going contention about the HS2 project discussed below.

The objectives of integration and engagement are important for EU territorial policy, where reducing inter-regional disparities is a key driver of policy and infrastructure investment. For example the Interreg programme not only tackles live challenges, it also seeks to increase institutional and human engagement in cross-border cooperation. Under this programme the CORRIDESIGN research focused upon strategic infrastructure, economic development and urbanization in North-West Europe, involving teams from six countries. Some of its findings are pertinent here including:

- the lack of effective structures of decision-making between local, regional, national and transnational levels
- discontinuities between infrastructure providers, operators and regulators
- conflicts between the needs of local and long-distance movement
- the strong tendency of each locality to compete for exchange points to transport infrastructure, even when this will diminish the strategic function of infrastructure
- small local authorities being dominated by local 'parochial' concerns
- Myrdal's (1957) conceptual notions of *spread* and *backwash* were identified as critical issues in the study *and while* this is not the place to explore these concepts in any detail it is important to appreciate that the selection and location of quality 'exchange points' is critical to the functioning and impacts that will be experienced from any railway infrastructure development (Chapman et al. 2003).

Infrastructure and Localism in the UK

The idea of Localism has been passed into law in the UK though the Localism Act 2011, conferring powers to the local 'neighbourhood' level and abolishing a number of Regional bodies including Regional Development Agencies and Planning Assemblies. Significantly emphasis is placed upon speeding up the approval of major infrastructure projects, partly as a reaction to long delays experienced in the past, for example Heathrow Terminal 5 which took around a decade to pass through the Public Inquiry process to formal approval. A key ingredient of the streamlining is the introduction of National Policy Statements (NPS) which are intended to enable the arguments about strategic need to be tested by the NPS consultation, thus removing the debate about this from the detailed approval stage. Powers to designate Nationally Significant Infrastructure Projects (NSIP) are also introduced where thresholds of size or capacity will trigger a consent regime intended to speed the process. The existing Infrastructure Planning Commission (IPC) is also being drawn more tightly into government structures, contrasting with the earlier model where responsibility was delegated to independent IPC Commissioners.

There is also a changed emphasis for railway operations, moving from the Route Utilisation Strategy (RUS) which aimed to optimize use of existing capacity, to a Long Term Planning Process (LTPP) intended to exploit new possibilities. This shift from efficient use of existing infrastructure to expansion responds to increasing passenger numbers and the quest for economic growth. It is also proposed to devolve prioritization and funding of major local transport schemes to new Local Transport Bodies (LTBs). A key principle is that LTB consortia can take different forms and local areas can ' ... decide what collaborations are right for them and ... prioritize eligible transport interventions ... ' allowing operators to use their 'own knowledge of passenger needs to develop service patterns' (Secretary of State for Transport 2012). While diverse approaches at the local level may lead to disparity in service provision and confusion over political and operational accountability, they could produce opportunities for smaller branch lines and networks (Nelson 2011). Even so there are difficult questions about their links to larger rail investments, sustainable transport and carbon reductions (Kells 2012).

Two other innovations are the Community Infrastructure Levy (CIL), which will allow local authorities to set a tariff for new commercial developments in order to help fund new infrastructure, and the Duty to Cooperate (DtC) which places a statutory responsibility upon local authorities and other public bodies to collaborate across borders ' … on environmental issues (like flooding), public transport networks (such as trams), or major new retail parks' (DCLG 2011) although no arrangements are made to facilitate collaboration or resolve differences.

Railway Development and Localism

To gain an appreciation of the impact that localism could have on railway infrastructural developments three small scale case-studies have been undertaken. Having been conducted for this chapter they are inevitably limited, however even at this early stage a number of issues are suggested. The cases explore three contrasting spatial scales, and in each case a leading practitioner in the project has reflected upon the potential effects of a rise in Localism. The first case is the High Peak and Hope Valley Community Rail Partnership (HPHVCRP) which explores the opportunities for direct engagement of local people in the development and running of railways in their area. The second concerns the Evergreen 3 project which creates a new route from London to Oxford. The third examines the interface between a high-speed railway development linking London and the North of England and the local interests at the first terminal city, Birmingham.

Community Rail and Local Engagement

Community Rail partnerships involve local people, organizations and communities in improving local rail services and facilities. They operate on a small geographical scale and are concerned with local economic and social development. The distances and number of stations served by community rail routes are varied, and they don't normally carry major commuting or freight traffic. The lines are generally rural, low speed with one train operator providing most services. The infrastructure is owned and maintained by Network Rail, the UK rail infrastructure authority. Community Rail Partnerships (CRPs) make a major contribution by working with the railway operator for the area, local councils and other community organizations, but they are not directly responsible for primary service provision. They are guided by a national development strategy (SRA 2004) and they are supported by the Association of Community Rail Partnerships (ACoRP). A number of 'Community Rail Routes' have been designated which allows some flexibility in operating standards and EU regulation. Designations involve consultation with key local and rail industry stakeholders and facilitate a flexible approach to management of franchises, timetables and fares. The High Peak and Hope Valley Community Rail Partnership (HPHVCRP) presents some valuable insights and is the first case study.

The members of HPHVCRP are Derbyshire County Council, Northern Rail, Transport for Greater Manchester, The Peak District National Park Authority and High Peak Borough Council, along with community groups, and they share the aim of improve rail services and stations, and increase their use in the area. While the issues facing the Partnership have not really changed with the increasing emphasis on Localism the level of local engagement here illustrates what might be achieved more widely. Figure 9.3 illustrates the HPHVCRP area and its strategic location between several major cities.

The primary objectives of HPHVCRP are to improve the speed, frequency and quality of the services provided; and to improve stations and the station experience. The Partnership also has ambitions to provide rail access to communities currently without services, for example by opening a new station at Gamesley on the Glossop line and reopening the station at Chapel-en-le-Frith Central, on the current freight-only line. There are also ambitious ideas about reopening lines between Matlock and Buxton and Chinley where improved infrastructure could provide a major catalyst for the local area.

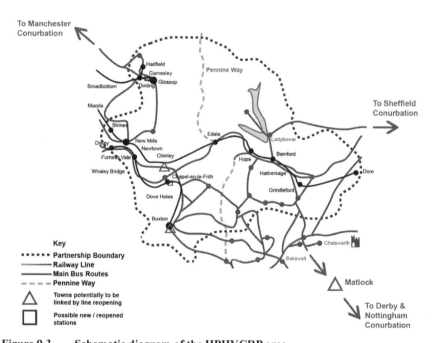

Figure 9.3   Schematic diagram of the HPHVCRP area
Source: Drawn by Ken Cronin.

In the shorter term all of the lines in the Partnership area have services which could be faster and more frequent without undue expense. While not perhaps in the operational front line it is also planned to improve the stations and station experience as many are in a very poor state. Financial resources are important as many practical improvements need investment. Sources include the County Council Local Transport Plan, the train operator, Network Rail and neighbouring Local Authorities, but in order to access this lobbying may play a very important role. For example the HPHVCRP has promoted just under £1 million improvement work at Buxton station with funding from Network Rail, Northern Rail, Derbyshire County Council and the National Stations Improvement Programme.

> While not unique to railways it is all about people and relationships, building up contacts and knowing who to ask. In my experience there are opportunities all around us. They come and go, but if you know what you want and seize the opportunity when it arrives, a great deal can be achieved. (Rose 2012)

Developer contributions under Section 106 (S106) of the Town and Country Planning Act are another source of funding. For example when planning applications for new housing or commercial developments have been considered a transport contribution has been negotiated, and as a result there is £400,000 set aside for a new station at Gamesley.

A key challenge, even within a small area, is identifying local communities and stakeholders. Private stakeholders may have extended linkages, for example Northern Rail appears at first to be private, but in fact is 50 per cent owned by the Dutch Government. Arriva who run many rail and bus services in the UK, is owned by DB, the German Railways and most freight trains in the UK are now operated by DB Schenker, also part of German Railways. Changing government priorities also present a significant challenge. Proposals for devolution of powers to LTBs and new approaches to franchising are two examples of the significant churn in institutional arrangements and structures. For those in CRPs a considerable amount of time is spent keeping up to date and responding to government consultations, all of which is essential for longer term results, but actually reduces the time spent on action.

Importantly success is not simply measured in major investments or changes. Small scale improvements are equally significant and these very personal steps are the real fruits of engagement. For example for many years residents had complained about the lack of an 1814 stopping train from Sheffield. If commuters missed the 1714, they had to wait for the 1914, by which time their children might be in bed. Volunteer experts got together and worked out how to add this train, and eventually after a lot of hard work and persuasion it started running in 2011. As Mike Rose said, 'There was some party in the Hope valley that night!' Many improvements to assist people with disabilities to access services freely have also been achieved, but there is more to do.

Local commitment is critical to Community Rail Partnerships and encouraging and coordinating voluntary contributions from local people, including the many retired railway workers keen improve the railway in the area, is invaluable. Station Friends groups do much work to improve assets which, while belonging to the state, are run by a private company. It is estimated that there are around 4,000 volunteers working in community rail in the UK and that they contribute over 1.2 million hours of work; with a benefit of some 4.6 times that of the cost of funding for the Partnerships (DfT 2012).Could this kind of engagement be stimulated at other scales of railway development and delivery?

Augmenting Railway Infrastructures and Local Engagement

The creation of a second London-Oxford rail link by Chiltern Railways (CR) as part of its Evergreen 3 project significantly augments existing railway infrastructure. The first stage involved a major upgrade of the existing route and was mostly undertaken using permitted development rights with relatively little public engagement. The second stage connects the London-Birmingham route to the lightly used Bicester Town-Oxford line at Bicester as illustrated in Figure 9.4. Because of its scale the second stage of the project required approval under the Transport & Works Act 1992, although as discussed below a potential alternative was considered.

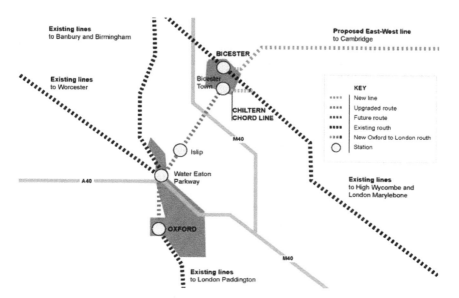

Figure 9.4   Schematic diagram of Evergreen 3 stage 2
Source: Drawn by Ken Cronin.

CR held a number of public exhibitions seeking public views, and at key locations where alternative solutions were viable public opinion was sought as to which option was preferred, before a formal application was made in January 2010. Over 300 objections were lodged mostly about specific attributes rather than the overall concept of the scheme. CR then worked with each objector to establish whether adjustments could be made to overcome the problems. In late 2010 objectors and supporters were able to present evidence to a public inquiry, which was adjourned until June 2012 to follow up on outstanding issues. Again objectors were able to present evidence. CR had considered an alternative approach using a mixture of individual planning applications and the exercise of their permitted development rights to bring the project forward, which might have acquired the parcels of land needed to be acquired at reasonable costs by individual negotiations with landowners. One of the reasons this was not pursued was because ' … it would have meant the planning applications would have been considered in isolation, outside of the wider context of a scheme that aims to link regional centres … ' (Barker 2012).

A sizeable proportion of the objections to the project concerned perceived noise or vibration at individual residential properties and in one case a concentration of objectors in north Oxford requested that the speed of trains be limited to 30 mph past their houses. Clearly this would conflict with the aim of providing a fast reliable link between the population centres. Despite efforts by CR to explain the operational difficulties and the precedent that such speed limitations would set for services throughout the entire railway network many local people refused to believe what the operator said, instead choosing to accuse it of trying to confuse them or maximize profits at the expense of health, safety and house prices. A number of objectors labelled the promoters as 'fat cats' and accused them of attempting to do everything in the cheapest possible way. While it is true that CR looked for value for money in their designs, they did not automatically default to using the cheapest solution to the detriment of local communities, and they clearly wanted to provide buildings, bridges etc. that sit comfortably in their environs. However as Stephen Barker has said the company did not have ' ... a bottomless pit of cash to pay for the most expensive cladding materials, endless miles of cycle lanes or many of the other "nice to have" things that some people have suggested we should provide' (Barker 2012). This issue will be returned to in the next case where the potential for railway infrastructural developments to play a major role in reconnecting communities and developing quality landscapes is being promoted by some the professionals who have taken an interest in the project.

While it is natural for stakeholders to seek high standards, for example in detailed design or landscape treatment, with no financial responsibility or accountability it is possible that they may make unreasonable demands, making difficulties for private promoters of railway infrastructural projects companies which can only undertake projects where they believe there will be an adequate return on investment.

A major ' ... issue in relation to localism is the inevitable conflict between the understandable desires of a local population to protect, conserve and enhance their local environment and community and the strategic aims of regionally (or nationally) important infrastructure schemes' (Barker 2012). There is also a danger that objections can be motivated by issues unrelated to the proposed scheme which is used as a means to advance another, unrelated cause. Despite these problems it is clear that local input can have a positive effect and early consultation work can give a better understanding of local problems and allow local people to suggest improvements, for example by influencing the appearance of stations, precise location of bridges, routes of diverted rights of way, and landscaping. As Barker (2012) has concluded ' ... local communities can, and indeed should, influence certain elements of a scheme but it needs to be done in a controlled and constructive manner and influence has to be limited to those aspects that have a local focus'. He would now favour facilitated workshops at which small groups of local residents or their representatives could provide their input, with a facilitator helping them to explore technical issues and gain a deeper understanding of what they could and could not expect to influence.

The project won permission in October 2012 when the Transport Secretary approved the Transport and Works Act order and the first trains are planned to run between Oxford and London Marylebone by 2015. Approval in 2¾ years from the formal application could be considered reasonable given the number of important stakeholder issues that needed to be addressed. However for the duration of this period, CR had to fund a team of experts (legal, environmental, town planning, engineering etc.) to support the application process at a cost of many millions of pounds.

> All of this expenditure has been 'at risk', with no certainty that approval would ever be granted. Such a costly and risky process does little to attract private investment in infrastructure'. (Barker 2012)

Developing High-Speed Rail and Localism: HS2 and Birmingham

HS2 is only the second high-speed railway in the UK. The first route linked London to the Channel Tunnel and the high speed network in Europe. HS2 is planned to link London to the north of England in two phases as illustrated schematically in Figure 9.5. Phase 1 will be a line from London to central England with a new terminal in Birmingham, and phase 2 a Y shaped configuration of lines which will link to Manchester and Leeds. A critical feature is that the proposals prioritize high speed working through London to remove the barrier to long distance movement caused by the Capital (Chapman et al. 2003). As the first major city outside London to be connected by HS2, Birmingham offers an opportunity to explore Localism in the context of already dense development and complex movement patterns.

High Speed2

.... High Speed 1 (2007)
━━━━━━ High Speed 2 (phase1)
━━━━━━ High Speed 2 (Phase2)
⋅⋅⋅⋅⋅⋅⋅⋅⋅ Channel Tunnel
━━━━━━ LGV Nord

Figure 9.5   Schematic diagram of HS2 route and phasing
Source: Drawn by Ken Cronin.

HS2 is seen locally as critical for Birmingham as it will increase capacity and support growth and a modal shift from air and road to rail. As a business city Birmingham depends upon first class transport links to attract international investors who expect high speed connections. HS2 is also critical for the long term viability of the existing transport network because the existing West Coast Main Line is currently biased to long-distance passenger services and HS2 should release capacity to expand commuter, regional and freight services. This would also enable more freight trains to operate and allow space for new regional services linking towns currently without direct rail services.

The project will have major social, economic and environmental impacts and the new HS2 stations are predicted to increase pressure on the existing transport network. While consultation with communities close to the proposed route has been undertaken no public engagement was undertaken earlier to consider strategic options although consultation has been undertaken on alternative paths within the overall strategy. As a result alternative strategic proposals are still being put forward and legal challenges have continued about environmental concerns and the lack of adequate consultation. However a government commitment to proceed with HS2 was given in 2012 and it is proposed to grant permission for the project using a Hybrid Bill. This approach allows parliament to deal with projects of strategic importance even though many of the impacts will be primarily at local level, thus normal planning and public engagement processes will be replaced by other, possibly more limited, processes.

The project is being implemented by HS2 Ltd, a company formed for the purpose, and community engagement has continued through Community Engagement Forum (CEF) meetings to identify local priorities and opportunities for community benefits. These have involved a number of individuals, local residents, local authorities, action groups, environmental and heritage organizations, and business representatives. Birmingham City Council sees its participation as critical because, while ' … HS2 Ltd is focused on mitigation of impacts … it is incumbent on the City Council and West Midlands partners to take the lead in exploring potential local improvements' (Jones 2012).

An innovative new approach that has been proposed is that the landscape context of HS2 should be considered as a catalyst for economic, physical and ecological transformation to promote greater community cohesion and economic development, spatial quality and identity. In this Wide Area Iconic Landscape Concept (Moore 2009) community benefit is an intrinsic component and not merely an afterthought, because while projects cannot be expected to mitigate all impacts, engagement beyond the operational considerations of the infrastructure can help to secure much wider benefits. While the remit of the project sponsors ' … is to build a railway and mitigate its impacts (and not with) "betterment"' (Jones 2012) this approach presents the opportunity to pursue both.

Many areas along the HS2 route have expressed significant opposition but Birmingham sees it as vital to the city. Without it continued growth in long-distance rail demand could push out local and regional services in favour of more profitable Inter City Services, hitting regional commuters, damaging local economies and stifling economic growth and job creation. Here the conflicting interests between those areas that will experience environmental impacts and those which will benefit from high speed services are clearly manifested.

Key Conclusions from the UK Context

The intentions for Localism and the Big Society as espoused by the Coalition Government in the UK suggest high ideals which if achieved have the potential to transform the relationships between people and government. The HS2 project shows the potential for railway infrastructural developments to galvanize local engagement and community development well beyond the operational level of the project. Evergreen 3 shows the value of local engagement in problem solving and enhancing detailed design decisions, HPHVCRP shows great value of volunteering and local inputs. But it is doubtful whether these potential added values can be widely achieved unless the idea of Localism is properly integrated and resourced.

There are also hazards that could frustrate the achievement of Localism. For example the Evergreen 3 project revealed the potential difficulties that may be caused by unrealistic local aspirations, limited appreciation of the needs of an efficient railway operation, and distraction by unrelated local political issues. HS2 shows the complex spatial dynamics that are involved in railway infrastructural projects and the very different costs and benefits for different places and regions. These tensions cannot be resolved at the local level, but neither do most issues need resolution at a national level. Thus there is an imperative for effective strategic planning and integration between multiple overlapping functional geographies. Without this conflicts of interest could prove very divisive between people and places.

The wide range of differently constituted local bodies being introduced in the UK, each having partial, or even overlapping, areas of spatial responsibility could result in poor coordination, especially if these bodies have uncertain or short term institutional status. These shifting institutional structures produce new geometries of power in which most responsibility for coordination depends on central government, inevitably centralizing responsibility. Lack of integration here could open loopholes to be exploited for individual, commercial or short-term gain, possibly at the expense of local places and people. This national-local polarization and reliance upon diverse and slightly ad hoc intermediate bodies appears too simplistic to tackle the complexities facing contemporary societies. It is interesting therefore those proposals for a new approach based upon the devolution of powers to city regions are already being considered, in part to address these multi-scalar issues. Thus Localism and the Big Society are work in progress and while the aspirations have great potential there are real risks that reality could fall far short of the vision, especially for railway infrastructure development where coordination and integration are so important to success.

Contemporary developments in the UK make an interesting study as the increasing emphasis on Localism presents new opportunities and challenges. Could it lead to a longer term progressive change in the way modern societies conduct their affairs, or could it be a parochial experiment that ends in failure? It has been argued that more equal societies are more stable and contented and that there is an ' ... almost unstoppable historical trend towards greater equality' (Wilkinson and Pickett 2009: 260). Could Localism present an opportunity for greater equality, or could it exacerbate differences? Hall (2012: 40) illustrates a key challenge by describing the experience of ' ... taking the east line out of Paris, Europe's highest speed railway, (when) you'll speed across France in an hour – but crossing into Germany, disconcertingly (find) this becomes a stopping train, with shoppers and students hopping on and off as you amble from station to station'.

One of the striking features of Localism in the UK are that the diverse bodies are being enabled at the local level, while the hierarchy of local and regional bodies which previously mediated tensions between scales of interest has been dismantled. This is significant as railway infrastructures and operations bear little resemblance to the institutional structures of government and depend upon complex multi-scalar relationships and sophisticated networks for success. The concept of multi-level governance having ' ... continuous negotiation among nested governments at several territorial tiers ... ' (Trip et al. 2000: 54) addresses some of this complexity but it has been rejected in the UK in favour of a much more widely 'polarized' relationship between central government and local entities and communities. Will this be able to effectively sustain the ' ... complex interplay of government agencies, non-governmental organisations and private companies' that is needed? (Ipenburg et al. 2001: 58).

Networks of actors and stakeholders are increasingly important at every scale and it is important they connect effectively with public decision-making processes. Klijn and Koppenjan (1999) have shown that successful networks develop rules of engagement that contribute to their longer term sustainability and bring the actors more closely together albeit that this closeness may perversely make it difficult for other actors to participate. Such networks have specific and often relatively narrow objectives when placed in the wider context of policy although they can become ' ... aggregated into a number of advocacy coalitions' (Sabatier 1987: 650). However could the institutional rescaling under Localism produce ' ... new constellations of governance articulated via a proliferating maze of opaque networks, fuzzy institutional arrangements, ill-defined responsibilities and ambiguous political objectives and priorities?' (Swyngedouw 2005: 2000). Will it undermine the aim of integration between urbanization, development and infrastructure?

Future Directions

Integration is fundamental for effective railway infrastructural development and as illustrated in Transit Orientated Development (TOD) (Dittmar and Ohland 2004, Hall and Ward 1998) and 'Corridor Design' (Zonneveld and Trip 2003) efficient networks and transport patterns, and walkable neighbourhoods at key nodes are critical features for future sustainable development. Thus evaluation of performance and functionality of these complex systems is critical (Chapman et al. 2003) if the impacts of 'spread' and 'backwash' (Myrdal 1957) are to be understood by decision-makers, especially for older industrial cities like Birmingham where the spread of economic activity and development from the historic centre to the regions could lead to hollowing-out and urban sprawl while backwash effects could reinforce the critical mass of centre (Chapman et al. 2003). Here ' ... the analysis and regulation of competition between growth poles ... ' may be critical to the future sustainability of settlement and transport patterns (Chapman et al. 2003). But can this be achieved if Localism is a dominant force? Would it be possible to resolve conflicts between long- and short-distance traffic; improve multi-modal integration; address competitive pressures and inequalities between places; reverse decentralization, urban sprawl, and the need to travel? (Chapman et al. 2003). Community Rail Partnerships do show how local citizens can play a valuable role at the local level but can similar approaches really become a catalyst for community engagement and environmental, economic and social change at a wider scale?

The evidence so far is that communities can play a constructive role at the local level but it is less clear how they can do so at regional, national and transnational levels. Indeed there is evidence that well-coordinated and articulate local voices may pose serious obstacles to strategic initiatives. A key issue is the time that projects can take to deliver because the views of those being consulted could be set in ' ... a very different context in 5, 10 or 15 years time' (Jones 2012). Thus keeping communities and stakeholders engaged over such a long period is a key challenge. While statutory processes do give opportunities for people to have their say this is frequently about detail after key strategic decisions have been taken. Are there other ways that local communities can contribute more creatively? Could we ' ... design social structures that foster learning' (Wenger 1998: 225) ' ... with *individuals* ... engaging in and contributing to ... their communities' and 'communities ... refining their practices' (Wenger 1998: 7). The processes of social learning employed in Seattle in the development of its Sustainability Codes (Holden 2008) show what could be done. It is not possible to explore this example in depth here but the goals adopted in the case of Seattle clearly illustrate the potential scope and ambition for social learning. The goals included:

- educating ourselves and other citizens about the values, principles and practices of sustainability
- providing a forum for dialogue about the meaning and practice of sustainability
- seeking to establish sustainability as a key criterion in planning and decision-making
- facilitating the development of cooperative partnerships in efforts to move towards sustainability
- monitoring sustainability through developing indicators of economic, cultural and environmental health
- identifying, encouraging and linking existing efforts for sustainability
- working together to build a more sustainable way of life.

Can railway infrastructural developments be conceived and developed with these ideas in mind from the beginning?

Railway infrastructural development has major strategic significance at all spatial scales, including the local, but as illustrated by the short outlines reported above it is evident that there are widely different needs, attitudes and practices internationally. Nevertheless it is clear that by linking places more effectively the fortunes of towns and cities and their users as well as their nations and international relations can be improved very significantly.

However, as revealed by the quite haphazard development of the British Rail system in its early years, there are dangers that ill-conceived investment will fail to achieve its full potential or even that the resultant railway system may become unsustainable. Any failure to integrate the functions between different parts of inevitably complex and interdependent systems, within which there are inevitable tensions between the aspirations of local interests and wider strategic goals, could significantly diminish the viability of the system overall. Much more comparative research is needed internationally, but there is already some evidence that integrated systems of spatial planning and governance can substantially assist in mediating tensions and positively assist in the effective development of railway infrastructures. For example could the experiences of China encourage a new high-speed railway development in other continents, including North America? Could the experiences of citizen engagement and local taxation in the United States enable better development and alignment of local and regional rail infrastructures in other countries? And can more active processes of involvement help to produce vibrant and diversified gateways, ecological landscapes, pedestrian friendly environments and low carbon economies?

References

Albrechts, L. 2004. Strategic (spatial) planning reexamined. *Environment and Planning B: Planning and Design*, 31(5), 743–58.

Arnstein, S.R. 1969. A ladder of citizen participation. *Journal of the Amercian Institute of Planners*, 35(4), 216–24.

Aspen Environmental Group 2006. *Sonoma-Marin Area Rail Transit Project – Final Environmental Impact Report*. San Rafael, CA: Sonoma-Marin Area Rail Transit District.

Barker, S. 2012. *Personal Correspondence*. September 2012.

Booth, P. 1996. *Controlling Development: Certainty and Discretion in Europe, the USA and Hong Kong*. London: UCL Press.

British Transport Commission. 1963. *The Reshaping of British Railways*. London: Her Majesty's Stationery Office.

Carpenter, J. and Brownhill, S. 2008. Approaches to democratic involvement: widening community engagement in the English planning system. *Planning Theory and Practice*, 9(2), 227–48.

Chapman, D. 2011. Engaging places: localizing urban design and development planning. *Journal of Urban Design*, 16(4), 511–30.

Chapman, D. and Cassar, G. 2004. Valletta. *Cities*, 21(5), 451–63.

Chapman, D., Pratt, D., Larkham, P., and Dickins, I. 2003. Concepts and definitions of corridors: evidence from England's Midlands. *Journal of Transport Geography*, 11(3), 179–91.

Cherry, G. 1974. The development of planning thought, in *The Spirit and Purpose of Planning*, edited by M.J. Bruton. London: Hutchinson.

Cheng, Y.S., Loo, B.P.Y. and Vickerman, R. 2013. *High-speed Rail Networks and Economic Integration in China and Europe*. Paper to the World Conference on Transportation Research, Track E1- Ex post Evaluation at the Macro, Regional and Project Level, Rio, 15–18 July 2013.

Cheung, P.T.Y. 2011. Civic engagement in the policy process in Hong Kong: change and continuity. *Public Administration and Development*, 31, 113–21.

City of Larkspur. 2012. *Public Workshop Summary Report: Larkspur SMART Station Area Plan – Public Workshop #1*. Greenbrae, CA: BMS Design Group and the City of Larkspur.

Collins, K. and Ison, R. 2006. *Dare we Jump off Arnstein's Ladder? Social Learning as a New Policy Paradigm*. Paper to the PATH (Participatory Approaches in Science & Technology) Conference, Edinburgh, 4–7 June 2006.

Cooke, B. and Kothari, U. 2001. *Participation: The New Tyranny?* London: Zed Books.

Cullingworth, B. and Nadin, V. 2006. *Town and Country Planning in the UK*. London: Routledge.

Department for Communities and Local Government (DCLG). 2010. *Memorandum from the Department for Communities and Local Government*. London: DCLG.

DCLG. 2011. *A Plain English Guide to the Localism*. London: DCLG.

Department for Transport (DfT). 2012. *Community Rail Development Strategy*. Available at: http://www.dft.gov.uk/topics/community-rail [accessed: 22 November 2012].

Dittmar, H. and Ohland, G. 2004. *The New Transit Town: Best Practices in Transit-Oriented Development*. Washington, D. C.: Island Press.

Docherty, I. 1999. *Making Tracks: The Politics of Local Rail Transport*. Aldershot: Ashgate.

EUROCITIES. 2004. *The Pegasus Files: a Practical Guide to Integrated Area-based Urban Planning.* Brussels: EUROCITIES.

Hall, P. 2012. Ending European rapid rail breaks. *Planning,* 1935, 40.

Hall, P. and Ward, C. 1998. *Sociable Cities: the Legacy of Ebenezer Howard.* Chichester: Wiley.

Hansen, M. 2013. Protesters oppose plans for housing near Larkspur SMART station, demonstrate disapproval at meeting. *Marin Independent Journal,* 12 March 2013.

Healy, P. 1992. Planning through debate: the communicative turn in planning theory. *Town Planning Review,* 63(2), 143–62.

Holden, M. 2008. Social learning in planning: Seattle's sustainable development codebooks. *Progress in Planning,* 69, 1–40.

Home, R. 1997. *Of Planting and Planning.* London: E & FN Spon.

Innes, J. and Gruber, D. 2001. *The Impact of Collaborative Planning on Governance Capacity. IURD Working Paper Series.* Berkeley: Institute of Urban and Regional Development, University of California, Berkeley.

Ipenburg, D., Romein, A., Trip, J.J., de Vries, J. and Zonneveld, W. 2001. *Transnational Perspectives on Megacorridors in North West Europe.* Delft: Delft University of Technology.

Jones, M. 2012. *Personal Correspondence.* September 2012.

Kells, G. 2012. Devolving transport governance. *Tripwire,* 68, 6.

Klijn, E.H. and Koppenjan, J. 1999. *Network Management and Decision-making in Networks: A multi-actor Approach to Governance,* NIG Working Papers, Enschede: University of Twente.

Lippmann, W. 1922. *Public Opinion.* New York: Harcourt Brace Jovanovich.

Loo, B.P.Y. and Liu, K. 2005. A geographical analysis of potential railway load centers in China. *Professional Geographer,* 57(4), 558–79.

Leung, C.K. 1980. *China: Railway Patterns and National Goals.* Chicago: University of Chicago.

Moore, K. 2009. *Overlooking the Visual: Demystifying the Art of Design.* London: Routledge.

Myrdal, G. 1957. *Economic Theory and Under-developed Regions.* London: Duckworth.

Nelson, J. 2011. Devolution. *Passenger Transport,* 15 September.

Rose, M. 2012. *Personal Correspondence.* July 2012.

Sabatier, P. 1987. Knowledge, policy-orientated learning and policy change – an advocacy coalition framework. *Science Communication,* 8(4), 649–92.

Secretary of State for Transport. 2012. *Reforming our Railways: Putting the Customer First.* London: The Stationery Office.

Simmons, J. 1968. *The Railways of Britain.* London: Macmillan.

SRA. 2004. *Community Rail Development Strategy.* London: Strategic Rail Authority.

Swyngedouw, E. 2005. Governance innovation and the citizen: the Janus face of Governance-Beyond-the-State. *Urban Studies,* 42(11), 1991–2006.

Tanner, M.S. 2004. China rethinks unrest. *The Washington Quarterly,* 27(3), 137–56.

Trip, J.J., Romein, A. and de Vries, J. 2000. *Background Report and Theoretical Framework: Corridesign.* Delft: Delft University of Technology.

U.S. Department of Transportation (US DOT). 2014. *National Transportation Statistics.* Washington, D. C.: Research and Innovative Technology Administration, Bureau of Transportation Statistics.

Ward, S.V. 2000. Re-examining the international diffusion of planning, in *Urban Planning in a Changing World: The Twentieth Century Experience,* edited by R. Freestone. London: E & FN Spon, 40–55.

Wenger, E. 1998. *Communities of Practice: Learning, Meaning, and Identity.* Cambridge: Cambridge University Press.

Wilkinson, R. and Pickett, K. 2009. *The Spirit Level: Why More Equal Societies Almost Always Do Better.* London: Penguin.

Zonneveld, W. and Trip, J. 2003. *Megacorridors in North West Europe: Investigating a New Transnational Planning Concept.* Delft: DUP Science.

Chapter 10
Regional and Local Line Rail Freight Transport in North America

John C. Spychalski

Operation of rail freight service in North America, measured by line (route) length and traffic volume, is concentrated on the systems of two railway companies in Canada, two in Mexico, and seven in the United States. Within the full structure of the North American railway network, the systems of these 11 carriers are dominant but not exclusive. Feeding shipments into and delivering shipments from the 11 are regional and local railways ranging from a half-dozen in Mexico to more than 30 in Canada and 558 in the US (AAR 2011, Harris and Tee 2010). This chapter examines conditions that have driven the creation and evolution of regional and local railways and shaped their operational and commercial policies, practices, and performance, primarily onward from the 1970s.

Local and Regional Railways: Defined Characteristics

Before going further, characteristics commonly used to distinguish regional and local railways from the 11 dominant carriers need to be noted. The Surface Transportation Board (STB), the US federal agency responsible for administering economic regulation of the railway industry, designates three classes of freight railways, based on operating revenue. These designations are commonly applied to railway companies domiciled in Canada and Mexico as well as those based in the US. The thresholds for these classes are adjusted annually for inflation. In 2010, they were US$398.7 million or more for Class I carriers; US$31.9 million or more and below US$398.7 million for Class II carriers, and less than US$31.9 million for Class III carriers. Carriers in Class II are commonly identified as regional, and those in Class III as local or short line. A combination of distance and revenue is also used as a definitional mark. The Association of American Railroads, the trade association for Class I carriers, specifies that a regional railway as distinguished from a local railway must have a length of at least 563 km (i.e., km of line/route as distinguished from km of track) and/or earning annual revenues between US$40 million and the Class I threshold of US$398.7 million. Still another distinction is between 'line-haul' and 'switching and terminal' railways. Strictly defined, a line-haul carrier's system, whether classified as Class II regional or Class III local, consists of track designated as line km that extends between two or more rail yards or terminals. Switching carriers serve as providers of pick-up and delivery service by moving rail shipments over short distances between private sidings of rail freight shippers and consignees and connections with line-haul rail carriers. In addition, some provide intra-plant switching service for large volume users of rail service. Terminal railways concentrate largely or exclusively on operation of freight marshalling (classification) yards and related support services (e.g., inspection and refuelling of locomotives and inspection and minor repair of freight rolling stock) for line-haul railways. In practice, functional distinction between these categories is blurred. Regional and local railways often provide services that fall within two or more of the categories (ASLRRA 2012, AAR 2011).

Historical Origins

Small local short-distance line-haul railways were the first type to appear during the initial phase of North American railway development circa 1827–1850. North America's first rail common-carrier (public service), the Baltimore and Ohio Railroad, was incorporated in 1827 and began operation on 21 km of track in 1830. However, from the outset, the B & O's founders envisaged building a much longer-distance main line that would link the city of Baltimore with the Ohio River. Ultimately, the B & O built west all the way to Chicago and St. Louis (Stover 1987). In contrast, the present-day link between Buffalo and Albany, New York within CSX Transportation's 33,789 km Class I rail system first came into existence piecemeal between 1830 and the early 1840s with the founding of seven different railroad companies. Apparently more by fortuitous happenstance than initial intent of most of their founders, the lines of each of the seven were built within an overall end-to-end alignment. This alignment, coupled with response to growing demand for longer-distance rail freight (and passenger) service, readily enabled consolidation of the seven lines under ownership and operation by a single company in 1853 (Harlow 1947). Both similar and dissimilar patterns of structural evolution have been replicated many times down through the now more than 160 year-long existence of the North American railway industry. The systems of the relatively few Class I carriers that exist today are the products of recurring consolidation of hundreds of smaller railways, both local and regional. Despite this evolutionary trend however, many short-distance rail firms, including some established in the nineteenth century, have either remained in existence under their own identity or have come and gone without acquisition by a larger rail firm (Locklin 1960, Levine et al. 1982, Saunders 2001).

1976–1980 and Beyond: Into a New Phase of Development within a Changing Environment

The period between 1976 and 1980 marked the start of a significant turning point in the evolution of local and regional line-haul railways, primarily in the US but also to lesser degrees in Canada and Mexico. At the end of 1980, approximately 240 local and regional line-haul railways were in operation in the US. By the end of 2010, the total number in existence had more than doubled to 558. Included within that total were 537 local carriers operating 50,838 km of line, and 21 regional carriers operating 16,744 km of line. Added together, the 67,582 line km operated by local and regional carriers constitute approximately 30 per cent of the total km of line (222,968) in operation in the US in 2010 (ASLRRA 2012, AAR 2011).

Comprehensive time-series data and supporting information for participation in total North American rail freight shipments by local and regional railways do not exist. However, some insight is provided by a study of all rail shipments made between July 1, 2005 and June 30, 2006. The study revealed that about 25 per cent of all rail shipments moved at least part of their journeys on a local or regional line, and also that local and regional carriers ' … participated in more than 40 per cent of all shipments other than coal and intermodal' (ASLRRA 2012). These findings support the view that local and regional railways collectively provide a wide array of customers with access to the Class I railway network. Simultaneously the findings indicate that local and regional railways collectively provide Class I railways with access to a substantial number of customers and thus also to traffic and revenue that they would not otherwise obtain. The following facts offer a general sense of the spatial reach of this access capability: In the US, local and regional carriers presently serve points in 49 states and account for approximately 40 per cent (line/route kilometres) of the national network (ASLRRA 2012). In Canada, they operate in seven provinces and comprise almost 20 per cent of the national network (Harris and Tee 2010, Railway Association of Canada 2011). In Mexico, they operate almost 30 per cent of the national network within 14 states (Harris and Tee 2010).

This dramatic upsurge in the local and regional railway sector stemmed from several landmark changes in the transport political and business environment. Foremost among the changes was decline, onward from 1945, in the financial performance and condition of the railway industry taken as a whole. Causes of the decline included increasingly intense and pervasive (by length-of-haul, points served, and type of commodity moved) competition from other modes of transport operating on government-funded infrastructure, excessive labour costs, heavy taxation of railway land and equipment, severe regulatory constraints on commercial freedom, and managerial deficiencies internal to railway companies. The decline culminated with bankruptcies of major railway companies. Most notable was that of the Penn Central Transportation Company (PC), in 1971. Soon thereafter, bankruptcy also befell most of the other rail carriers that competed and connected with PC in the region bounded by Chicago and St. Louis in the Midwest, the Ohio and Potomac Rivers on the south, and the Atlantic Coast and New England in the Northeast. Near the close of the 1970s, two more – Chicago Rock Island & Pacific (Rock Island), and Chicago, Milwaukee, St. Paul & Pacific (Milwaukee Road), prominent in length but financially the weakest of those operating in Midwestern and western states, also entered bankruptcy (Gallamore 1999, Healy 1985, Spychalski 1997a).

These large corporate failures coupled with rising concern about the future viability of still-solvent railways gave impetus to liberalization of rail firms' commercial behaviour. In the US, significant reductions in the scope of economic regulation of railways were made by passage of the Railroad Revitalization and Regulatory Reform Act (3R Act) (1976), the Staggers Rail Act (1980), and the Northeast Rail Services Act (NERSA) (1981). In Canada, such reductions occurred with passage of the National Transportation Act (1987) and the Canada Transportation Act (1996). In some instances, moves toward liberalization were also accomplished by changes in the administration of established regulatory law. Additionally, railway privatization in Canada and Mexico made achievement of unsubsidized financial and higher-quality freight service performance objectives rather than fulfilment of socio-political purposes the primary driver of railway managerial action (Perrit et al. 1983, Spychalski 1997b, Canada Transportation Act 1996).

Primary Catalysts for Growth in Regional and Local Line Formation

Deregulation and privatization enabled Class I railways to pursue improvement of their financial performance and condition by extensive rationalization of their network operating patterns, asset capital and maintenance costs, and labour costs. A liberalization action of great importance for driving the surge in formation of regional and local line formations in the US during the 1980s was the exemption of Class I railways from having to provide income protection payments to union-represented employees as a condition for sale of a light-density line (Wilner 1991). Similarly, the Supreme Court of Canada ruled that sale of track to a new operator was not subject to the successor rights provision in Canada's federal labour code that compels new owners of firms in other industries to preserve labour agreements entered into by previous owners. The court accepted the argument that a sale of track ' ... to a new operator was covered by provincial rather than federal law ... ' (Freudmann and Watson 1996). Since only British Columbia and Saskatchewan had successor rights laws in effect, spatial applicability of the incentive provided by the court's ruling was significant.

For Class I railways, transfer of underperforming line assets to regional and local railways offered a potentially and often virtually assured means for continuing to obtain a portion of the revenues derived from traffic originating and terminating on such lines. Regional and local carriers could and can perform shorter-distance and/or lighter-density line-haul and shunting movements profitably because they typically possess labour cost advantages that cannot be obtained easily if at all under the work rule and compensation terms prevalent in Class I railways' labour agreements. Strength in retention of existing traffic and development of new sources of traffic and revenue is another advantage of regional and local lines' business conduct. The scope and scale of their service territories and train operations enables the building and maintenance of relationships with small and medium sized customers in ways for which Class I railways lack incentive and strong capability (Due 1984, 1987, Rund 2006).

Accomplishing Local and Regional Formation: Mechanisms and Initiatives

Acquisition for continuing (or reinstatement of) operation of track cast off by rationalization and restructuring of Class I rail systems posed (and continues to pose) challenges and opportunities for private sector investors, rail service-dependent industrial and commercial firms, and public sector officials at local, state/provincial, and federal levels. While the goal of preserving operation of rail service was (and presumably still is) common among actors in each of these three categories, the primary motivation for doing so differs between them.

Lines Formed Exclusively or Largely by Private Sector Investor Initiatives and Resources

Why have private investors willingly and even enthusiastically acquired lines that had been seen as either unprofitable or insufficiently profitable by a former Class I owner? In theory, a private sector investor obviously would do so only on expectation of being able to earn an acceptable rate of return on the amount of investment required to (1) acquire the line, (2) fund whatever rehabilitation or upgrading track and related rail infrastructure that might be required, and (3) put in place the managerial and other human resources and physical assets needed for business operation. In some instances, this appears to have been the only motivation. In other instances, additional inducements have also had influence. A need for job preservation stemming from shrinkage of employment on downsized Class I railways and/or the desire to 'be one's own boss', and/or simply wanting to remain in the railway industry out of keen interest in the nature of the work, have drawn persons from operating, middle management, and even senior executive levels on Class I carriers to participate in new local and regional rail ventures. Some start-up leaders were persons employed in state rail planning work who possessed entrepreneurial instincts and saw promising opportunities.

A few new start-ups were begun by 'railfans not otherwise qualified' – i.e., persons having strong affinity for the palpable traits of railway equipment, infrastructure, and operations, but with little or no management expertise in the railway industry (Due 1984).

Lines Formed by Rail Service Users

Ownership of common carrier (public service) local and regional railways by non-transport firms is not a new phenomenon. More than a century ago, companies in the steel, aluminium, mining, and forest products industries began establishing subsidiaries to construct and operate line-haul rail lines intended primarily but not exclusively for fulfillment of their own high-volume freight transport requirements. The incentive for doing so was obvious when an existing Class I carrier was unable or unwilling to commit the resources required for new line construction. However, doing so could also enable access to more than one Class I line-haul railway, thereby enhancing the local rail line shipper-owner's bargaining power in obtaining more favourable commercial terms from Class I lines. A classic historic case in point was the Elgin, Joliet & Eastern Railway (the J), formerly owned by a subsidiary of the United States Steel Corporation (USS). The J's line-haul route formed an arc encircling the outer reaches of the Chicago area, and featured connections with all Class I railways entering Chicago. USS steel works were dominant users of the J's service. However, the J also served numerous other shippers located along its route and functioned as an intermediate connecting railway for the interchange (exchange) of car load (wagon load) and full train-load consignments between its various Class I connectors (Harris and Tee 2010).

New construction of shipper-owned line-haul rail lines became a rarity during the latter half of the twentieth century. However, shipper-consignee involvement in the start-up of local railways on lines already in existence surged in number during the 1980s, in the wake of rationalization actions by Class I carriers. In some instances, shippers acquired threatened lines by means of outright cash purchase from Class I railways, and either contracted out operation of the service to an independent local-line rail operating firm or established a wholly-owned subsidiary or unit within their own business organization to operate the service. Their primary motivation for choosing either of these two approaches was preservation of transport service critical to continued economic viability of facilities essential to performance of their own business functions. In essence, profit per se from operation of the service on a line thus preserved was subordinate; the cost of operating and maintaining the line was viewed as an additional unavoidable cost of doing business in non-rail fields ranging from mining and raw material processing to manufacturing (Due 1984, Levine et al. 1982).

Lines Formed by Local and State Governments

Large portions of the total mileage of lines made available for disposal by Class I railways in the years immediately preceding and following 1980 were not attractive for purchase by private sector parties. Their existing and prospective levels of traffic yielded earnings seen as insufficient for justifying any level of investment required to acquire, upgrade, and maintain them for continued operation. Hence, the only alternative to their abandonment was purchase, either directly by municipalities or states, or by creation of quasi-independent public authorities funded with grants from local, state, and federal sources. Proclivity for such public sector intervention to acquire and preserve threatened lines is driven fundamentally by the complex of underlying conditions that shape (1) political will of elected officials, (2) vision of such officials and their professional support staff toward future as well as existing transport service needs and the potential role of rail in helping to meet those needs, and (3) public funding capability.

These conditions vary over time within and between individual states (provinces) and municipalities. State and local officials generally recognize the need for maintenance and improvement of local and regional road transport infrastructure. However, they often tend to view rail freight service as a business-to-business activity exclusive to the private sector. Also, efforts to restore to frequent use lines that have become little-used or dormant although still physically intact often arouse opposition from adjacent land owners and/ or from environmental and recreational interest groups that prefer either 'reversion of the track to nature' or conversion to hiking/cycling trails. Conversely, on the positive side, political acceptance of an activist role for government in preserving rail infrastructure and service thereon has in some localities been made possible by private sector influence of public policy formulation, and by augmenting public funds with private sector loans and contributions. Use of shipper/consignee bargaining power can also assist a public agency by reducing the cost of acquiring track from a Class I railway. In one example, a large rail freight shipper ' ... used its leverage to persuade Conrail to drop its initial asking price by about $1 million ... ' for a line that a newly-formed public rail authority was negotiating to buy from Conrail (NADO Research Foundation 2008).

Institutional Structure: Ownership and Operation

The structure for ownership and operation of local and regional railways in North America is heterogeneous. An enumerated view of its distinctive components follows.

First: Private sector ownership of service operation within a single area on a single system, on infrastructure (track and terminals) owned at least in part by the service operator. A prime specimen within this 'stand-alone' category is the Providence & Worcester Railroad Company, which began operation on a 69 km line that it owns between its namesake cities, and has grown to an 877 km system in central and southern New England, providing freight service by means of trackage (running) rights on lines operated primarily for passenger service by Amtrak and Metro-North Railroad (Harris and Tee 2010).

Second: Private sector holding company (shares either closely held or publicly traded) with subsidiaries operating service at two or more locations on track owned by the operating subsidiary and/or by either another railway company, a public authority, or a department of a state or local governmental unit (see Table 10.1). The holding company phenomenon receives further attention in a later section.

Third: Private sector local rail line operator (either a 'stand alone' entity or a subsidiary of a local/regional railway holding company) providing service on track leased from a Class I railway owner. A note on this point: Class I railways have sold much unwanted track to local short lines by means of either a negotiated selling price or competitive bidding. However, some have determined that lease rather than sale of such lines offers the best chance for enabling the local line operator to become economically viable and, by so doing, prevent total loss of revenue from shipments originated and terminated on the local lines (The Thoroughbred). Additionally, retention of underlying ownership of leased-out track would likely ease a return to operation by the Class I lessor if warranted in future by a favourable change in revenue conditions.

Table 10.1   Prominent regional/local railway holding companies

Company Name	No. of Operating Subsidiaries	Total km of Line Operated (All Subsidiaries, Approximate)	Share Capital Ownership	
			Privately Held	Publicly Traded
Anacostia & Pacific Company, Inc.	6	1,296	X	
Genessee Valley Transportation Company, Inc.	4	482	X	
Genesee & Wyoming, Inc.*	105	21,834		X
Iowa Pacific Holdings, Inc.	9	830		
OmniTRAX, Inc.	17	4,089	X	
Patriot Rail Corporation	6	534	X	
Pinsley Railroad Company	5	333	X	
Pioneer Railcorp.	18	938		X
Railroad Development Corporation*	1	1,106	X	
Rio Grande Pacific Corporation	4	1,098	X	
R.J. Corman Railroad Group	12	1,286	X	
Transtar, Inc.	7	600	X	
Vermont Rail System	5	370	X	
Watco Companies, Inc.	22	2,500	X	
Totals:	221	37,296	11	2

Note: * Company also holds investments in regional and/or local railways outside North America.
Source: Author's compilation of data extracted from Harris and Tee 2010, and web sites and annual reports of companies listed.

Fourth: Private sector company providing service and maintenance and renewal of infrastructure on property obtained under long-term concession from a national government (in Mexico, e.g., Linea Coahuila Durango SA de CV [CFM], operator of secondary lines in the states of Chihuahua, Coahuila, Durango, and Zacatecas).

Fifth: Private sector company operating service on track and related infrastructure components owned largely or exclusively by either a quasi-independent public authority, or directly by a state or municipality. An example is the North Shore Railroad System (NSHR), which operates local line-haul and switching service on ex-Conrail lines owned by the SEDA-COG Joint Rail Authority at five different locations in central Pennsylvania (NADO Research Foundation 2008).

Sixth: Public sector entity (public authority, province, state or municipality) ownership and operation – e.g., (1) in the US, (a) the South Carolina Division of Public Railways, which owns and operates one line-haul local railway and two switching railways serving state port authority-owned ocean terminals, and (b) the Alaska Railroad, a quasi-public corporation owned by the State of Alaska which operates a 750 km-long main line; and (2) in Canada, the provincially-owned Ontario Northland, operator of a 1,086 km rail system serving a sparsely-populated sector in eastern Ontario (Harris and Tee 2010).

Seventh: Ownership in whole or in part by one or more Class I railways. Two contemporary examples in this category are (1) the Indiana Rail Road Company, a 177 route-km line-haul carrier in the states of Indiana and Illinois in which CSX holds 85 per cent of the share capital (Rund 2006); and (2) the Indiana Harbor Belt Railroad, an 87 route-km Chicago-area terminal, switching (shunting) and inter-railway traffic interchange facilitator in which Class I carriers CSX and Norfolk Southern each own a 25.5 per cent share, and Canadian Pacific owns 49 per cent.

Performance Determinants: Strengths, Weaknesses, Opportunities, and Threats

Taken at face, the post-1976 upsurge in the total population of regional and local railways mirrors success. However, as with almost all sectors of business that have experienced boom-level growth of entry by new firms, the evolutionary fabric of the regional and local railway sector has been (and continues to be) coloured by a mix of strength-driven successes, weakness-driven failures, and a changing array of opportunities and threats. A synopsis of this mix is presented in Table 10.2 within the context of a SWOT analysis framework. The synopsis is based on (1) substantial experience-based qualitative evidence presented in several survey- and case-based studies and in railway trade publications (see, e.g., Due 1984, Due et al. 2002, Hemphill 2004, NADO Research Foundation 2008, Rockey 1987, Rund 2006, Bowen 2012, Vantuono 2012), and (2) the results of several efforts to measure statistically the relative significance of conditions and actions affecting success and failure (e.g., Wolfe 1988, 1989a, 1989b, Grim and Sapienza 1993).

Performance Determinants: Discussion

Of the strengths identified in Table 10.2, payment of a reasonable purchase price for track and related infrastructure required to establish (or expand) either a regional or local railway merits being listed first, given the truism that the price paid (plus all additional expenditures required for provision of adequate customer service and all other basic business expenses) must not exceed whatever limit is required for survival as a going concern. Executives who have achieved success with local and regional railway ventures stress that this limit should be set by a conservative estimate of traffic volume, revenue and cash flow. Experience with regional and local railway formation has demonstrated that the weakness of paying an excessive purchase price as a result of excessive optimism in making such estimates generally results in venture failure and either cessation of service or sale of the railway's assets to a successor entity at a price in closer alignment with the intrinsic earning power (cash flow generation) of the line (Babcock et al. 1994).

Initial and future capital and operating expenses per km of railway line can vary significantly, depending on a diverse array of cost determinants, including gradient, curvature, climate, roadbed drainage and soil conditions, locomotive and wagon axle weights, and train operating speeds. Thus, whether a specific level of traffic density per km of line is either a strength or weakness depends on the revenue and hence cash flow that the traffic generates per km of line, and the capital and operating costs specific to the segment

Table 10.2   Determinants of performance for regional and local railways

STRENGTHS	WEAKNESSES
• Reasonable purchase price for track and related infrastructure.	• Excessive purchase price for track and related infrastructure.
• Adequate extant and prospective traffic density and revenue level.	• Inadequate extant and/or prospective traffic and revenue levels.
• Diversified traffic and revenue base.	• Dependence on one or very few shippers/ consignees and commodity types.
• Quality, depth and breadth of human resource base.	• Inadequate human resource base. Inflexible labour agreement provisions.
• Flexibility in use of operating, mechanical, and maintenance personnel.	• Hostile work environment.
• Constructive employee relations policies.	• Inability to acquire financial capital in amounts and on terms required.
• Adequate financial capital for required commitment conditions.	• Lack of access to federal, state, and/or local government assistance.
• Access to federal, state, and/or local government assistance.	• Inability to obtain required insurance coverage.
• Availability of required insurance coverage.	• Inadequate track and related infrastructure.
• Adequate track and related infrastructure.	• Captive to one connecting rail carrier.
• Access to more than one connecting rail carrier.	• Inadequate service by connecting railway on interchange of traffic.
• Adequate service from connecting railways on interchange of traffic.	• Insufficient cooperation from Class I connectors on retention and development of traffic.
• Constructive sales and marketing relationships with connecting Class I railways.	• Inability to withstand economic recessions.
• Ability to withstand economic recessions.	• Inability to fund costs imposed by extraordinary forces of nature.
• Ability to fund costs imposed by extraordinary forces of nature.	

OPPORTUNITIES	THREATS
• Return of manufacturing with rail service potential to North America from elsewhere.	• De-emphasis of wagon-load vis-à-vis intermodal and train-load traffic by connecting Class I railways.
• Provision of originating and terminating service for long-haul wagon-load traffic captured from road haulers by Class I railways and/or obtained from new sources.	• Changes in environmental regulations that impede freight traffic retention and development.
	• Public hostility toward service restoration on dormant lines and construction of new lines.
• Growth in domestic energy development, production, and uses.	• Fiscal constraint-driven loss of government assistance for infrastructure renewal.
• Capacity and network limitations of competing transport modes.	• Cost of compliance with unfunded government safety mandates – e.g., installation of positive train control.

of line being operated. In numerous instances, track and other infrastructure components on lines spun off by Class I railways were in poor physical condition. This made substantial expenditures for capital asset renewal an almost immediate necessity for efficient and safe operation by the regional or local carrier (e.g., Rund 2006).

A published comprehensive accounting of the fate of all local and regional railways that were in existence in 1980, together with those formed between that year and 2012, does not exist. Also, financial data and detailed qualitative information for many of the companies involved cannot be accessed publicly. It thus is not possible to readily obtain a full detailed view of the success/failure experience in this sector of the North American railway industry with time-series-based measures such as:

1. survival rates for companies;
2. percentage of track continued in service up to the present day versus track abandoned and removed; and
3. profitability, liquidity, and solvency of companies taken in the aggregate.

However, available information does enable several observations about the sector's post-1980 evolution.

The formation of local and regional carriers on track sold by Class I railways stood at its highest level between 1980 and the mid-1990s. Initially, many of the sales were made to either a single buyer or a small group of investors. However, as the 1980s wore on, proliferation in the number of lines offered for sale drew increasing interest from holding companies led by executives with strong rail management expertise, established relationships with Class I railways, and the critical practical skills required to start up operation of service quickly or even seamlessly upon cessation of operation of the line by the Class I seller. Second, the stock of light-density Class I-owned lines available for sale naturally dwindled greatly in the wake of the many sales made during the 1980s. This, coupled with labour cost-saving reductions in train operating crew sizes that Class I carriers were finally able to achieve after many years of struggle, and emergence of various difficulties in relationships between Class I officials and officials of some of the relatively new local lines, brought Class I line sales to almost a standstill in the mid-1990s (Hemphill 2004, Due et al. 2002). Formations have resumed since then, albeit at a modest level in comparison with those of the immediate post-1980 boom years.

Leading causes of failure have included loss of all traffic from a dominant or sole customer, inability to fund needed renewal of track and/or bridges and other infrastructure components damaged or destroyed by acts of nature, and inept management. In some instances, failure resulted in permanent cessation of service and lifting of track, whilst others were followed by preservation of track and continuation of service under a new owner. For firms categorized as successful, performance has ranged from survival at a financially marginal level to very strong (e.g., Murray 2013, Danneman 2013, Rund 2006).

As noted previously, numerous local and regional rail lines that began operation as stand-alone independent entities have been acquired by holding companies (Table 10.1). Conditions driving the move toward holding company ownership appear to include:

1. desire of the original owner or owners to retire from active business management and shift their personal financial capital to other investment alternatives;
2. greater depth and breadth of managerial and technical support staff; and

3.   strengthening of bargaining power in relations with Class I railways, suppliers of material and equipment, and customers.

Another phenomenon involving change in ownership structure is acquisition by a Class I railway of a line previously sold, either by the same or a different Class I carrier, to a local or regional rail firm. In some instances, a return to Class I ownership has been driven by strategic network-building initiatives. A leading example is acquisition of a regional carrier, Wisconsin Central Transportation Company (WCT), by the Canadian National Railway (CN). This gave CN a link between the western portion of its network and Chicago, Illinois, a location that CN already served with links extending in a southwesterly direction from Ontario, and northward from New Orleans, Louisiana. Subsequently, CN also purchased the aforementioned local Elgin, Joliet & Eastern Railway. The arc of the J's route around the outer edge of the Chicago metropolitan area gave CN a less congested route for moving traffic more efficiently to and from connections with both its own lines and other railways in the Chicago area. In other instances, relief from capacity constraints resulting from traffic growth has moved Class I railways to reacquire lines that they formerly owned. A case in point is BNSF Railway's buy-back of a line in the state of Washington that it had sold to a local railway. By doing so, BNSF regained a second route into the Pacific Northwest coastal area to accommodate growth in traffic that had reached levels thought to be unachievable when the line was sold.

Stakeholders in the local and regional railway sector are presently confronted by a variety of significant threats. Arguably of greatest significance, measured in terms of both capital and maintenance expenditure requirements and sustentation of revenue-generation capability, are two essential infrastructure-related matters. First is upgrading of the quality and load-bearing capacity of track and bridge structures to accommodate higher train operating speeds and increases in the weight-carrying load capacity of freight cars from the former standard of 263,000 lbs. (119,297 kg) to 286,000 lbs. (129,730 kg), and in some instances, to 315,000 lbs. (142,884 kg). This need stems from the fact, noted previously, that many of the lines transferred to the local railway sector by Class I carriers had been left to decline into poor and/or functionally obsolete condition by their former Class I owners due to light-density traffic and revenue levels. For local and regional railways in the US, a second pressing infrastructure need is compliance with federal government-mandated (but *not* government-funded) installation of Positive Train Control (PTC) technology on lines carrying toxic and hazardous commodities and/or passengers. The burden for such compliance appears to exceed what can be sustained solely by operating revenues in the local and regional railway sector taken as a whole. This poses the need for supplemental support with funds from external public sector sources. Some states have modest local railway capital assistance grant programmes in place that can be drawn upon. Existing sources for federal funding assistance are limited to a loan programme administered by the Federal Railroad Administration and by a rail track maintenance tax credit provision (Hemphill 2004).

Several threats to revenue generation by local and regional railways have emerged and/ or grown in significance in recent years. One is dissonance with some (not all) connecting Class I railways over the optimum length of trains for movement of bulk commodities such as grain and coal. A case in point is the imposition by a US Class I carrier of large minimum shipment-size requirements, such as 110 cars (wagons), for movements of corn and wheat. Confinement of such movements to full trainloads (moving directly between loading and unloading points without intermediate shunting) enables fuller realization of economies of scale at the train operating unit level, lower terminal operating and capital costs, and possibly also, greater economies of density from more intensive utilization of available track capacity. However, the Class I carrier's economic gain obviously will be achieved at the cost of an economic loss to a connecting grain-carrying local railway if the local line's customers' logistics conditions prohibit aggregation of their grain shipments into unit trains for hand-off to the Class I carrier and delivery to a single consignee and a single destination. Further, loss of grain traffic revenue could impair adequate coverage of a local railway's track and bridge maintenance and renewal costs and thus threaten loss of rail service for shippers of other types of products. Elimination of a local railway as a gathering carrier for single and small multiple-car (wagon) grain shipments could also occasion negative externalities. Harvested grain that previously moved from farms to small and medium-capacity grain elevators served by the local railway would instead move longer distances by truck to large-volume grain elevators capable of loading trainload-size grain shipments, thus triggering increases in road congestion and road infrastructure costs.

Another traffic and revenue generation threat is posed by acceleration of Class I railways' efforts to grow intermodal traffic by means of improvements in the speed and consistency of transit time and increases in the location, size, and technological features of intermodal terminals. Line-haul movement of a container or trailer on a Class I railway, preceded and followed by truck movement to and from the Class I carrier's intermodal terminals, presents a competitive alternative to all-rail movements that begin or end their journeys on a local or regional railway.

An issue that straddles the boundary between a weakness and a threat is posed by contractual terms for transfer of ownership (or operation under lease) of a line from a Class I railway to a regional or local railway that prohibit the regional or local carrier from interchanging freight traffic with any railway other than the Class I seller/lessor, even if a track connection with another railway is in place. This captivity provision obviously serves the business interest of the Class I seller/lessor by enabling it to retain all revenue from all traffic moved to and from the connecting regional or local carrier, and prevent erosion of its pricing power over such interchange traffic. The provision also provides the Class I carrier with an incentive to sell or lease out operation of a marginal line rather than letting it deteriorate toward closure. However, captivity to a single provider of connecting service precludes access to alternative price and service quality offerings from one or more other Class I railways that might be more advantageous for customers of the regional or local carrier. Also, it denies the regional or local carrier and its customers a means for counteracting actions by the Class I carrier that would impact negatively on the retention, development, and economic viability of interchange traffic (Massa 2001).

A revenue-generating strength of local and regional railways formed in the first one to two decades after 1980 was 'being close to the customer'. That is, having personnel at both senior and subordinate levels living and working in the areas served has enabled strong knowledge of shippers' transport service needs and 'short chains of command' for responding promptly and flexibly to those needs and for successful pursuit of new rail business opportunities (ASLRRA 2012). However, growing concentration of local and regional lines under holding company ownership (Table 10.1) poses the challenge of *not* letting authority, responsibility, and capability for effective business development and customer service (as has typically been manifested by managers of stand-alone local lines) be weakened or lost by immersion in the centralized corporate bureaucracy of a parent company. A related additional challenge is delineation and application of criteria for measuring the performance of resident managers of holding company-owned local lines that will strike a proper balance between minimization of operating and maintenance costs on the one hand, and effectiveness of revenue retention and development actions on the other.

Standing in contrast to the just-mentioned threats and others are numerous successful grasps of opportunities for maintaining and increasing traffic and revenue generation. Many, too great in number to cite completely, have been reported in railway industry trade news media and other sources over time (see, e.g., Rund 2006, NADO Research Foundation 2008, Bowen 2012, 2013, Blanchard 2009a, 2009b, 2012, Frailey 2012, Vantuono 2012). These successes helped local and regional railway freight revenue grow 34 per cent, from US$2.815 billion to US$3.775 billion, between 2002 and 2006. Going forward from 2006, the Great Recession that began in 2007 caused a 12.87 per cent decline to US$3.289 billion in 2010. That this decline still left revenue 16.83 per cent above that earned in 2002 indicates substantial durability in the earning power of local and regional carriers (ASLRRA 2012). Such strength in the face of recessionary economic conditions is remarkable, given that general merchandise freight, rather than finished motor vehicles, coal, and intermodal movements, dominate the aggregate local and regional railway traffic base. It is also remarkable given that the traffic bases of most individual local and regional lines are dominated by very few customers and very few types of commodities (ASLRRA 2012).

Despite their concentrated traffic bases, local and regional carriers often make important economic contributions to the areas that they serve by providing customers in those areas with transport service at levels of cost and load size-carrying capability that road freight operators cannot match. Discontinuance of railway freight service in such a situation would force closure of a rail customer's facility, termination of employment at the facility, and hence also a reduction in economic strength within the locale of the facility. Market place dynamics naturally ensure a continuum of turnover at varying rates over time among the more than 10,000 customers that are collectively served by North American local and regional railways. On the positive side of this turnover, case studies reveal successes in developing new sources of traffic to offset losses from closures of manufacturing plants and distribution centres, and depletion of mines, quarries, and other sources of traffic for which rail service is essential and well-suited (NADO Research Foundation 2008). Also, the average local and regional railway reportedly ' ... secured 1.3 new customers from 2009 to 2010 and expected to serve 3.2 customers between 2011 and 2012' (ASLRRA 2012).

On occasion, opportunities for new sources of significant increments in rail freight traffic and revenue arise without scant evidence in advance of their emergence and growth. Dramatic contemporary cases in point involve ethanol production and distribution, Marcellus Shale natural gas exploration and development, and Bakken Shale crude oil exploration and distribution. Since 2009, both Class I railways and at least 15 local and regional railways have benefited strongly from movements of equipment and materials required for the support of horizontal drilling and hydraulic fracturing of sedimentary rock formations to tap trapped deposits of natural gas and crude oil. Limitations in the capacity and geographic coverage of crude oil-carrying pipelines have presented lucrative opportunities for both Class I and regional and local railways in the US and Canada. Reportedly, 97,135 wagon loads of crude oil moved by rail in the first quarter of 2013, which is 166 per cent more than in the first quarter of 2012, and 922 per cent more than what was carried within all of 2008 (Sneider 2011, Stagl 2013, Bowen 2013, Phillips and Loder 2013).

Summary and Conclusions

Extensive rationalization of Class I railway systems during the last quarter of the twentieth century created the foundation for formation of a majority of today's local and regional railways within the North American railway network. Thousands of kilometres of line segments deemed uneconomic for retention were shed as their Class I owners exercised market-driven commercial freedom granted by curtailment of economic regulation in the US and Canada and privatization of national government-owned railways in Canada and Mexico. Establishment of new local and regional railway lines burgeoned between the end of the 1970s and the mid-1990s. Some were founded by entrepreneurs and investor groups with the expectation of achieving profitable operation at a level commensurate with both the earning of an acceptable return on invested capital and full sustainment of funding requirements for capital asset renewal and whatever capacity expansion might be required to accommodate traffic growth. Others were acquired by non-transport businesses as a cost of doing business to preserve access to the Class I railway network for movement of their in-bound materials and out-bound products. Still others, beset by traffic levels too low to attract purchase by private-sector entities, were acquired variously by state, provincial, and local-area governments, and by agencies thereof such as quasi-independent public authorities. In some instances, commitments of public sector resources for line purchases were made in partnership with contributions from private sector entities having business needs for continuation of rail freight service. Founding of new local and regional lines declined to very few per annum in the 1990s and beyond as the number of Class I-owned lines remaining available for sale or lease dwindled, and as some Class I carriers changed their policies toward relationships with non-Class I lines.

Structural change within the local and regional railway sector since the 1980s has been confined largely to significant growth in holding company ownership of lines that were founded initially as independent stand-alone entities. The question of whether, how, and to what extent this shift in ownership is and/or ultimately will be beneficial for all stakeholders in the supply and use of local and regional railway service is open for debate. Reversion of local and regional lines to Class I ownership constitutes a structural change of lesser magnitude. Some local and regional lines have in several instances been purchased by Class I carriers to achieve network expansion objectives keyed to revenue growth and/or improvements in operating efficiency and effectiveness.

In conclusion, the collective success that has been achieved with establishment and on-going operation of local and regional railways during the past three decades has far outweighed occurrences of venture failure. Such railways now comprise a vital subset of the North American railway network. In that role, they have preserved railway freight service in numerous areas where it almost certainly would have disappeared permanently, provided Class I railways with valuable access to customers located away from their own lines, contributed to the economic viability of the localities served, and hold strong potential for continuing to do so long into the future.

References

American Short Line and Regional Railroad Association (ASLRRA). 2012. *Short Line and Regional Railroad Facts and Figures*. 2012 Edition. Washington, DC: ASLRRA.

Association of American Railroads (AAR). 2011. *Railroad Facts*. 2011 Edition. Washington, DC: Association of American Railroads.

Babcock, M.W., Prater, M. and Morrill, J. 1994. A profile of short line railroad success. *Transportation Journal*, 34(1), 22–31.

Banham, R. 1996. Rail lines spin off unwanted track. *Journal of Commerce*, 2 December, 1C–2C.

Beier, F.J., and Cross, J. 1993. Shortline-client relationships: can local carriers be more than small railroads? *Transportation Journal*, 33(2), 5–14.

Blanchard, R. 2009a. Facing a raging storm together. *Trains Magazine*, 69(6), 24–31.

Blanchard, R. 2009b. America's energy independence rides the rails. *Trains Magazine*, 69(6), 44–9.

Blanchard, R. 2012. Short distances, big opportunity. *Trains Magazine*, 72(9), 24–33.

Bowen, D.J. 2012. High green for Vermont railway. *Railway Age*, 43–5.

Bowen, D.J. 2013. Mighty mite stands tall in Texas. *Railway Age*, 27–33.

Canada Transportation Act. 1996. Part III, 111–29.

Danneman, T. 2013. Survivor. *Trains Magazine*. 73(6), 22–33.

Due, J.F. 1984. New railroad companies formed to take over abandoned or spun-off lines. *Transportation Journal*, 24(1), 30–51.

Due, J.F. 1987. Abandonment of rail lines and the smaller railroad alternative. *Logistics and Transportation Review*, 23(1), 109–34.

Due, J.F. and Leever, S.D. 1993. The post-1984 experience with new small and regional railroads. *Transportation Journal*, 33(1), 40–52.

Due, J.F., Leever, S.D. and Noyes, T. 2002. The experience with new small and regional railroads, 1997–2001. *Transportation Journal*, 42(1), 5–19.

Frailey, F.W. 2012. Bob Bryant's big little railroad. *Trains Magazine*, 72(1), 42–51.

Freudmann, A. and Watson, R. 1996. Canada's court rules against union in short-line case. *Journal of Commerce*, 15 January 1996, 2B.

Gallamore, R.E. 1999. Regulation and innovation: lessons from the American railroad industry, in *Essays in Transportation Economics and Policy – A Handbook in Honor of John R. Meyer*, edited by J. Gómez-Ibáñez, W.B. Tye and C. Winston. Washington, DC: The Brookings Institution. 493–529.

Grim, C.M. and Sapienza, H.J. 1993. Determinants of shortline railroad performance. *Transportation Journal*, 32(3), 5–13.

Harlow, A.F. 1947. *The Road of the Century*. New York: Creative Age Press.

Harris, K. and Tee, J. 2010. *Jane's World Railways. 2010–2011*. 52nd Edition. Alexandria: Jane's Information Group.

Healy, K.T. 1985. *Performance of the U.S. Railroads since World War II*. New York: Vantage Press.

Hemphill, M.W. 2004. The plight of the short line railroad. *Trains Magazine*, 64(3), 30.

Levine, H.A., Rockey, C.F., Eby, C.C. and Dale, J.L. 1982. *Small Railroads*. Washington, DC: Economics and Finance Department, Association of American Railroads.

Locklin, D.P. 1960. *Economics of Transportation*. 5th Edition. Homewood: Richard D. Irwin.

Massa, S. 2001. A tale of two monopolies: why removing paper barriers is a good idea. *Transportation Journal*, 41(2–3), 47–60.

Murray, T. 2013. A recipe for success. *Trains Magazine*, 73(6), 42–9.

NADO Research Foundation. 2008. *Short Line Railroads: Saving an Endangered Species of Freight Transport – Case Studies, Experiences and Lessons Learned from Regional Development Organizations*. Washington, DC: National Association of Development Organizations.

Perritt, H.H. 1983. Ask and you shall receive: the legislative response to the northeast rail crisis. *Villanova Law Review*, 28(2), 271–377.

Philips, M. and Loder, A. 2013. All aboard the crude express. *Bloomberg Businessweek*, 21–2.

Powell, E. 2009. Big power for the little guys. *Trains Magazine*, 60(6), 34–7.

Railway Association of Canada. 2011. *2011 Rail Trends*. Ottawa: The Railway Association of Canada.

Rockey, C.F. 1987. The formation of regional railroads in the United States. *Transportation Journal*, 27(2), 5–13.

Rund, C. 2006. *The Indiana Rail Road Company*. Bloomington: Indiana University Press.

Saunders, R. 2001. *Merging Lines: American Railroads 1900–1970*. DeKalb: Northern Illinois University Press.

Sneider, J. 2011. Positive energy by the carload. *Progressive Railroading*, 20–30.

Spychalski, J.C. 1997a. From ICC to STB: continuing vestiges of U.S. surface transport regulation. *Journal of Transport Economics and Policy*, 31(1), 131–6.

Spychalski, J.C. 1997b. Rail transport: retreat and resurgence. *The Annals of the American Academy of Political and Social Science*, 553, 42–54.

Stagl, J. 2013. Rails, tales and western shales. *Progressive Railroading*, 56(5), 25–30.

Stover, J.F. 1987. *History of the Baltimore and Ohio Railroad*. West Lafayette: Purdue University Press.

Vantuono, W.C. 2012. The entrepreneurial Indiana Rail Road. *Railway Age*, 47–9.

Wilner, F.N. 1991. *The Railway Labor Act & the Dilemma of Labor Relations*. Omaha: Simmons-Boardman Books.

Wolfe, K.E. 1988. The downside risk: an analysis of local and regional railroad service failures. *Journal of the Transportation Research Forum*, 29(1), 124–37.

Wolfe, K.E. 1989a. Financial and demographic conditions associated with local and regional railroad service failures. *Transportation Quarterly*, 43(1), 3–28.

Wolfe, K.E. 1989b. Long-run financial and demographic differences between failed and successful local and regional railroads. *Transportation Journal*, 28(3), 13–23.

SECTION V
Making Ends Meet: Economic Dimensions

Chapter 11
Exporting Railway Technologies

Tin Kin Ho

Railway: An Integrated System

Since the first commercial railway services more than 200 years ago, the working principles of running trains on rails and keeping them apart safely have largely remained but the technologies have evolved with time to cater for higher speed, increasing service intensity and rising passenger expectation. It has to be noted that a railway system is not just an engineering or technology artefact but a catalyst of change in the society it serves. While this chapter focuses primarily on technologies, social and economic factors, strategic management and business goals that take full advantage of technologies are also considered.

Railways are huge and interconnected systems in which millions of engineering components click in harmony to produce the desired operation for service provision. A railway system can be broken down into a number of sub-systems which are complex in their own right and interact with others physically and functionally. There are various schools of thoughts on how a railway system is dissected. From a technology viewpoint, the trains can be regarded as the anchor. They link up with the civil engineering system through tracks while signalling and power supply systems are the media for one train to communicate with other trains and the stations provide the input/output interfaces with the passengers. The obvious drawback of this categorization is that maintenance, one of the technology-intensive activities, is pushed into the background implicitly.

Train Traction

Horse-drawn carriages provided traction for the very first generation of railways. Steam engines quickly stepped in to offer an untiring source of traction when the industrial revolution commenced. Locomotives with coal-heated steam boilers were the characteristics of the trains. The development of railways in the nineteenth century helped shape the countries, notably the UK and US, who subsequently dominated the world economically and technologically. In the late nineteenth and early twentieth century, diesel engines and electric traction motors arrived on the scene and gradually replaced steam engines. They are still the mainstream traction technology today.

Diesel engines enable more efficient fuel carriage and combustion (Swanston and Towell 1961). Their advantages are particularly evident on large railway networks where long-distance journeys to remote destinations are frequently required. They are still used extensively in passenger and freight services. Mechanical, electric and hydraulic transmissions have been employed with diesel engines. Hybrid systems combining diesel engines, electric motors and an energy storage system are being developed for freight trains to reduce fuel consumption (Sun et al. 2012).

Electric railways started with battery-propelled trains in the early nineteenth century and DC motors were the natural choice of traction to go with DC voltage sources. With the subsequent trackside electrification, DC motors remained commonly adopted because of compatibility with both DC and AC power supplies and simple speed control (Hill 1994a). DC motors however have their own intrinsic limitations. The presence of commutation and brush gear to reverse current flow implies high levels of wear-and-tear and thus maintenance costs. High power DC traction motors must be cooled with forced ventilation.

AC motors (or 3-phase induction motors) are well known for high torque-to-weight ratio, low maintenance, better efficiency and reliability in operation but they require a 3-phase AC supply and variable-voltage-variable-frequency speed control at high power rating for traction purposes (Hill 1994b). The breakthrough did not arrive until the high-power solid-state power electronics devices of thyristors and gate-turn-off (GTO) thyristors became available in the 1970s. Applications of AC motors then picked up rapidly in the 1980s.

A traction motor reverses the energy conversion role and becomes a generator when a train brakes. In the early days, the regenerated energy was dissipated in a resistor bank. Power electronic devices came to the rescue again and diverted the regenerated energy back to the power feeding network. As the energy has to be dissipated somewhere, another train accelerating nearby is the ideal recipient through the network with energy receiving capability.

Civil Structure

Railways are characterized by exclusive tracks and the purpose of civil structures is to provide a stable, durable and reliable passage on which rail tracks are laid. Technologies on tunnelling, reclamation, excavation and construction for railways are applicable in civil structures for other purposes. Railways have however played a vital role in advancing technologies in those areas. Bridges are one example.

When railways were growing fast in the US during the nineteenth century, a large number of bridges were required to take trains over rivers and canals. Civil engineers at the time had not encountered the substantial load demand of a train and the length of a bridge required in some cases. As the trains moved at higher speed and carried more loads, stronger and safer bridges kept driving the technologies. From wooden arched-stiffened truss to cast iron girder and truss spurs, railway bridges expanded in size and strength. While cast iron was brittle and prone to sudden failures, wrought iron was adopted until stronger and lighter steel was available when the steel-making process matured in the mid-nineteenth century (Unsworth 2010). The basic forms of steel railway bridges have largely remained the same for more than a century. Improvements have been made in the material, construction methodology, structural design and analysis.

Another key component of railway tracks is the sleepers whose function is to spread train axle load to the substructure underneath and maintain train gauge within the possible limits. Their form and shape have not changed and the materials range from wood and pre-stressed concrete to composite materials to suit operational conditions (Kaewunruen and Remennikov 2009). Applications of technology focus on impact capacity, structure design and condition monitoring. Ballast is the largest component of the track by weight and volume. It acts as the interface between the sleepers and subgrade, providing lateral and longitudinal stability to the track. It also allows drainage of rainwater from the track (Cope 1993). Hard angular stone is considered to be the best materials for ballast. Others, like ashes, sand, or even oyster shell have been adopted. A two-layered system (Claisse et al. 2006), with smaller ballast stone on the top level, has been experimented with to reduce noise levels from track, extend track life and keep maintenance down.

Power Supply

The first electrified railway started operation in 1837. Electrification has become the mainstream traction power source with no emissions in the vicinity it is used and a mature technology in electricity distribution and the traction system. Both DC and AC sources are commonly adopted in railway electrification. DC is derived from the AC utility network through rectifiers. The choices between DC and AC, feeding setup arrangement and line-side equipment are influenced by the technical considerations, such as route characteristics, locations of power sources, network configuration and traction technology (Hill 1994c).

DC supply is mainly employed in urban metro systems with a lower voltage, from 600 V to 3 kV. It fits with the early adoption of DC traction motors but the high current needed to deliver the traction power implies shorter distances between feeding stations. Leakage current through the rails accelerates rail corrosion and the high current also induces potentially high touch voltage on the rail.

Single-phase transmission is established for each power feeding section in an AC supply system. To make use of the 3-phase utility supply, the 3 phases are connected to successive sections. Higher voltages, typical 15 kV or 25 kV, are favoured for long-distance transmission. One of the issues of AC supplies is electromagnetic interference (Hill 1997) on signalling equipment and other trackside facilities because of the significant physical separation between the incoming current (overhead cable) and return current (rail). Special feeding arrangements, with booster transformers and autotransformers, were introduced to force the return current to another overhead cable (Hill 1994c).

Technology on traction stays in parallel with the development of utility power transmission and distribution, with particular attention on fault management and electromagnetic compatibility. Maintenance strategy is another topical issue as reliability is pushed to the forefront of service provision while operation cost is under scrutiny. Further technological developments include efficient capture of regenerative energy and effective deployment of energy storage systems to supplement the power supply from the utility.

Signalling

The prime purpose of signalling is to ensure sufficient separation among trains to avoid collision and to safeguard human lives and railway assets. The signalling concept has effectively been the same for the last 200 years: a line is divided into a number of blocks and each block can only be occupied by one train at any one time. The simplicity is imperative for the train drivers and signal engineers alike in putting the concept into practice (Hill 1995). Advances in technology mainly contribute to the implementation of signalling systems, improving headway, i.e. packing more trains on the line while upholding safety. To stop two trains from colliding, two functions are undertaken by signalling: (a) location detection of the train ahead, and (b) instructions to the train behind.

Train detection is performed by track circuits (Hill 1996) in most systems. It is a large electrical circuit with the rail within a signalling block as the conductor. The axles of a train presence in the block act as short circuit to the source and trigger the 'occupied' status of the block. Sources in track circuits have moved from DC to the increasingly higher frequency of AC signals to attain electromagnetic compatibility with the traction system. Coding has also been introduced to enhance the fail-safe features in communication. Track circuits rely on the integrity of a physical circuit which may be subject to harsh working conditions, such as flooding. Axle counters, which detect and match the number of train axles going in and out of a signalling block to determine the occupancy of the block by magnetic circuits, has provided an alternative to this in recent decades.

Instructions to the train behind are devised according to the occupancy status of the signalling ahead and conveyed to the train through trackside equipment. Semaphore signals and then coloured lighting have been widely employed. The instructions can be implicit and the drivers have to exercise their experience and route knowledge to operate the trains. In systems where tight headways are required, such as metros, explicit speed instructions are embedded in the signals (Nock 1995). Trackside visual signals become redundant when train operation is automated where signalling information is distributed to the trains by secured communication links.

Signalling is a safety-critical system and the ultimate guardian against human mistakes and equipment failures. Modern operation demands the highest standard of safety from the Safety Integrity Levels defined by the International Electromechanical Commission's standard (Smith and Simpson 2010). It is now a common practice in many countries that a Safety Case has to be established and vigorously examined before a revenue-generating operation is commissioned.

System Integration

The above systems are functionally and physically interconnected and interdependent as they gel together to give the resulting railway operation. For example, adoption of a traction drive system determines the power demand over a given service requirement and thus the power feeding arrangement, i.e. locations and ratings of substations. The braking characteristics imply the maximum braking distance of the train, leading to the signalling block length. A holistic approach is important throughout the life cycle of each sub-system, from design, specification, implementation, operation, maintenance and decommissioning, to consider the direct impacts and knock-on effects to other sub-systems. A system engineering approach facilitates an effective management process of system integration with accountability (Hitchins 2007).

Driving Force of Railway Technologies

Railways are a relatively conservative industry which is compelled to observe very stringent safety and service requirements in order to meet public expectations and regulatory obligations. High-capital investment and slow, if not low, return also prompt prudent considerations before adopting innovations and technologies. As a result, railways are not usually regarded as a hi-tech industry and new technologies have to be initiated somewhere else.

Innovations in railways are always driven by the demand in service and operation over time. For example, in order to increase line capacity to accommodate additional demand, signalling may be required to shift up a gear from fixed-block to the moving-block concept to squeeze a tighter headway. The advantages of computer automation, such as Automatic Train Operation (ATO), are fully exploited to eliminate variations in driving behaviour. Trains running at a higher speed call for innovations on traction drive systems, train body structure and aerodynamics, track geotechnical engineering, communication and noise and vibration management.

Railway service requirements have evolved from the basics of simple service availability of moving goods or people from one point to another two centuries ago to a sophisticated matrix of reliability, safety, comfort, regularity, accessibility, customer satisfaction and added-value entertainment. This escalation of intensity of service provisions and complexity of operation in modern-day railways is thus another driving force behind technology development. With the high infrastructure investment on railways, technologies for asset condition monitoring and innovations for asset management strategies have to be introduced in order to preserve the asset worth and extend its life time.

Innovation seldom leads to a wholesale transformation of operations or a new generation of railway. Maglev (Thornton 1973) was the nearest example of a novel technology turning railways into an entirely new running paradigm. However, it has not genuinely taken off as a commonly adopted real-life operation as there have been very few revenue-generating Maglev systems around the world (Holmer 2003). On the other hand, technologies, particularly proven ones, are often drawn in by the industry to sustain the increasing service and operation demands. The transformation of railways through technology advances tends to be subtle, incremental and accumulative.

Driven by demand, the operators, government or private companies, turn to consultants or major manufacturers to come up with system designs and solutions to meets their requirements. It then triggers the manufacturers' in-house research and development teams who undertake applied research to meet the specific design requirements or at times enlist the support from universities or research institutes to explore fundamental research. As a new technology goes through the process of commissioning, testing and verification of its practical applications, it becomes mature as a next-generation product with a track record to back up its credibility in subsequent contracts. The intellectual property rights of the developed technologies, usually in the form of patents, remain with the vendors for the protection of their commercial interests. From this point, the research and development team may review functionality enhancements and performance upgrades with the products regularly, but the trigger for a fresh round of technology drive is likely to come from the next surge of service and operation demand in one form or another. High-Speed Rail is a classic example of technology being pushed to the next level in the pursuit of mass transport services over long-distance inter-city commuting amid competition with air transport. At a small scale, technology to facilitate fast, reliable and secure personal mobile communication for passengers on-board the trains while overcoming electromagnetic interference with the signalling system in enclosed and open areas is another demand-driven development.

Technology Transfer

In railway applications, technology is not attained or transferred as an individual entity. Instead, it is embedded in systems, products or services provided by the major manufacturers and consultants, as the components of the railway system to support its operation and management. Examples include rolling stock, train control systems, signalling communication and traction drive equipment. Technology transfer thus occurs when such systems and products are acquired through development of new systems and refurbishments of the old ones. These systems are hardly of simple plug-and-play configurations and they require the full process of specification, design, building, testing, commissioning, and sometimes further training for operating personnel, in order to ensure integration into the overall system. Given the recent intensified investment in rail development and its revitalisation worldwide, the multi-million-dollar procurement contracts underline prominently the importance of exporting railway technology to the growth of domestic economies and employment opportunities.

Like many other infrastructure systems, projects to design and construct railway systems are managed by different approaches to integrate the system functions within time and cost constraints. The impact on technology transfer within individual systems varies. The discussion here will look at the two common approaches: (i) a whole-system development as a 'turnkey' project by a single undertaker on behalf of the operator; and (ii) active participation of the operator in the design, specification and construction processes to ensure fit-for-purpose technologies and a compatible asset life cycle from a system perspective.

Turnkey

The turnkey approach to project development has been widely adopted by railway operators since late 1980s. It is structured in a number of ways and the idea is to pull together the suppliers of the components of the system under a single consortium which assumes the overall responsibility for design, construction, equipment, financing and even operation of the rail system. The system in fully proven operation is then handed over to the operator upon completion or even after a period of operation. There are three broad categories of turnkey implementation (Middleton 1989): design-build, turnkey and build-operate-transfer (BOT) and they provide different degrees of flexibility in cost and time, risk and responsibility management, as well as opportunities for technology development and transfer. Figure 11.1 illustrates the processes and participating parties in these categories. Variations to suit specific requirements of individual systems are common while the framework remains the same.

With the design-build approach, the engineering consultant, on behalf of the operator, undertakes the preliminary design work before calling for bids from third-party design-build contractors. Here, an operator is referred generally to the company or agency, which may be owned and run by government, the private sector or a public-private partnership, to build and operate a railway system. The successful bidder then completes the final design and construction and takes up the responsibility of designing, furnishing and installation of the equipment and systems. Coordination and integration of the work from the contractors, and the financing and operation of the whole project is still the responsibility of the operator and its consultant. It is not too far away from the traditional approach under which fully developed plans and specifications for individual components of a system are prepared for lump sum competitive biddings. The operator has a fair degree of control on and access to the technology details but limited involvement in technology development. Knowledge transfer is made possible if the operator chooses to do so. However, the suppliers are likely to stick to their off-the-shelf products and systems and then manipulate the interfaces to fit the specifications.

The consultant for the operator prepares the same preliminary design work in a standard turnkey approach. The whole project is then raised for tendering as a single package. Within the agreed price and timeframe, the successful contractor is responsible for the full design, specifications and sourcing for the entire system, coordination of construction, installation of all components, system integration and commissioning and testing of the sub-systems. The contractor usually operates the system for the first few years to ensure smooth and reliable services before handing it over to the operator. Technology selections are completely the contractor's decision and technology transfer is confined at the product

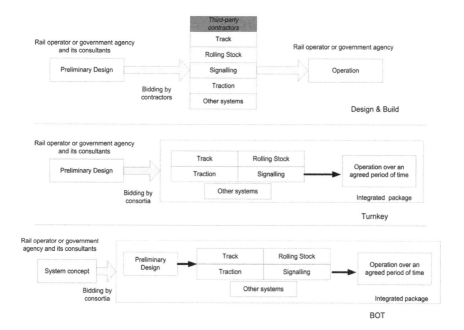

Figure 11.1   The 3 categories of Turnkey projects
Source: Author.

application level. The actual know-how remains with the suppliers and any add-ons or modifications of technology to suit the specific system requirements are not necessarily shared with and made available to the operator.

Build-operate-transfer (BOT) is a common approach to encourage the private sector to participate in public infrastructure project development, particularly in Third World countries. Based on a preliminary design and specification, the BOT team literally takes over the entire project and oversees the complete process of construction, equipment, system integration and even financing of the project. When the system is ready for operation upon commissioning and testing, the BOT team carries on with the operation and assume the responsibility of service provision and maintenance. The system is ultimately transferred to the operator after an agreed period of time. The operator is supposed to inherit a system in sound operating order according to the design and specification it imposed at the very beginning. The design and system details are given and likely well documented but the technology decisions and their impacts to the system long-term technical and economic cost benefit are out of the hands of the operator.

Turnkey projects often offer the advantages of cost and time reduction and better risk management. In systems where just-in-time project completion and service readiness is of utmost importance, turnkey approach becomes a preferred option. It also speeds up technology export from which the manufacturers are able to build considerable track records for their products for further spread of related technologies.

Active Operator Participation

In a system where the operator is more experienced in design, construction, operation and maintenance, the operator tend to play a more prominent role in the process. External consultants and suppliers are still in their usual places to provide services and products in the competitive bidding exercise but the operator has its engineers and project managers to oversee progress and enforce the design and specifications to meet the unique requirements of the system. As a result, the suppliers, together with the engineering team of the operator, have to come up with a fit-for-purpose solution which may push beyond the technologies incorporated in the off-the-shelf products. The operator then retains the knowledge of the technology development and has access to the details of the technology. In some cases, the operator even shares the intellectual property rights for the future application of the technology. It is also possible for the operator to nurture in-house expertise in order to extend its business to consultancy services or even take part in system development and the operation on public-private partnerships for other railway systems (Black 2006).

The motivation of active participation by the operator is more than attaining the technology know-how. The technical details on design principles, structures and system integration allow a better understanding of the life cycles of the system and its components under the unique system operational conditions. A railway system is a significant capital investment and its life cycle is measured in decades. The return is usually implicit and slow. The investment can only be protected when the asset worth is maintained throughout the life cycle. Applying the appropriate technologies to suit the purposes and understanding the design and the supporting system components are crucial to maintain the system in a reliable revenue-generating condition. They also inform refurbishment and extension planning when different components, such as rolling stock, track and signalling, vary in the lengths of their life cycles.

A system with components at various stages of their lives have to work together to provide the desired functionalities, which is a sizable challenge, let alone managing the transition of replacing or renewing one of the components while keeping the service going. It affects not only systems with a long history, but also relatively young systems going through a system upgrade or mid-life refurbishment. When the Hong Kong MTR decided to upgrade its signalling system from fixed-block to moving-block in the mid-90s (i.e. after 20 years of operation), it had to ensure system compatibility with existing rolling stock and power traction systems and their future additions or upgrades. The upgrade work was carried out within limited hours between active operations, stringent health and safety requirements and the parallel presence of both old and new systems. The knowledge of the system design, structure and integration became profoundly valuable during this exercise. The active involvement of the operator throughout the system life cycle, known as a cradle-to-grave approach, unearths the necessary knowledge to facilitate asset worth preservation with appropriate asset management measures.

Export for Expansion and Survival

Railways are a specialized industry in which the technologies are not necessarily applicable to other industries. The technology providers have to seek a wider market to sustain the economy of scale for continuing research and development investment. Exporting technologies worldwide is the natural course of action for the industry to expand, if not just to survive. A few examples of railway technology export are discussed here.

The UK was the first country to export railway technology. It was the pioneer of railway development in the nineteenth century which coincided with the heyday of the British Empire. Colonies around the world were exploited for natural resources or as trading outposts and railways were the essential vehicles to facilitate these purposes. British railway construction, equipment and operation principles were inevitably imported as there was no local knowledge. This exploration of the world market brought substantial economic benefits to the British railway industry and hastened further development of technologies for domestic demand. The railway operations, such as signalling, in Australia, India and Hong Kong, are still under significant early influence from the British practices, despite decades of development of their own.

High-Speed Rail (HSR) is a classic example of a railway technology export. Germany was among the first developers of HSR in the early twentieth century. The first regular commercial service started in 1935 between Hamburg and Berlin. The trains were powered by diesel engines and they reached a maximum speed of 160 kph. The progress encouraged development across Europe but it was brought to an abrupt halt by the war. Inspired by the technology advances in Europe, Japan made a major breakthrough in the 1960s with its first Shinkansen service between Tokyo and Osaka. The electric trains hit over 250 kph. It took nearly 10 years for Japan to perfect its HSR craft and turn the concept into a commercial service. The technologies include rail and sub-track structures, train body, traction equipment and signalling. The French version of HSR is TGV, which was developed in the 1970s. The service commenced in 1981 between Paris and Lyon. Powered by electric cars, the service ran at speeds of over 250 kph, and by 2011, it rose to 320 kph (Hazell 1994). Germany, Japan and France are the trend-setter of HSR technologies. After a few decades of expansion, their HSR networks have almost come to a saturation point and the technologies have become mature for export.

At the turn of the century, China was desperate to revitalize its aging railway network in order to support economic growth and HSR was the perfect solution. The original plan was to develop domestic HSR technologies but the first batch of HSR systems were far below the performance requirements. In order to jump-start the development, technologies from Germany, France and Japan were brought in (Chan and Aldhaban 2009). It was a timely opportunity for these countries to export their technologies and grow their HSR industries. Siemens and Bombardier (Germany), Alstrom (France) and Kawasaki (Japan) are the major suppliers. On the other hand, having envisioned a much bigger HSR network than any other country, China was still keen on developing its own HSR technologies. With most of the technology procurements, terms were inserted to ensure technology transfers. The China Railways Highspeed (CRH) started the first services in 2007 with imported trains but it now has a train fleet from its own development. With the initial push from imported technologies, not only is China able to cut short the development stage and expand its HSR network, it is also in the position of exporting HSR technologies nowadays (China Briefing 2012, GE 2009). China is exporting to Germany (aluminium alloy for trains walls and floors), Bangladesh (trains, network control systems, traction inverters and auxiliary inverters), the US (partnership to increase speed of US network and provide China with fuel-efficient and low-emission locomotives) and others including Russia, Turkey and Saudi Arabia.

The story is similar with Maglev technology. Germany and Japan are pioneers of Maglev technology but they do not have their own operational services. China runs the most well-known fully commercial Maglev system in the world at Shanghai airport and the technologies were imported from Germany (Bohn and Steinmetz 1984). However, the opportunities for exporting further are rather limited as the construction cost of Maglev can hardly be justified. However, the development of Maglev technology pushes significant advances in related areas, such as superconducting, which have found successful applications in energy storage systems and medical equipment.

Australia is an emerging player of railway technology exports in recent years. With the mining boom, Australia is at the forefront of heavy haul rail technologies, such as bogie design, rail-wheel interface condition monitoring and car loading/unloading systems. Level crossing accidents accounted for 30 per cent of rail-related fatalities in Australia. Warning systems, communication with train drivers, active and passive boom-gate control systems and real-time surveillance have been developed to manage the risks at level crossings. The heavy haul and level-crossing technologies were again initiated by domestic demand. Export is possible when they become mature and proven and the financial return and experience feedback keep them as the leader of the technologies. The priority markets for the Australian rail industry include Latin America, China, Indonesia and South East Asia (source from website available at www.austrade.gov.au/Railways-overview).

In addition to hardware and software systems, an important domain of 'technologies' is the soft skills or know-how of system development, system integration, safety practices, system assurance and risk management. The sources of the skills are not just the commonly known international standards and practices (International Electrotechnical Commission 1999, 2000), but the specialized experts with a thorough understanding of the standards and vast experience to implement them rigorously in practice (McCormack et al. 2006, Daw 2004). The skills are fundamental to modern-day railway system planning, construction and operation. International consultancy companies are the key suppliers and they set up offices around the world to look for bidding opportunities. When a contract is awarded, experts are flown in to provide the services. Freelance consultants, formerly working for the major consultancies, railway operators or even government regulation agencies, are also in the market to supply these soft skills and they work for the global market. There is also an increasing trend of successful railway operators setting up their own branch of consultancy business in order to maximize the utilization of the expertise pool within the organizations.

For example, the Hong Kong Mass Transit Railway, backed by its highly efficient operations and hard earned experience over the last 30 years, developed the affiliated consultancy branch with in-house experienced experts to support the franchise operation bidding and co-development of new metro lines around the world (Hoyle 2010, Anonymous 2010). Technology export is thus realized through the company's participation in international operation projects. The consultancy service is also extended to various aspects of metro projects in developing countries. This initiative allows the company to extend its business arm beyond running domestic railways, and to retain the in-house expertise accumulated through development and expansion of its own systems.

Challenges and Opportunities

Paradigm Change

Railways provide mass transportation services to move people and goods from one location to another with an agreed schedule. Railways were a natural monopoly from the very beginning because of the shear scale of capital investment. Quite often, railway development and operation relied so heavily on public funding or subsidy that it was turned into a public service. Lack of long-term planning and coordination, combined with poor management, saw the service deteriorating in the 1970s and 1980s. Service quality becomes the Achilles heel, if not a liability, of the operating agencies and thus the responsibility of a ministry of the government.

The gradual decline in the importance of rail in the decades after World War II was accelerated by the fact that roads took over as the dominant means of land transport and aviation did the same for long-distance travel. Despite misgivings, railways had not been pushed to extinction and remained a provider of transport and a vital part of the economy. At the turn of the new millennium, the continual trend of urbanization, growing concern on carbon emission and seemingly unstoppable road congestion have prompted the re-emergence of railways. Rail is now seen as the environmentally friendly and financially viable transportation to support economic growth. Numerous high-speed rails to connect cities, metros and light rails to facilitate inner-city connectivity and freight corridors to move raw material commodities are now in various stages of planning, construction and operation worldwide.

With the developments of societies and changes of the user behaviour and expectation, the role of rail has shifted from being a public service and rail technologies must keep pace with this trend. In the past, railways were government undertakings and not open to questioning. Railway operators determined the service quality and travelling environment while the end-users were allowed limited or no input. As the population grew and its distribution expanded with the city size over the last few decades, demand of railway services to support and sustain social and economic growth rises gradually. The change of service requirement on a railway system is characterized by the increasing intensity and complexity in the service.

The intensity comes from the service demand, traffic volume and frequency and hence the scale and coverage of the rail network. They pile pressure on the infrastructure assets which were built or acquired for a lower intensity. While investment is not readily available, railways have to deal with the legacy problems. One of the challenges is to preserve the infrastructure asset worth and maximize capacity utilization. The operator is also the steward of the assets and charged with the responsibility of harnessing the productivity out of the available assets through appropriate technologies and management.

Complexity is signified by the number of stakeholders in railways and the roles they play. Railway service provisions are now scrutinized by the regulators, media and public. High service quality, affordable ticket fares and stringent compliance of reliability, safety, accessibility and contingency measures contribute to the landscape of modern-day rail service operation. Regulatory requirements are mandated as a result of previous accidents or incidents involving fatalities. Other safety regulations are pushed in because of advances of knowledge and availability of technologies. Social and health concerns, such as SARS, avian flu and anti-terrorism (Staples 2004), also lead to the sophistication of the operation, which put additional burden on the operators.

The complexity is further aggregated by the withdrawal of public funding or the introduction of private sector involvement. Without government funding, construction and operation have to be financially sustainable and various business models, such as public-private partnership, open market, franchises, come to the fore. Competition creeps in and the passengers or freight forwarders are regarded more as customers, or even clients, who have to be managed and supported in order to ensure profitability. Rail service has now evolved to a customer-oriented service and the key drivers of technologies or innovations must be originated from customer needs.

The focus of railway service provision is now on (1) protecting asset investment and extending asset life cycle, (2) satisfying the needs of the customers in a whole-journey experience and (3) integrating the railway system into a broader infrastructure system to contribute to economic growth and social well-being. This paradigm shift has set the operators on a different pathway of pursuing technologies.

The railway system is no longer regarded as an engineering system, but a functional entity to serve the community, with constant interactions with society and individuals. The 'technologies' must go beyond engineering and science and spill over to studies on the areas of human dynamics and management.

Future Development

With the new paradigm, technologies are not only about applying cutting edge engineering technologies or high-end products, but also taking advantage of appropriate technologies to meet the demands of the service. A simple example to illustrate this change is the quest of shortening travel time on railways.

In the past, travel time was usually reduced by trains running at high speed, which calls for higher power traction equipment, signalling to allow tighter headway and shorter braking distance, and track structure and train body design to bear the stress of higher speed operation. They all demand substantial upgrades of the infrastructure and tremendous amounts of investment even for a small portion of travel time reduction. However, if the passengers have found their journeys well-occupied by efficient personal work or carried out in relaxing entertainment over their mobile devices, they do not look at the travel time as wasted time. The hard saved time through infrastructure upgrade would have become insignificant. Instead, only the investment to provide secure, fast, reliable, accessible and free mobile connection, as well as rich content entertainment and information updates, is adequate to turn the lost time in commuting into productive time for personal lives and business opportunities.

In order to look into the crystal ball on how future technologies for railways pan out, the characteristics of railway system have to be understood, railways are complex infrastructure systems with the following dimensions:

1. sub-system diversity
2. interactions with human users and other infrastructure systems
3. physical dispersion of infrastructure and assets
4. rigidness of operation
5. regulations and standards compliance.

Railways are huge heterogeneous systems with a large number of sub-systems interfacing and interacting organically to provide the transport services. The sub-systems are diverse in size, technology, age and phase in their respective life cycles. It is not uncommon to have a brand new train fleet with the latest sophisticated power electronics traction drive package and car-body design running on a line which is about to replace its 30 years old signalling system. There are bridges and tunnels along the line built more than 100 years ago and they are expected to last for decades to come. The diversity presents the challenge of attaining the maximum productivity of the system as a unit while managing their conditions with affordable cost and maintaining reliability, safety and comfort of the services. The 'technology' required is the scientific understanding of the technical and economic life cycles of the sub-systems and a system perspective, in terms of functionality and performance, of how they interweave through system integration (McCusker 2006).

Railways are the people's transportation and the interactions with human users are crucial to shape railway operation. A simple analogy is the influence of human behaviour on the design of the latest mobile phones and the thousands of new demand-driven apps to enhance the interfaces. For railways, real-time information exchanges, contactless ticketing, station and train designs have been moving forward with technologies to improve the interface with users. Studies on perception of crowdedness and the psychology behind tolerance to crowding among individuals in a transport environment (Cox et al. 2006) are riding on the next wave. Egress management may be the early purpose but capacity management and passenger comfort is now the main driver. Interactions with other infrastructure systems give rise to technologies to address safety issues at level crossings with road traffic and energy management with the electricity networks.

As railway lines are connections among cities, assets spread along the way over very long distances, which makes control and maintenance very difficult. Technologies on reliable remote sensing and secure communications are critical to ensure just-in-time information on asset conditions and support decision-making process in operation. The scattering of assets and operation also put the chain of commands for the staff to the test. Supervision, management and boundaries between central and local decisions and actions have to be specified and articulated effectively. Management strategies and policies to engage all staff members and raise awareness on duties and responsibilities fall into the domain of management and corporate governance.

Because of the complexity and physical arrangement in a railway system, the operation follows very rigid sequences of actions in which one event can only take place when another specific event is completed. Interlocking in signalling system to control signals and point machines collectively according to train movement is a typical example. When limited slack is available in the process, the operation is more vulnerable to disruption. Suitable amount of margins have to be introduced to absorb unexpected occurrence of disruption and to uphold robustness and resilience of the operation. Applications of operations research techniques on process planning, schedule optimization and disturbance recovery are on the forefront of the technology.

Regulations and standards are at first set out to help railways deal with the intrinsic complexity with traceable accountability and standardized procedures. They are also intended to generate interoperability across systems in some cases. Further regulations and standards emerge from the experience of operations with tragic failures or incidents involving heavy casualties. However, not every system is subject to the same requirements of regulations and standards. This variation leads to opportunities for the implementation of know-how of these regulations and standards to become the soft skills of railway technologies. System assurance practices on risk management and reliability evaluation, together with safety case formulation, are the most sought-after form of expertise.

References

Anonymous. 2010. MTR to operate Stockholm metro. *International Railway Journal,* 49(3), 15.

Black, R. 2006. Line 4 takes shape as PPP Progresses. *Metro Report: A Railway Gazette Yearbook,* 162, 10–11.

Bohn, G. and Steinmetz, G. 1984. The electromagnetic levitation and guidance technology of the transrapid test facility Emsland. *IEEE Transactions on Magnetics,* 20(5), 1666–71.

Chan, L. and Aldhaban, F. 2009. *Technology Transfer to China: With Case Studies in the High-Speed Rail Industries.* Paper to the Portland International Conference on Management of Engineering and Technology, Portland, 2–6 August 2009.

China Briefing. 2012. *On the Fast-Track: Technology Transfer in China* [Online]. Available at: www.china-briefing.com/news/2012/09/03/on-the-fast-track-technology-transfer-in-china.html [accessed: 30 August 2013].

Claisse, P.A. and Calla, C. 2006. Rail ballast: A conclusion from a historical perspective. *Proceedings of Institute of Civil Engineers: Transport,* 159(2): 69–74.

Cope, G.H. 1993. *British Railway Track: Design, Construction and Maintenance.* 6th Edition. Barnsleys: The Permanent Way Institution.

Cox, T., Houdmont, J. and Griffiths, A. 2006. Rail passenger crowding, stress, health and safety in British. *Transportation Research A,* 40(3), 244–58.

Daw, S. 2004. *Rail Systems Delivery – Long Term Thinking For a Long Term Environment.* Paper to the IEEE Seminar: On the Right Line – Systems Engineering for the Railway Industry, London, January 2004.

GE. 2009. *GE and China MOR Sign Strategic MOU to Advance High-Speed Rail Opportunities in the U.S.* [Online]. Available at: www.defence.pk/forums/chinese-defence/39409-chinas-advance-high-speed-rail-technology-will-export-u-s-after-export-russia.html [accessed: 30 August 2013].

Hazell, A.B. 1994. *Recent Developments in European High Speed Rail.* Paper to the ASME/IEEE Joint RailRoad Conference, Chicago, 22–24 March 1994.

Hill, R.J. 1994a. Electric railway traction Part 1 electric traction and DC traction motor drives. *Power Engineering Journal,* 47–56.

Hill, R.J. 1994b. Electric railway traction Part 2 traction drive with 3-phase induction motors. *Power Engineering Journal,* 143–52.

Hill, R.J. 1994c. Electric railway traction Part 3 traction power supplies. *Power Engineering Journal,* 275–86.

Hill, R.J. 1995. Electric railway traction Part 4 signalling and interlocking, *Power Engineering Journal,* 201–6.

Hill, R.J. 1996. Electric railway traction Part 5 train detection, communications and supervision. *Power Engineering Journal,* 87–95.

Hill, R.J. 1997. Electric railway traction Part 7 electromagnetic interference in traction systems. *Power Engineering Journal,* 259–66.

Hitchins, D.K. 2007. *Systems Engineering: A 21st Century Systems Methodology.* Chichester: John Wiley & Sons.

Holmer, P. 2003. Faster than a speeding bullet train. *IEEE Spectrum,* 40(8), 30–34.

Hoyle, J. 2010. Victoria … a state of contrast. *International Railway Journal,* 50(1), 28–30.

International Electrotechnical Commission. 1999. *Railway Applications – The Specification and Demonstration of Reliability, Availability, Maintainability and Safety (RAMS), European Standards.* Geneva: International Electrotechnical Commission.

International Electrotechnical Commission. 2000. *Railway Applications – Electromagnetic Compatibility. Emission and Immunity of the Signalling and Telecommunications Apparatus, European Standards.* Geneva: International Electrotechnical Commission.

Kaewunruen, S. and Remennikov, A.M. 2009. Impact capacity of pre-stressed concrete sleepers. *Engineering Failure Analysis,* 16, 1520–33.

McCormack, L.M., Seller, S., White, R.D., Hutchison, R. and Hooper, B.W. 2006. *Railway Electrical Systems Integration: Practical Applications of 'V' Cycle of Electromagnetic Compatibility.* Paper to the IET Seminar on EMC in Railways, Birmingham, UK, 28 September 2006.

McCusker, A. 2006. *Best Practices in Asset Management to Achieve Superior Performance and Productivity Breakthrough.* Paper to the Conference on Railway Engineering, Melbourne, Australia, 2006.

Middleton, W.D. 1989. Time to talk 'Turnkey'? *Railway Age,* 190(9), 65–74.

Nock, O.S. 1995. *Railway Signalling.* London: A & C Black.

Smith, D. and Simpson, K. 2010. *Safety Critical Systems Handbook: A Straightforward Guide to Functional Safety. IEC 61508 (2010 Edition) and Related Standards.* Amsterdam: Elsevier.

Staples, J. 2004. Anti-terrorist moves to protect the Tube are inadequate. *The Safety and Health Practitioner,* 22(5), 20.

Sun, Y., Cole, C., Spiryagin, M.R., Godber, T. and Hames, S. 2012. *Energy Storage System Analysis for Heavy Haul Hybrid System.* Paper to the CORE2012: Global Perspectives: Conference on Railway Engineering, Brisbane, Australia, 10–12 September 2012.

Swanston, A.D. and Towell, B.W. 1961. Diesel railway locomotives. *Students' Quarterly Journal,* 139–46.

Thornton, R.D. 1973. Design principles for magnetic levitation. *Proceedings of the IEEE,* 61(5), 586–98.

Unsworth, J.H. 2010. *Design of Modern Steel Railway Bridges.* Boca Raton: CRC Press.

Chapter 12
Property Models for Financing Railway Development

Siman Tang and Hong K. Lo

Introduction

Mass transit railway services are instrumental in meeting the mobility and accessibility needs of the general public, and in supporting the demographic and economic development of a city, especially for transit-oriented metropolitan areas. Indeed mass transit railway projects are often a top contender of many cities to meet their increasing demand for travel. It is ideal if the services have not only affordable fares and expedient quality satisfactory to the public, but are also financially sustainable.

Despite the global trend of privatization, mass transit railway services, as public goods, remain largely provided and operated by the public sector. Hong Kong is one of the few exceptions where mass transit railway services are operated by private companies or corporations according to prudent commercial principles. Furthermore, rail transit services in Hong Kong are reputed for their quality and profitability, superbly addressing the accessibility needs of the city, and often serve as benchmarks for new projects in other cities around the world.

In this chapter we analyse the provision of rail transit services in Hong Kong from three perspectives. Firstly, we give, by way of background, an outline of the transport and land use policies set forth by the government, illustrating the importance of these policies in shaping the supply of rail transit services over time and integrating the development of transport facilities and property so as to exploit the synergy between them and to ensure the financial viability of privately provided rail transit services. This analysis is mainly conducted through a review of relevant policy documents and statistical reports published by the Hong Kong government. Particular reference is also drawn from the previous studies of Tang and Lo (2008).

Secondly, given the operation of rail transit services according to commercial principles together with the competitive nature of the public transport market in Hong Kong, we can reasonably assume that the services are operated at optimal levels. With that assumption, we assess the profitability of the leading railway operator in Hong Kong by analysing its annual reports, with an aim to understand whether it manages to achieve an acceptable return to investment, and if so, how this is achieved. An understanding of how the railway company has maintained service quality in a financially sustainable manner is important for contemplating privatization of rail transit services.

Finally, we investigate how the experience of Hong Kong can be applied to build up an integrated railway and property development model that can secure the financial viability of a railway development project on the one hand and the provision of a quality rail transit service on the other, through the partnership participation between public and private sectors. In particular, we outline four alternative partnership models between the public sector, private railway operator and property developer for the provision of mass transit railway services. We also introduce the influence diagram approach as a means to assess and portray how the roles of the different parties in building, funding and owning a mass transit railway may influence the accomplishment of financial, transportation and construction objectives of a project. Twelve questions are eventually identified to summarize the key issues that should be considered when making the decision of the extent to which each party should be involved, or more exactly which one is to build, fund and own the railway.

Transport and Land-Use Policies

The Policy of Giving Priority to Mass Public Transit

The limited space and high population density of Hong Kong have long shaped its transport policy of giving priority to mass carriers, especially those off-street modes that do not occupy road space, and controlling the growth of private car ownership and usage. New private cars in Hong Kong are subject to a first registration tax ranging from 40 per cent to over 100 per cent of the cost of the vehicle. Private car users also need to pay substantial fuel tax and high garaging charges due to the limited number of available parking spaces especially in urban areas. The high acquisition and running costs have succeeded in maintaining the ownership rate below 80 private cars per 1,000 people, compared to almost 800 passenger cars per 1,000 people in the United States (International Road Federation 2013). These measures have also kept the use of private cars at about 11 per cent of total daily passenger journeys, compared to 33 per cent in New York (Singapore Land Transport Authority Academy 2011). As a result, the substantial demand for public transportation has driven the rapid development of public transit services and laid the foundations for the prosperous mass transit market in Hong Kong.

In May 1979, the Hong Kong government published its first White Paper on internal transport policy, which considered that the mobility of people could be best met by an integrated, multi-modal system in which public transportation should be given greater priority (Environment Branch 1979). Accordingly, the Mass Transit Railway (MTR) was constructed in the late 1970s to provide an off-street, efficient means of travel through urban areas. The Kowloon-Canton Railway (KCR) was also electrified in 1982 to provide a transit service for the suburban New Territories area and to support the development of new towns to accommodate the growing population. Both railways were corporatized to operate on prudent commercial principles in accordance with their respective Ordinances, although they were wholly owned by the government. MTR was privatized in October 2000, and since then its shares have been traded on the Stock Exchange of Hong Kong.

The second White Paper on transport policy issued in 1990 continued to emphasize the improvement of transport infrastructure including new railways. At the same time, the adjusted emphasis on service proliferation and competition was revealed by the guiding principles of applying the policy of inter-modal coordination more flexibly and deriving maximum benefit from improved public transport services through competition between modes (Transport Branch 1990). In 1994, echoing the policy of expanding the railway infrastructure as a means for improving mobility, the Hong Kong government issued the first Railway Development Strategy, which set out development plans for four new rail lines or extensions (Transport Branch 1994). These new rail lines were opened for use in the early 2000s.

In October 1999, the government of Hong Kong published 'Hong Kong Moving Ahead', which outlined a revised set of transport strategies towards service rationalization and consolidation for the next two decades, including better integration of transport and land use planning and better use of rail as the backbone of the passenger transport system. One notable objective was to increase the proportion of rail-based public transport journeys from 33 per cent in 1997 to 40–50 per cent by 2016 (Transport Bureau 1999). In accordance with this objective, the second Railway Development Strategy was issued in May 2000, laying out a planning framework for expanding Hong Kong's railway network through to 2016 (Transport Bureau 2000).

Table 12.1   Mass railway transit services and patronage

	1980s and 1990s			2000s onward		
	1984	1999	Average annual growth rate %	2000	2011	Average annual growth rate %
Rail car-km (million)	66	197	7.6	196	284	3.4
Rail-based passenger trips (million)	491	1,181	6.0	1,185	1,644	3.0
Public passenger trips (million)	3,008	3,771	1.5	3,852	4,354	1.1

Source: Transport Department 2012.

As a result of the transport policies discussed above, rail-based mass transit services in Hong Kong had been developing rapidly since MTR began operating in 1979, and continued to expand through the 1980s and 1990s and then into the new century (Table 12.1). The share of mass transit railway in passenger journeys using public transport has also been increasing towards the target set forth by the government of Hong Kong, reaching more than 45 per cent in 2011.

The transport policy of giving priority to mass public transit has ensured that the traffic demand for rail transit services would not be diluted by private modes of transport, so the huge public investment in railway infrastructure would be paid back within a reasonable return period. In this way, the policy allowed for the creation of a 'win-win' situation benefitting both the transport operators and the travelling public. Under this policy, the government was able to rely on the private sector to provide rail transit services according to the user-pay principle without direct subsidies.

The Policy on Land Use Development

The tremendous economic growth in the past few decades has established Hong Kong as a world-class city and a major global financial centre. But Hong Kong is a small place, with a total land area of 1,104 square kilometres (Information Services Department 2012), which is slightly smaller than Los Angeles. Furthermore, because of the hilly landscape and large number of outlying islands, only a relatively small portion of land can be developed. In response to these constraints, Hong Kong has been expanding its usable land by reclamation, but despite this effort, it has become more densely populated due to population growth over time, mainly by immigration. Counting only the usable land, the population density in Hong Kong is around 36,000 persons per square kilometre, almost 11 times that of Los Angeles, six times that of London, five times that of Tokyo, or 35 per cent more than that of Manhattan New York. Such a high population density requires an efficient transportation system to support mobility and economic development. On the other hand, this high density provides the essential ingredient for the development of a mass transit railway.

Land scarcity and population expansion require the Hong Kong government to use land resources effectively. The land-development strategies, in turn, have catalysed sustained high-density development over the years. The limited supply has caused rapid increases in the prices of land and property, with the average price index of private domestic premises recording a four-fold increase in the past quarter of century (Census and Statistics Department 2011). The prosperous real estate market has thus formed one of the most important pillars for the economic growth of Hong Kong. On the other hand, further development of the existing central business districts around Victoria Harbour through land reclamation and replacement of low-rise buildings with modern skyscrapers has generated tremendous converging traffic demand from various residential areas and new towns to these central districts, while the construction of high-density residential estates around railway stations has created a large pool of potential passengers to support the operation of rail transit services and recover investments in railways. Conversely, the rail service provides a convenient and accessible mode of travel for nearby residents. Synergistically, the improved accessibility brought about by the rail service helps boost the value of properties built on top of railway stations. In the end, the high urban density resulting from Hong Kong's land development strategies, especially along the railway corridors, provides ideal conditions for the development of integrated rail and property projects.

Financial Viability of Rail Transit Service

How MTR Earns a Viable Profit

The provision of financially sustainable accessibility via mass transit railways has been difficult to achieve in many countries around the world. The success of Hong Kong in providing financially viable rail service, therefore, serves as an important reference. A remarkable aspect of mass transit railway service in Hong Kong is that all railway services are operated according to prudent commercial principles. The profitability consideration, however, has not resulted in unaffordable fare as characterized by virtually reduced fare level over the years after price escalation is taken into account (Transport Bureau 1999), but not surprisingly, has driven the operator to strive for the utmost operating efficiency and continuous service expansion for business growth (Figure 12.1). It is therefore important to know how the private operations can manage to achieve financial viability without government subsidies.

To study the financial viability of railway service in Hong Kong, we analyse the account book of the operator, MTR, with an aim to assess how it has maintained profitability while providing quality services over the years. It is a listed company with its operating and financial data available with sufficient details in its annual reports. The financial viability analysis considers three aspects: (1) income derived purely from the core business of providing rail transit service, (2) income from (1) plus income from other commercial activities that complement railway operations, and (3) income from (2) plus income from property development and management, through the 20 years before its merging with KCR in 2007 which had significant impact to its financial profile and makes a trend analysis beyond that not meaningful. The results of painstakingly working through the annual reports of MTR and segregating the financial data according to these three aspects are presented in Figure 12.2.

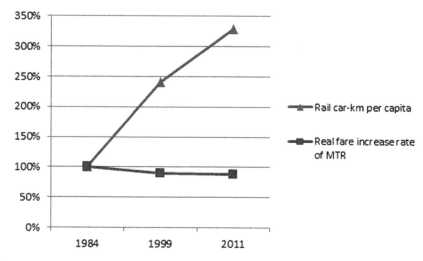

Figure 12.1   Rate of MTR real fare increases and rail transit service supplies over years

Source: (MTRCL 1986–2011).[1]

On average, the proportion of fare revenue in the total income of MTR had reduced from 80 per cent in the first 10 years (1986–1996) to 50 per cent in the last 10 years (1996–2006). In other words, over the years, MTR had become less dependent on its fare-box income. The high proportion of non-fare revenue reflects the strategy and financial needs of MTR for business development in addition to railway operations, which enhances its financial performance while paying for capital investments. MTR would not have been able to sustain financially had it relied on fare revenue alone. Figure 12.2 shows that the railway has not ever been able to earn enough fare revenue to pay for high capital depreciation and financing costs, which have been similar in magnitude to operating costs over the past 20 years. The exception was the few years prior to the completion of the Airport Railway in 1998 when the investment to build the urban lines in 1970s and 1980s had been paid off. Thus, the profitability of MTR has relied heavily on non-fare recurrent revenue from commercial activities in stations, such as kiosks and advertising, as well as railway consultancy services (i.e. the difference between the middle and bottom lines in Figure 12.2).

---

1   Figures were estimated from MTRCL Annual Reports as source data.

Nevertheless, despite more than doubled non-fare revenue over the last 10 years (1996–2006), MTR still suffered from operating loss (after accounting for capital depreciation) in the years subsequent to the opening of the Airport Railway and then the Tseung Kwan O Line in early 2000s. This is obviously not commercially viable. Hence, the financial viability of MTR has been largely dependent on earnings from property development on top of train stations (after deduction of the land premium paid to government for property development), including profits from property sales and recurrent revenue from rental and management of associated shopping arcades (i.e. the difference between the top and middle lines in Figure 12.2). This significant source of income allows MTR to pay for the capital investment on railway infrastructure development and asset replacement. Without the income from property development, MTR would be unable to earn a viable return and would have to seek alternative support from the government for its continuous service improvement and network expansion. In other words, the non-fare income is crucial to the financial viability of a mass transit railway without funding support from government – even one with high levels of patronage and good operating efficiency like MTR.

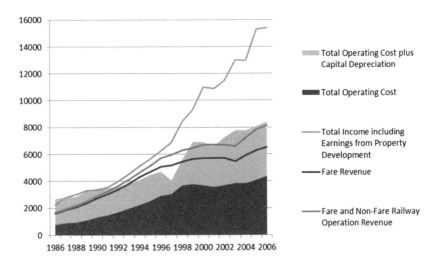

Figure 12.2   The cost and turnover of MTR over the past two decades
Source: (MTRCL 1986–2006).[2]

Synergy between Rail Transit Service and Property Development

The success of Hong Kong in the provision of mass transit services via the private sector, with financial viability secured by cross-subsidization through property development, sets forth a unique public-private partnership service supply model. The experience of Hong Kong sheds light on a business model that goes beyond the core business and successfully extends and integrates railway operations with different sorts of commercial opportunities, offering an innovative way for providing and financing rail services. This integration creates synergy between property development and rail transit service. The rail service

---

2   Figures were estimated from MTRCL Annual Reports as source data.

improves the accessibility of the adjacent real-estate properties and hence increases their values, while at the same time the real-estate properties generate traffic for the rail service and hence increase its fare revenue. Higher fare revenue can in turn support better service quality, leading to still higher levels of patronage. This synergy may offer a way to break the vicious cycle of declining rail transit service and pave the way for improving the accessibility on public transport via financially viable railway service.

Financing of Mass Transit Railway Projects

Prevailing Railway Development Model in Hong Kong

The capital investment required for a rail transit project is huge as compared with other transport infrastructure. Even worse is the thin likelihood, as per experience of many countries, that fare revenue alone is sufficient to support the operation of a rail transit system and hence sustain its viability in the long run. The participation of the private sector in either construction or operation, or both, of rail transit projects has been one of the key considerations to improve the financial viability of the projects, especially being encouraged by the success of the prevailing railway development model in Hong Kong. This model goes beyond the traditional ways of engaging the private sector in constructing or operating the railway; but rather builds on a tripod relationship among government, railway company and property developer, in which the railway company builds, funds, owns and operates the railway, and jointly develops real estate property on top of railway stations together with a private developer. By doing so, the railway company cross-subsidizes the infrastructure investments with profits from property development, which ensures the financial viability of the entire synergistic transit-property project. Although the government has no direct involvement, it plays the crucial role in formulating necessary transport and land use policies, setting up legislative framework, initiating and coordinating strategic railway development, and monitoring service quality (Tang and Lo 2008, 2010a).

The participation of the private sector in developing rail transit projects is often considered as a way to shift certain risks, management, finance, or otherwise, from the public sector to a private partner, who may be in a better position to manage the risks (International Tunnelling Association 2004, Oncala 2004, Zhang 2005). Nevertheless, the success of a rail transit project requires a 'win-win' situation for all stakeholders, wherein all partners, public or private, achieve their different objectives. The partnership cannot sustain if any partner has to endure long-term losses, which will in turn jeopardize the project as a whole. In other words, the success of a rail transit project often involves an appropriate sharing of risks and returns among the public and private partners. It is therefore interesting to analyse whether the prevailing PPP model in Hong Kong, or any alternative model, is more likely to meet the objectives of a project. In this section, we study four alternative PPP models (Tang and Lo 2010b), and assess how the different extents of involvement among government, railway company and property developer in building, funding, owning and operating the railway may enhance the likelihood of its financial viability, timely completion and fulfilment of the transportation needs.

Alternative Public-Private Partnership Models

Having the unlikely scenarios excluded, the tripod partnership model between the public sector, private railway company and property developer can be formed in four alternative ways (Tang and Lo 2010b). With the nomenclatures following the standard pattern of BFOOD, representing 'Build', 'Fund', 'Own', 'Operate' and 'Develop Property', and with subscripts R (rail), G (government) or D (developer) indicating the responsible partner, the four alternatives are then denoted as: $B_R F_R O_R O_R D_{R/D}$, $B_R F_G O_R O_R D_{G/R/D}$, $B_G F_G O_G O_R D_{G/D}$ and $B_D F_D O_G O_R D_D$ accordingly. Based on this nomenclature scheme, we summarize in Table 12.2 the roles of each partner in these four models.

$B_R F_R O_R O_R D_{R/D}$

The $B_R F_R O_R O_R D_{R/D}$ model is exactly the common model in Hong Kong, where the railway company builds, funds, owns and operates the railway, and jointly develops real estate property on top of railway stations together with a private developer. The government has no direct involvement except in policy formulation, strategic planning, legislative approval and service monitoring.

$B_R F_G O_R O_R D_{G/R/D}$

In the $B_R F_G O_R O_R D_{G/R/D}$ model, the railway company is involved to a lesser extent. It owns the rail transit system, and is involved in building and operating the railway. On the other hand, the government funds the project and develops real estate property in conjunction with a private developer. The West Rail in Hong Kong was a typical example. The railway was built by KCR with direct funding from the government in the form of an upfront equity injection. While KCR remained the owner and operator of the railway, it only acted as the agent for the government to develop real estate property on top of railway stations and was obliged to return all its share of profit to the government (Finance Bureau 1998). In this model, the government, instead of the railway company, bears the financial risk on payback to the infrastructure investment, due to the cyclical nature of the property market or prolonged delay in developing the real estates.

$B_G F_G O_G O_R D_{G/D}$

In contrast, in the $B_G F_G O_G O_R D_{G/D}$ model, the government is heavily involved in almost every aspect including property development, probably in conjunction with a private developer. The only exception is operation of the rail service where the railway company is involved. Heavy involvement of the government remains the most common approach for rail transit projects developed all over the world (Amos 2004, World Bank 2007). In Singapore, the entire mass rapid transit system was built by the Land Transport Authority and respectively licensed to SMRT Corporation and SBS Transit Limited for operation of different lines of the system, while transit oriented property development was implemented through another two government entities namely the Housing and Development Board and Urban Redevelopment Authority (Cervero and Murakami 2008). The electrification of East Rail in Hong Kong was another example. In this model, as the private sector plays the least role compared with the previous two models, the efficiency benefits as anticipated from private participation (Amos 2004, Zhang 2006) might not be realized.

Table 12.2   Roles of public and private partners in alternative public-private partnership models

Model	Government	Railway Company	Property Developer
1. $B_R F_R O_R O_R D_{R/D}$			
Build	—	yes	—
Fund	—	yes	—
Own	—	yes	—
Operate	—	yes	—
Develop Property	—	yes	yes
2. $B_R F_G O_R O_R D_{G/R/D}$			
Build	—	yes	—
Fund	yes	—	—
Own	—	yes	—
Operate	—	yes	—
Develop Property	yes	—	yes
3. $B_G F_G O_G O_R D_{G/D}$			
Build	yes	—	—
Fund	yes	—	—
Own	yes	—	—
Operate	—	yes	—
Develop Property	yes	—	yes
4. $B_D F_D O_G O_R D_D$			
Build	—	—	yes
Fund	—	—	yes
Own	yes	—	—
Operate	—	yes	—
Develop Property	—	—	yes

$B_DF_DO_GO_RD_D$

The private developer is most heavily involved in the $B_DF_DO_GO_RD_D$ model, building and funding the rail transit project, and solely developing the real estate property. Upon completion of the project, the developer transfers the ownership of the railway to the government, who then appoints a railway company to run the service as an operating agent under some concessionary agreement. While this model is not practiced in Hong Kong, such cases, albeit infrequent, do exist in other parts of the world, such as the Hopewell Saga Project in Bangkok. The failure of the Saga Project gave a clear lesson of the insecurity of linking rail transit infrastructure development to the profitability of property developer (Gwilliam 2002). Indeed, the rare occurrence of this model perhaps can be attributed to the fact that a mass transit railway project takes more or less 10 years from inception to completion (Mak and Mo 2005), which is often beyond the strategic planning period of a property developer in committing financial resources, having to endure long-term financial risks due to the cyclical and vulnerable property market. In addition, property developer is likely to put more emphasis and higher priority on property development as its core business due to the significantly greater profitability as compared with that of a rail transit project.

Analysis of Alternative Models

Influence diagram approach

For each alternative PPP model, there are various intertwined factors affecting the outcome of a new rail transit line. Assessment of the likelihood of success in meeting the objectives of a rail transit project is often too complex without a systematic way of analysing the interactions among the factors. We make use of the influence diagram approach to describe and portray the interrelations between the decisions and outcomes while considering the PPP model. The point is to have a complete picture of all relevant factors that may have positive or negative influences in pursuit of the objectives of a project, so that one can assess the combined effects of all influences and eventually come up with decisions towards achieving the objectives. With the help of a graphical model to conduct the analysis, the result is to identify key issues that decision makers should be aware of when deciding the extent of involvement of the public and private sectors.

Decisions: In whichever PPP model, the railway company is in the position of operating the railway (either as the owner or an operating agent), and the property developer either jointly with a partner or solely developing real estate property on top of railway stations. In other words, the choice among the alternative PPP models mainly involves the decisions of which of the three parties to 'build', 'fund' and/or 'own' the mass transit railway.

Objectives: The objectives of government, railway company and property developer to build, fund and/or own a mass transit railway project may vary, but can largely be summarized into financial, transportation and construction aspects. While profit maximization is obviously the key objective of private investment, a publicly funded project would also very likely have one of its objectives to ensure good value or return for the investment. In quantitative terms, the financial objective may hence be a certain internal rate of return or profit margin, the payback period of certain portion of the capital investment, or simply the capital expenditure within budget. The transportation objectives of railway company or property developer are usually more specific, represented by the forecast level of patronage or market share, whereas the government often has more generic transportation objectives, like reduction of congestion, increase of accessibility and mobility, increase of the use of public transport, etc. Quantitatively, these objectives can be stated as a certain per cent increase in the public transport market share, increases in usage in terms of total passenger journeys, or increases in average speed, etc. Last but not least, the construction objective is usually timely completion of the project according to the pre-defined safety standards and design intents, regardless of which party is building the project.

Influential variables: The decision on who to build, fund and own the railway does not produce the outcomes directly, but indirectly through the interactions between certain variables that have significant influences on a project's success. The variables interact with one another and eventually affect the likelihood of achieving the project objectives. The following provides a brief description of these variables.

Capital cost: The huge capital investment required for a rail transit project results in tremendous influence of the variable of capital cost on the financial risk of the project, and eventually the fare level of the railway in order to ensure financial viability and avoid burdening the government budget (Asian Development Bank 2005). The significance of this variable can be reflected by its feedback effect on the decision of which of the public and private partners to fund the project, as well as its bearing on the final scope of the design and method of construction.

Design and construction: Design and construction of a railway determines its scale, service standard, efficiency; and hence variables including capital cost, service quality and operating cost.

Fare level: The price is beyond doubt a major factor affecting the attractiveness of a rail transit line. However, one should be cautious that a low fare attracting high patronage is not necessarily an optimal fare, which should be affordable from users' perspective and also viable from the operator's point of view. Besides, the transformation of time into monetary term often involves theoretical assumptions; in reality, people taking public transit services tend to be much more concerned with their out-of-pocket costs.

Patronage: The demand for travel is the most fundamental element that determines whether a sound revenue stream exists to assure the financial viability of a transport infrastructure project in the long run. The number of passengers also reflects whether the investment succeeds to increase accessibility (Lo et al. 2008) and achieve the transportation objectives.

Productivity and operating cost: Financial viability depends on profitability in the long term and profit is a simple subtraction between revenue and cost. The influence of productivity and hence the operating cost on the financial objective of a rail transit is therefore obvious.

Project completion: Project completion is a variable having direct influence on the accomplishment of all the objectives. In case of prolonged project delay, one can expect that the total capital cost will escalate and more likely exceed the budget, and that transportation problems, such as road congestion and suppressed demand due to insufficient public transport facilities, cannot be timely resolved.

Public acceptance: While public acceptance or political pressure from different stakeholders may affect decisions on the extents of involvement of each public and private sector, a decision with recognized benefits to society as a whole, through wide consultation and public communication, can also influence public acceptance. In any event, it is generally considered that a railway with good public acceptance is likely to be more heavily used and vice versa.

Service quality: The service level of a rail transit, in terms of its waiting time, travel time, transfer time, point-to-point connectivity and reliability (Lo et al. 2008), is a major determinant of patronage. It is largely the performance of the railway as a result of the committed service standard, its design and construction, as well as how effective and efficient the operation is managed.

Influence diagrams

The influence diagrams developed for the 'build', 'fund' and 'own' decisions are respectively presented in Figures 12.3, 12.4 and 12.5. The diagrams are developed based on the assumptions that decisions are made under due consideration of the current and foreseeable macro-economy and property market as well as under the framework of prevailing transportation and land use policies. For simplicity, the associated decision and objectives are not shown in the diagrams. Rectangular nodes are used to represent variables under direct influences of the decision under consideration, shaded rectangular nodes to denote variables dependent on other variables as well, and oval nodes to signify variables directly affecting the accomplishment of objectives. Inside each node, the intended positive outcome(s) of the variable is (are) shown in the lower part of the node.

The decision of 'who builds': The decision of who builds directly influences the variables of capital cost, design and construction, and project completion, and through them and their dependent variables, influences the objectives of a mass transit railway (Figure 12.3).

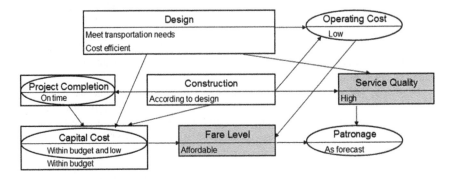

Figure 12.3   Influence diagram of the 'Build' decision
Source: Author.

It is generally considered that higher efficiency and cost consciousness of private companies are likely to have positive influence on the variables of capital cost and project completion, or in other words more likely to enable the project being built on time and within budget (Higton 2005, OECD 2000). However, one should be cautious that financial instability, lack of technical expertise and ineffective project management of the private partner who builds the railway are among the common reasons why a railway project cannot complete on time (Zhang 2005). On the other hand, stringent cost control measures put in place to ensure the project to be within budget sometimes may compromise the fundamental transportation objectives. In Hong Kong, the strong commitment of the public sector and the legal framework are essential tools to assure the railway company in fulfilment of its obligation in construction and operations of the railway, and in meeting the transportation needs.

A report of OECD (2000) points out that the greater involvement of the operator in the planning, design and construction stages of a rail transit project, the less risk that the railway is designed and built at the expense of its long term operating efficiency and service quality. The report also gives warning on the potential moral hazard that the construction contractor may not fully carry out its contractual obligations and build the railway to the design intent, because the contractor cares more about the cost than the operating difficulties which are to be faced by the operating party. The result is often less operating efficiency, and hence greater financial burden in the long run especially when significant rectification and improvement work is required to put the railway back to the required service standards. In other words, the decision on whether the owner and/or the operator to build the railway, or at least to be substantially involved in its design and construction, is likely to have significant implication on the outcome of the project and whether its objectives can be effectively met.

The key issues that the 'build' decision should address can be summarized as below:

1. Whether there exist financially and technically competent private partners to build the railway?
2. Whether there are effective regulatory and/or administrative measures to ensure that the private builder will make an appropriate balance between cost efficiency and transportation objectives of the project?
3. Whether the owning and/or operating partner is in a position to have early involvement in or take charge of building the railway?

The decision of 'who funds': The decision of who funds directly influences the variables of capital cost, design, fare level, project completion and public acceptance, and through them and their dependent variables, further influences the objectives of a mass transit railway (Figure 12.4). The influence of this decision on the financial and transportation objectives is apparently greater than that of the 'build' decision because its dependent variables, such as fare level and public acceptance, have direct or indirect influences on these objectives.

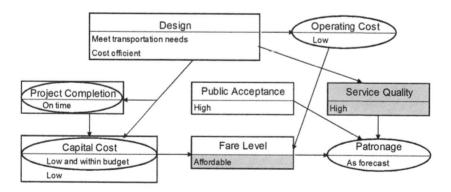

Figure 12.4   Influence diagram of the 'Fund' decision
Source: Author.

According to a global study on metro systems by Halcrow Fox (2000), effectiveness of organization and management is the dominant factor influencing metro capital cost, and the private sector is generally more capable of reducing the implementation time and construction cost of metro systems. In fact, there were plenty of precedents of government-led transport infrastructure projects whose capital costs were substantially under-estimated, causing sizeable cost overruns (OECD 2000). This is one major reason in support of the involvement of the private sector in developing mass transit railways.

In Hong Kong, property developers are excluded from funding the transit part of transit-property projects. This is to avoid the risk wherein the property market or profit from property development is directly linked to transit infrastructure project, hence affecting the completion time of a project. The Jubilee Line extension of London Underground (OECD 2000) and Hopewell Saga Project of Bangkok (Gwilliam 2002) are typical examples of railway projects with heavy involvement of property developers on funding and construction. They were either extensively delayed or defaulted due to the cyclical slump of the vulnerable property market causing the respective developers to defer or withdraw their investments. They demonstrated the extra risks of connecting the prosperity of land and property market and hence the profitability of developers to transport infrastructure development (OECD 2000).

Timely completion of the property part of a synergistic transit-property development project is equally important; profits from property development are crucial for paying back the infrastructure investment. In Hong Kong, the West Rail is an exceptional case, with the property development lagging far behind schedule. While the railway began operating at the end of 2003, only one of the planned property development projects at its stations has been completed and all others are still in planning or tendering stage after 10 years. As mentioned above, the railway was built by KCR with direct funding support from the government. In exchange, the government is entitled to all the share of profit from property development (Finance Bureau 1998). To the contrary, although the KCR Ma On Shan Line was opened one year later, three property development projects have been completed. It is interesting to note that the Ma On Shan Line was also built with direct funding support from the government, but the government is not entitled to any share of profit from the associated property development. While there can be various reasons to explain the delay of property development along the West Rail, this financing arrangement inevitably induces an additional risk on the project as a whole, arising from the difficulty and complexity in managing the distribution of capital and benefit between the public and private sectors (Tang and Lo 2010b).

Rail transit infrastructure is traditionally regarded as public goods, and is often provided by the government as social welfare (Zhang 2005). The greater extent of involvement of the private sector, especially if the user-pay principle is adopted, which will result in higher fares in the absence of indirect subsidy, the greater effort and longer time are likely to be required to win public acceptance and support. The school of thought that advocates the user-pay principle argues that a new rail transit system should not cause additional burden to taxpayers who do not enjoy the benefit. The implication of the 'fund' and 'own' decisions on public acceptance can therefore vary, depending on which school of thought prevails, whether the decision can be justified from financial and social perspectives, whether the private partner's return can be effectively regulated, and how the government, its policies and the consultation process influence the stakeholders.

The above discussions on the 'fund' decision can be summarized by the following key issues that the decision makers should contemplate:

1. Whether the public sector can implement the project with lower capital cost and manage the capital investment in an equally efficient manner as the private sector?
2. Whether the core business of the funding private partner is vulnerable to the macro-economic conditions, especially the property market?
3. Whether the investing partner will have to rely on effort of other partners for return on investment?
4. Whether the funding arrangement can gain public acceptance?
5. Whether the investing partner's return and influence on meeting the transportation needs can be effectively regulated?

The decision of 'who owns': The decision of who owns directly influences the variables of design, fare level, productivity, public acceptance and service quality, and through them and their dependent variables, indirectly influences the financial and transportation objectives of a mass transit railway (Figure 12.5). As its dependent variables influencing the financial objective are quite different from those of the 'build' and 'fund' decisions, it is difficult to say which decision has greater influence on this objective. Nevertheless, the greater influence of the 'own' decision on the transportation objective is more apparent, because of its direct influence on more variables with influential effects on patronage.

It is widely believed that private companies, because of their commercially oriented objectives, are more operationally efficient and innovative in the use and management of assets and resources than public organizations. Occasionally, the public sector may have to accomplish other imperatives, such as maintaining certain minimum service frequency or providing employment opportunities, at the expense of operating efficiency and productivity (Higton 2005). In this regard, it is important for decision makers to realize whether the public sector would be facing such political pressure when deciding which partner to own the railway.

The vision of the owner often determines the level of sophistication of system design and hence the service standard of the rail transit. As it is reasonable to expect that the government, railway company and property developer, as owner of the railway, will have different visions from both social and commercial perspectives, the decision of ownership is likely to make a considerable difference on the concerned variables.

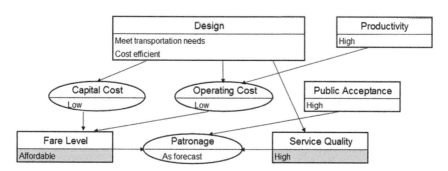

Figure 12.5   Influence diagram of the 'Own' decision
Source: Author.

The involvement of the private sector in providing public transit services often results in tariff increases, such as in London. One can expect that higher fares are needed to strengthen revenue and to pay for the increased spending on service enhancements. While tariff increases are likely to have negative impact on patronage, the increased efficiency and improved services may offset the adverse effect and eventually result in net increases in both passengers and fare revenue. The experience of Hong Kong shows that high efficiency and affordable fare can go hand-in-hand with profit maximization (Tang and Lo 2008).

In contrast, the public sector may have other concerns on top of financial ones when setting fares. The decision of the Beijing municipal government to reduce the metro price to a flat fare of ¥2.00[3] per trip was, following the policy of the national government, partially to contain inflation and partially to encourage shifts to this more environmentally friendly mode of transport. The implication of this example on the ownership decision is, therefore, whether the public sector would like to retain the control of fare setting in the long run, for the sake of social or political reasons.

A summary of the key issues of the 'own' decision is listed as below:

1. Whether the owner has an obligation to take care of social interest, even at the expense of operating efficiency?
2. Whether the envisioned service standard is aligned between the public and private sectors?
3. Whether it is essential for the public sector to retain control setting fares?
4. Whether the ownership arrangement can gain public acceptance?

Concluding Remarks

The experience of Hong Kong reveals that the private sector can provide quality railway services at affordable fares. However, it is also clear that, even at high levels of patronage and operating efficiency, the fare revenue alone is unable to recover the capital investment for a mass transit railway and to generate a viable return. The success of Hong Kong in the provision of mass transit services via the private sector, with financial viability secured by cross-subsidization through property development, sets forth a unique public-private partnership service supply model, which can serve as a benchmark for new projects. The experience of Hong Kong sheds light on a business model that goes beyond the core business and successfully extends and integrates railway operations with different sorts of commercial opportunities, which not only generate significant non-fare income but also enhance the overall service quality. It is advisable for countries or cities opting for new railway projects to set out clear objectives and to formulate the service supply model to meet the objectives. The model should include the form of contribution by the public sector, the involvement of the private sector, and the way to ensure the financial sustainability of the project.

However, the objectives of a rail transit project are often in multiple dimensions in that their accomplishment or not is the result of the complex interactions between different influential variables. The influence diagrams presented in this chapter portray the interrelations of these influential variables in a systematic and holistic manner, and serve to illustrate which public or private partner among government, railway company

---

3   Equivalent to approximately 30 US cents.

and property developer to build, fund and own the railway respectively may more likely accomplish the objectives. The experience of Hong Kong shows that it is not just the role of each public or private partner, but rather the effectiveness of managing the variables, maximizing their positive influences and minimizing negative impacts, that determine the success or failure of a rail transit project. Provided that relevant data are available, in terms of probabilities of the outcomes as a result of the decisions, the influence diagrams can be easily transformed for quantitative assessment of the likelihood of achieving the various objectives. For accuracy, this will require a large number of case studies to populate the different PPP models so that quantitative results can be derived. This is an important and meaningful exercise that can be built up over time.

References

Amos, P. 2004. *Public and Private Sector Roles in the Supply of Transport Infrastructure and Services.* Transport Sector Board, The World Bank Group.

Asian Development Bank. 2005. *People Republic of China: Application of Public Private Partnerships in Urban Rail-based Transportation Project.* Technical Assistance Report, 39527.

Cervero, R. and Murakam,i J. 2008. *Rail + Property Development: A Model of Sustainable Transit Finance and Urbanism.* UC Berkeley Centre for Future Urban Transport.

Census and Statistics Department. 2011. *Hong Kong Annual Digest of Statistics.* Hong Kong Special Administrative Region Government.

Environment Branch. 1979. *Keeping Hong Kong Moving: The White Paper on Internal Transport Policy.* Hong Kong Government.

Finance Bureau. 1998. *Equity Injection for Implementation of West Rail Phase I Project.* Submitted to Provisional Legislative Council Panel on Financial Affairs and Panel on Transport. Hong Kong Special Administrative Region Government.

Gwilliam, K. 2002. *Mass Rapid Transit in Cities on the Move: A World Bank Urban Transport Strategy Review.* The World Bank, 109–24.

Halcrow Fox. 2000. *World Bank Urban Transport Strategy Review – Mass Rapid Transit in Developing Countries: Final Report.*

Higton, N. 2005. *Using PPP to Deliver Successful Rail Projects.* Presented at the Conference on Public Private Partnerships – Opportunities and Challenges, Hong Kong.

Information Services Department. 2012. *Hong Kong Yearbook 2011.* Hong Kong Special Administrative Region Government.

International Road Federation. 2013. *World Road Statistics.*

International Tunnelling Association, Working Group Number 13. 2004. Underground or aboveground? Making the choice for urban mass transit systems. *Tunnel and Underground Space Technology*, 19, 3–28.

Lo, H.K., Tang, S. and Wang, D. 2008. Managing the accessibility on mass public transit: The case of Hong Kong. *Journal of Transport and Land Use*, 1(2), 23–49.

Mak, C.K. and Mo, S. 2005. *Some aspects of the PPP approach to transport infrastructure development in Hong Kong.* Presented at the Conference on Public Private Partnerships – Opportunities and Challenges, Hong Kong.

Mass Transit Railway Corporation Limited (MTRCL). 1986–2011. *Annual Report.*

Organisation for Economic Co-operation and Development (OECD). 2000. *Integrating Transport in City – Reconciling the Economic, Social and Environmental Dimensions.* Paris: OECD Publications.

Oncala, A.A. 2004. Brazil turns to PPP for infrastructure investment. *International Financial Law Review*, 23(11), 26–8.

Singapore Land Transport Authority Academy. 2011. Passenger transport mode shares in world cities. *Journeys*, November 2011.

Tang, S. and Lo, H.K. 2008. The impact of public transport policy on the viability and sustainability of mass railway transit – Hong Kong experience. *Transportation Research A*, 42(4), 563–76.

Tang, S. and Lo, H.K. 2010a. On the financial viability of mass transit development: The case of Hong Kong. *Transportation*, 37(2), 299–316.

Tang, S., and Lo, H.K. 2010b. Assessment of public private partnership models for mass rail transit – an influence diagram approach. *Public Transport – Planning and Operations*, 2(1), 111–34.

Transport Branch. 1990. *Moving into the Twenty-first Century: The White Paper on Transport Policy in Hong Kong.* Hong Kong Government.

Transport Branch. 1994. *Railway Development Strategy.* Hong Kong Government.

Transport Bureau. 1999. *Hong Kong Moving Ahead.* Hong Kong Special Administrative Region Government.

Transport Bureau. 2000. *Railway Development Strategy.* Hong Kong Special Administrative Region Government.

Transport Department. 1999. *Third Comprehensive Transport Study Final Report.* Hong Kong Special Administrative Region Government.

Transport Department. 2003. *Travel Characteristics Survey 2002 Final Report.* Hong Kong Special Administrative Region Government.

Transport Department. 2012. *Annual Transport Digest.* Hong Kong Special Administrative Region Government.

World Bank. 2007. *Reforming Transport: Maximizing Synergy Between Public and Private Sectors.*

Zhang, X. 2005. Critical success factors for public private partnerships in infrastructure development. *Journal of Construction Engineering and Management*, 131(1), 3–14.

Zhang, X. 2006. Public clients' best value perspectives of public private partnerships in infrastructure development. *Journal of Construction Engineering and Management*, 132(2), 107–14.

Chapter 13
Intermodal Transportation

Brian Slack

Introduction

By the late 1960s the US rail industry was in crisis. A major cause of this crisis was the loss of business to other modes. Passenger traffic was declining as automobiles and air transport drew away a large share of the market. In the freight business the railroads were losing the higher value (and higher revenue-generating) goods to trucking. A transport mode that had laid the basis for the industrial and agricultural development of the US was facing financial collapse. This trend has been repeated also in many other parts of the world.

The late 1970s marked a watershed for US railroads, however, and since then they have experienced something of a reversal of health in the freight business. A new sub-market has been created, that of intermodal traffic, based largely on the maritime container. In addition to providing a new traffic source, intermodal traffic involved a major restructuring of the railroad industry and its organization. This success has led other countries to consider whether intermodal transportation can provide a comparable stimulus to their domestic rail industries.

In this chapter the factors behind the growth of intermodal transport in the US and Europe are reviewed. The trajectory of development in North America and elsewhere has not been smooth, however. In the US its growth has produced capacity and congestion problems for the railroads. Questions about the concentration of ownership have come forward and there are moves to promote competition. In Europe, intermodal transport enjoys mixed results. Regulatory reform has sought to open access to new players with varying degrees of success. For Europe, some of the big issues facing intermodal transportation include its absence from many regions, and the imbalance between the established national companies and the new entrants.

Defining Intermodal Transport

Many freight movements are multi-modal. As products move from source to market combinations of trucking, water transport, air freight or railroads may be used. Here the individual items are loaded and unloaded as separate stages in a transport chain, with each segment being organized separately. In intermodal transport the goods are typically placed in a container that is designed to hold many products and be transferred easily from one mode to another. This simple concept, however, required a number of technical and organizational innovations that had to be put in place before it could become successful.

First, the ease of transfer was made possible by the early decision of the International Standards Organization (ISO) to establish the world-wide standards for the dimension of the boxes. Had this not been agreed upon a mix of proprietal and national dimensions would have made its transferability costly and complex. The standards established a width of 8 feet, a height of 8 feet and two lengths of 20 feet and 40 feet. The size of the container thus determined the unit of counting boxes as multiples of 20 feet (twenty foot equivalent units or TEUs) (Levinson 2006).

Second, containerization required new equipment to hand that would be capable of transporting them, since regular ships or trains were not designed to maximize container numbers. In addition, it required the design and purchase of equipment that could lift the containers and transfer them between the modes. These represented significant capital investments.

Third, it required an organizational readjustment since goods now could be transported across many separate modes. In order to achieve better integration of the transport chain there had to emerge companies who could organize the services and assume legal responsibility for the transfers and shipments with through bills of lading. In some cases shipping lines took the lead, but over time the importance of third parties such as forwarders achieved prominence.

Tracing the Development of Rail Intermodalism: the Success of the US

In the US the railroads were initially cautious about the container (Bowen and Slack 2007). They had already invested in 'piggyback' where road trailers are loaded onto rail flat cars for shipment. This system of 'Trailer on Flat Car' (TOFC) had been adopted to counteract the loss of traffic to the trucking industry, but the system was slow and cumbersome, with terminal facilities established in traditional freight yards located in every major market, and the trucking industry saw it as a competitor and were reluctant to cooperate. Furthermore given the difficult financial health of the industry, US railroads were in no position to invest in a new capital intensive system.

The shipping industry was the first mode to adopt the container mainly as a means of reducing the time and costs of loading and discharging ships (Levinson 2006). It was the mode that experienced the highest terminal charges and thus the benefits of containerization were quickly realized. The US shipping lines were among the first to adopt the container and the first trans-Atlantic service was initiated in 1965. Onward delivery from ports, however, was captured largely by the trucking industry.

Significant change occurred after 1980. Growing imports from Asia (principally Japan, Taiwan and later China) prompted a market shift. Up until that time containerized trade was focused on the North Atlantic. Goods shipped from the emerging Asian markets and destined for the major US East Coast markets passed through the Panama Canal en route for New York. This represented a costly trade route for the shipping lines, since many ships had to be assigned to the service because of the length of time of each voyage (>35 days), and because of the tolls on the Canal. A much shorter route from Asia to US West Coast ports would be feasible if the containers could be sent by rail to Eastern markets. Not finding the US railroads ready to commit themselves, some shipping lines, most notably the US carrier American President Lines (APL), arranged with a manufacturer to produce and lease special flat cars and to contract with rail companies such as Southern Pacific to haul dedicated container services from West Coast ports to a number of terminals in the East, which the shipping lines leased and operated. Initially the railroads provided locomotives only, the services being at the financial risk of the shipping lines. The shipping lines achieved economies by reducing overall delivery times by 10 days over the all-water route to New York, and they were able to make better deployment of their ships, since the Trans-Pacific ocean crossing required 18 days only.

The success of this land bridge service was based not only on the emergence of a new trade route, but also by several other factors that came into play:

- The financial difficulties of the US Railroads, and the collapse of a large railroad company, the New York Central, forced the US government to completely change the regulatory environment. A series of reforms, culminating in the Staggers Act of 1980, allowed the US Railroads to abandon the passenger business, permitted ownership between different transport modes; allowed railroads to abandon uneconomic routes; gave the railroads more flexibility in managing personnel; and freed rate structures (Breeautigam 1993).
- The great distances from the West Coast ports to Eastern markets made truck transport largely uncompetitive, thus giving the railroads a more or less captive market.
- APL pioneered the use of double stacking, by which the capacity per train was doubled without an equivalent increase in fuel costs.

Freed from regulatory constraints the railroads took an ever larger interest in containerization, and this created a new traffic category, container on flat car (COFC) which rapidly overtook TOFC in importance. Over time the railroads developed and expanded the number of intermodal services from all West Coast ports. Because they acted as wholesalers of the service they were seen by trucking firms as not competing for the business of their clients, and some of the major trucking groups began to use rail intermodal for long distance haulage of their containerized traffic. Furthermore the railways made no move to provide door-to-door service.

The success of the intermodal system built on Western traffic was slower to be extended in the East. The Eastern port cities themselves are major markets, making rail distribution from local ports uncompetitive, but there were several other problems, including the poor access to the railroad terminals from East Coast ports, and bridge and tunnel clearances that impeded double stack services. Over the years these latter issues have been addressed, and today there are well established corridors linking East Coast ports with Mid-West markets.

A further development in intermodal transport in the US was the development of domestic containerization (Slack 1994). Although the initial impetus for intermodal rail was the import-export market, traffic imbalances resulted in many empty containers being hauled back to the ports. The shipping lines saw an opportunity to offer space for goods being shipped from interior centres to coastal markets. Because trucking dimensions are larger than ISO containers by as much as 80 per cent domestic traffic was at a cost disadvantage. They developed a range of container sizes for particular market conditions, including containers that are 48 and 53 feet long. Initially conceived for domestic traffic these domestic containers have impacted on import freight and has led to a new activity in port markets: that of transloading (Rodrigue 2008). Here, goods in maritime containers arriving by ship are transloaded into larger domestic containers for shipment inland. The maritime containers may be thus loaded with export goods or returned overseas empty. For the shipping lines this is an advantage since their propriety containers are returned quickly into service.

The Contemporary Situation of Rail Intermodalism in the US

By the first decade of the twenty-first century, rail intermodal in the US was a mature system. It had a number of specific features:

- As shown in Figure 13.1, traffic reached a peak of 12 million TEUs in 2007, fell during the recession, but has grown again to nearly 12 million TEUs in 2011. It focused on a number of corridors linking the main cities and coastal ports. There are over 200 daily double stack services between the major markets.
- Geographically, the main focus is Chicago, the traditional core of the US Rail network, where the Eastern and Western railroads meet.
- Few existing freight yards are configured for intermodal block trains that typically carry 400 containers. New terminals have been established on greenfield sites that may be over 4000 metres long but only a few hundred metres in width.
- Intermodal terminals typically serve a market area within a radius of 350 km. This market is served by trucks.
- National trucking companies such as Yellow and J.B. Hunt have adopted domestic containers to ship goods between domestic markets by rail.
- Many of the new terminals have attracted significant logistics activity. Distribution centres, frequently comprising major clusters such as San Bernadino California, Joliet Illinois and Alliance Texas, have emerged as important new centres of regional development (Cidell 2011).
- While the US railroads are still heavily involved in bulk traffic, such as coal, intermodal has become a significant component of rail revenues, and in the case of some companies has now become the most important component. Since deregulation the US railroads have been profitable and their efficiency has improved (Chapin and Schmidt 1999).

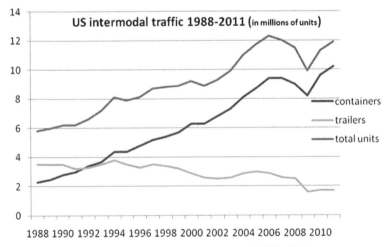

Figure 13.1   Growth of intermodal traffic in the US, 1961–2011
Source: Data from American Association of Railroads.

How Transferable is the US Experience?

The *resurgence* of the US rail industry has led other countries to consider intermodal transport as a means of revitalizing their own domestic railroads. Europe, in particular, has been active in seeking solutions to its flagging rail industry. Figure 13.2 shows the rail modal split comparison between US and EU15 from 1950 to 2000. In the 1950s the rail share of total freight ton-miles was 60 per cent in both Europe and the US. By 2000 the share of railroads in the EU15 was 8 per cent, while in the US it had increased to 38 per cent from a low of 30 per cent in 1980.

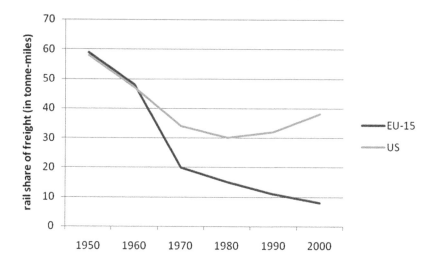

Figure 13.2   Rail modal split comparison between US and EU15

Source: Adapted by the Author from Vasaallo and Fagin 2007.

Public policy in Europe has been striving to counteract this decline for over 20 years. Concern is expressed at the growing dominance of trucking, which is seen as undesirable for environmental and congestion reasons. The response has been to address regulatory constraints, technological issues and to offer subsidies to promote intermodality.

- As in the US, regulatory issues constrained the rail industry. But whereas in the US the move was to free the private rail companies to set rates, to manage the closure of uneconomic tracks, and to allow the financial participation in multimodal operations, in Europe the main thrust has been to try to promote competition between rail operators. To achieve greater competition, as a spur to economic efficiency, the move has been to separate the ownership and management of the tracks and infrastructures from rail operations, and to open up rail freight operations to competing companies. This was the approach initially adopted in the UK with some differences. In the rest of Europe any company could enter the freight business if it could satisfy safety and operational conditions.

- The European rail transport system is fragmented, having evolved out of national systems. Each country has its own signalling, locomotive power units and operating systems. Between France and Spain there are different track dimensions. The EU has been investing in harmonizing technical requirements and establishing European norms for equipment and infrastructure.
- Recognizing the need to shift traffic from road to rail, the EU has instituted several programmes to subsidize companies to transfer their business to rail. First was PACT (Pilot Actions for Combined Transport) that was introduced in 1997 was designed to encourage a shift from road to rail intermodal specifically (in Europe, intermodal is referred to as combined transport). After its term ended in 2001, it was renewed and extended as the Marco Polo Programme, in which because of disappointing results of the PACT programme eligibility was extended to include Short Sea Shipping. In addition, the EU and member states have been taxing road transport in an attempt to halt its growing market share.

Despite these interventions the modal split in Europe is still heavily oriented towards trucking, the exception being some of the newer EU members such as Estonia and Romania. Its market share continues to fall overall. Some of the reasons reflect differences between the US and Europe (Vassallo and Fagin 2007):

- Rail lines are used primarily for passengers, and the number of available slots for freight trains is determined by the priority for passenger trains. Signalling is based on short, high speed trains, and precludes lengthy freight trains.
- Distances between major markets are much smaller in Europe than the US. The average length of haul for road and rail in Europe is 132 km compared with 386 km in the US. This gives a clear advantage to trucking in Europe (Vassallo and Fagin 2007).
- Although there has been an attempt to provide trans-European corridors, rail networks in Europe still reflect the fact that they were developed separately by each country. Technical standards and working conditions still reflect national conditions that make longer haul movements complex (Ghijsen et al. 2007). For example, permitted length of trains and weights differs from one country to the other, and the number of hours a train driver can work is also country-specific.
- Most European countries use electric power for their locomotives which draw power from overhead cables. These preclude double stacking.

A Contemporary Overview of Intermodal Transport in Europe

As Beuthe (2007) and others have mentioned it is extremely difficult to obtain a comprehensive picture of intermodal transport in Europe. Several groups publish data on traffic, but none are comparable. For example, UIRR, an association of traffic intermediaries who engage in shipping freight intermodally include trucks, trucks with accompanied drivers, swap bodies and containers in their data and make assumptions about the equivalents in TEUs. Its data indicates growth from 5,211,000 TEU equivalents in 2000 to 6,428,000 TEU equivalents in 2011. Some of this growth is accounted for by its enlargement through adding new members. On the other hand, ICF (INTERCONTAINER-INTERFRIGO) the operating arm of the European railroads experienced a decline in traffic, from 961,000 units in 2000 to 396,000 units in 2008, and resulted in the company going into receivership in 2010. In the UK intermodal traffic volumes have grown from 3.05 million TEUs in 1985 to 7.99 million TEUs in 2004 (Woodburn 2007).

Prior to the EU liberalization programmes for railways in continental Europe the pattern of intermodal traffic was relatively simple. The national railroads controlled rail operations, but there were some operations for international traffic organized by members of the UIRR. Since the separation of track from operations (applied unevenly however), and with the opening up of traction to new entrants, the patterns have become more complex. As Debrie and Gouvernal (2006) indicate, intermodal transportation services now comprise different permutations of track operators, traction providers, and service operators. While most track operators manage the track for each national system, there has been an extension of their business activity outside. For example, DBNetz, the track provider in Germany has purchased the freight operations in Denmark and Holland and several small traction providers in Italy. The Swiss National Railroad (not bound by EU legislation) has purchased interests in German and Italian rail companies and terminals.

In Europe the former national rail companies dominate the provision of traction in the member states. Their dominance is being challenged by new entrants, but as examined in detail in the next section, their market share remains small. On the other hand some traction providers, are involved with partners in offering intermodal services in which it is sharing commercial risks. Thus DB with its freight arm, DB Schenker Rail, has partnered with others to provide services to the Czech Republic (Metrans service) and Poland (Polzug service).

Most important and diverse are the service providers, the companies that offer customers intermodal services between certain markets and must take the commercial risk in such endeavours (Debrie and Gouvernal 2006). As noted above some traction providers provide such services, but there are many other players participating. It is noteworthy that many are focused on the ports, port traffic provide a large volume of container traffic for hinterland markets. Because of this traffic potential several actors in ports and international shipping offer rail services from certain ports. Most extensive are the rail services operated by terminal operators in Bremen and Hamburg. HHLA, a major terminal operator in Hamburg is a partner in the Metrans and Polzug services. Its competitor, Eurogate, a company jointly owned by Eurokai, a Hamburg Terminal operator, and BLG, a Bremen logistics company, operates a network of services from the German ports in a north-south direction. Within Germany it does not use DB for traction, but in Switzerland and Italy it uses locomotives from the State railways. The European Rail Shuttle (ERS) is a major operator out of the port of Rotterdam. Founded in 1994, it is owned by Maersk and provides service to markets in Central and Eastern Europe as well as Italy. It uses traction from the state railways, but because of dissatisfaction with the quality of the service from DB it has established its own traction provider to provide some of its services within Germany. CMA-CGM is another shipping line mounting its own services from ports and maintains its own intermodal terminals in Ludwigshafen and Lyon.

In the UK the situation has evolved with some differences. It has already been noted that the freight sector was treated differently from the passenger section, with the former British Rail freight subsidiary, Freightliner taking over intermodal freight activity in an executive buyout. Over time new companies have entered the container freight market, including EWS, GBRail Freight, DRS and Fastlane and traffic growth has been quite significant over the last 30 years, as noted above.

A feature of both the US and Europe is the importance of port traffic as a base for intermodal rail services. The concentration of containers at major ports provides the scale advantages that are necessary to maintain viable rail services. As international traffic grows, this has become a vital driver of intermodal transport in Europe. However, it must be realized that the modal split for container traffic in the largest European ports is still not in favour of the rail mode. For example, the rail share of shipments to and from the port of Rotterdam is only 10 per cent, and declining, compared with 57 per cent by road and 33 per cent by barge. Even for Hamburg the rail share is only 17 per cent and road transport is the dominant mode at other European ports.

Challenges and Issues

The US

In the US, despite the apparent success of rail intermodal business a number of issues have emerged. The railroads were able to absorb the new traffic initially because the railroads had overcapacity in trackage, labour and equipment in the immediate post-deregulation period (Plant 2002). However, the growth of traffic began to impact on certain parts of the chain. Improvements had to be made in equipment, track, signalling, IT and terminals. The railroads are spending a significant part of their revenues on such improvements. A recent study revealed that between 1996 and 2005 the capital expenditures of US railroads averaged 17 per cent of revenue. In comparison US manufacturing spent three per cent of revenue on average on maintenance and expansion (Fritelli 2004).

Two areas in particular have experienced congestion: access to ports and interchanges in Chicago. The rail intermodal terminals in major port cities were built on new sites in suburban locations some distance from the ports. Linking the port terminals with these facilities has become a challenge. While on-dock rail connections have been built in several US ports, such as Seattle, their connections with the rail intermodal yards are tenuous and subject to delays, so that many containers are trucked instead to the yards, a trend that in Los Angeles-Long Beach resulted in massive road congestion. In the case of Chicago the problem is that it is historically the point where the Western railroads meet the Eastern railroads. Each company has its own intermodal yards, and although there is a belt line railway that links the terminals, it is usually faster to haul containers between yards by truck, a practice called 'rubber tire interchanges'. Since 500 freight trains pass through Chicago each day which represents 46 per cent of all intermodal traffic in the US, this volume produces significant congestion on urban highways in the metropolitan region (CREATE 2013).

Because these two cases have produced significant urban traffic impacts, public funds have been made available to address the problems. Solutions involve financing by the railroads themselves as well as local, state and federal governments. This type of funding arrangement was behind the construction of the $2.4 billion Alameda Corridor in Los Angeles, a dedicated 32 km rail freight corridor from the ports to the rail intermodal yards, that, being in a trench for part of the way, avoids level crossings (Guiliano 2007). In the case of Chicago, 70 projects have been identified to ease the traffic problems for both road users, rail passenger traffic, and rail freight, that will be focused on 4 major corridors. Again, public and private investment is being allocated to the CREATE programme that is apportioned as to the benefits each contributor will receive: freight railways, AMTRAK, and local communities in the metropolitan area, the State and federal governments (CREATE 2013).

The involvement of public money in rail projects is generating some controversy in the US. Recent studies have shown that expected growth of rail freight in the US will give rise to serious congestion, unless remedial steps are taken (Cambridge Systematics 2007). In Figure 13.3, the level-of-service grades A–C (below capacity), D (near capacity), E (at capacity) and F (above capacity) correspond to the volume/capacity ratios of 0.0–0.7, 0.7–0.8, 0.8–1.0 and >1.0 respectively. It is estimated that to solve the bottlenecks will cost $135 billion by 2035. Predicted traffic growth and increased revenues will enable the companies to invest $95 billion over that time period. Thus, the size of the investments would be beyond the capacity of the railroads, and will require public contributions to make up the shortfall (Fritelli 2004).

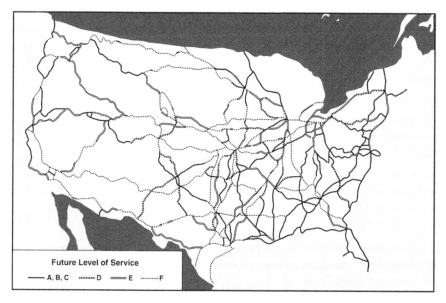

Future Level of Service
— A, B, C   .... D   ═══ E   .... F

Figure 13.3   Future capacity constraints in the US rail network, 2035
Source: Cambridge Systematics 2007. Redrawn by Tina Tsang.

Questions are being raised as to why should a private industry receive public subsidies of this magnitude? Public investments in roads benefit public access, whereas investments in railways benefit giant corporations who restrict access to their tracks (Plant 2002). There are those who point to Europe where open access to tracks to promote competition has been at the heart of railway reform. These questions are being framed by a more general concern about the concentration of ownership in the US rail industry. In 1975 there were 56 Class I railroads. According to Larson and Spraggs (2000), there were four in the US, although two Canadian Class I railroads operated in the US as well. The massive concentration in control has resulted in there being only two railroads in Western US (Union Pacific (UP), and Burlington Northern and Santa Fe (BNSF) – the latter being privately owned by Warren Buffet), and two railroads in the East (CSX) and Norfolk Southern (NS). While the early mergers and acquisitions that occurred immediately after deregulation have been shown to be positive, since the remaining companies obtained greater scale economies (Larson and Spraggs 2000, Chapin and Schmidt 1999), there is some evidence to suggest that the Class I railroads are now so large that they have exhausted available economies of system size and are at or near the point of exhausting economies of density (Pittman 2009).

Europe

The goal of promoting competition in rail freight in Europe by opening up the system to competition has achieved mixed results in the EU. The legislated separation of tracks from operations has been applied differentially in different countries. In Germany for example DBNetz is separate from DB in name only. The single most important issue is the market power of the former railroad operators, which has made it very difficult for new entrants to establish themselves. In Germany, for example, despite 111 companies possessing the right to haul freight DB and its freight arm, DB Schenker Rail, yields enormous power. A recent study that surveyed the new start-up traction providers found that all entered the market because of dissatisfaction with the services of DB Schenker Rail. However, they report that access to slots is difficult and cumbersome, with DB Schenker Rail having advantages because of its established service agreements with DBNetz (Slack and Vogt 2007). Further constraints were financial, in that it was difficult to obtain bank loans because the service contracts with clients were short term, while DB Schenker Rail because of its enormous size as part of DB had no such difficulties, and furthermore received large government subsidies. The rationalization of DBNetz took into account the needs of DB as a whole, and closed many branch lines and sidings not used by DB Schenker Rail but some of which were used by the new entrants to access their customers' sites. A further issue is energy costs. New entrants have to pay for electricity consumption to DBNetz, but because their consumption is significantly less than DB Schenker Rail they are charged a higher unit rate. The fact that these issues have been reported for many years indicates the challenges new entrants have in facing limit competition.

Intermodal traffic is able to compete successfully against other modes where traffic density is high, so that frequent and high capacity trains can be used. It has already been noted that international traffic from ports creates such conditions. However, this means that the traffic is restricted to a few corridors only. Smaller local markets cannot be served. An important objective of EU policy is to promote regional development and reduce regional disparities, yet rail intermodal acts in a contrary fashion to this goal (Spiekermanfl and Wegener 1996). There is much debate in Europe about 'single wagons', about how to ensure that even small loads can be carried by rail to and from smaller markets (Vogt 2012). From a commercial perspective however, such markets cannot be served directly by rail intermodal. In the US, for example, local deliveries are truck hauled. In Europe there is a concern that once on a truck the containers will stay on them for the entire journey.

Despite the promising growth of intermodal traffic in the UK, which is largely based on shipments to and from the ports, and despite the entry of new service providers, there is high market concentration there too. EWS accounts for 66 per cent of the market (Woodburn 2007). As in Europe, traffic growth in absolute terms must be considered in the context of modal share. In the UK the share of rail shipments from the ports is still small compared to road shipments. For example in Felixstowe, the largest port, rail had a 22 per cent market share in 2004, and for Tilbury the share was 17 per cent (Woodburn 2007).

Common Issues

The overarching issue for rail intermodal everywhere is service quality. The goods carried in containers or other intermodal units are of much higher value than the typical commodity mix of rail freight. Customers demand competitive rates as well as fast and reliable services. While rail may offer competitive pricing over longer distances, the question of on time delivery and service quality remains a real and perceived problem. When trucks are used customers know that the goods will be delivered directly to their destination with a high degree of certainty. Because the rail alternative requires the container to be delivered to the rail yard and stored while the trains are assembled, transported to a rail terminal near the destination point, and the containers then loaded onto trucks for final delivery, there exist numerous possibilities in this transport chain for delays and damage to contents.

These issues are magnified because of a widespread perception that rail transport offers poor quality service. This is a perception that is historic, because railroads did offer poor service when they were the only mode to offer long distance freight transport. Subsequently their freight operations were oriented towards bulk traffic where operational and market requirements are far less demanding. This image has been reinforced by more events including the congestion in US West Coast ports in 2004 that was accentuated by a lack of rail equipment to haul containers, and the failure of most PACT projects in Europe because the railways failed to live up to performance guarantees.

Thus, intermodal transport requires a new approach for the railways. They have to assure that locomotives and wagons are available on time where required and in situations where daily or weekly fluctuations in demand occur. The railways are used to dealing with customers who establish long term contracts to haul large volumes of bulk freight. The change requires a profound organizational and cultural shift in rail management. Intermodal competes with road not just on price, since the customers are likely to be sensitive to reliability and on time performance. Logistics requires that the chain is transparent, that goods are tracked and that schedules are respected.

There are indications that railroads are responding to these challenges. In the US the railroads are publishing performance indicators (AAR.org). At the same time, different levels of service provision are being reflected in rates. Speediest deliveries are being offered at premium rates, while slower shipments can benefit from discounts. Premium rates include performance guarantees, with a schedule of penalties for late deliveries. In addition, third party companies are now offering tracking and tracing for containerized rail freight. These are features that the trucking industry has offered for many years, but are necessary steps for the railroads if they are to expand their market share.

Conclusion

Intermodal rail has developed significantly over the last 30 years in the United States and Europe. The traffic has grown in both continents, but there are still obstacles to its ability to provide an alternative to road transport, in Europe at least. It works best in high traffic corridors where goods have to be transported over long distances. Port-based traffic provides the initial opportunities for such shipments in most cases. These market and geographical conditions are not present in most parts of the world. In much of East and South East Asia, which is the largest market for containers, as well as South America, the regional markets are coastal. This makes it almost impossible for rail to compete over other modes. In China too, development up until recently has been coastal, but with the westward expansion of industrial activity, the China market on the surface at least would appear to provide opportunities for rail intermodal developments.

Evidence presented in this chapter suggests however that market and geographical conditions are not the most important factors determining the success of rail intermodal traffic. The industry has been shaped significantly by political factors, including regulatory changes. A major factor for its success in the US was the removal of passenger operations from the railroads and their freedom to operate with only regulatory oversight. Elsewhere, railroads operate both freight and passenger trains, two very different systems, in which passenger operations usually take priority. In Europe, public policy has been directed mainly at promoting competition, a process that is taking a long time to be realized, especially given the market power of the incumbent national railroads. In the meantime the market share of rail is slipping, and it will be very difficult to reverse this trend without attention to other factors.

The history of rail intermodalism demonstrates that geographical, market size and policy factors are important, but that the key to its further development is a focus on serving customers with a service that is reliable as well as cost competitive. Intermodal rail has a role to play in logistics chains, where information about the shipments is available in real time, and where customers can plan their supply chains with a high degree of certainty that goods will be delivered on time. The railroads have focused a lot on 'hard' issues, such as infrastructure, but these 'soft' issues are critical if they are to attract more customers. Fortunately, there are encouraging signs that in the US in particular, but also to some degree in Europe a customer focus will help rail intermodal compete more effectively.

References

Beuthe, M. 2007. Intermodal transport in Europe, in *Globalized Freight Transport*, edited by T. Leinbach and C. Capineri. London: Elgar, 54–99.

Bowen, J and Slack, B. 2007. Shifting modes and spatial flows in North American freight transportation, in *Globalized Freight Transport*, edited by T. Leinbach and C. Capineri. London: Elgar, 17–53.

Braeutigam, R.R. 1993. Consequences of regulatory reform in the American railroad industry. *Southern Economic Journal*, 59(3), 468–80.

Brendt, E.R., Friedlander, A.F., Chiang, J.S.W. and Vellturo, C.A. 1993. Cost effects of mergers and deregulation in the US rail industry. *Journal of Productivity Analysis*, 4(2), 127–44.

Cambridge Systematics, Inc. 2007. *National Freight Infrastructure Capacity and Investment Study* [Online]. Available at: www.AAR.org [accessed: 7 Jan 2013].

Chapin, A. and Schmidt, S. 1999. Do mergers improve efficiency? *Journal of Transport Economics and Policy*, 33(2), 147–62.

Cidell, J. 2011. Distribution centers among the rooftops: The global logistics network meets the suburban spatial imaginary. *Journal of Urban and Regional Research*, 35(4), 832–51.

CREATE. 2013. *Keeping the Go in Chicago* [Online]. Available at: www.createprogram. org [accessed: 7 Jan 2013].

Debrie, J. and Gouvernal, E. 2006. Intermodal rail in western Europe: actors and services in a new regulatory environment. *Growth and Change*, 37(3), 444–59.

Frittelli, J. 2004. *Intermodal Rail Freight: A Role for Federal Funding?* Washington, DC: Congressional Research Services.

Ghijsen, P.W.TH., Semeijn, J. and Linden, H. 2007. Rail freight in Europe: different perspectives on achieving higher service levels. *Transportation Journal*, 46(4), 42–57.

Guiliano, G. 2007. The changing landscape of transportation decision making. *Transportation Research Board*, 2036, 5–12.

Larson, P.D. and Spraggs, H.B. 2000. The American railroad industry: 20 years after staggers. *Transportation Quarterly*, 54(2), 31–45.

Levinson, M. 2006. *The Box.* Princeton: University of Princeton Press.

Pittman, R. 2009. *Railway Mergers and Railway Alliances: Competition, Issues and Lessons for Other Network Industries.* Economic Analysis Group Discussion Paper (02) [Online]. Available at: http://ssrn.com/abstract=1410132.

Plant, J.F. 2002. Railroad policy and intermodalism: policy choices after deregulation. *Review of Policy Research*, 19(2), 13–32.

Rodrigue, J-P. 2008. The Thruport concept and transmodal freight distribution in North America. *Journal of Transport Geography*, 16(4), 233–46.

Slack, B. 1994. Domestic containerisation and the load centre concept. *Maritime Policy and Management*, 21(3), 229–36.

Slack, B. and Vogt, A. 2007. Challenges confronting new traction providers of rail freight in Germany. *Transport Reviews*, 14(5), 399–409.

Spiekermanfl, K. and Wegener, M. 1996. Trans-European networks and unequal accessibility in Europe. *European Journal of Regional Development (EUREG)*, 4(96), 35–42.

Vassallo, J.M and Fagin, M. 2007. Nature or nurture: why do railroads carry greater freight share in the United States than in Europe? *Transportation*, 34(2), 177–93.

Vogt, A. 2012. Wagonload must become Europe-wide to survive. *International Railway Journal*, July, 40.

Woodburn, A.G. 2007. The role for rail in port-based container freight flows in Britain. *Maritime Policy and Management*, 34(4), 311–30.

SECTION VI
Looking Forward

Chapter 14
The Resilience of Railways

Claude Comtois

The opportunities for the constituents of rail transport to become highly competitive are likely to be manifold in the next decade. A series of issues are raised by this focus. How are railways responding to changes in the global economy? How are these developments affecting the capacity of railways to meet demands? How selected components of railway transport system affected by particular stresses or stimuli? Above all, how to enhance the capacity of railways?

The chapter initially considers the concept of resilience within a framework embedding governance and infrastructures. This is followed by selected empirical case studies of railway vulnerabilities. Particular attention is given to formulating railway challenges in terms of supply chain, shifting market conditions, border crossing and gateway competitiveness. The chapter then examines the working agenda in assisting in the development of resilient railways.

Railway Vulnerabilities

Railways represent a complex infrastructure system. This complexity can be portrayed *spatially* by the geographical span of railroads from local to transcontinental networks, *sectorally* in terms of passenger and freight transport, *technically* in terms of level of automation, capacity and speed, *politically* in jurisdictional control, and even from an *ideological* point of view in the formulation of policies related to the different functions of railways.

The capacity of railways to adapt to change, to moderate negative externalities, to realize opportunities or to cope with various impacts is a key issue in sustaining their competitiveness. This suggests analyzing railways in terms of system-wide property. Such a framework requires an integrated approach articulating how interactions between the different components of the railway system are affected by patterns of change and by the causal chain through which modifications of these interactions might enhance the vulnerability of the railways.

Vulnerability implies uncertainties and risks about future events resulting in disruptions and damages (Haimes 2006). Fundamentally, uncertainty implies that an unforeseen event may occur in the future, but the likelihood of its occurrence is totally unpredictable. In sharp contrast, a risk represents an event to which a probability of occurrence can be measured. Arguably, risks come in a broad diversity of forms, scope, size and scale. Risks are neither time nor space constrained. Operational, social or legal risks can trigger systems failures. The impact of disruptions can range from negligible to complete failure of the system.

A review of the literature suggests that understanding the vulnerability of transport systems has focused on issues of crisis management (Chang 2000, Porfiriev 2001, Mansouri et al. 2010), security (Comfort 2005, Sarathy 2006), network design (Murray-Tuite 2006,

Iakovou et al. 2007), planning process (Pitera 2008, Taneja et al. 2010, Winkelman et al. 2010), environmental sustainability (Instanes et al. 2005, McCarthy et al. 2005, Sivell 2008) and organizational framework (Cetin and Cerit 2010, Therien 2010). These academic authors have contributed extensively to questions relating to risk assessment processes in system engineering, management science, operational research and ecology. These approaches are essentially concentrating on predictable events, rare events of unknowable occurrence and the cost of disruption.

In the context of railway systems, resilience refers to the capacity to meet demands while confronted with disruptive situations. The objective is not to jettison the approaches presented above, but rather to offer a fresh perspective to assess the resilience of railway systems in terms of governance and infrastructure. The analysis of railways provides a unique opportunity to explore the relationship between institutional reforms and transport infrastructure renewal. Institutions recognize the role of public state actors and private business entrepreneurs in capital investment, asset ownership, operations and commercial risks. The evaluation of change in railway governance assesses the kinds of competition that can be introduced in the railway sector and the concomitant need for regulatory intervention (Williamson 2002). The infrastructure component integrates *corridors* that concentrate communication axis, *interfaces* that act as compulsory passages for various activities and *thresholds* that organize directions. In analyzing change in the physical component of railways, emphasis is given to the shift in goods and people flows, influences of technological advances and variation in the hierarchical networks of nodes and links (Lakshmanan and Anderson 2002).

Moreover, railways cannot be seen in isolation. There is a need to recognize the interplay between geographical scales (Rimmer 1988). The articulation of railways from peripheral hinterland into the global logistics system underpins the emergence of a world railway system. There is thus a need to provide a knowledge base to ensure the fluidity and reliability of railways as part of a global system. An analysis of the changes at different geographical scales underlines the extent to which railways are subordinated to a global network of transport-land use activities. From this perspective, four factors are deemed essential to increase the resilience of railway system. First, a global approach to railway resilience suggests an understanding of supply chain. Second, shifting market conditions have been a neglected topic in analysing the resilience of railways at the continental level. Third, progress in transport and logistics is prompting countries to pay increasing attention to their border crossings, especially as some forwarders have deemed them unreliable because of breaks in railway gauge and the lack of harmonization of customs regulations. Fourth, world regions cannot avoid intermodalism. This function rests on the most important markets, those that generate the highest revenues and offer the greatest potential for growth. The establishment of synergies between different modes is critical to the resilience of railways. Railway challenges at different geographical scales – global, continental, national and regional – can be illustrated with selected case studies.

Railway Challenges

African Railways and Global Supply Chain

For the past 30 years, globalization, liberalization and privatization processes have transformed the railway industry. At the global scale, the railway industry is experiencing a restructuring similar to the container shipping industry and the airline industry. Some railway companies have developed overseas operations as independent businesses. The Canadian National Railways has opened offices in the port city of Shanghai and the capital city of Beijing, China with a view to take advantage of increased trade between Asia and North America. Others have developed international organizations with separate railway companies coming together within a holding. Operations abroad are appendages to headquarters. There is central control over strategic issues such as technology, financial budgets and capital investment decisions, but decentralized decision-making to deal with local or regional issues (McMillan 2007). Genesee & Wyoming Inc. owns and operates short line and regional freight railroads in the United States, Canada, Australia, the Netherlands and Belgium.

In terms of governance, the colonial policies in Africa distorted the traditional trade routes. For the Europeans, the main axis of travel in Africa was north-south while for Africans, the east-west routes were considered the main corridors. The routes which once crossed through Africa were thus fragmented by politics. More importantly, the old caravan routes were neglected in favour of highway development in the main cities catering essentially for local traffic. The economies of many African countries were shaped with domestic markets in mind. The influence of colonial powers and the establishment of political boundaries barred traditional routes (Hilling 1996). As a result, the trade that once bounded together the peoples along both coasts of the continent almost disappeared. The basic problems of the railway sector are the lack of maintenance, the poor quality of the equipment and the important break-of-gauge between rail networks which implies additional transshipment. Acknowledging the need to improve railway performance and efficiency, African governments have embarked on major railway reforms in the forms of concessions. All of the African railway concessions are integrated concessions with a strong dominance of freight transport and ancillary passenger service provision. Most of the concessions have been associated with substantial infrastructure investments, notably by international lending agencies and concomitant increase in labour and assets productivity (Bullock 2005).

Africa's rail transport system issued from colonization and was completed after five decades of development under the direction of politically independent states which presents several inadequacies. More specifically, the rail transport system is marked by contradictions (Pelletier 2012). Territorially, the networks are characterized by the importance of penetration axis from core regions, and problems of accessibility in the periphery. Figure 14.1 shows that technologically, the rail transport sector is influenced by the number of tracks and variations in gauge. The distribution of the rail network is very uneven with 15,223 km in Mediterranean Africa, 45,799 km located between the tropics and 20,247 km in South Africa. Many cities are linked only by a low-capacity single track. Rail gauge determines the rolling stock's loading capacity. There are five different gauges used in Africa. Countries such as Algeria and Tunisia display more than one gauge. Only 14 per cent of the continent's rail network has the standard gauge of 1,435 m with less than 2 per cent located south of the Sahara. Socially, there is a strong inequality of access between urban and rural inhabitants.

The global supply chain depends heavily on ocean transport for the exchange of goods among members of the world community. Even though on a world scale, foreign trade in African countries is marginal in terms of value, weight or volume; Africa is becoming an important actor in commercial relations for simple reasons of demographic growth. The interplay between infrastructure and institution in the unfolding integration of Africa within the global supply chain suggests that the competitiveness of the railway supply chain system in Africa is conditioned by the objectives of stakeholders and the transport network in which they are embedded.

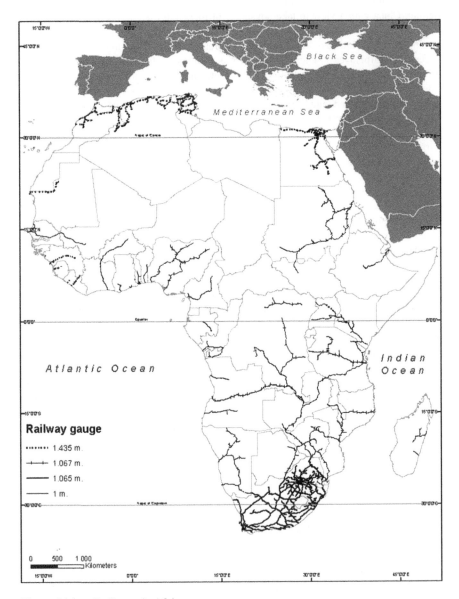

Figure 14.1   Railways in Africa

Source: For railway lines, available at: http://market.weogeo.com; for railway gauge, CIA *The World Factbook*, available at: https://www.cia.gov/library/publications/the-world-factbook/fields/2121.html, drawn by Dominique Goyer.

Globally, distribution centres are increasingly being located in inland locations with a view to benefit from the lower rental costs inland and to avoid congestion and drayage connectivity at ports. This is leading to increasing demand from manufacturers and retailers for rail transport services. Many shippers are using innovative methods and techniques to better package products for shipping, loading railcars and ocean containers to maximum capacity. Africa rail cargo handling is often incompatible with ocean transport facilities (Elbadawi et al. 2006). Many ports are affected by congestion, inadequacy of storage facilities and high rail transit costs. The successful integration of Africa within global supply chains will increasingly depend on the growing market share of the railway system and an efficient intermodal transport system. Competitiveness refers to the attainment of positive supply chain outcomes resulting from functional interdependency of individual participating stakeholders. This suggests that African railway operators must create competitive advantage in both Africa's export and import markets by integrating production and logistics functions at inland regional transport hubs.

North American Railways and Shifting Market Conditions

At the continental scale, the reduction of obstacles to international trade including the establishment of economic blocs, such as the North American Free Trade Agreement (NAFTA) and EU, favoured the establishment of three types of rail connections across the land mass of the largest continent. Landbridge applies to traffic transiting across a continent bound to overseas destinations. This is the case of Asian traffic bound for Europe. Cargo is shipped across the Pacific Ocean, carried by rail over North America and transferred to vessels for ocean sailing across the Atlantic. The second type is a dedicated rail corridor involving the freight shipments from one side of a continent to the other. This can be exemplified by traffic movement from Montreal to Los Angeles. For freight, railway carriers haul containers by means of owned or leased equipment and operate partially over their owned tracks or negotiate right of way on tracks owned by other freight railways. For passenger movement, the journey involves the use of a different number of route segments between cities. The third type is regional traffic that may use the overland rail corridor for a portion of its journey, such as the traffic between Germany, Belgium and the Netherlands.

The liberalization and deregulation process profoundly affected the governance of the North American railroad market (Thompson 2003). First, mergers and acquisitions led to a reduction in the number of Class 1 rail carriers from 11 in 1990 to 7 in 2013. The largest carriers in Canada are Canadian National and Canadian Pacific. In the United States, five companies qualify to be Class I railroads: BNSF Railway, CSX Transportation, Kansas City Southern Railway, Norfolk Southern Combined Railroad Subsidiaries and Union Pacific Railroad. Second, the commercial trend to reduce costs and offer a better service led Class 1 rail carriers to abandon part of their network. This process contributed to the emergence of new short-line railways. There are currently 30 regional and over 500 local railways operating in the United States and Canada. Third, railroad restructuring prompted a burgeoning market for new railway entities including terminal and yard operators and train operating companies. Fourth, the benefits of transporting different commodities between numerous pairs of origins and destinations prompted the private sector to focus on freight traffic. The North American railway passenger services are essentially publically-owned and subsidized. These public companies operate almost entirely over private freight railway tracks.

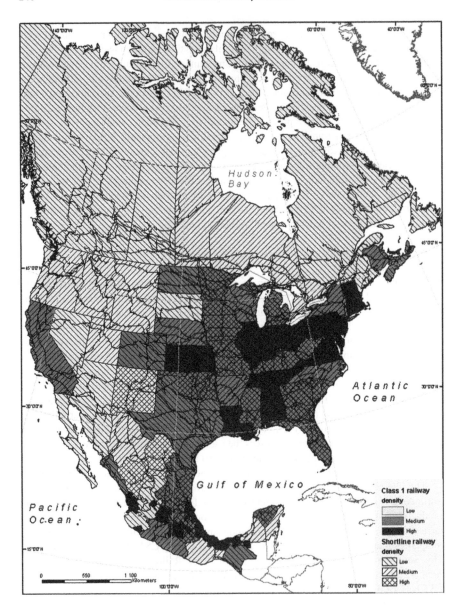

Figure 14.2   Railway densities in North America
Source: For Class 1 railway lines, available at: http://www.geobase.ca; for secondary railway lines, available at: http://market.weogeo.com, drawn by Dominique Goyer.

In 2012, the length of railway route available for train service in North America totalled 271,344 km. This figure does not take into account the number of parallel tracks. In sharp contrast to other continent, the railroad network is highly integrated and exhibits significant development since 1996 (Figure 14.2). Railways have implemented the use of longer trains, more cars per train and heavier cars. Increasing yard capacity is permitting additional blocks and higher network fluidity. Technology development is also assisting operators in lowering costs and increasing productivity (Kohn 2011). This is particularly relevant in sustainable development strategies. Railways are more fuel-efficient than trucks on a ton-km basis and are contributing to a more socially efficient and sustainable allocation of transportation resources. It is estimated that rail saves 45–80 kg CO_2 for each 1,000 ton-km transferred from truck.

Rail transportation is facing significant requirements to support oil and gas mining utilities and consistent service delivery (CAPP 2012). The dynamics of North America's oil market are rapidly changing. Growing conventional, oil shale and oil sands production in Western Canada and Mid-continent United States suggests that North American supplies will exceed domestic consumption. Oil producers are thus looking for new markets associated with expanding production. On the continent, Eastern Canada and the Gulf Coast which currently export internationally are prime candidates. Overseas, the outlook for demand for oil in China, Japan and India remains very strong. Pipelines are the dominant mode of transportation. But the existing pipeline network is reaching capacity and provides limited access for deliveries to selected land refineries or coastal terminal locations for offshore exports. The construction or expansion of pipeline infrastructure is confronted with important environmental restrictions. This is leading to increasing opportunity for railway as the alternative mode for transporting crude oil. The average revenue per ton for a given length of haul that can be earned by Class 1 railways to move oil is higher than most other bulk commodities. Shifting market conditions are having an impact on the transportation practices of shippers. Exports of selected dry bulk commodities such as grain are hampered by railway capacity constraints. The benefits of competition and market forces in the rail freight industry in a deregulated environment can hinder selected railway services and railcar allocation. For stakeholders, the main challenge to shifting market conditions requires the creation of buffers in the system in terms of extra inventory or excess transportation capacity with a view to mitigate potential interruptions of flows.

Chinese Railways and Border Crossing

Liberalization has forced governments to reconsider and amend policies with a view to instil competitiveness in national rail transport markets. As part of this ongoing evolution, many railway enterprises underwent corporate restructuring. In Canada, the national railway company was transferred from the public to the private sector. Liberalization of the European railway sector is leading to the restructuring of national public institutions with new stakeholders in terms of infrastructure providers, passenger and freight train operators and maintenance contractors (IBM Business Consulting Services 2004). New statutory bodies are emerging to oversee the railway sector in terms of governing access to operational service facilities and in issuing licenses, safety certificates and approval of rolling stock. Restructuring involves significant changes in asset ownership, technological development, network access, routing patterns and fare structures (Amos and Bullock 2006). The major impact can be found in rail market growth, productivity of rail system, network development process in terms of high-speed passenger train corridors and connection with cross-border merger of rail freight operations.

China's railway system is organized under the Ministry of Railways. In 2004, China's State council approved The Mid- and Long-Term Railway Network plan to extend the railway network from 61,404 to 100,000 route-km by 2020. This suggests the construction of approximately 2,400 km of rail per year. Considering that the infrastructure and technological requirements of the rail network and terminals are beyond railway internal earnings, the Central government also formulated a railway policy framework. Central to this reform, the government initiated a policy of separating government administration of the railways from enterprise management. China's railways underwent corporate restructuring. Operations were streamlined and responsibilities for the various core businesses were assigned to specialized entities. Accounts for passenger and freight transport businesses would be reported separately. As part of this ongoing evolution is the state policy to grant concessions for over 100 secondary railway lines to joint ventures composed of provincial governments, regional rail administrations and enterprises. In pursuing the goal of growth in an environment of intense competition, the government also introduced industry regulations to permit foreign direct investments in railway development. Plans are currently being set afoot to call upon private investors to have greater access to state-controlled businesses.

The continued development of railways is a deep-seated ideological issue for all Chinese leaders (Comtois 1990). Railways play a key role in strengthening China's transactional environment. The central government through five year plans undertook sustained efforts to develop the rail network. Reconstructing the traditional transactional networks resulted in the formation of a unified interior market. This allowed the commercial environment to be closely integrated with political power. The importance of these efforts arises from several considerations:

1. to facilitate central government control over the entire country;
2. to reduce regional disparities by reaching out to areas populated by minority nationalities;
3. to improve the defence support system;
4. to facilitate the exploitation of minerals, mostly combustible, located in the interior;
5. to transport grain, coal and wood;
6. to increase the regional exchanges of goods; and
7. to disperse the industrial base of the country in order to promote regional economic development.

The last 20 years saw the extension of railway corridors towards border areas suggesting that Chinese leaders are following the ambitious plans of Sun Yat-Sen (Rimmer 1997).

China's railways are challenged by trade facilitation for long-haul goods movement and border-crossings. China has 10 rail border crossings with North Korea, Russia, Mongolia, Kazakhstan and Vietnam (Figure 14.3). The analysis of cross-border trade reveals key diagnostic features. First, China's cross-border trade has been increasing at an average annual growth rate of 8 per cent over the past 20 years. Second, over 50 per cent of China's border trade is with Russia through the Manzhouli and Suifenhe gateways. Third, there is marked imbalance in cross-border trade with almost 90 per cent of rail exchange volume being import to China. Fourth, trade is essentially composed of bulk commodities. The main products for imports are wood, crude oil and minerals, while exports are essentially composed of coal and construction materials. China's railways underpin the country's transactional space. China's rail border-crossings have to be seen in the broader context of attempts to reconstruct the chains of transactions necessary to organize outward cargo movements and to distribute inbound goods (Rimmer and Comtois 2006). China will be pivotal in providing access to and from major ports for landlocked countries in Asia. China's railways are pawns in geopolitical processes. As China's gateways are now emerging as critical logistics service centres that rationalize distribution systems to fit new trading patterns, the rail network development and border crossings throughout the country have far-reaching geopolitical implications. This suggests that the organizational and structural reforms are concomitant with the need for China's railway to closely mirror the corporate practices of emerging global railway operators and logistics providers.

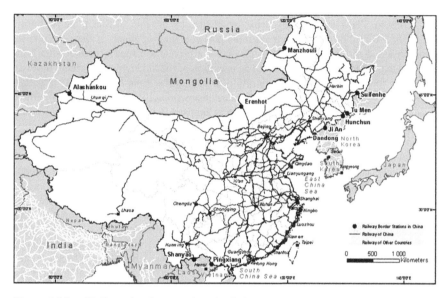

Figure 14.3   Railway border crossings in China

Source: Zhongguo Dituce, 1990–2005; Zhongguo Jiaotong Nianjian, 2011. Drawn by Dominique Goyer.

Panamanian Railways and Gateway Connectivity

At the regional level, railways are operating in an environment of intense competition and consolidation. This dynamic is portrayed spatially and sectorally. Spatially, railway systems represent an infrastructural arena. The terminals, corridors, engineering structures and fleet illustrate the cumulative connections between infrastructure, industrial production and the man-made environment. These infrastructures have a long life span. Much of this equipment has significant value symbolizing important amortized capital investment. The maintenance, modernization and adaptation of rail infrastructure exercise a profound spatial imprint on urban and rural land use changes. Sectorally, the relative weight of passenger and freight rail transport underpins the extension of rail connections to air, road and sea transport. The accessibility, intermodality and frequency of rail services are instrumental in answering the demand for capacity, fluidity and reliability imposed by the transport industry. Railways play a vital role in local and regional development strategies. They maintain the growth, performance and organization of transport gateways and corridors as the archetypical modern growth machine.

The dynamics of the Panamanian railway are the result of major institutional changes (Slack 2008). These include reversion to local control over Canal operations after the transfer of sovereignty from the United States and massive concession programs resulting in foreign investment in port, road and rail facilities. The Hong Kong conglomerate Hutchison Port Holdings has invested US$200 million to increase the terminal capacity at Cristobal and committed another US$300 million to upgrade terminal facilities at Balboa to accommodate post-Panamax ships. Stevedoring Services of America and Motores Internacionales S.A. developed a US$220 million facility at Manzanillo. This was complemented with another US$85 million terminal facility by the Taiwanese shipping line Evergreen Marine at Coco Solo. Plans are currently being established by the Port of Singapore Authority for a US$500 million project to build three port container terminals at the old Rodman naval base and at Farfán port. A concession for a private toll road Corredor Norte was awarded to the Mexican firm PYCSA. The operation of the toll highway Corredor Sur was granted to the construction and engineering firm ICA also from Mexico. The Brazilian construction company Odebrecht financed the construction of Panama City's $183 million coastal highway. The Panama Canal Railroad Company, a joint venture between Kansas City Southern Industries (KCSI) and MI-JACK, a manufacturer and operator of inter-modal facilities has won the concession to reconstruct and operate the interoceanic railway between the ports of Balboa and Cristobal with an extension to the newly constructed port of Coco Solo. The plan involved US$60 million to upgrade the track and equipment. Global forces and international stakeholders are shaping the future of Panama.

The privatization process opened up the country's transport infrastructures to foreign investments. This has transformed the canal from a deepwater crossing between the Caribbean Sea and the Pacific Ocean into a global maritime complex. The presence of leading international terminal operators has contributed to increasing container throughput. Global container carriers such as Maersk, MSC and Cosco have channelled a higher proportion of their Latin American relay cargo to the container terminal facilities of Panama. The strategic importance of the Panama Canal is underpinned by its role as a transshipment hub and drop-off point with many boxes originating/destined from countries outside of Panama. On the Pacific coast the port of Balboa is handling 3.2 million TEUs. The Caribbean entrance to the Canal has three major container ports: Manzanillo, Cristobal and Colon with container throughput of 1,900, 1,000 and 500 thousand TEUs in 2011 (Containerisation International 2012). This unique transportation complex offers shippers a wide range of distribution opportunities. Railways are critical in maintaining the growth, performance and organization of the Panama Canal from the perspective of a system extracting the maximum potential from existing infrastructure. Between 30–40 per cent of traffic is moved by rail from one end of the canal to the other. Kansas City Southern offers 10 train services per day with a capacity of 8,000–9,000 TEUs per week. The objective is to use the rail connection as a conveyor belt to integrate Panama's port terminals as a transportation-based trade gateway.

The transformation of the Canal Zone into Latin America's fully-fledged transportation hub is confronted with serious challenges. The expansion of Panama's port terminals with capacity to handle and transship goods and the related growth in traffic volume has been underpinned by rail linkages (Figure 14.4). Services disruptions in any component of the system impact the entire network with cascading effects. Evidence suggests that problems of stocking capacity, labour issues or difficulties in the transfer of information at port terminals are affecting railroad operations resulting in major delays to vessels being discharged. Internal efficiency, unimpeded accessibility and expansion capacity are key drivers affecting the competitiveness of gateways. The Panama Canal is experiencing strong competition in the regional container handling market. Cartagena in Columbia, Kingston in Jamaica and Manzanillo in Mexico are expanding and upgrading their facilities to accommodate the largest container vessels transiting the Caribbean or feeders servicing north-south traffic of South America. All-land alternatives are also being considered to challenge the Panama Canal. These include a road link between the ports of Limon Sarapiqui and Peñas Blancas in Costa Rica, a landbridge between the ports of Punta Mono and Puerto Corinto in Nicaragua, a superhighway connecting the Honduran port of Cortes on the Atlantic with the Port of La Union on El Salvador's Pacific Coast, a multimodal inter-oceanic corridor linking City Pedro de Alvarado in Moyuta with Port Santo Tomás de Castilla in Guatemala and rail connections between the ports of Salina Cruz and Coatzacoalcos in Mexico. The success of Panama as an exceptional transportation-based gateway increasingly depends on clusters of value-added services within a highly integrated multi-modal network where rail linkages play a key role. Problems could become more acute as the Panama Canal Authority is carrying out studies to consolidate its position as transshipment and logistics hub by developing new port terminals in the Corozal area in Panama City and Margarita Island near Colon.

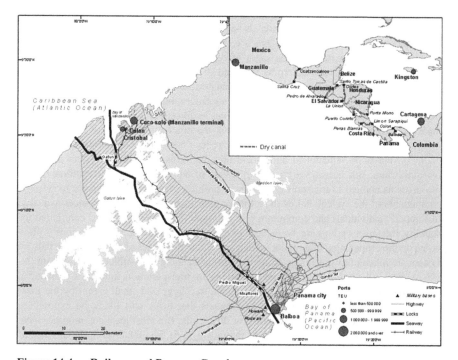

Figure 14.4   Railway and Panama Canal
Source: For railway lines and roads, available at: http://market.weogeo.com; for dry canal, available at: http://www.siteselection.com/issues/2013/mar/central-america.cfm; for container traffic, Containerisation International 2012. Drawn by Dominique Goyer.

Railway Resilience

The Context

Collectively, analyses of global supply chains, shifting market conditions, border crossings and gateway connectivity at different geographical scales reiterate the extent to which the resilience of railway system is tied to governance and infrastructure. The analysis of African, North American, Chinese and Panamanian railways reveal several broad diagnostic feature of the vulnerability of railways. First, growth in rail traffic is an unavoidable part of economic globalization. The global reach of supply chains illustrates the critical function of railways in providing transportation services beyond maritime ranges. Second, railways can participate in a number of parallel and even competing business processes that can change over time. As level of service along the rail transportation chain is extremely difficult to predict and transportation output cannot be stored, capacity is a perennial issue for railways. Third, major preoccupations in rail infrastructure development address the strengthening of transport nodes and corridors in relation to public or corporate transactional activities. This process creates network hierarchy and distribution bias affecting the rail traffic fluidity. Fourth, new and denser infrastructures, based on multi-layered links, have intensified the conditions of the rail system. Problems are expressed in terms of congestion that closes or impedes access to routes or passages affecting the network economy. The potential confluence of these issues underpins the need to increase the resilience of the railway system in an effort to mitigate effects of internal perturbations or external influences.

Transport systems are confronted with an environment of constant changes. This trend has led to the wide-spread adoption of optimization techniques and efficiency measures. Traditionally the objective is to seek the efficient allocation of resources. But it is not clear if optimal solutions maintain or reduce resilience (Gibbs 2009). First, most of these approaches attempt to understand how perturbations affect a system in a state of equilibrium. But railways are never in a state of equilibrium. Second, optimal use of resources as applied to transport management problems could reduce choices to selected components of the system. A key to resilience is to focus on increasing choices available to shippers, individuals and communities as the more the railway system is configured for stability, the fewer options are available. Third, the adoption of optimal allocations is often based on the propagation of cumulative impacts. Some properties or features of the railway system are inherent to specific geographic scales and cannot be combined or scaled-up.

As with all anthropic activities, operations of transportation industries generate a wide range of local impacts while being shaped to a large and small extent by the local communities as an objective reality. This means that firms will likely be exposed to different sets of local forces and will behave differently. But most local communities have lost sight of the system-wide property of the railways. At the global level, the absence of unified international standards on resilience poses problems for integrating the principles of resilience into country policies and effective implementation programs. Ultimately, a resilient railway system would be modular, provide redundancy and display shifting network hierarchy. No technology, policy or modelling approaches will ever allow that objective to be achieved.

The Framework

The adoption of resilient principles requires anticipating rather than following policy needs. Considering rail transport institutional frameworks and infrastructure as units of analysis, the development of effective design principles for a resilient railway system begins with a better understanding of *institutional infrastructure adaptation*. Institutional infrastructure adaptation suggests that the various factors affecting infrastructure adaptation are subject to a firm's prior experience with disruption impacts, various regulatory standards and evolving technologies, thus suggesting that the "corporate learning process" is ultimately a major determinant of adaptation rationale and resilience. In the absence of universal consensus towards a unified resilience-based approach and practice, institutional infrastructure adaptation describes the range of possibilities for an institution to implement resilience. This perspective suggests that the organizational environment in which resilience is implemented contributes to the nature and direction of a firm's organizational strategy. The resilience trajectory pursued by the firm is dependent on the cumulative effect of previous experience, know-how and organizational assets. Resilience thus becomes a functional capacity. By embedding resilience, a railway firm can counteract vulnerability to disruptions, limit exposure to risks and minimize the impact of changes or disruptive events on performance.

The measurement of resilience is difficult. Quantification requires an assessment of the cost of actions to prevent disruptions, the economic losses of a disruptive event, and the expenditure to achieve recovery. Performance measure is the main path towards achieving resilience. In the context of the rail industry, the challenge requires the development of benchmarks adapted to evolving railway conditions and the dynamic transformation of corporations. For a complex and changing organization such as railways, benchmarking involves a small number of activities each having indicators that need to be considered simultaneously for assessment. A performance indicator is a number that indicates the extent to which the railway system, a rail function or some internal process is performing as it ought to. The development of performance indicators often employs an Input-Process-Outcome (IPO) framework. Inputs represent what a railway starts with – physical infrastructure and manpower. Process refers to what railways do with the inputs – transport and trade facilitation processes governing physical flows. Outcomes are the throughput, revenue and service effects of the railway activities on customers – cost, supply, on time delivery, incomes, etc. The interaction of input characteristics and railway structures and processes all take place within an external environment (demographic, economic, social, regional or political factors) which affects railways but are beyond their control or influence. There are many railway indicators, descriptors or management statistics concerning railway inputs, process and outcomes. Most of these are not performance indicators. Measures such as volume of traffic, number of employees, yard dimension or length of block train are input characteristics. Meaningful performance indicators link railway infrastructures and processes (governance of physical flows) to business logistical systems and practices independent of input characteristics (size of rail terminal).

Indicators are not measures of input, process or even outcome per se. They are not measures of anything and everything that can be counted. Performance indicators are more than simple management statistics describing various aspects of the railway system. It is possible to compare railways on the volume of traffic, length of block trains or employment figures. But these do not really represent the railway transportation and trade facilitation system that are totally within the control of the railway industry. Traffic volume or length of block trains are a function of the world economic conditions or demand while number of employees is closely related to a combination of input factors and skills.

The Method

Performance measurement has been used for several decades. Performance indicators are not superficial or peripheral to railways. They can be used to improve the performance of railway core business and above all to keep pace with changes in the railway business or even auditing system (i.e. ISO 14000). Good data and appropriate indicators lead to a better understanding of the weak link in the railway operations system. Above all, the production of performance indicators for railways allows the formulation of infrastructure investment priorities. Table 14.1 indicates five groups of functional areas impacting on railway activities in which improvement is required and that need assessment through 20 indicators.

Transportation demand indicators focus on the volume of traffic that flows through the railway system in terms of railcar availability. The usefulness of transportation supply indicators depends on plans elaborated and targets that have been set. Indicators must have a purpose: Remedy a problem? Fix cost? Set price? Equipment productivity needs to meet industry targets. Such indicators provide a diagnostic on productivity and provide a link between product and process to technological innovation. The best assessment is the level of productivity that can be maintained over the long term. As a result the targets are best met using a working time sheet. Labour skills, attitudes or motivations are encompassed in general productivity indicators. Employment figures from the operation and management of the railway industry sector need to be considered as indicators for their multiplier effect on the expenditures of the railway system, the supplier industries and the economy in general. The logistical system structure of railways requires the establishment of a service quality index. The objective is to measure how many times the railways met expected time of arrival and departure for trains. The scale ranges from 0 per cent when the port is closed to 100 per cent when the customer is satisfied. Environmental indicators have become an unavoidable part of benchmarking process in the marine industry. Climate change and greenhouse gas emissions are a reality. But no standards are agreed upon on measuring polluting emissions. Evidence based on field work suggests that initially the salient aspects of air emissions as measured by the volume of particulate matters generated by the railway activities should be considered to provide a base for subsequent analysis.

Obviously, these performance measures can be refined while some may be more crucial than others. The objective is to provide insight in the design of a resilient railway system as indicators will identify and quantify vulnerabilities. Performance monitoring is one of several quality enhancing activities designed to improve quality and accountability for railways. The indicators suggested should meet certain standards with a view to evaluate the corporate levers for effectively building and deploying knowledge and skills required for resilience. The development of indicators demands clarity on quality aspects notably scientific rigour in terms of feasibility, robustness, usability, transparency and readability.

- Feasibility involves issue to the extent to which the data needed for constructing the indicator exists.
- Robustness is the quality of the indicator to withstand changes in operational environment or conditions without affecting its functionality to overall indicators.
- Usability denotes the ease with which port stakeholders can easily employ indicators with low rate of error.

Table 14.1   Selected indicators for railway performance

Rail functional sector	Indicator	Data needed	Units of measurement
Transportation demand	Throughput	Throughput	Tonnage/ passenger
	Rail car availability	Number of cars available for loading	Cars
Transportation supply	Terminal design capacity	Maximum possible throughput	Tonnage/ passenger
	Terminal utilisation rate	Actual vs maximum potential throughput by terminal	%
	Terminal operations	Terminal operating hours	hours
	Terminal productivity	Throughput per terminal	Tonnes/ passenger per hectare
	Fleet design capacity	Maximum possible throughput by type of train	Tonnes
	Fleet utilisation rate	Total availability of train minus down time	Hours
	Fleet operations	Train operating time	Hours
Transportation supply	Fleet productivity	Throughput and train operating time	Tonne/ passenger/ hour/train
Employment	Labour generation	Direct and indirect employment generated by rail activities	Manpower hours
	Labour income	Annual wage and benefits	$
	Labour productivity	Throughput, working time, income	Tonne/passenger/hours/$
Transport fluidity	Rail loading utilisation rate	Actual throughput vs maximum car capacity	% and standard deviation
	Rail loading time	Variation in loading time	% and standard deviation
	Train cycle time	Time train takes to make trip from source back to source	Hours or days
	Rail operations at terminal	Rail start and end date time at terminal	Hours
	Rail schedule reliability	Train scheduled arrival date time vs train actual arrival date time	% and standard deviation
	Train space occupation	Length of cars and throughput handled	Metres per tonnage/ passenger/train length
Environment	Air emission	Throughput and air contaminants	Particulate matter (PM) concentration/ tonnes

Source: Author.

- Transparency pertains to the level a customer is involved in the decision-making process of indicators accepting goals and operations of indicators.
- Readability refers to the intelligibility of an indicator and the ease with it is understood by a stakeholder.

Benchmarking is the first step towards building a more resilient railway system as vulnerabilities often emanates from poor performance and incapacity or unwillingness to adapt to changing conditions. The successful implementation of a resilient railway system must consider several factors. First, benchmarking should be more than numbers and figure tables. Benchmarking is more than a statistical exercise based on the collection of indicators. An agreed corporate strategy shared among all railway stakeholders is a prerequisite. The input is then information gathering on the internal and external environment impacting on railway system. Second, performance accounting should provide guidance for improvement. Such a task should identify drivers and constraints that impact on improvement. Third, understanding best practices sometimes generate more meaningful results than a rigid prescriptive model. But there are few references about best practices and how best practices changes given new trade, new policy, new technology, etc. Non-quantitative information might convey a better assessment of the situation. All this suggests qualitative assessment of changes in the operating environment of the railway system is a necessary complement to quantitative indicators. Fourth, the proposed framework formulates a pattern of instrument based on industry self-regulation in the context of market liberalization. Should the industry fail to answer the need for resilience, then increasing pressure will request public policy initiative and concomitant movement towards more assertive government instruments.

Conclusion

This chapter has developed a conceptual framework by coupling governance and infrastructure in order to explore the measures required to assess railway competitive functions that can have a determining impact on stimulating resilience.

Application of governance and infrastructure at different geographical scale has drawn attention to railway corridors, interfaces and thresholds as an objective reality while being shaped to a large or small extent by the way states and corporations have incorporated them. The series of case studies has highlighted a number of areas for improving the conceptual underpinnings and providing methodological refinements for understanding the resilience of railway transport system and identifying adaptation strategies. The complexity of globalization processes, the shifts in trades, emerging significant geopolitical concerns, and more importantly, the current business and economic environment are calling for some form of evaluation mechanisms demonstrating the maintenance and improvement of standards. The studies suggest that railways are part of a global system.

The global nature of railways has increased the exposure to risks. The vulnerability of each stakeholder can be transferred to other chain stakeholders. The number of possible disruptions within the railway system is almost infinite. The best approach to reduce vulnerability is coordinated efforts. Ideally, the resilience framework should be global in scope, encompass both internal and external risks with a view to develop a vast portfolio of capacities in a cost competitive way.

All stakeholders acknowledge that any attempt to understand changes and reduce vulnerability issues in railways requires benchmarking. The development of performance indicators has great benefit in terms of information and assessment. These indicators can be used as negotiation languages between stakeholders sharing different anticipations of changes and various opinions on possible futures that can be reasonably imagined. Benchmarking permits legitimizing decisions prior to the full resolution of vulnerabilities.

Looking ahead, there is a persistent gap between communities focusing on safety, security and sustainability issues and railway authorities concerns with economic development and cost competitiveness. This gap is a major source of difficulties in elaborating transition towards resilience. The main challenge for railway stakeholders consists in searching for compromise between the cost of failure and the cost of resilience that often implies the development of performance indicators and a modification of firm's organizational strategies. Railway transportation systems are critical infrastructures enabling economic activities for a broad range of entities within a society, through the transfer of goods and passengers between destinations in a safe, secure and efficient way. The railway transport system operates in a complex environment and is thus exposed to a variety of disruptions. In this context, the analysis of railway resilience can serve as a test bed to assess the global system of transport.

References

Amos, P. and Bullock, R. 2006. *Managing Economic Interfaces in Multi-Operator Railway Environments. Report to the Ministry of Railways China.* Beijing: World Bank.

Bullock, R. 2005. *Results of Railway Privatization in Africa.* Transport Paper TP-8. Washington, DC: World Bank, Transport Sector Board.

Canadian Association of Petroleum Producers (CAPP). 2012. *Crude Oil Forecast, Markets and Pipelines.* Calgary: CAPP.

Cetin, K.C. and Cerit, A.G. 2010. Organizational effectiveness at seaports: a systems approach. *Maritime Policy and Management*, 37(3), 195–219.

Chang, S.E. 2000. Disasters and transport systems: loss, recovery and competition at the Port of Kobe after the 1995 earthquake. *Journal of Transport Geography*, 8(1), 53–65.

Comfort, L.K. 2005. Risk, security and disaster management. *Annual Review of Political Science*, 8, 335–56.

Comtois, C. 1990. Transport and territorial development in China, 1949–1985. *Modern Asian Studies*, 24(4), 777–818.

Containerisation International. 2012. *Top 100 Container Ports 2012.* London: Informa.

Elbadawi, I., Mengistae, T. and Zeufack, A. 2006. *Market Access, Supplier Access, and Africa's Manufactured Exports: an Analysis of the Role of Geography and Institutions.* World Bank Policy Research Working Paper 3942. Washington, DC: World Bank.

Gibbs, M.T. 2009. Resilience: what is it and what does it mean for marine policy makers? *Marine Policy*, 33, 322–31.

Guillaume, J. 2008. *Les Transports Maritimes dans la Mondialisation.* Paris: L'Harmattan.

Haimes, Y.Y. 2006. On the definition of vulnerabilities in measuring risks to infrastructure. *Risk Analysis*, 26(2), 293–6.

Hilling, D. 1996. *Transport and Developing Countries.* London: Routledge.

Iakovou, E., Vlachos, D. and Xanthopoulos, A. 2007. An analytical methodological framework for the optimal design of resilience supply chain. *International Journal of Logistics Economics and Globalization*, 1(1), 1–20.

IBM Business Consulting Services. 2004. *Rail Liberalisation Index.* Berlin: IBM.

Instanes, A. et al. 2005. Infrastructure: buildings, support systems, and industrial facilities, in *Impacts of a Warming Climate*, edited by C. Symon, L. Arris and B. Heal. New York: Cambridge University Press, 908–44.

Kohn, H.M. 2011. *Trends in Rail Technology*. Paper to the 46th annual Conference of the Canadian Transportation Research Forum, Gatineau, 29 May–1 June 2011.

Lakshmanan, T.R. and Anderson, W.P. 2002. *Transportation Infrastructure, Freight Services Sector and Economic Growth*. Boston: Boston University, Centre for Transportation Studies.

Lasserre, F. 2006. *L'éveil du Dragon. Les défis du Développement de la Chine au 21ᵉ Siècle*. Québec: Presses de l'Université du Québec.

Mansouri, M., Nilchiani, R. and Mostashari, A. 2010. A policy making framework for resilient port infrastructure systems. *Marine Policy*, 34(6), 1125–34.

McCarthy, J.J. et al. 2005. Climate change in the context of multiple stressors and resilience, in *Impacts of a Warming Climate*, edited by C. Symon, L. Arris and B. Heal. New York: Cambridge University Press, 945–88.

McMillan, C. 2007. *The Strategic Challenge: from Serfdom to Surfing*. Concord: Captus Press.

Murray-Tuite, P.M. 2006. *A Comparison of Transportation Network Resilience under Simulated System Optimum and User Equilibrium Conditions: Proceedings of the 2006 Winter Simulation Conference, California, 3–6 December, 2006*, edited by L.F. Perrone, F.P. Wieland, J. Liu, B.G. Lawson, P.M. Nicol and R.M. Fujimoto, Monterey: IEEE Computer Society Press, 1398–405.

Pelletier, J.F. 2012. *L'intégration des Corridors dans les Chaînes d'Approvisionnement Internationales: Analyse de cas Africains*. Thesis, Département de géographie, Université Paris Est.

Pitera, K.A. 2008. *Interpreting Resilience: an Examination of the Use of Resiliency Strategies within the Supply Chain and Consequences for the Freight Transportation System*. Thesis. Department of Civil and Environmental Engineering, University of Washington.

Porfiriev, B. 2001. Managing security and safety risks in the Baltic Sea region: a comparative study of institutional crisis policy models. *Risk Management*, 3(4), 51–62.

Rimmer, P.J. 1988. Transport geography. *Progress in Human Geography*, 12(2), 271–81.

Rimmer, P.J. 1997. China's infrastructure and economic development in the 21st century. *Futures*, 29(4/5), 435–65.

Rimmer, P.J. and Comtois, C. 2006. Les passages transfrontaliers de la Chine, in *Défis du Dragen: less défis du Développement de la Chine*, 147–68.

Sarathy, R. 2006. Security and global supply chain. *Transportation Journal*, 45(4), 28–52.

Sivell, P.M., Reeves, S.J., Baldachin, L. and Brightman, T.G. 2008. *Climate Change Resilience Indicators*. Guildford: Transport Research Laboratory.

Slack, B. 2008. The crossroad at the crossroads, panama and the challenge of containerized trade, in *Les Transports Maritimes dans la Mondialisation*, 79–89.

Symon, C., Arris, L. and Heal, B. 2005. *Arctic Climate Impact Assessment*. Cambridge: Cambridge University Press.

Taneja, P. et al. 2010. Implications of an uncertain future for port planning. *Maritime Policy and Management*, 37(3), 221–45.

Therien, M. 2010. Stratégies de résilience et infrastructures essentielles. *Téléscope*, 16(2), 154–71.

Thompson, L. 2003. Changing railway structure and ownership: is anything working? *Transport Reviews*, 23(3), 311–55.

Williamson, O. 2002. The theory of the firm as governance structure: from choice to contract. *Journal of Economic Perspective*, 16(3), 171–95.

Winkelman, S., Bishins, A. and Kooshian, C. 2010. Planning for economic and environmental resilience. *Transportation Research A*, 44(8), 575–86.

Index

'(t)' following page number denotes table, '(f)' denotes figure.

accessibility 3, 10, 23–4, 27, 29, 30, 31, 35, 60, 69, 102, 117, 130–40, 145, 189, 195, 201, 204, 207, 210–11, 237, 243–4
accountability 154,158, 188, 197, 248
acquisition(s) 11, 41, 68, 104, 168–80, 202, 227, 239
Adelaide 46
adjacency 23–4, 35
Africa(n) 4, 57, 70, 135, 236–9, 246
agglomeration 24, 36, 78, 118
air transport/transportation 6, 7, 9, 23, 26–7, 29–30, 40, 70, 95–106, 189, 219
airline 59, 68, 95–106, 237
airport terminal(s) 26–7, 30, 46
Alaska 173–4
Albany 168
Algeria 237
alternative fuel(s) 6
Amsterdam 27, 64(t), 97, 99–101
Antwerp 117, 120(t)
Argentina 4, 40(t), 70, 140(t)
Asia(n) 9, 29, 70, 87, 90, 110, 131, 135, 136, 220, 229, 237, 239, 242
Australasia 70
Australia(n) 7, 39–44, 46, 47, 48–9, 50, 51, 52–3, 110, 112(f), 114, 136, 193, 194, 237
Austria 65, 104, 110
automation 188, 235
automobile(s) 4, 5–6, 9, 29, 57, 80, 86–7, 88, 129–30, 150, 219

Balboa 244
Baltimore 168
Bangkok 90, 210, 214
Bangladesh 193
bankruptcy 45, 104, 169
Beijing 29, 75, 216, 237

Belgium 27, 30, 61–4, 104, 123, 132, 146, 237, 239
benchmark(s) 98, 201, 216, 247–51
Berlin 80, 193
Bettembourg 122
Birmingham 102, 154, 157, 159–60, 162
black 131, 135
border regions 60, 64, 69
Boston 30
Bradford 99
Brazil(ian) 4, 110–11, 114, 140(t), 244
Bremen 225
Brisbane 46, 49
British Columbia 170
Brussels 24, 30, 61, 64, 99, 100, 101(t), 103
Buffalo 168
Build-Operate-Transfer (BOT) 139, 190–91
Build-Own-Operate (BOO) 139
Build-Own-Operate-Transfer (BOOT) 139
Burlington 227
Busan 29

California 10, 30, 150, 222
Canada (Canadian) 8, 40, 42, 47, 110, 114, 118, 133, 134–5, 167–80, 237, 239–41
Canada Transportation Act (1996) 169
canal 4, 23, 70, 85, 152, 186, 220, 243–5
Canberra 46, 49
capacity building 50, 52
capital markets 4
carbon dioxide (CO_2) 9, 51, 76, 80, 82–4, 109, 115, 241
carbon emission(s) 6, 9, 195
Cartagena 244
central business district (CBD) 27, 30, 46, 86, 204
Charleroi 64

Chicago 32, 78(t), 118, 168–9, 171, 174,
    177, 222, 226
children 10, 52, 130
China/People's Republic of China (PRC)
    4, 11, 24, 29, 40, 47, 57, 75, 90, 91,
    49, 98, 105, 110, 115, 117, 140(t),
    151–2, 163, 193, 194, 220, 230,
    241–3
Channel Tunnel 59, 61, 64, 69, 102, 159
citizen participation 146–7
climate change 6, 48, 52, 75, 91, 95, 248
Coatzacoalcos 245
code-sharing 97, 104
co-location 24, 27, 31, 34–6
Cologne 97, 99, 101(t)
Colon 244–5
colony/colonies/colonial/colonization 4,
    41–4, 57, 148, 193, 237
combined transport 115–23, 224
competition 40, 41, 43, 48, 49, 50, 53, 58,
    59, 68, 69–70, 95–9, 103–5, 113,
    116, 122, 169, 189, 195, 202, 219,
    223, 227, 228, 230, 236, 241–4
congestion 3, 5, 29, 30, 48, 68, 81, 83,
    86–7, 91, 95, 97, 102, 105, 109,
    116, 117, 118, 178, 195, 210–11,
    219, 223, 226–7, 229, 239, 246
connectivity 24, 27, 34, 19, 100, 103, 152,
    195, 211, 239, 243, 246
consultancy/consultant 152, 189–90, 192,
    194, 205
container on flat car (COFC) 221
containerization 34, 61, 109, 115–23,
    220–21, 229
Copenhagen 64, 76, 78, 83–5, 86
Cortes 245
cost-benefit analysis 131
Costa Rica 245
Cristobal 244
cross-border freight traffic/cross-border
    passenger traffic 9, 61–7
Curitiba 76, 78(t)
cycling 3, 82, 83–4, 90, 172
cyclist 79, 84
Czech Republic 225

daily necessities 130
Darwin 43
decision-making 48, 52, 145, 146–9, 153,
    162, 197, 237, 250
Denmark 61, 64, 85, 225

deregulation 28, 59, 65, 68, 70, 96, 104,
    139, 169, 222, 227, 239, 241
Deutsche Bahn (DB) 68, 97, 120(t), 156,
    225, 228
developmental line 41
disabled 10, 131, 132–3, 134–7, 149
disparity(-ies) 60, 69, 152–4, 228, 242
door-to-door 65, 109, 117, 119, 121, 123,
    221
double stack 11, 33, 117, 221–2, 224
Dunkerque 64
Dusseldorf 99, 101(t)

east coast of Australia 46, 49
East Indies 41, 42
East/Eastern Europe 65, 110, 115, 225
Eastern Africa 135
economic development 3–4, 47, 49, 52, 57,
    76, 86, 115, 129, 132, 138, 152,
    153, 160, 201, 204, 242, 251
Edinburgh 99, 101(t), 102
Edo 41–2
education 6, 10, 76, 129, 131
efficiency 29, 33–5, 43, 44, 113, 131–3,
    138, 140, 180, 186, 204, 206, 208,
    211, 212–13, 215–16, 222–3, 237,
    244, 246
egalitarianism 129
elderly 10, 130–31, 133
electric railways 185
electrification 7, 59, 186, 187, 202, 208
Emmerich 121
energy consumption 6, 89, 90
engagement/public engagement/community
    engagement 10, 145–63
environment 3, 6, 8, 10, 35, 47–8, 50,
    51–2, 73, 76, 79, 82–3, 86, 95, 100,
    105, 109, 115, 116, 121, 122, 145,
    150, 152, 154, 158, 160, 163, 172,
    175(t), 195, 216, 223, 241, 248–9
environmental sustainability 9, 236
equity 3, 41, 89, 208
Eskilstuna 137
Estonia 224
ethnic minorities 10, 131, 149
Europe 5, 6, 12, 24, 31, 33–4, 40, 57, 78,
    80, 84, 90, 95–8, 100, 102, 105,
    110–13, 115–16, 117, 121–3, 129,
    130, 132–3, 134, 137, 149, 193,
    219, 223–6, 227, 228–30, 239, 241;
    see also European Union

European Commission 6, 60, 97, 109
European Union (EU) 9, 30, 45, 51, 59–70,
    95, 98, 104, 110, 115, 122, 152–3,
    154, 224–5, 228, 239
export 4, 11, 50, 51, 58, 114–15, 119, 221,
    239, 241, 242

Felixstowe 228
financial viability 11, 201, 204–7, 211, 216
Finland 30, 61
Florida 30
forced car ownership (FCO) 130
France 5, 27, 30, 40(t), 57, 59, 61, 63–5,
    69, 95, 104, 110–12, 114, 122, 123,
    130, 132, 193, 224
freight corridor 35(t)–6, 122, 195, 226
freight logistics network 48
freight transport 4, 9, 12, 25, 61, 67,
    109–23, 167–80, 229, 235, 237,
    242
Fukuoka 45, 136

gateway 46, 48, 100, 152, 163, 235, 242,
    243–6
gauge(s) 8–9, 39–43, 45, 48, 49–50, 59,
    186, 236, 237, 238(f)
Germany 11, 27, 30, 40, 42, 57, 59, 60, 61,
    65, 68, 110–12, 121–2, 193–4, 225,
    228, 239
Genesee and Wyoming (Genesee &
    Wyoming) 43, 173(t), 237
Glasgow 99, 101(t), 102
global cities 77–8, 80, 88
Global South 5, 90
globalization 6, 23, 31, 46, 236, 246, 250
Gothard 122
governance 39, 41–5, 48, 87, 99, 139,
    145–7, 152, 162–3, 197, 235–7,
    239, 246, 250
Great Britain 57, 131
Great Southern Railways 43
Greece 132
green logistics 9
green TOD 81–3, 90
greenhouse gas(es)/GHG 6, 52, 90, 150,
    248
Guangzhou 29
Guatemala 245

Hamburg 85, 101(t), 117, 193, 225–6
health care 130
health impact assessment (HIA) 135

heritage 160
high-density environment 9, 29, 79, 134,
    138, 151, 204
high-speed rail/high-speed railway(s)/
    HSR/HSRs 5, 7, 8, 9, 10, 12,
    24–7, 29–31, 35–6, 39, 42, 45–6,
    49, 60, 61, 69–70, 95–106, 137–8,
    145, 151, 154, 159–60, 163, 189,
    193
highway 4, 7, 31, 47, 59, 60, 83, 150, 226,
    237, 244, 245
hinterland 29, 33, 41, 60, 96, 115–16, 119,
    225, 236
Hokkaido 45, 46
Holland 225; *see also* Netherlands
Hong Kong 11, 27, 47, 76, 78(t), 80, 88–9,
    91, 136, 138, 139, 151–2, 193,
    201–12, 214, 216–17, 244
horizontal equity 132
Hourglass model 96
HS2 102, 153, 159–61
hub airport(s) 96–7, 102, 104,
    105(footnotes)
Hub and Spoke (H&S) 96, 117
hub(s) 24, 26, 29–30, 35(t), 75, 79, 95,
    98, 100, 239, 244–5; *see also* hub
    airport

IC ticketing system 51
India 4, 24, 29, 40, 42, 57, 70, 110, 112(f),
    115, 117, 140(t), 193, 241
Indonesia 39, 40(t), 41, 42, 44, 46–8,
    49–51, 52–3, 194
Indonesian Economic Development Plan
    2011–2025 47, 49
Indonesia Infrastructure Initiative 44,
    49–50
industrialization 3, 6, 7, 57
influence diagram 202, 210, 212–13,
    215(f), 216–17
Infrastructure Australia 47, 48–9
inland load centre(s) 6, 24
innovation 53, 58, 68, 113, 146, 154,
    188–9, 196, 219, 248
institutional framework 44, 47, 247
institutional obstacles 139
integrated hub model 96–7
integration 4, 7, 8–9, 27, 29, 30, 35–6, 39,
    60, 70, 86, 89–90, 95–106, 115,
    119, 122, 137, 149, 152–3, 161–2,
    188–92, 194, 197, 203, 206, 220,
    237, 239

interchange(s) 8, 39, 46, 49, 136, 171,
    175(t), 178, 226
international container port strategy 51
International Union of Railways 46, 47
inter-city transport 8, 9, 26, 27, 29, 30, 39,
    40, 90–91, 110, 189
inter-modal transfers 79
intermodalism/intermodality 6, 11, 23–5,
    27, 28, 31–6, 46, 79, 97, 99, 109,
    115, 118–23, 149, 175(t), 178–9,
    219–30, 236, 243–4
Ireland 110, 132
Italy 4, 30, 61, 65, 122, 123, 225

Jakarta 46, 49, 90
Jamaica 244
Japan 3, 11, 24, 29, 39–42, 44–6, 47, 48,
    49, 51–3, 70, 95, 98, 110, 112(f),
    114, 123, 134, 135(t), 136–7,
    138–9, 193, 220, 241
Japan(ese) National Railways (JNR) 42,
    45, 53
Java North Coast line 50
Jeumont 64
job(s) 10, 78, 80, 84, 116, 130, 133, 135,
    137–8, 160, 170
journey time(s) 9, 49, 57, 85
JR Central 45–6, 51–2, 53
JR Freight 45, 51
just-in-time 113, 116, 191, 197

Kalgoorlie 44
Kalimantan 50
Kansai 46
Kansas City 239, 244
Kaohsiung 29
Kawasaki 51, 193
Kazakhstan 242
Kingston 244
knowledge transfer 78, 148, 190
Kobe 51
Kortrijk 64
Kyoto Protocol 9
Kyushu 45, 46

La Union 245
laissez-faire 99
Lampung 50
land acquisition 34, 47, 49–50, 157
land conservation 9
land development 76, 80, 87, 88, 90, 118,
    204

land use(s) 24, 30, 75, 79, 86, 89, 138, 148,
    151, 201, 202–4, 207, 212, 236, 243
landlocked countries/landlocked territories
    57, 59, 242
Latin America/South America 4, 70, 135,
    194, 229, 244–5
Law no. 23/2007 44, 50
Le Havre 117, 120(t)
Leeds 99, 102, 159
legislation 117, 122, 139, 225
liberalization 95–6, 104, 139, 169, 225,
    236, 239, 241, 250
life cycle 188, 190, 192, 196–7
Light Railway Act 1910 45
Lille 30, 61, 64
Limon Sarapiqui 245
line-haul 167, 168, 170, 171, 173–4, 178
Lithuania 61
livability 3, 83, 85, 135, 140
localism 10, 145–63
locomotive(s) 11, 50, 60, 117, 167, 174,
    185, 193, 220, 224–5, 229
logistics 24, 34–6, 48, 51, 68, 79, 81, 113,
    117–23, 178, 222, 225, 229, 230,
    236, 239, 243, 245, 247–8; *see also*
    green logistics
London 8, 11, 30, 59, 61, 64(t), 68, 80, 88,
    99–102, 154, 156–8, 204, 214, 216
Los Angeles 10, 203–4, 226, 239
Lötschberg 122
Louisiana 177
low cost carriers (LCCs) 95, 103(t), 104,
    105
Ludwigshafen 225
Lufthansa 27, 97
Lyon 40, 101(t), 122, 193, 225

MAGLEV 40, 52, 98, 189, 193–4
Malmo 64
Malta 148
Manchester 99–103, 155, 159
Manzanillo 244–5
Manzhouli 242
massification 117, 123
Mediterranean Africa 237
Melbourne 46, 49, 78(t), 88, 130
mergers 10, 11, 227, 239, 241
metropolitan areas 6, 26, 29, 45, 46, 49, 52,
    61, 64, 70, 81, 109, 137, 149–50,
    177, 201, 226
Mexico 4, 114, 140(t), 167–9, 173, 180,
    239–41, 244–5

Milan 59
military 4, 60
Milwaukee 169
Minneapolis 137–8
Minnesota 135
mobility 3, 6, 9, 10, 23, 25, 29, 35, 36, 46, 48, 75, 87, 90, 130, 132, 134, 201–2, 204, 210
modal shift 9, 34, 98, 109, 110, 113, 115–16, 121–3, 160
mode substitution 95–102, 105–6
modernization 40, 42, 44, 69, 91, 243
modernization paradigm 3
Mongolia 242
Montreal 118, 239
Moyuta 245
MTR 47, 88–9, 136, 138–9, 192, 202–6
Myrdal's spread and backwash 153, 162

Nagoya 40, 45, 46, 51, 51–2, 53
Namibia 134
National Competition Policy 43, 53
National Railway Master Plan 49–50, 53
National Transportation Act (1987) 169
Netherlands 10, 30, 61, 104, 110, 121, 237, 239
network capacity 146
network effects 23–4, 35, 60
New Orleans 177
New York 12, 30, 80, 202, 204, 220–21
New Zealand 43, 133
Newcastle 99, 100, 101(t)
Nicaragua 245
noise 3, 5, 9–10, 150, 157, 186, 188
non-renewable energy/non-renewable resource 5, 6, 82
North America 11, 24, 30, 32–4, 41, 57, 116, 117, 123, 129–30, 134–5, 149, 163, 167–80, 219, 237, 239–41, 246
North Platte 32
North-West Europe 153
Norway 30, 110

Ocean transport 237, 239
OECD 5, 110(footnotes), 130, 213–14
Ohio 168, 169
Oil crisis 6
Oil depletion 6
Open-skies 96
Operating cost 174, 205, 211
Oregon 79

Osaka 29, 39, 40, 45–6, 51–2, 95, 193
Owen's stages of mobility 3
Oxford 154, 156–8

Pacific National 43
Panama 220, 243–6
Paris 27, 40, 61, 64, 68, 88, 99, 100–101, 103, 118, 161, 193
patronage 95, 203(t), 206–7, 210, 210–11, 215–16
pedestrian(s) 75, 79, 81, 83–4, 89, 131, 135, 149–50, 152, 163
Pedro de Alvarado 245
Peñas Blancas 245
Pennsylvania 173
performance monitoring 248
peripheral regions 137, 140, 152
periphery 10, 60, 69, 83, 137, 146, 237
Perpignan 122
Poland 65, 110, 112(f), 225
politics 4, 8, 23, 35, 42, 49, 51, 53, 76, 87, 100, 110, 115, 137, 145–6, 151, 161–2, 169, 171, 172, 211, 215–16, 230, 235, 237, 242, 247, 250
pollution 3, 5–6, 9, 82, 86, 89, 91, 150
Portland 79
privatization 11, 43, 45, 50, 68, 70, 139, 169, 180, 201–2, 236, 244
productivity 4, 31, 43, 46, 48, 53, 76, 115, 122, 132, 138, 195, 196, 211, 215, 237, 241, 248–9
profitability 10, 11, 28, 42, 44, 49–51, 69, 80, 88–9, 96, 121, 138, 160, 170, 176, 180, 195, 201, 204–7, 210, 211, 214, 222
public participation 133, 147, 149
public-private partnership (PPP) 31, 34, 39, 41, 46, 47, 50, 53, 139, 190–92, 206–17
public transport 5, 75–8, 80–82, 87, 88, 106, 129–34, 137, 149, 154, 201, 202–3, 207, 210–11
Puerto Corinto 245
Punta Mono 245

Quality of life 3, 78, 130
Queensland 44, 48

rail deficit 41
rail line 23, 28, 43, 46, 48, 80, 85, 121, 171, 172, 176, 202, 224

Rail & Property development model/
rail-cum-property model 11, 138,
201–17
Rail Track Corporation 43–4
railway alliances 98, 103
railway infrastructure 9, 11, 44, 46, 47,
139, 145, 153, 156, 161–2, 163,
202, 203, 206, 247
railway institution 39, 41–5, 53
railway investments 4, 5, 89
Railway Nationalization Act 44
regions 23, 24, 26, 28, 29, 57, 59, 60, 64,
69–70, 138, 152, 161, 162, 219,
236, 237; *see also* peripheral regions
regulations 44, 50, 59, 139, 175, 195–7,
236, 242
regulatory environment 23, 52, 65, 68–9,
98, 221
reliability 34, 48, 57, 68, 109, 113, 116,
121, 186, 187, 189, 195, 197, 211,
229, 236, 243, 249(t)
resilience 197, 235–51
Rio+20 75
risk 34, 41, 51, 70, 116, 119, 158, 161, 190,
191, 194, 197, 207–8, 210, 211,
213–14, 220, 225, 235–6, 247, 250
river navigation 4
road transport 6, 9, 28, 35, 50, 59, 109–10,
113–19, 122–3, 134, 172, 224, 226,
229
role of leadership 53
rolling stock 43, 45, 46, 50–51, 53, 68,
167, 189, 192, 237, 241
roll-on/roll-off terminals 26
Romania 224
Rostow's Stage of Growth 3, 58
Rotterdam 10, 117, 120(t), 121, 225, 226
Russia 4, 8, 40, 57, 110–12, 115, 140(t),
193, 242

safety 9–10, 44, 130, 132, 151, 158, 175,
187–8, 189, 192, 194, 195, 197,
211, 223, 241, 251
Saint Paul 135
Salina Cruz 245
San Diego 135
Santo Tomás de Castilla 245
Saskatchewan 170
Saudi Arabia 193
scale economies 114, 228
Scandinavia (Scandinavian) 75, 76, 83,
86, 110

Scotland 102
sea transport 6, 42, 243
seamless 8, 39, 43, 46, 48, 51, 97
Seattle 163, 226
Semarang 42
Seoul 29, 90
Shanghai 8, 27, 40, 98, 193, 237
Sheffield 156
Shenzhen 75, 90, 151
Shikoku 45
Shinkansen 39, 40, 42, 45–6, 52, 53, 138,
139, 193
signalling system 9, 11, 49, 59, 68, 187,
189, 192, 196, 197
social equity 3, 10, 76, 129–40, 149
social exclusion 129–34
social learning 145, 147, 163
social saving(s) 3–4, 58
South Africa 40(t), 133, 140(t), 237
South Korea 29, 110, 114
Southeast Asia/South East Asia 76, 135,
194, 229
Soviet Union 110
Spain 4, 27, 30, 98, 133, 224
spatial imbalance 10
spatial clustering 78
spatial integration 149
spatial planning 148, 151, 163
spatial structure 23, 29, 35
special discount membership service 46
St. Louis 168, 169
standards 44, 154, 158, 194, 196, 197, 211,
213, 219, 224, 246–7, 248, 250
Stockholm 76–8, 80–83, 86, 90, 137
structuring effects 23–36
suburbanization 4, 118
sufficientarianism 129
Suifenhe 242
Sumatra 42, 50
supply chain 35, 48, 116, 117, 230, 235,
236–9, 246
Surabaya 49
sustainability 3, 6–7, 8, 9, 10, 11–12, 35,
39, 47, 52, 76, 138, 162–3, 216,
236, 251
sustainable development 3, 48, 52, 116,
129, 152, 162, 241
sustainable mobility 6, 46, 48, 90
sustainable transport 3, 5–6, 46, 48, 75, 95,
129, 132, 154
Sweden 30, 61, 80–83, 137
Switzerland 61, 104, 110–12, 122, 225

Sydney 46, 49
Sydney Airport 46

Taaffe-Morril-Gould model 3, 4
Taipei 29
Taiwan (Taiwanese) 29, 220, 244
Tanggung 42
Tarcoola 43
tariff(s) 8, 39, 59, 154, 216
Tasmania 41, 43
technology transfer 189–92, 193
telecommunication 6
TEN-T (network) 60, 61, 68, 152
terminals 8, 23–36, 46, 69, 117–19, 121–2,
        146, 167, 172–3, 178, 220–22, 225,
        226, 242, 243–5
TEU(s) 116, 117, 118, 220, 222, 224–5,
        244
Texas 30, 222
TGV 40, 49, 95, 104, 193
Thruport 8
Tilbury 228
Tokaido Shinkansen 39, 42, 45, 46, 53
Tokyo 29, 39, 40, 41, 45–6, 51–2, 80, 95,
        193, 209
toll 47, 81, 83, 87, 122, 220, 244
Tournai 64
traffic injuries 3, 5
Trailer on Flat Car (TOFC) 220
transcontinental networks 235
transit-oriented development (TOD) 6, 9,
        47, 75–91, 134, 135, 151, 162
transport disadvantaged 10, 129–31,
        132–3, 134
transport externalities 5
TRANSRAPID 40
transshipment 8, 29, 39, 59, 68, 113, 121,
        237, 244–5
Tunisia 237

turnkey 190–91

UIC Declaration on Sustainable Mobility
        and Transport 46, 48
underinvestment 134
United Kingdom (UK) 5, 10, 40, 59, 61, 65,
        68–9, 70, 98(footnotes), 100–102,
        110–12, 114, 122, 123, 130, 131,
        133, 134–5, 139, 145–6, 149,
        153–62, 185, 193, 223, 225, 228
universal design 131–3, 136–7
urban agglomerations 118
urban form 76, 80, 90
USA/United States/US 3–4, 8, 40, 42, 57,
        60, 76, 90, 96, 110, 112(f), 114,
        130, 131, 133–5, 137, 148–51,
        163, 167–80, 185, 186, 193, 202,
        219–30, 237, 239–41, 244
utilitarianism 129

vertical equity 132
vibration 157, 188
Victoria 48
Vietnam 242
vulnerability(-ies) 197, 210, 214–15,
        235–6, 246–51

walkable 162
walking 3, 79, 81–2, 84, 89, 131
Washington 30, 177
Western Europe 29, 65, 104, 145, 148, 149,
        152–3
women 10, 130

Yokohama 41, 42, 51
youngsters 10, 130

zero-car households 129–30
Zevenaar 121

For Product Safety Concerns and Information please contact our EU
representative GPSR@taylorandfrancis.com Taylor & Francis Verlag GmbH,
Kaufingerstraße 24, 80331 München, Germany

Printed and bound by CPI Group (UK) Ltd, Croydon, CR0 4YY
08/05/2025
01864528-0002